I0882718

Formalism and Pragmatism in American Law

The Social Sciences of Practice

THE HISTORY AND THEORY OF LEGAL PRACTICE

Series Editor

Philip C. C. Huang
(*University of California, Los Angeles and Renmin University of China*)

VOLUME 2

The titles published in this series are listed at *brill.com/ssop*

Formalism and Pragmatism in American Law

By

Thomas C. Grey

BRILL

LEIDEN | BOSTON

Library of Congress Cataloging-in-Publication Data

Grey, Thomas C., author.
Formalism and pragmatism in American law / by Thomas C. Grey.
pages cm. — (The social sciences of practice : the history and theory of legal practice ; v. 2)
Includes bibliographical references.
ISBN 978-90-04-27288-0 (hardback : alk. paper) — ISBN 978-90-04-27289-7 (e-book) 1. Law—United States—Philosophy. 2. Legal positivism. 3. Realism. 4. Pragmatism. I. Title.

KF380.G74 2014
340'.1—dc23

2014006671

This publication has been typeset in the multilingual 'Brill' typeface. With over 5,100 characters covering Latin, IPA, Greek, and Cyrillic, this typeface is especially suitable for use in the humanities.
For more information, please see brill.com/brill-typeface.

ISSN 2214-952X
ISBN 978 90 04 27288 0 (hardback)
ISBN 978 90 04 27289 7 (e-book)

Copyright 2014 by Koninklijke Brill NV, Leiden, The Netherlands.
Koninklijke Brill NV incorporates the imprints Brill, Brill Nijhoff, Global Oriental and Hotei Publishing.
All rights reserved. No part of this publication may be reproduced, translated, stored in a retrieval system, or transmitted in any form or by any means, electronic, mechanical, photocopying, recording or otherwise, without prior written permission from the publisher.
Authorization to photocopy items for internal or personal use is granted by Koninklijke Brill NV provided that the appropriate fees are paid directly to The Copyright Clearance Center, 222 Rosewood Drive, Suite 910, Danvers, MA 01923, USA. Fees are subject to change.

This book is printed on acid-free paper.

Contents

Author's Biography

Thomas C. Grey, Sweitzer Professor of Law, Emeritus, at Stanford Law School, is a leading legal theorist and historian of the development of modern American legal thought. He has written extensively on the development of such strains of legal thought as pragmatism, formalism, and realism with particular attention to the jurisprudence of Oliver Wendell Holmes Jr. Earlier in his career, he wrote significant articles on constitutional law, history, and theory, with special emphasis on the "unwritten constitution" of unenumerated constitutional rights. He also taught torts to first-year students for more than 30 years before his retirement in 2007.

Professor Grey is a fellow of the American Academy of Arts and Sciences and is the recipient of an honorary law doctorate from Chicago-Kent College of Law. Before joining the Stanford Law School faculty in 1971, he served as a clerk to Justice Thurgood Marshall of the U.S. Supreme Court and Judge J. Skelly Wright of the U.S. Court of Appeals for the District of Columbia Circuit.

Series Foreword

Philip C. C. Huang 黄宗智

The social sciences in China and the U.S. have come to be rather heavily dominated by abstract theorizing divorced from practical realities. What this series proposes to emphasize instead is actual economic and legal, and historical and social practices, and the theoretical logics evidenced therein. The theoretical works included in the series proceed not from theory to practice, but rather from practice to theory; the empirical studies included are ones of important theoretical implications.

We propose to include selected major works in each of five sub-series, to be published simultaneously in both English and Chinese, or, where the work is already available in one language (English or Chinese), then its translation into the other. The five sub-series include one each in the history and theory of legal practice, the economic history and economics of practice, and the social history and sociology of practice. The fourth series consists of broader cross-disciplinary works in historical political economy, in the tradition of the likes of Adam Smith, Karl Marx, and Max Weber. The fifth series includes major innovations evident in Chinese economic, legal, social, and political-economic practices that have yet to receive full theoretical elaboration.

The typical social science study today proceeds from a certain theoretical position, and asks a question derived from that particular perspective, with the intention of proving (or, sometimes, disproving) the posited "hypothesis." This may be done explicitly or implicitly, but always with a host of assumptions, often unspoken, even unconscious.

Since almost all existing social science theories have originated from the West, such an epistemological approach often comes with the belief that the Western experience (e.g., capitalism and democracy and formalist law) and the theoretical abstractions therefrom are universally applicable. When applied to the developing non-Western world, the research can become mainly a matter of finding inadequacies in the subject country or region, often with implicit or explicit advocacy for development in the direction of the Western "model." This is most evident, for example, in the disciplines of economics and jurisprudence, the most formalistic and ideological of the "modern" disciplines.

Our "social sciences of practice," however, calls for inverting that epistemological process, to proceed not from (Western-originated) theory (and hypotheses derived therefrom), but rather from the practical realities of the subject country. Non-Western countries, faced with the economic-military as well as cultural-intellectual expansion of the West in modern times, have been placed unavoidably into a historical situation of conflicting tugs between tradition and (Western) "modernity," the indigenous and the imported, East and West. What exist in practice are almost of necessity paradoxical when seen from the perspective of Western theory.

We start with practice because, unlike theory, practice is anchored in the subject country's own social-economic and political contexts, perspectives, and discourses. And problems seen through practice rather than theory are far more likely to be of indigenous concern to the subject country itself rather than just theoretical / epistemological concern to the West.

Practice, in fact, tells first and foremost about paradoxes—or the co-existence of pairs of seemingly contradictory and mutually exclusive realities that are both true and real, like (globalized) commercialization without development, or capitalism without democracy, or Westernized formalist legal codes without their judicial practice. It challenges the very validity of commonly used (Western) theories that presuppose a cause and effect relationship between those, and therefore cries out for new theoretical formulations. In addition, unlike theory, which tends to be dominated by deductive / formal (and Western-originated) logic, and hence insists on logical consistency, practice readily accommodates the seemingly contradictory. It demands conceptualization and theorizing in terms of its own logic—such as, for example, China's "feeling for the stones while crossing the river."

The perspective from practice is one that calls for taking historical process as the point of departure, and for theoretical formulations therefrom. Such practical and theoretical concerns do not mean, however, the simple rejection or disregard of Western social science theory, but rather deliberate dialoguing with existing theory, and also deliberate borrowing from and developing the West's multiple alternative theoretical traditions. Such research can in fact highlight the need to combine "mainstream" formalist theoretical traditions with alternative Western theoretical traditions to conceptualize Western experience itself—e.g., combining the jurisprudential traditions of "classical orthodoxy" with legal pragmatism (and Marxism and postmodernism) to understand the past and present of American law, or the Smithian with the Marxist and substantivist to understand the economic history of the West. Better yet, to uncover the operative theoretical logics of those combinations that exist in practice and to search for ways to go beyond the either/or juxtaposition of binaries that are seen to be mutually exclusive.

Our series proposes to include such works in economics, law, sociology, and political economy, as well as works on such Chinese innovations that have already been made in practice but have yet to receive full theoretical formulation and attention. Our goal is to develop a series of works guided by problematics and theoretical conceptions that are better suited to Chinese concerns and realities than typical "mainstream" formalist studies.

Introduction

This book was launched when Prof. Philip Huang contacted me offering to arrange translation and Chinese publication of a selection of my articles. I did wonder whether my writings, mostly about American law, could have much to say to a Chinese audience. But given Prof. Huang's intimate involvement with both legal systems throughout his distinguished scholarly career, I accepted his flattering judgment that they might, and I am very grateful to him for making the necessary arrangements. The result is this selection from my writings, for which I agreed to write this introduction.

Prof. Huang's 2007 article "Whither Chinese Law?"[1] helped me understand why he thinks Chinese law students and legal academics might be interested in these writings of mine. That article provides a lively summary of the struggle between Westernizers and proponents of indigenous tradition in the course of Chinese jurisprudence over the last century, illustrated by a number of instructive case studies. It then answers the question posed by its title by urging acceptance of the coexistence of the competing schools rather than the triumph of any one of them as the best way into the future for Chinese law. In support of this recommendation, Prof. Huang offers an analogy to what he sees as a comparable development in modern American legal thought and practice. "If the essence of modernity in American law is indeed the coexistence of its classical orthodoxy with legal pragmatism, then the essence of China's modernity lies perhaps in the coexistence of Western formalism with Chinese practical moralism."[2]

Much of my own scholarly career has been devoted to writing about classical orthodoxy and pragmatism in 19th and 20th century American legal thought. In two of the articles included here, "Langdell's Orthodoxy" (1983) and "Holmes and Legal Pragmatism" (1989),[3] I have tried to provide accounts of these jurisprudential tendencies that were accurate and as sympathetic as possible. Viewed as tendencies, they are readily seen in tension with each other, so that the history of modern American legal thought is a narrative of their ongoing struggle.

1 33 *Modern China* 1 (2007).

2 *Id.* at 29.

3 **1983, 1989.** See Bibliography of Principal Publications, at end, where articles are identified by bolded dates, followed by full citations. I use the bolded dates as citations in these footnotes, inviting readers seeking original sources to look to the Bibliography.

© KONINKLIJKE BRILL NV, LEIDEN, 2014 | DOI 10.1163/9789004272897_002

At the same time, I argue that legal pragmatism, understood as the theory of law articulated by Oliver Wendell Holmes Jr., in harmony with the general pragmatist philosophy of John Dewey, is a jurisprudence that supports what Prof. Huang describes as the "essence" of modern American law—that is, the "coexistence" of the classical tendency with the practical and flexible pragmatic tendency. To avoid terminological confusion, I prefer to keep the term "legal pragmatism" for this overarching jurisprudential account, which makes space for both of the competing tendencies. I label the tendencies themselves formalist and legal realist. Classical orthodoxy is then a jurisprudence that attempts to subject the whole domain of law to the formalist tendency. (I believe Chinese law may have felt the influence of something like this jurisprudence at the time of the adoption of the German Civil Code, one of the great embodiments of classical European legal science.) In my view, such a universal formalism cannot be a successful general account of law, though the tendency which animates it, the drive to make law coherent and predictable, is a necessary aspect of any successful legal system.

The heart of legal pragmatism as I understand it, following Holmes, is a view of law as an enterprise that is practical in two senses. First, it is "constituted of practices—contextual, situated, rooted in shared expectations;" second, it is "instrumental, a means for achieving socially desired ends, and available to be adapted to their service."[4] The first sense, emphasizing practice, suggests the historical school of jurisprudence; the second, emphasizing practicality, suggests the analytical-utilitarian school. These were regarded as rival jurisprudential approaches in the 19th century, but it was Holmes's insight that they were partners rather than rivals, each stating important but partial truths about law. Thus Holmes promoted legal pragmatism as a "both-and" rather than an "either-or" theory—a synthesis of historical and analytical jurisprudence, law as both guided by past practice and looking forward in a practical spirit to future consequences.

The historical school urged that law is founded in customs and community social norms, which represent the collective wisdom of experience, and are unlikely to be improved by rationalist schemes of legal reconstruction. The analytical school saw law as the articulate command of a present legislative sovereign, with the power and the duty to shake off the dead hand of the past and consciously shape law to achieve the present and future greatest happiness of the greatest number. A characteristic aphorism of Holmes's captured his synthesis of the two approaches, emphasizing the descriptive power of the historical school and the normative force of analytical utilitarianism: "historic

4 1989 at 805.

continuity with the past is not a duty, it is only a necessity."[5] Especially in a time of rapid historical change, conscious reform is an essential corrective to increasingly outmoded traditions; but the complexity of social life makes it impossible to rebuild a whole system of law from the ground up.

If I read Prof. Huang rightly, it is possible to see those who would draw primarily on indigenous sources to develop Chinese law as the heirs of the historical school, while those who would mainly look to the West for legal progress might remind us of the utilitarian reformers who followed Jeremy Bentham. If that much is conceded, then Prof. Huang's exhortation of Chinese lawyers to accept and indeed welcome the coexistence of both these approaches can remind us of Holmes, the advocate of "both-and" over "either-or."

My articles on Langdell and Holmes represent my attempt to construct from historical materials two ideal types of legal thought, the pure formalism of classical orthodoxy, and the inclusive practicality of legal pragmatism.[6] The other three articles in this book are efforts to examine some of the larger conceptual structures of three of the main divisions of law: constitutional law, property law, and tort law.

In "Do We Have an Unwritten Constitution?"[7] I argue that though the conventional answer to the question posed would be No (the British have an unwritten constitution, Americans have a written one), an affirmative answer better fits the realities of American practice. Of course we Americans do live under the written constitution adopted in 1789 and amended twenty-seven times since, and we regard it as what it declares itself to be, "the supreme law of the land."[8] But supplementing the supreme written constitution, we also have an unwritten constitution, authorized or at least tolerated by the founding document, and developed by our courts through a kind of common-law process over more than two centuries.

The unwritten constitution shows itself most dramatically when American courts strike down statutes on the ground that they violate fundamental rights, even rights that have never been formally articulated and protected through original constitutional adoption or later amendment. Examples are the rights of privacy and freedom of choice in matters of sexual intimacy, nowhere declared in the constitution, but over the last half century invoked

5 *Id.* at 807.

6 Other articles of mine addressing Holmes's pragmatism are **1992**, **1995**, **1997**, and **2000b**; others addressing legal pragmatism apart from Holmes's thought are **1991c**, **1996b**, and **2003**.

7 **1975**.

8 U.S. Const., Art. VI.

by the courts to invalidate laws prohibiting contraception, abortion, and gay sexual relations.

This article (and others of mine pursuing the theme of the unwritten constitution)[9] harmonize with pragmatist legal theory in their critique of universalized formalism and their emphasis on practice and practical reason as sources of fundamental legal norms. The formalist approach to American constitutional law over the last half century has been embodied in the linked ideas of textualism and originalism. Textualists believe that the only legitimate source of constitutional norms is enacted constitutional text. Originalism adds that the meanings of broad and potentially flexible constitutional provisions are fixed by how their original framers and ratifiers understood them.

Posed against these are two persistent practices, judicial articulation and enforcement of unenacted constitutional limitations, and adaptive interpretation of broadly phrased constitutional provisions, both carried on though evolutionary common-law-style adjudication. A recurrent practical case for this common-law "living constitution" is that something like it is required if constitutional government in the United States is to be workable. The country and its constitution are old, formal constitutional amendment is extremely difficult, and times and circumstances change, so there must be some leeway for constitutional development through interpretive adaptation as well as amendment.

This said, the thrust of my writings on the unwritten constitution is not that its legitimacy is beyond question; the arguments between broad adaptive interpretation and strict construction of the constitution recur in every generation. One of our best-established practices is that these opposed interpretive attitudes coexist with each other in continuing tension.

"The Disintegration of Property"[10] argues that one of the great subdivisions of law in both the common and civil law worlds, the law of property, is losing its coherence through its internal logical tensions, exacerbated by economic and technological developments characteristic of advanced capitalism and the information age. This loss of coherence means the decline of property as an operative concept central to our legal system.

In its classical stage, property law was organized around the paradigm of absolute ownership, famously described by Blackstone as "that sole and despotic dominion which one man claims and exercises over the external things of the world, in total exclusion of the right of any other individual in the

---

9 See 1978, 1984, 1988a, 1988b.

10 1980a.

universe."[11] This reflected a popular conception of property which still has considerable force—it's mine, not yours or his, and that means I can do with it what I want.

In an 18th century economy of small farmers and shopkeepers, much or even most property might come roughly under this description. But both the "sole and despotic dominion" and the "external things" in Blackstone's definition create problems for the internal coherence of conception of property founded on ownership.

First, it seems that Blackstone's dominion if it is to be despotic must include full freedom of disposition, partial as well as complete. An owner can keep and use his property, or sell it, give it away, or abandon it. But he may find it convenient to dispose of some rather than all of his ownership rights. He can lease it, in effect selling his right of possession and use for a limited time. He may also want to sell off rights to particular uses, grazing rights to his land, or rights to the minerals under the ground. He may want to sell off half his ownership, or transfer that ownership to a partnership or corporation, with himself a partner or stockholder. Reflection suggests that an owner's full freedom of disposition allows for a virtually complete fragmentation of the ownership of the object over time, among uses, and among different stakeholders. From this insight emerges the "bundle-of-rights" conception of property offered by the American realists, no longer sole dominion over a thing by its owner, but rights and duties among persons with respect to a thing. How much of the bundle constitutes ownership? It seems that any answer must be arbitrary, and the ideal of full ownership thereby loses some of its hold.

Second, why must property right apply only to "things," material objects? In a mature market economy more and more property becomes intangible: "shares of stock in corporations, bonds, various forms of commercial paper, bank accounts, insurance policies" as I enumerated these in 1980. At the time, I added as an afterthought "not to mention more arcane intangibles such as trademarks, patents, copyrights..." The extraordinary growth of the information economy in the last few decades has made intellectual property not arcane at all, but increasingly one of the most important forms of wealth.

A consequence of this loss of centrality to the "thing-ownership" paradigm has been the fragmentation of property discourses among legal specialists, who now distinguish property rights from other rights in a variety of ways, detailed in my article. These conflict with each other, and mostly display little resemblance to sole and despotic dominion over things. This multiple

11 **1980a** at 75.

fragmentation of the concept makes it a fair question whether we might not just as well do away altogether away with "property" as one of the master terms of our legal discourse.

One of my last articles, and the only one I wrote on a subject that I taught for the full length of my academic career, "Accidental Torts" analyzes the emergence of tort as a fundamental legal category in the common-law world in the late 19th century. This piece illustrates two important features of legal pragmatism: first, contrary to what many legal realists contend, the conceptual architecture of the law has real practical importance; and, second, that architecture, once generally accepted and used as the framework within which law is taught, can come to seem inevitable, the only rational way to arrange our knowledge of the law. But often this is not the case. Torts, universally recognized today as a major subdivision of law, is a good example of this; it might never have become a basic legal category, and in the future it might well no longer be one. Legal architecture is more historical and conventional than it is natural and eternal.

In the article, I examine the period 1870–1890, a time when American and English civil procedure had recently been reformed to do away with the archaic common-law forms of action. The forms of action had long been used as the main organizing categories for legal knowledge. Their abolition prompted the best legal minds of that period to set to work creating a new taxonomy of substantive law categories. These categories would identify the subjects of introductory law study, and provide organizing titles under which indexers could classify authoritative legal materials and commentators could identify and organize the doctrine expounding those materials. Lawyers would then come to think of law as naturally falling into those subdivisions.

A consensus gradually emerged that criminal law, property, and contracts would be basic categories; these were installed as first-year courses in the leading American law schools. There were already recognized treatises on these subjects, and casebooks were quickly assembled as teaching tools. Torts was a candidate to join them as a fundamental department of the law, but its status was seen as more debatable.

Holmes was one of the young intellectual lawyers who took an interest in the project of providing a conceptual doctrinal structure for the substantive law. He regarded the project as practical, but also what he called "philosophical;" the best scheme of categories would classify the law in the way that best revealed its nature and content. At first he rejected the idea that torts would be one of the basic divisions, writing that tort was "not a proper subject for a law book."[12] But he changed his mind, and two years later published an article

12 2001 at 1232.

entitled "The Theory of Torts," outlining a conceptual structure for the field, most of which we still use to this day.

Analogies from Roman and civil law favored making torts a basic category, but the analytical jurisprudence of Bentham and Austin, which Holmes and his young contemporaries considered the most advanced form of legal thought, pressed against this conclusion. Torts could not be fundamental because it was not a substantive law category but only a remedial one, covering wrongful acts for which an award of compensatory damage was the law's response. But not all such wrongful acts; contract law supplied substantive law defining the wrong of breach of contract, and then providing compensatory damages as the standard remedy. That left tort as an ungainly catch-all category apparently lacking coherence or practical significance: the law of civil liability for those wrongs not arising out of contract.

Holmes was at first convinced by this argument, but he came to recognize that there were civil suits based on substantive law not covered by criminal law, contracts, or property: those involving personal injury or property damage accidentally caused by one person to another. His insight was that there was a single legal concept around which a coherent body of law governing accidental injury could be built, the concept of negligence, or failure to exercise ordinary care.

Previously, writers on tort had tended to center the subject around the action for trespass, which governed suits for assault and battery. These intentional torts were mostly also crimes, and the substantive law governing these concepts was in effect already provided by criminal law. But negligence, while considered a kind of wrongdoing, was the least culpable form of faulty conduct, rarely treated as criminal. Suits for compensatory damage provided the normal remedy for injury caused by ordinary negligence. The tort concept of negligence as Holmes formulated it was not a blameworthy subjective state of mind, carelessness, but rather was any conduct that fell below the standard of reasonable safety.

Holmes then placed this objective concept of negligence at the center of the field of tort law, covering the great mass of cases. It was flanked by two less important subcategories of torts. On the more culpable side were the intentional torts like assault and battery, serious wrongdoing that was usually criminal as well as tortious and that justified punitive as well as compensatory damages in civil suits. On the less culpable side was a category that Holmes created, drawing on a scattering of common-law precedents, namely strict liability for extrahazardous activities. Thus storing explosives in a town was not per se negligent, but for reasons of public policy an explosion would subject the defendant to tort liability for injuries even no particular failure of reasonable care could be shown.

Holmes's idea of building tort law around negligence came to be generally adopted, at least in part because of a practical factor that he did not mention in his own writings on the subject. Liability for negligently caused accidental injury had existed for centuries, but had produced only a scattering of cases. However the industrial revolution meant that in the period in which Holmes was writing, accidental injuries involving solvent defendants were becoming much more numerous as the rapid growth of railroads, streetcars, and machine-driven factories took an increasing toll on passengers, travelers, and workers, stimulating an equally rapid growth in the number of lawyers who made their living bringing or defending suits for these injuries.

There is no evidence in any of Holmes's early writings on tort law that he was motivated to build the subject around the negligence cause of action by the upsurge of industrial accidents. Indeed he may not even have been aware of this social phenomenon. Throughout his long career, Holmes often bemusedly noted in his extensive correspondence that he did not know much about what was going on in the world of business and politics around him; he did not even read the newspapers.

Rather he was driven by a passion to devise an intellectually satisfying classification for the substantive law, one that could meet his need to win renown for philosophically significant work in the very worldly profession he had stumbled into. In that quest, his imaginative centering of tort law around the problem of accidental injury happened to coincide with an extraordinary growth of those injuries that he may not even have been aware of. Torts might not have become a basic category of our law without this coincidence; as I argue in my article, there were plausible alternative ways of classifying substantive law during this period that did not include torts as a basic category. Today tort law appears to many law students to be naturally and necessarily a basic category of our law, but it may have stumbled into that status in the first instance as Holmes stumbled in the law—by accident.

I have discussed the five articles selected for this book in what seems to me a logical order. The first two articles begin with the most abstract question—should classical orthodoxy or pragmatism be our favored account of basic legal method? Having argued in favor of pragmatism, I then go on to consider three high-level conceptual questions that arise within the working law: does the United States have an unwritten constitution? is property still viable as a central organizing concept in our legal system? and, how did torts become a major legal category? Answers: yes, decreasingly so, to a surprising extent by accident. In each case, I accept that the contrary answer is fairly arguable, so that a full account of existing law must include the arguments for that position.

Dealing with legal issues at this level of abstraction assumes that conceptual and categorical issues like these are of enough practical importance to make them worth debating. Legal pragmatism is often conflated with legal realism, but on this issue they differ. Pragmatists think the conceptual architecture of the law is of real practical importance, even if the relatively abstract categories and concepts lawyers use lack the geometric properties ascribed to them by classical orthodoxy. Holmes certainly thought so; his famous book *The Common Law* is organized around the categories of crime, tort, contract, and succession, and in that book and other writings he contributed significantly to the doctrinal foundations of those subjects. By contrast, legal realists see doctrinal disputation at the level of high-level principles and basic categories as insignificant, not affecting concrete results, a waste of time.[13]

So I think connecting the five articles selected to form this book in the way I have just outlined can add to the understanding of American legal pragmatism. But in the book, these articles are placed, not in the logical sequence in which I have treated them here, but rather in the chronological order of their publication. I originally selected these five articles, not as an exposition of my views on legal pragmatism, but as representative selection from my whole body of scholarly work, revealing its development over time.

I actually did not formulate the account of legal pragmatism set out in the 1989 Holmes article until after I had written the three articles on the constitution (1975), on property (1980), and on classical orthodoxy (1983). When I wrote the last of these, I was already launched on a comparison of Langdell's jurisprudence with Holmes's, but I did not see the links between Holmes's legal theory and philosophical pragmatism, particularly Dewey's version of it, until the middle years of the 1980s, when I read extensively in pragmatist philosophy, first Richard Rorty and then Dewey himself.

Going further back, I had studied Anglo-American analytical philosophy as an undergraduate at Stanford and Oxford, and I went to law school at Yale at a time when Ronald Dworkin was teaching there. I was intrigued by his insistence that American constitutional law could be studied partly as an exercise in applied moral and political philosophy. When I joined the faculty at Stanford in 1971, I taught both constitutional law and jurisprudence, the latter a traditional course in analytical philosophy of law. My first published article was a review-essay of the analytical moral philosopher John Rawls's then-new book

13 For more on Holmes's conceptualism see **1989** at 816–826, and for a more detailed treatment, see **2000b**. Other important American pragmatist legal thinkers like Roscoe Pound and Benjamin Cardozo shared Holmes's interest in the conceptual architecture of the law.

A Theory of Justice; it was meant to serve as a kind of introduction to Rawls for academic lawyers.[14]

My early work on the unwritten constitution was stimulated by my interest in public welfare law; I had taken a course in the subject at Yale, and briefly taught a similar course for a few years at Stanford. This was during the short period when there was a flurry of interest in interpreting the Equal Protection Clause of the US Constitution to support movements in the direction of judicially enforceable constitutional social rights in the United States, comparable to those included in a number of post-World-War-II European constitutions. Rawls's book argued for material guarantees as a matter of justice, while Dworkin argued that philosophical argument about justice should inform constitutional interpretation. I wrote a law review article myself framing a philosophical argument somewhat different from Rawls's for material guarantees, and briefly noting that it might translate into constitutional law.[15]

In the late 1970s my interests in legal theory moved away from analytical philosophy, as I was influenced by the interpretive turn in American legal scholarship, and also by the work of critical legal scholars. I had planned a book on the historical development of the unwritten constitution throughout American history, but abandoned it as I found myself less drawn to this kind of doctrinally oriented historical scholarship. The 19th century development of unwritten constitutional doctrine was devoted in large part to constitutional protection of property rights, and the combination of my historical researches on that period with the influence of critical writers led to "The Disintegration of Property." In the following years, I wrote two more pieces on constitutional law that moved away from my earlier doctrinal orientation, one, influenced by social theory, a perspective on emerging protections of sexual freedom, and the other, influenced by philosophical hermeneutics, working through the analogy between theories of constitutional and scriptural interpretation.[16]

In this same period, the early eighties, I reconstituted my Jurisprudence course, oriented toward analytical philosophy, into a new course called Modern American Legal Thought,[17] organized chronologically and emphasizing writings by lawyers and law teachers rather than philosophers. It was out of my preparation for this course that "Langdell's Orthodoxy" emerged, as well as my engagement with the thought of Holmes. That led to study of the

14 **1973.**

15 **1976.**

16 **1980b, 1984.**

17 Later summarized in **1996d.**

American pragmatist philosophers, especially Dewey, and thus to "Holmes and Legal Pragmatism."

I've given this brief account of the twists and turns in my scholarly interests and the influences on my work that culminated in my writings on legal pragmatism so that a reader of the five articles that make up this book will not unduly be surprised at the shifts in tone and intellectual style from one of them to another. History and philosophy have been the two outside disciplines that have in varying ways shaped my work on the law, and while my interest in philosophy tempts me toward a logically coherent retroactive account of my work, history, the narrative of human events, reminds me to give fair weight to the illogical, arbitrary, and personal factors. The law itself is also an amalgam of order-seeking philosophy on the one hand, and disorderly one-damned-thing-after-another history on the other. I have found that, for me at least, pragmatism as a philosophy of law has best been able to make sense of the coexistence of these two aspects of human life.

Do We Have an Unwritten Constitution?

Thomas C. Grey

In reviewing laws for constitutionality, should our judges confine themselves to determining whether those laws conflict with norms derived from the written Constitution? Or may they also enforce principles of liberty and justice when the normative content of those principles is not to be found within the four corners of our founding document? Excluding the question of the legitimacy of judicial review itself, that is perhaps the most fundamental question we can ask about our fundamental law.

I The Pure Interpretive Model

For many years this most basic question has not much engaged the explicit attention of constitutional scholars or of the courts or judges themselves, with at least one important exception. That exception was Mr. Justice Black. Throughout his long and remarkable career on the bench, the most consistently reiterated theme of his constitutional jurisprudence was the need for fidelity to the constitutional text in judicial review, and the illegitimacy of constitutional doctrines based on sources other than the explicit commands of the written Constitution.[1]

It now appears that as a final mark of Mr. Justice Black's achievement, his jurisprudential view of constitutional adjudication may be returning to favor. In the last few years, distinguished commentators on constitutional law have begun to echo Mr. Justice Black's central theme, criticizing constitutional developments in terms that have scarcely been heard in the scholarly community for a generation.

---

* This article originally appeared in *Stanford Law Review*, Vol. 27, No. 3 (Feb. 1975), pp. 703–718. Author's Note: I would like to thank Professors John Ely and Hans Linde for their thoughtful comments on an earlier draft of this Essay.

** A.B. 1963, Stanford University; LL.B. 1968, Yale University. Associate Professor of Law, Stanford University.

1 *See, e.g., In re* Winship, 397 U.S. 358, 377 (1970) (Black, J., dissenting); Griswold v. Connecticut, 381 U.S. 479, 507 (1965) (Black, J., dissenting); Rochin v. California, 342 U.S. 165, 174 (1952) (Black, J., concurring); Adamson v. California, 332 U.S. 46, 68 (1947) (Black, J., dissenting).

© KONINKLIJKE BRILL NV, LEIDEN, 2014 | DOI 10.1163/9789004272897_003

The criticism has centered around the new "fundamental interest" branch of equal protection doctrine, and the emerging libertarian right of privacy in familial and sexual matters. The strand of criticism that I wish to focus on here has not alleged the impolicy of the new doctrines, or their lack of internal coherence or principled articulation—those are the familiar themes of contemporary constitutional commentary. Rather it has urged that because the new developments rest on principles not derived by normal processes of textual interpretation from the written Constitution, they represent a wholly illegitimate mode of judicial review.

This is the strand of criticism that sounds in the jurisprudence of Mr. Justice Black. It has been put most forcefully by Solicitor General (then Professor) Bork:

> [T]he choice of "fundamental values" by the Court cannot be justified. Where constitutional materials do not clearly specify the value to be preferred, there is no principled way to prefer any claimed human value to any other. The judge must stick close to the text and the history, and their fair implications, and not construct new rights.[2]

Mr. Bork calls this the requirement of "neutral derivation" of constitutional principle, and makes clear that he regards it as additional to the requirement of "neutral application" of principle so much debated in the 1950's and 1960's.[3]

In a thoughtful and stimulating review and extension of that familiar "neutral principles" debate, Professor Hans Linde has likewise urged a return to the commands of the constitutional text as the sole legitimating source for judicial review:

> The judicial responsibility begins and ends with determining the present scope and meaning of a decision that the nation, at an earlier time, articulated and enacted into constitutional text....[4]

The last example of this recent trend that I will cite—though not the last I could cite—is Professor John Ely's powerful assault on the Supreme Court's

---

2 Bork, *Neutral Principles and Some First Amendment Problems*, 47 IND. L.J. 1, 8 (1971).

3 *Id.* at 7.

4 Linde, *Judges, Critics, and the Realist Tradition*, 82 YALE L.J. 227, 254 (1972). Professor Linde has urged the same viewpoint with respect to the application of state constitutional provisions. Linde, *Without "Due Process": Unconstitutional Law in Oregon*, 49 ORE. L. REV. 125 (1970).

recent decision in the Abortion Cases.[5] Professor Ely charges that in those decisions, based on a right of "privacy" drawn by no imaginable arts of construction or interpretation from the constitutional text, the Court has violated its "obligation to trace its premises to the charter from which it derives its authority." He goes on:

> A neutral and durable principle may be a thing of beauty and a joy forever. But if it lacks connection with any value the Constitution marks as special, it is not a constitutional principle and the Court has no business imposing it.[6]

Professor Ely takes care to characterize the Bork and Linde articles as "espousing the general view of constitutional adjudication espoused here."[7]

I do not think that the view of constitutional adjudication outlined by these commentators is sufficiently broad to capture the full scope of legitimate judicial review. It seems to me that the courts do appropriately invoke values not articulated in the constitutional text, and appropriately apply them in determining the constitutionality of legislation.

This view, it seems to me, tacitly underlies much of the affirmative constitutional doctrine developed by the courts over the last generation. The trouble is that the view has been too tacit. It has not been clearly stated and articulately defended, as basic constitutional doctrine should be. Nor, for that matter, has the opposing general view received adequate theoretical statement and defense—except by Mr. Justice Black. Unfortunately, the professional world concerned with constitutional law has not taken Mr. Justice Black's theoretical position sufficiently seriously. Perhaps there was too much of a tendency to accept at face value the great Justice's pose as a rather old-fashioned and simple-minded country lawyer, with sound intuition and a good nose for the concrete issues, but lacking any claim to jurisprudential sophistication.

---

5 Roe v. Wade, 410 U.S. 113 (1973); Doe v. Bolton, 410 U.S. 179 (1973).

6 Ely, *The Wages of Crying Wolf: A Comment on* Roe v. Wade, 82 YALE L.J. 920, 949 (1973) (footnote omitted).

7 *Id.* at 949 n. 147. Professor Ely disagrees, however, with many of Mr. Bork's criticisms of the Warren Court.

For other recent constitutional commentary in which the Bork-Ely-Linde view is expressed or implied, *see* Epstein, *Substantive Due Process by Any Other Name: The Abortion Cases*, 1973 SUP. CT. REV. 159; Winter, *Poverty, Economic Equality, and the Equal Protection Clause*, 1972 SUP. CT. REV. 41.

If the articles by Messrs. Bork, Linde, and Ely mark the emergence of an important trend—as I suspect they do—this basic theoretical issue will no longer be swept under the rug. These critics simply cannot be dismissed as unsophisticates or out-of-date legal primitives.

The truth is that the view of constitutional adjudication they share with Mr. Justice Black is one of great power and compelling simplicity. That view is deeply rooted in our history and in our shared principles of political legitimacy. It has equally deep roots in our formal constitutional law; it is, after all, the theory upon which judicial review was founded in *Marbury v. Madison.*[8]

The chief virtue of this view is that it supports judicial review while answering the charge that the practice is undemocratic. Under the pure interpretive model (as I shall henceforth call the view in question), when a court strikes down a popular statute or practice as unconstitutional, it may always reply to the resulting public outcry: "We didn't do it—you did." The people have chosen the principle that the statute or practice violated, have designated it as fundamental, and have written it down in the text of the Constitution for the judges to interpret and apply. The task of interpretation of the people's commands may not always be simple or mechanical; there is no warrant to condemn Mr. Justice Black or his allies with the epithet "mechanical jurisprudence." But the task remains basically one of interpretation, the application of fixed and binding norms to new facts.[9]

II Beyond Interpretation

The contrary view of judicial review, the one that I espouse and that seems to me implicit in much of the constitutional law developed by the courts, does not

8 5 U.S. (1 Cranch) 137 (1803).

9 The pure interpretive model should not be confused with *literalism* in constitutional interpretation, particularly with "narrow" or "crabbed" literalism. The interpretive model, at least in the hands of its sophisticated exponents, certainly contemplates that the courts may look through the sometimes opaque text to the purposes behind it in determining constitutional norms. Normative inferences may be drawn from silences and omissions, from structures and relationships, as well as from explicit commands. Thus I do not see the sort of constitutional reasoning described by Professor Charles Black in his STRUCTURE AND RELATIONSHIP IN CONSTITUTIONAL LAW (1969) as necessarily going beyond the interpretive model.

What distinguishes the exponent of the pure interpretive model is his insistence that the only norms used in constitutional adjudication must be those inferable from the text—that the Constitution must not be seen as licensing courts to articulate and apply contemporary norms not demonstrably expressed or implied by the framers.

deny that the Constitution is a written document, expressing some clear and positive restraints upon governmental power. Nor does it deny that part of the business of judicial review consists of giving effect to these explicit commands.

Where the broader view of judicial review diverges from the pure interpretive model is in its acceptance of the courts' additional role as the expounder of basic national ideals of individual liberty and fair treatment, even when the content of these ideals is not expressed as a matter of positive law in the written Constitution. It must at once be conceded that such a role for our courts is more difficult to justify than is the role assigned by the pure interpretive model. Why, one asks, are the courts better able to discern and articulate basic national ideals than are the people's politically responsible representatives? And one recalls Learned Hand's remark that he would find it "most irksome to be ruled by a bevy of Platonic Guardians, even if I knew how to choose them, which I assuredly do not."[10]

These grave difficulties no doubt explain, although they do not excuse, the tendency of our courts—today as throughout our history—to resort to bad legislative history and strained reading of constitutional language to support results that would be better justified by explication of contemporary moral and political ideals not drawn from the constitutional text. Of course, this tendency of the courts in no way helps to establish the legitimacy of noninterpretive judicial review. Indeed, standing alone it tends to establish the opposite; for if judges resort to bad interpretation in preference to honest exposition of deeply held but unwritten ideals, it must be because they perceive the latter mode of decisionmaking to be of suspect legitimacy.

However, the tendency to slipshod history and text-parsing does not stand alone. The courts do not only effectuate unwritten ideals and values covertly. Rather, in a very large proportion of their important constitutional decisions, they proceed in a mode that is openly noninterpretive. If this assertion seems at first glance surprising, it may be so partly because of the way in which constitutional law is taught in our law schools.

In the academic teaching of constitutional law, the general question of the legitimacy of judicial review is addressed largely through the vehicle of *Marbury v. Madison*. Students examine the arguments made for judicial review by Chief Justice Marshall, and perhaps contrast them with some of the counterarguments of later judges or commentators. The discussion concludes with the point that, whatever the validity of those arguments as an original matter, history has firmly decided in favor of judicial review. Thereafter, debates about judicial review focus on the question of how "activist" or how "deferential" *it*

10 L. HAND, THE BILL OF RIGHTS 73 (1958).

should be. *It* is always assumed to be the single unitary practice established and justified in *Marbury*.

This seems to me a seriously misleading way of proceeding. *Marbury* defends (and its detractors attack) what I have here called the pure interpretive model of judicial review. The case itself involves the close interpretation of a technical and explicit constitutional provision, which is found, upon conventional linguistic analysis, to conflict with a statute. The argument for judicial review as a general matter is made in terms appropriate to that sort of case. Chief Justice Marshall's stress is on the *writtenness* of the Constitution, and on its supremacy in cases of clear conflict with ordinary law.[11] His heuristic examples all involve obvious conflicts between hypothetical (and unlikely) statutes on the one hand, and particularly explicit constitutional commands on the other.[12]

All this makes *Marbury* a most atypical constitutional case, and an inappropriate paradigm for the sort of judicial review that has been important and controversial throughout our history, from *Dred Scott*[13] to the *Legal Tender Cases*[14] to *Lochner*[15] to *Carter Coal*[16] and on to *Brown v. Board of Education*,[17] *Baker v. Carr*,[18] and the Death Penalty[19] and Abortion[20] cases in our own day. In the important cases, reference to and analysis of the constitutional text plays a minor role. The dominant norms of decision are those large conceptions of governmental structure and individual rights that are at best referred to, and whose content is scarcely at all specified, in the written Constitution—dual federalism, vested rights, fair procedure, equality before the law.

11 5 U.S. (1 Cranch) 137, 176–78 (1803). Although the argument proceeds in terms of instances of purely interpretive judicial review, the underlying principle—that the courts must give precedence to constitutional law over ordinary law—is not itself found in or easily inferred from the text. Nevertheless, the argument for that principle still seems to be in the interpretive mode, based as it is on the intentions inferable from the framers' adoption of a written constitution.

12 For example, Marshall asks rhetorically whether the courts should enforce a statute generally imposing a duty on exports from a state, or an avowed bill of attainder or ex post facto law. *Id.* at 179.

13 Dred Scott v. Sanford, 60 U.S. (19 How.) 393 (1857).

14 79 U.S. (12 Wall.) 457 (1871).

15 Lochner v. New York, 198 U.S. 45 (1905).

16 Carter v. Carter Coal Co., 298 U.S. 238 (1936).

17 347 U.S. 483 (1954).

18 369 U.S. 186 (1962).

19 Furman v. Georgia, 408 U.S. 238 (1972).

20 Roe v. Wade, 410 U.S. 113 (1973); Doe v. Bolton, 410 U.S. 179 (1973).

The question of the legitimacy of this very different sort of judicial review is scarcely addressed, much less concluded, by the arguments of *Marbury v. Madison*. To approach that question, we might better examine the debate between Justices Chase and Iredell in *Calder v. Bull*.[21] And if exposure to the matchless rhetoric of John Marshall is desired, *Fletcher v. Peck*[22] provides an excellent example. In that case, the Georgia statute is struck down on two alternative grounds. The first is a strained interpretation of the contract clause, comparable in flimsiness to some of the poorer interpretive efforts of the Warren Court. The second ground is expressed in the Court's conclusion that the statute violates "general principles which are common to our free institutions"—in particular, the principle of the inviolability of vested rights.[23] Conspicuously absent is a dissent arguing that this principle is nowhere stated in the constitutional text. Indeed, the other opinion in the case—that of Justice Johnson—expresses agreement with the result on the ground of "general principles," but disavows the strained reading of the contract clause.[24]

The parallel between *Fletcher* and most contemporary judicial review is striking. Today, the Court will formally invoke one of the majestic generalities of the Constitution, typically the due process or equal protection clause, as the textual basis for its decision. Even this much specificity is not always vouchsafed us. Thus we are told of the constitutional "right to travel" that the Court has "no occasion to ascribe the source of this right to . . . a particular constitutional provision."[25] And in the Abortion Cases, the Court's reference to the textual cover for the "right of privacy" is strikingly casual:

21 3 U.S. (3 Dall.) 386 (1798). Chase: "I cannot subscribe to the omnipotence of a state legislature, or that it is absolute and without control, although its authority should not be expressly restrained by the constitution, or fundamental law of the State. . . . There are certain vital principles in our free republican governments, which will determine and overrule an apparent and flagrant abuse of legislative power. . . ." *Id.* at 387–88 (majority opinion).

Iredell: "It is true, that some speculative jurists have held, that a legislative act against natural justice must, in itself, be void; but I cannot think, that under such a government, any court of justice would possess a power to declare it so. . . .

"[T]he ideas of natural justice are regulated by no fixed standard; the ablest and the purest men have differed upon the subject; and all that the court could properly say, in such an event, would be, that the legislature, possessed of an equal right of opinion, had passed an act which, in the opinion of the judges, was inconsistent with the abstract principles of natural justice." *Id.* at 398–99 (concurring opinion).

22 10 U.S. (6 Cranch) 87 (1810).

23 *Id.* at 139.

24 *Id.* at 143 (concurring in part).

25 Shapiro v. Thompson, 394 U.S. 618, 630 (1969) (footnote omitted).

> This right of privacy, whether it be founded in the Fourteenth Amendment's concept of personal liberty and restrictions upon state action, as we feel it is, or, as the District Court determined, in the Ninth Amendment's reservation of rights to the people, is broad enough to encompass a woman's decision whether or not to terminate her pregnancy.[26]

It should be clear that in these cases the Court is quite openly *not* relying on constitutional text for the content of the substantive principles it is invoking to invalidate legislation. The parallel reliance on the ninth amendment and the due process clause in the Abortion Cases is instructive on the point. The ninth amendment on its face has no substantive content.[27] It is rather a license to constitutional decisionmakers to look beyond the substantive commands of the constitutional text to protect fundamental rights not expressed therein. In this case at least, the due process clause is being used in the same way.

Much of our substantive constitutional doctrine is of this kind. Where it arises "under" some piece of constitutional text, the text is not invoked as the source of the values or principles that rule the cases. Rather the broad textual provisions are seen as sources of legitimacy for judicial development and explication of basic shared national values. These values may be seen as permanent and universal features of human social arrangements—natural law principles—as they typically were in the 18th and 19th centuries. Or they may be seen as relative to our particular civilization, and subject to growth and change, as they typically are today. Our characteristic contemporary metaphor is "the living Constitution"—a constitution with provisions suggesting restraints on government in the name of basic rights, yet sufficiently unspecific to permit the judiciary to elucidate the development and change in the content of those rights over time.

This view of constitutional adjudication is at war with the pure interpretive model. As Mr. Justice Black said often and forcefully enough, he had no truck with the notion of changing, flexible, "living" constitutional guarantees.[28] The

---

26 Roe v. Wade, 410 U.S. 113, 153 (1973). Students of the aesthetics of pseudo-interpretation may debate whether or not this formulation is preferable to the Court's celebrated shuffle in Griswold v. Connecticut, 381 U.S. 479 (1965), through the "emanations" and "penumbras" of the Bill of Rights.

27 "The enumeration in the Constitution, of certain rights, shall not be construed to deny or disparage others retained by the people." The uses and limits of the ninth amendment as a "source" of constitutional rights are analyzed by Mr. Justice Goldberg in Griswold v. Connecticut, 381 U.S. at 486 (concurring opinion).

28 *See, e.g.*, Harper v. Virginia Bd. of Elections, 383 U.S. 663, 670 (1966) (Black, J., dissenting).

amendment process was the framers' chosen and exclusive method of adapting constitutional values to changing times; the judiciary was to enforce the Constitution's substantive commands as the framers meant them.

This is not to say that the interpretive model is incompatible with one limited sense of the concept of a "living" constitution. The model can contemplate the application of the framers' value judgments and institutional arrangements to new or changed *factual* circumstances.[29] In that sense, its proponents can endorse Chief Justice Marshall's view of the Constitution as "intended to endure for ages to come, and consequently, to be adapted to the various crises of human affairs."[30]

But the interpretive model cannot be reconciled with constitutional doctrines protecting unspecified "essential" or "fundamental" liberties, or "fair procedure," or "decency"—leaving it to the judiciary to give moral content to those conceptions either once and for all or from age to age. That sort of "interpretation" would drain from the interpretive model its animating strength. Once it was adopted, the courts could no longer honestly defend an unpopular decision to a protesting public with the transfer of responsibility: "We didn't do it—you did." No longer would the Court's constitutional role be the technical and professional one of applying *given* norms to changing facts; instead the Court would assume the large and problematic role of discerning a society's most basic contemporary values.

III The Implications of the Pure Interpretive Model

Let me now give some examples, confined to the area of individual rights, of the numerous and important substantive constitutional doctrines which seem to me unjustified under a consistently applied pure interpretive model of judicial review. First and most obvious is virtually the entire body of doctrine developed under the due process clauses of the 5th and 14th amendments. If those

29 Presumably it is in this sense that Professor Linde can describe judicial review as "a task of construing the *living* meaning of *past* political decisions" without any sense of internal inconsistency. He notes that some constitutional provisions "obviously contemplate changing applications in step with economic and technological developments, or with changes in the relation of the individual to social agencies." Linde, *Judges, Critics, and the Realist Tradition, supra* note 4, at 254–55 (emphasis added).

Similarly, Professor Ely argues: "Surely the Court is entitled, indeed I think it is obligated, to seek out the sorts of evils the framers meant to combat and to move against their fundamental twentieth century counterparts." Ely, *supra* note 6, at 929 (footnote omitted).

30 McCulloch v. Maryland, 17 U.S. (4 Wheat.) 415, 427 (1819).

clauses can be seen as having any specific normative content attributable to their framers, it is probably only that given to them by Mr. Justice Black.[31] In his view, due process requires only that deprivations of life, liberty or property be authorized by law duly enacted, rather than carried out by arbitrary executive action. A slightly more ambitious, though highly implausible, narrow interpretation is that adopted by the pre-Civil War Supreme Court—that the clause prohibits departures from the settled course of procedure familiar in the English courts in 1791.[32]

On the interpretive model, then, all the rest of due process doctrine must go. First, what many regard as the core of due process doctrine—its flexible requirement of "fundamentally fair" procedures in criminal and civil proceedings—cannot be reconciled with the interpretive model. These doctrines are developments of the "living constitution" concept *par excellence.*[33] In addition, everything that has been labeled "substantive due process" would be eliminated. It is these doctrines on which the proponents of the interpretive model have most often focused their attacks. Much of the force behind their position derives from the deeply felt opposition to the constitutionalization of laissez-faire economics epitomized by *Lochner v. New York*,[34] and they typically unite in opposition to contemporary doctrinal developments that remind them too much of *Lochner.*[35]

---

31 *See In re* Winship, 397 U.S. 358, 377–85 (1970) (dissenting opinion). As Mr. Justice Black notes in that opinion, his separate position that the 14th amendment incorporates the Bill of Rights is not based on construction of the due process clause alone, but on "the language of the entire first section of the Fourteenth Amendment, as illuminated by the legislative history surrounding its adoption." *Id.* at 382 n. 11.

32 Murray's Lessee v. Hoboken Land & Improvement Co., 59 U.S. (18 How.) 272, 277 (1856).

33 *See, e.g., In re* Winship, 397 U.S. 358, 377 (1970) (Black, J., dissenting); Goldberg v. Kelly, 397 U.S. 254 (1970) (Black, J., dissenting).

34 198 U.S. 45 (1905).

35 It now seems that the ultimate punchline in the criticism of a constitutional decision is to say that it is "like *Lochner.*" Professor Ely has even minted a generic term, "to *Lochner,*" to describe whatever-it-was-so-awful-the-Court-did-in-*Lochner*. Ely, *supra* note 6, at 944. *Cf.* Winter, *supra* note 7, at 102: "Make no mistake about it, *Lochner v. New York* is alive and well in *Shapiro v. Thompson.*"

Lochner is only one of thousands of decisions in the history of the Court that invoke a non-interpretive mode of constitutional adjudication; if it was a bad decision, as I think it was, it by no means follows that the general mode of adjudication it represents is illegitimate. There are many bad decisions in the mode of pure interpretation.

It is an often overlooked point that Mr. Justice Holmes in his classic *Lochner* dissent did not use the case as an occasion to reject noninterpretive adjudication generally, or even substantive due process as such; quite the contrary: "I think that the word liberty in

A striking point often overlooked by contemporary interpretivists is that the demise of substantive due process must constitutionally free the federal government to engage in explicit racial discrimination. There is no textual warrant for reading into the due process clause of the fifth amendment any of the prohibitions directed against the states by the equal protection clause.[36]

Equally strikingly, the application of the provisions of the Bill of Rights to states cannot be justified under an interpretive model—unless one strains to accept, as the Court clearly has declined to do, the flimsy historical evidence that the framers of the 14th amendment intended this result.[37] Freedom of speech, freedom of religion, and the requirement of just compensation in the taking of property, as well as the procedural provisions of the fourth, fifth, sixth, and eighth amendments must then no longer be seen as federal constitutional restraints on state power.

All of the "fundamental interests" that trigger "strict scrutiny" under the equal protection clause would have to be discarded, if the interpretive model were to control constitutional adjudication. Most obviously, the large body of doctrine that has grown up around the interests in the franchise and in participation in the electoral process could not stand. If the values implicit in the equal protection clause are limited only to those that its framers intended at

---

the Fourteenth Amendment is perverted when it is held to prevent the natural outcome of a dominant opinion, *unless it can be said that a rational and fair man necessarily would admit that the statute proposed would infringe fundamental principles as they have been understood by the traditions of our people and our law.*" 198 U.S. at 76 (emphasis added).

36 *See* Bolling v. Sharpe, 347 U.S. 497, 499 (1954). Since *Bolling*, the Court has often applied equal protection doctrine to the federal government "under" the fifth amendment due process clause. *See, e.g.*, Shapiro v. Thompson, 394 U.S. 618 (1969), in which the Court invalidated a District of Columbia statute as a violation of due process, while relying upon the equal protection clause to invalidate similar state statutes. Since *Bolling*—at least as far as I have been able to discover—the Court has never even seriously discussed the possibility that the fifth amendment due process clause might not fully incorporate the requirements progressively imposed on the states under the equal protection clause.

37 The Court's refusal to adopt the "incorporation" theory is clear both from its refusal to apply the requirements of grand jury indictment and civil jury trial to the states, and from its statements in "selective incorporation" cases. *See, e.g.*, Duncan v. Louisiana, 391 U.S. 145, 149 (1968), which held that due process required the states to provide jury trial in serious criminal cases *because* "trial by jury in criminal cases is fundamental to the American scheme of justice ...." For the controversy over the intent of the framers, *compare* Fairman, *Does the Fourteenth Amendment Incorporate the Bill of Rights?*, 2 STAN. L. REV. 5 (1949), *with* Adamson v. California, 332 U.S. 46, 68 (1947) (Black, J., dissenting).

the time of enactment, the clause clearly does not speak to questions of eligibility for the franchise or of legislative apportionment.[38]

Thus far, it seems to me there is little room for disagreement that the premises of the pure interpretive model would require the conclusions I have drawn from it. For those who have not yet had enough, and coming to slightly more doubtful matters, there is serious question how much of the law prohibiting state racial discrimination can survive honest application of the interpretive model. It is clear that the equal protection clause was meant to prohibit *some* forms of state racial discrimination, most obviously those enacted in the Black Codes. It is equally clear from the legislative history that the clause was *not* intended to guarantee equal political rights, such as the right to vote or to run for office, and perhaps including the right to serve on juries.[39]

It is at least doubtful whether the clause can fairly be read as intended to bar any form of state-imposed racial segregation, so long as equal facilities are made available. Professor Bickel's careful study of the legislative history revealed little evidence of intent to prohibit segregation, which at the time was widespread in the North.[40] Professor Bickel did conclude that the original understanding of the amendment was consistent with the decision in the School Segregation Cases, but only in the sense that the general language of the clause *licensed* the courts (and Congress) to enforce evolving ideals of racial justice.[41] Yet this is a classic invocation of the notion of the "living constitution," and as such is not permitted by the interpretive model.

Finally, under the interpretive model, modern applications of the provisions of the Bill of Rights based on their capacity to grow or develop with changing social values would have to be discarded. Prominent among the discarded doctrines would be the prevailing view that the eighth amendment's prohibition of cruel and unusual punishments must be "interpreted" in light of society's "evolving standards of decency."[42] It is doubtful that much of modern first amendment doctrine could be defended on the basis of value choices

38 The numerous dissenting opinions of Mr. Justice Harlan in voting and reapportionment cases put the point beyond doubt. *See, e.g.*, Carrington v. Rash, 380 U.S. 89, 97 (1965) (Harlan, J., dissenting); Reynolds v. Sims, 377 U.S. 533, 589 (1964) (Harlan, J., dissenting).

39 *See generally* Bickel, *The Original Understanding and the Segregation Decision*, 69 HARV. L. REV. 1 (1955).

40 *Id.* at 58.

41 *Id.* at 62–65.

42 *See, e.g.*, Trop v. Dulles, 356 U.S. 86, 101 (1958).

attributable to the framers,[43] and similar doubts must cast a shadow on some of the law of the fourth amendment.[44] The doctrine that the sixth amendment guarantees appointed counsel for indigent defendants[45] is likewise in serious jeopardy, if historically intended meaning must be the only legitimate guide in constitutional adjudication.[46]

While one might disagree with this rough catalogue on points of detail, it should be clear that an extraordinarily radical purge of established constitutional doctrine would be required if we candidly and consistently applied the pure interpretive model. Surely that makes out at least a prima facie practical case against the model. Conservatives ought to be cautious about adopting any abstract premise which requires so drastic a change in accepted practice, and

---

43 *See generally* L. Levy, Legacy of Suppression (1960).

44 *See, e.g.*, Katz v. United States, 389 U.S. 347 (1967), in which the Court extended fourth amendment coverage to the recording of oral statements by electronic devices. Justice Black filed a lone dissent arguing—from an interpretive stance—"[s]ince I see no way in which the words of the Fourth Amendment can be construed to apply to eavesdropping, that closes the matter for me.... I will not distort the words of the Amendment in order to 'keep the Constitution up to date' or 'to bring it into harmony with the times.'" *Id.* at 373 (dissenting opinion).

45 Johnson v. Zerbst, 304 U.S. 458 (1938).

46 The instances of noninterpretive judicial review I have mentioned fall into three general groups. First are those instances where the courts have created (or found) independent constitutional rights with almost no textual guidance. Examples are the contemporary right of privacy, and the older liberty of contract. Second are those instances where the courts have given general application to norms that the constitutional text explicitly applies in a more limited way. Examples are the application of equal protection and contract clause principles to the federal government, and the application of the Bill of Rights to the states—"under" the conveniently all-embracing due process clauses. The third type is the extension or broadening of principles stated in the Constitution beyond the normative content intended for them by the framers. Examples are the School Segregation Cases, and the extension of the fourth amendment to cover eavesdropping.

Most of the ire of proponents of the pure interpretive model has been directed against the first of these types of noninterpretive review. However the other two types are equally illegitimate, given the logic of the interpretive model. The advantage of placing a controverted case in the third rather than the first grouping is that it is usually possible to argue, with at least a shadow of plausibility, that extension of a specific constitutional prohibition really involves only the application of old norms to changed facts, and not a change in the norms themselves. *See, e.g.*, the majority opinion in Griswold v. Connecticut, 381 U.S. 479 (1965), for an implausible attempt to base a nontextual right of marital privacy on an "interpretation" of various provisions of the Bill of Rights—thus converting a Type 1 case into a "less suspect" Type 3 case.

liberals presumably will be dismayed by the prospect of any major diminution in the courts' authority to protect basic human rights.

IV Beyond Interpretation: A Program of Inquiry

The uncomfortable results of adopting the interpretive model do not by themselves make a wholly satisfying argument for judicial review that goes beyond interpretation. Constitutional adjudication going beyond the norms implicit in text and original history requires its own affirmative justification. In this short Essay, I can only suggest the several levels on which this inquiry might proceed, and hint at some of the directions it might take.

A *The Question of Practical Wisdom*

First, one must consider the question of the wisdom and prudence of putting—or more accurately *leaving*—in the hands of judges the considerable power to define and enforce fundamental human rights without substantial guidance from constitutional text and history. How one views this question depends largely on how one evaluates the practical results, over the long run, of the exercise of this power. Arguments about institutional competence and the general propensities of judges become relevant here. Familiar in this context is the argument made in varying forms by constitutional commentators from Alexander Hamilton to Alexander Bickel that it makes some sense to give the final—or nearly final—say over the barrier between state and individual to the "least dangerous branch," the one that possesses neither purse nor sword.[47] But much can be said the other way, particularly through argument in the name of popular sovereignty, and through allusion to *Lochner* and its ilk.

B *The Jurisprudential Question*

Second, one can ask the jurisprudential question whether as a general matter the defining and enforcing of basic rights without external textual guidance is essentially a judicial task. Judges may be fine folk, but if what they are doing when they engage in judicial review on the basis of changing and unwritten moral principles is not adjudication, then they are sailing under false colors. For they have consistently told us that judicial review is genuinely incident to their traditionally assigned task of deciding litigated cases according to law.

---

47 *See* THE FEDERALIST NO. 78, at 504–05 (E. Earle ed.) (A. Hamilton); A. BICKEL, THE LEAST DANGEROUS BRANCH 23–28 (1962).

A rigorously positivist jurisprudence would hold that judicial decision not directed by the articulate command of a determinate external sovereign is not truly adjudication. Rather it is a species of legislation. But this sort of positivist also views the entirely traditional judicial task of common law development through case-by-case decision as a form of legislation.[48] If common law development is an appropriate judicial function, falling within the traditionally accepted judicial role, is not the functionally similar case-by-case development of constitutional norms appropriate as well? Granted that the supremacy of constitutional law over legislation, when contrasted with the formally inferior status of common law, makes a great difference. But the difference is in the hierarchical status of the judicial decision—which turns on a question of *authority*—and not in the intrinsic nature of the task.

C *The Question of Lawful Authority*

The question of authority is the third level of inquiry into the justification for noninterpretive judicial review. Even if this mode of judicial review produces good results in the eyes of some beholders, and even if it is not intrinsically unjudicial, there remains the question whether in our Constitution we have actually granted this large power to our judges.

In resolving this issue of legal authority, there seems to me only one plausible method of inquiry. We must apply the conventional and accepted categories of legal argument—original understanding, judicial precedent, subsequent history, and internal consistency—and see if they support judicial review that goes beyond interpretation.

I believe that when these tests are applied, constitutional adjudication of the sort objected to by Mr. Justice Black and the other proponents of the pure interpretive model will be seen to be a lawful and legitimate feature of our system of judicial review. Full development of the argument must await another occasion; it necessarily requires lengthy and detailed historical documentation. But a brief sketch may be useful here.[49]

---

48 I do not endorse this positivist analysis. It seems to me that traditional common law decision and constitutional decision according to the noninterpretive mode both can be seen as decision of cases according to law. The law in question consists of the generally accepted social norms applied in the decision of the cases, norms that are—contrary to the positivists' position—best seen as "part of the law," quite independent of their promulgation through defined lawmaking procedures. *See* Dworkin, *The Model of Rules*, 35 U. CHI. L. REV. 14 (1967); Wellington, *Common Law Rules and Constitutional Double Standards: Some Notes on Adjudication*, 83 YALE L.J. 221 (1973).

49 I have set out my sketch as a simple narrative, lacking the detail, the qualifications, and the analysis of conflicting evidence that the full argument requires. I have also left out

For the generation that framed the Constitution, the concept of a "higher law," protecting "natural rights," and taking precedence over ordinary positive law as a matter of political obligation, was widely shared and deeply felt. An essential element of American constitutionalism was the reduction to written form—and hence to positive law—of some of the principles of natural rights. But at the same time, it was generally recognized that written constitutions could not completely codify the higher law. Thus in the framing of the original American constitutions it was widely accepted that there remained unwritten but still binding principles of higher law. The ninth amendment is the textual expression of this idea in the federal Constitution.

As it came to be accepted that the judiciary had the power to enforce the commands of the written Constitution when these conflicted with ordinary law, it was also widely assumed that judges would enforce as constitutional restraints the unwritten natural rights as well. The practice of the Marshall Court and of many of its contemporary state courts, and the writings of the leading constitutional commentators through the first generation of our national life, confirm this understanding.

A parallel development during the first half of the 19th century was the frequent attachment of unwritten constitutional principles to the vaguer and more general clauses of the state and federal constitutions. Natural-rights reasoning in constitutional adjudication persisted up to the Civil War, particularly with respect to property and contract rights, and increasingly involving "due process" and "law of the land" clauses in constitutional texts. At the same time, an important wing of the antislavery movement developed a natural-rights constitutional theory, built around the concepts of due process, of national citizenship and its rights, and of the human equality proclaimed in the Declaration of Independence.

Though this latter movement had little direct effect on pre-Civil War judicial decisions, it was the formative theory underlying the due process, equal protection, and privileges and immunities clauses of the 14th amendment. Section 1 of the 14th amendment is thus properly seen as a reaffirmation and reenactment in positive law of the principle that fundamental human rights have constitutional status.

The late 19th century saw the most controversial phase in our history of unwritten constitutional law, with the aggressive development by state and federal judges of constitutional principles protecting "liberty of contract"

---

any documentation, on the theory that incomplete and necessarily misleading citation of sources is worse than none at all. The full-scale development of the historical argument sketched here awaits the completion of a forthcoming article.

against labor legislation, and restraining taxation and the regulation of prices charged by private business. The reaction to this tendency marked the beginning of sustained intellectual and political attack on the whole concept of unwritten constitutional principles.

Politically, emergent and eventually dominant social forces continued to press for the legislation that was being invalidated under these constitutional principles. Intellectually, the 18th-century philosophical framework supporting the concept of immutable natural rights was eroded with the growth of legal positivism, ethical relativism, pragmatism, and historicism.

Under the combined assault of these social and intellectual forces, the courts retreated from the doctrines of "economic due process," abandoning them in the 1930's. However, although the more sweeping attack on the whole tradition of unwritten constitutional principles gained some important adherents within the judiciary and still more among academic critics, it did not ultimately prevail.

For at almost the same time as the doctrines protecting the laissez-faire economy were passing out of constitutional law, the judiciary began the active development of new civil-libertarian constitutional rights whose protection was deemed "essential to the concept of ordered liberty"—for example, rights against state governments of freedom of speech and religion, rights to "fundamentally fair" proceedings, and rights to familial autonomy in childrearing and education.

The last generation has seen further development of constitutional rights clearly—and sometimes avowedly—not derived by textual interpretation, notably the right of privacy, the right to vote, the right to travel, and generally the rights resulting from application of "equal protection of the laws" to the federal government. The intellectual framework against which these rights have developed is different from the natural-rights tradition of the founding fathers—its rhetorical reference points are the Anglo-American tradition and basic American ideals, rather than human nature, the social contract, or the rights of man. But it is the modern offspring, in a direct and traceable line of legitimate descent, of the natural-rights tradition that is so deeply embedded in our constitutional origins.

To summarize, there was an original understanding, both implicit and textually expressed, that unwritten higher law principles had constitutional status. From the very beginning, and continuously until the Civil War, the courts acted on that understanding and defined and enforced such principles as part of their function of judicial review. Aware of that history, the framers of the 14th amendment reconfirmed the original understanding through the "majestic generalities" of section 1. And ever since, again without significant break, the courts have openly proclaimed and enforced unwritten constitutional principles.

V Conclusion

I recognize that there are a host of controversial assertions in this little historico-legal sketch. Had the natural-rights arguments that played so large a role in the American Revolution passed out of fashion and favor when the Constitution was framed? Was not the ninth amendment meant merely to express a principle of federalism? How clear are the natural-rights, anti-slavery origins of the 14th amendment?

Perhaps the most significant question raised is not one of historical fact so much as of legal principle and political theory. Conceding the natural-rights origins of our Constitution, does not the erosion and abandonment of the 18th-century ethics and epistemology on which the natural-rights theory was founded require the abandonment of the mode of judicial review flowing from that theory? Is a "fundamental law" judicially enforced in a climate of historical and cultural relativism the legitimate offspring of a fundamental law which its exponents felt expressed rationally demonstrable, universal, and immutable human rights?

These questions remain to be debated and further investigated before the legitimate pedigree of noninterpretive judicial review can be established. I certainly make no claim that they have been answered here. I have only argued in this Essay that very little of our constitutional law of individual rights has any firm foundation in the model of judicial review which traces from *Marbury v. Madison* to the jurisprudence of Mr. Justice Black. And I have suggested that the reflexive resort to variants of this model, so common a rhetorical response of constitutional scholars in the *Lochner* era, seems to be reviving today, and therefore requires more direct critical scrutiny than it has had in the recent past.

The Disintegration of Property

Thomas C. Grey

I

In the English-speaking countries today, the conception of property held by the specialist (the lawyer or economist) is quite different from that held by the ordinary person. Most people, including most specialists in their unprofessional moments, conceive of property as *things* that are *owned* by *persons*. To own property is to have exclusive control of something—to be able to use it as one wishes, to sell it, give it away, leave it idle, or destroy it. Legal restraints on the free use of one's property are conceived as departures from an ideal conception of full ownership.[1]

By contrast, the theory of property rights held by the modern specialist tends both to dissolve the notion of ownership and to eliminate any necessary connection between property rights and things. Consider ownership first. The specialist fragments the robust unitary conception of ownership into a more shadowy "bundle of rights." Thus, a thing can be owned by more than one person, in which case it becomes necessary to focus on the particular limited rights each of the co-owners has with respect to the thing. Further, the notion that full ownership includes rights to do as you wish with what you own suggests that you might sell off *particular aspects* of your control—rights to certain uses, to profits from the thing, and so on. Finally, rights of use, profit, and the like can be parceled out along a temporal dimension as well—you might sell your control over your property for tomorrow to one person, for the next day to another, and so on.

Not only can ownership rights be subdivided, they can even be made to disappear as if by magic, if we postulate full freedom of disposition in the owner. Consider the convenient legal institution of the trust. Yesterday A

* This article originally appeared in *Ethics, Economics and the Law of Property* edited by J. Roland Pennock and John W. Chapman (New York: New York University Press, 1980), pp. 69–85.

1 See the excellent explication of the "ordinary" conception of property in Bruce A. Ackerman, *Private Property and the Constitution* (New Haven and London, 1977), pp. 97–100, 113–67. *See also* A.M. Honore, "Ownership," in A.G. Guest, ed. *Oxford Essays in Jurisprudence* (London, 1961). [Relevant parts of the latter are summarized in Lawrence Becker's paper in the present volume (eds.).]

© KONINKLIJKE BRILL NV, LEIDEN, 2014 | DOI 10.1163/9789004272897_004

owned Blackacre; among his rights of ownership was the legal power to leave the land idle, even though developing it would bring a good income. Today A puts Blackacre in trust, conveying it to B (the trustee) for the benefit of C (the beneficiary). Now no one any longer has the legal power to use the land uneconomically or to leave it idle—that part of the rights of ownership is neither in A nor B nor C, but has disappeared. As between B and C, who owns Blackacre? Lawyers say B has the legal and C the equitable ownership, but upon reflection the question seems meaningless: what is important is that we be able to specify what B and C can legally do with respect to the land.

The same point can be made with respect to fragmentation of ownership generally. When a full owner of a thing begins to sell off various of his rights over it—the right to use it for this purpose tomorrow, for that purpose next year, and so on—at what point does he cease to be the owner, and who then owns the thing? You can say that each one of many right holders owns it to the extent of the right, or you can say that no one owns it. Or you can say, as we still tend to do, in vestigial deference to the lay conception of property, that some conventionally designated rights constitute "ownership." The issue is seen as one of terminology; nothing significant turns on it.[2]

What, then, of the idea that property rights must be rights in things? Perhaps we no longer need a notion of ownership, but surely property rights are a distinct category from other legal rights, in that they pertain to things. But this suggestion cannot withstand analysis either; most property in a modern capitalist economy is intangible. Consider the common forms of wealth: shares of stock in corporations, bonds, various kinds of commercial paper, bank accounts, insurance policies—not to mention more arcane intangibles such as trademarks, patents, copyrights, franchises, and business goodwill.

In our everyday language, we tend to speak of these rights as if they attached to things. Thus we "deposit our money in the bank", as if we were putting a thing in a place; but really we are creating a complex set of abstract claims against an abstract legal institution. We are told that as insurance policy holders we "own a piece of the rock"; but we really have other abstract claims against another abstract institution. We think of our share of stock in Megabucks Corporation as part ownership in the Megabucks factory outside town; but really the Megabucks board of directors could sell the factory and go

2 For modern property vocabulary, see Ackerman, op. cit., pp. 26–28. For the still common vestigial use of the notion of ownership by lawyers, see American Law Institute, *Restatement of the Law of Property* (St. Paul, 1936), vol. 1 pp. 25–27. Compare J.C. Vaines, *Personal Property*, 4th ed. (London, 1967), pp. 39–40.

into another line of business and we would still have the same claims on the same abstract corporation.

Property rights cannot any longer be characterized as "rights of ownership" or as "rights in things" by specialists in property. What, then, *is* their special characteristic? How do property rights differ from rights generally—from human rights or personal rights or rights to life or liberty, say? Our specialists and theoreticians have no answer; or rather, they have a multiplicity of widely differing answers, related only in that they bear some association or analogy, more or less remote, to the common notion of property as ownership of things.

Let me briefly list a number of present usages of the term property in law, legal theory, and economics.

1. The law of property for law teachers and law students typically is the whole body of law concerned with the use of land: the doctrines of estates in land, title registration and transfer, the financing of real estate transactions, the law of landlord and tenant, public regulation of land use (including zoning and environmental regulation), and public subsidy and provision of low-income housing. The only thing these doctrines have in common with each other is that they concern real estate as distinguished from other aspects of the economy.[3]
2. Lawyers (and some economists) identify property rights with rights *in rem* (rights good against the world), as distinguished from rights *in personam* (rights good against determinate persons). This distinction does not fit closely with popular notions of property; for example, the rights to life, bodily security, and personal liberty protected by criminal laws against murder, assault, and kidnapping are on this account "property rights." Neither the application of the distinction nor its purpose is very clear; for example, *in personam* contract rights shade into property rights as they become freely assignable, and assumable, and as "interference with contractual relations" is recognized as a tort.[4]
3. Some economists seem to adopt, implicitly, a purposive account of property, including among property rights all and only those entitlements whose purpose (in some sense) is to advance allocative efficiency by allowing individuals to reap the benefits and requiring them to bear the

3 I draw this point from conversations with colleagues who teach law school courses in property. Some of them do deal with a few aspects of the law of "personal property," particularly rules concerning original acquistion.

4 For the *in rem* vs. *in personam* distinction, *see, e.g.*, Felix Cohen, "Dialogue on Private Property," 9 *Rutgers Law Review* 373–74 (Fall 1954).

costs generated by their activities. Again, on this account rights to life, liberty, and personal security are included within the field of property. On the other hand, legal entitlements to transfer payments, such as are conferred by welfare and social security laws, are presumably excluded.[5]

4. By contrast, some modern legal theorists have stressed that a traditional purpose of private property has been to protect security and independence, and that public law entitlements to social minima serve this purpose in the modern economy, and hence should be considered a "new property."[6] This view has been embodied in the construction the courts have given to the constitutional requirement that persons not be "deprived of... property without due process of law." Protections offered to property have been extended to entitlements conferred by, for example, welfare and public education law.[7]
5. Another contrasting view of property is suggested by the prevailing interpretation of another constitutional provision, the prohibition against "taking" private property except for a public purpose and upon the payment of just compensation. Here, the kind of property that can be taken is confined to those conglomerations of rights that, in the popular mind, have been reified into "things" or "pieces of property." Thus, the Supreme Court recently held that designation of Grand Central Station as a historic monument, and the consequent prohibition of construction of a skyscraper over the station, did not "take" any property of the landowners—the right to use the airspace over the building, an economically valuable entitlement, was not sufficiently thing-like to be subject to the just compensation requirement.[8] (This body of "takings" law, which most nearly corresponds to popular conceptions of property as thing ownership, is difficult to rationalize in the terms of modern legal and economic theory.)[9]
6. Another specialized usage distinguishes between "property" and "liability" rules according to the nature of the sanctions imposed upon their violation. Property rules are enforceable by injunction or criminal

5 *See, e.g.*, Richard Posner, *Economic Analysis of Law*, 2d ed. (Boston and Toronto, 1977), pp. 27–31; Harold Demsetz, "Toward a Theory of Property Rights," 57 *Am. Econ. Rev. Papers and Proceedings* 347 (1967).

6 *See* Charles A. Reich, "The New Property," 73 *Yale Law Journal* 733 (April 1964).

7 Goldberg v. Kelly, 397 U.S. 254 (1970); Goss v. Lopez, 419 U.S. 565 (1975).

8 Penn Central Transp. Co. v. New York City, 438 U.S. 104 (1978).

9 See the discussion in Ackerman, op. cit., especially chap. 6. [*See also* Ackerman's essay in this volume (eds.).]

> sanctions or both—sanctions designed to prevent violation even when it would be cost-justified in terms of market valuation. Liability rules are enforced only by the award of money damages, measured by the market valuation of the resources lost to the victim. This conception departs widely from popular usage; thus, a person's ownership of his car, for example, is protected by both liability rules (tort doctrines of conversion and liability for negligent damage to property) and property rules (criminal laws against theft).[10]

The conclusion of all this is that discourse about property has fragmented into a set of discontinuous usages. The more fruitful and useful of these usages are those stipulated by theorists; but these depart drastically from each other and from common speech. Conversely, meanings of "property" in law that cling to their origin in the thing-ownership conception are integrated least successfully into the general doctrinal framework of law, legal theory, and economics. It seems fair to conclude from a glance at the range of current usages that the specialists who design and manipulate the legal structures of the advanced capitalist economies could easily do without using the term "property" at all.

II

It was not always so. At the high point of classical liberal thought, around the end of the eighteenth century, the idea of private property stood at the center of the conceptual scheme of lawyers and political theorists. Thus, Blackstone wrote: "There is nothing which so generally strikes the imagination, and engages the affections of mankind, as the right of property."[11] And the French Civil Code had as its "grand and principal object" (in the words of one of its authors) "to regulate the principles and the rights of property."[12] Kant began his discussion of law in the *Metaphysics of Morals* with an analysis

10 This usage was introduced by Guido Calabresi and A. Douglas Melamed, "Property Rules, Liability Rules, and Inalienability: One View of the Cathedral," 85 *Harvard Law Review* 1089 (1972).

11 Sir William Blackstone, *Commentaries on the Laws of England* 11th ed. (London, 1791), vol. II, p. 2.

12 Quoted by Richard Schlatter, *Private Property: The History of an Idea* (New Brunswick, N.J., 1951), p. 232, from J.G. Locre, *La Legislation Civil de la France* (Paris, 1827), vol. 31, p. 169.

and justification of property rights.[13] The earliest American state constitutions proclaimed property as one of the natural rights of man.[14]

The conception of property held by the legal and political theorists of classical liberalism coincided precisely with the present popular idea, the notion of thing-ownership. Thus, Blackstone described property as "that sole and despotic dominion which one man claims and exercises over the external things of the world, in total exclusion of the right of any other individual in the universe."[15] And, in perfect concord, the French Civil Code defined property as "the right of enjoying and disposing of things in the most absolute manner."[16]

It is not difficult to see how the idea of simple ownership came to dominate classical liberal legal and political thought. First, this conception of property mirrored economic reality to a much greater extent than it did before or has since. Much of the wealth of the preindustrial capitalist economy consisted of the houses and lots of freeholders, the land of peasant proprietors or small farmers, and the shops and tools of artisans.[17]

Second, the concept of property as thing-ownership served important ideological functions. Liberalism was the ideology of the attack on feudalism. A central feature of feudalism was its complex and hierarchical system of land tenure. To the rising bourgeoisie, property conceived as a web of relations among persons meant the system of lord, vassal, and serf from which they were struggling to free themselves. On the other hand, property conceived as the control of a piece of the material world by a single individual meant freedom and equality of status. Thus Blackstone denounced the archaisms of feudal tenure.[18] The French Civil Code marked the culmination of a revolution that abolished feudal property.[19] Hegel wrote that the abolition of feudal property in favor of individual ownership was as great a triumph of freedom as the abolition of slavery.[20] Jefferson contrasted the free allodial system of land titles in America with the servile English system of feudal tenure.[21]

---

13 Kant, *Philosophy of Law*, trans. W. Hastie (Edinburgh, 1887), pp. 81–84.

14 Quoted in Schlatter, op. cit., pp. 188–89.

15 Blackstone, op. cit., p. 2.

16 Code Civil, Art. 544, quoted in Schlatter, op. cit., p. 232.

17 *See* R.H. Tawney, *The Acquisitive Society* (New York, 1920), pp. 55–60.

18 Blackstone, op. cit. p. 77, where he said of the feudal institution of tenure by knight service: "A slavery so complicated, and so extensive as this, called aloud for a remedy in a nation that boasted of its freedom."

19 *See* Schlatter, op. cit., p. 222.

20 Hegel, *Philosophy of Right*, trans. W.W. Dyde (London, 1896), pp. 65–68.

21 Jefferson, "A Summary View of the Rights of British America," in Boyd et al., *The Papers of Thomas Jefferson* (Princeton, 1950–), vol. 1, pp. 121–135.

Third, ownership of things by individuals fitted the principal justifications for treating property as a natural right. In England and America, the dominant theory was Locke's; rightful property resulted from the mixing of an individual's labor with nature.[22] The main rival to Locke's theory within liberal thought was the German Idealist conception of Kant and Hegel, who saw original property resulting from the subjective act of appropriation, the exercise of the individual will over a piece of unclaimed nature. On this view, property was an extension of personality. Ownership expanded the natural sphere of freedom for the individual beyond his body to part of the material world.[23]

III

We have gone, then, in less than two centuries, from a world in which property was a central idea mirroring a clearly understood institution, to one in which it is no longer a coherent or crucial category in our conceptual scheme. The concept of property and the institution of property have disintegrated. I want to offer first a partial explanation of this phenomenon, and then some suggestions about its political significance.

My explanatory point is that the collapse of the idea of property can best be understood as a process internal to the development of capitalism itself. It is, on this view, not a result of the attack on capitalism by socialists, and not a result of the modifications of laissez-faire that we associate with the coming of a mixed economy or a welfare state. Rather, it is intrinsic to the development of a free-market economy into an industrial phase. Indeed, it is a factor contributing to the declining prestige, the decaying cultural hegemony, of capitalism. To say this is not to deny that the causation may run the other way as well. The decline of capitalism may also contribute to the breakdown of the idea of private property, so that the two phenomena mutually reinforce each other; but my purpose is to isolate a sense in which the disintegration of property follows from the workings of an idealized market economy.

The development from an economy of small property owners to an industrial economy proceeds by the progressive exploitation of the *division of labor or function* and the *economies of scale*. This development can be pictured as taking place through a series of free economic transactions, with the state playing only its classically liberal, neutral, facilitative role. Proprietors subdivide and recombine the bundles of rights that make up their original ownership,

22 Locke, *Second Treatise of Government* (London, 1964). chap. 5, "Of Property."

23 Kant, op. cit., pp. 62–64; Hegel, op. cit., pp. 48–53.

creating by private agreement the complex of elaborate and abstract economic institutions and claims characteristic of industrial capitalism, particularly the financial institutions and the industrial corporations. With very few exceptions, all of the private law institutions of mature capitalism can be imagined as arising from the voluntary decompositions and recombination of elements of simple ownership, under a regime in which owners are allowed to divide and transfer their interests as they wish.[24]

The few aspects of the modern private economy that require state action beyond the enforcement of private agreements are the newer forms of originally acquired intangible entitlements, such as patents, copyrights, and trademarks on the one hand, and on the other hand the privilege of corporate limited liability against tort claims. (Limited liability against claims by employees and creditors could be created by contract, as could the rest of the structure of the modern corporation.)[25] The intangible entitlements are of nontrivial but relatively peripheral significance to the functioning of mature capitalism. And although the corporation is the central institution of the modern economy, it is not likely that the corporate economy would collapse without limited liability in tort.

The transformation of a preindustrial economy of private proprietors into an industrial economy by the process suggested here presupposes that the entrepreneurs, financiers, and lawyers who carry the process through have the imagination to liberate themselves from the imprisoning concept of property as the simple ownership of a thing by an individual person. They must be able to design new forms of finance and control for enterprise, which can take maximum advantage of the efficiencies of scale and division of function, forms that fractionate traditional ownership and that create claims remote from tangible objects. Similarly, if the process is to go forward smoothly, the courts will have to free themselves from stereotypes about the appropriate forms of

---

24 The free creation of property interests by proprietors has in fact never been allowed to go this far; the types of property interests that could be carved out has typically been limited, often in the name of facilitating market transactions by prohibiting unduly complex holdings. See the discussion in F.H. Lawson, *The Law of Property* (Oxford, 1958), chap. 6. In the civil law systems of continental Europe, the law has allowed only quite limited formal freedom to create new property interests; this apparently is the outgrowth of a Roman law heritage, combined with a prejudice in favor of simple thing-ownership arising out of the association of complex forms of property with feudalism. See generally, John Merryman, "Ownership and Estate," 48 *Tulane Law Review* 916, 924–29 (June 1974).

25 See the analysis in Posner, op. cit., pp. 292–96.

control over the economic resources of the community, stereotypes founded on an economy of artisans, tradesmen, and family farms.[26]

The creation of new forms of enterprise and new structures of entitlement would require doctrinal formulation, at least by lawyers and courts. And where law, business, and finance are subjects of theoretical study, these new legal structures of economic organization would eventually become the focus of examination by commentators and scholars, particularly as they come to replace older forms of property as the chief economic institutions of the society. Leaving ideological considerations aside for the moment, it would not be surprising if the replacement of thing-ownership by abstract claim structures in the real world should eventually lead some theorists to the kind of analysis of the concept of property I sketched in the first section. Even if the analysis did not go that far, the basic need to teach lawyers the technical tools of their trade would suggest if not require some movement toward a bundle-of-rights formulation of property, as against the historical and popular thing-ownership conception. The main point is that all of these developments—the new economic structures, the legal forms through which they are organized, and the theoretical analysis of property that they suggest—can be plausibly seen as entirely *internal* to the capitalist market system; entirely consistent with full loyalty to that system; in no way fueled by the ethics, politics, or interests of socialism, collectivism, paternalism, or redistributive egalitarianism.

I must repeat that this account is not offered as an accurate narrative of historical events. (No society has practiced as pure an economic liberalism as this; industrial development has been subsidized, retarded, and actively shaped by government throughout.) But this account is intended to abstract out a plausible *partial* explanation, based on simplified assumptions, of the collapse of the idea of property between 1800 and today. I now want to turn to the ideological factors this simplified account has left out. If the internal logic of the market tends to fragment the concept of property in the ways I have suggested, what does a recognition of this development mean in political terms?

IV

The dissolution of the traditional conception of property erodes the moral basis of capitalism. Capitalism has commonly been conceived, by friends and enemies alike, as a system based on the existence and protection of private property rights. Given this conception, the view that property rights have intrinsic

26 See n. 24, above.

worth must strengthen the case for capitalism—at least so long as "property rights" are viewed as a single coherent category. But the phenomenon of the "death of property" breaks the connection between simple thing-ownership and the legal entitlements that make up the framework of the capitalist organization of the economy. And it is simple thing-ownership that has been justified in classical liberal theory, and I think in popular consciousness, as having intrinsic worth.

The theories that support an intrinsic moral right to property can be roughly divided into the labor and personality justifications for private ownership. The labor theory expresses the intuition that the individual owns as a matter of natural right the valued objects he has made or wrested from nature. Thus, the farmer naturally owns the land he has cleared and the crops he has grown; the artisan owns the tools he has fashioned, the raw materials he has gathered, and the products he has made.[27] The idealist "personality" theory rests on the different but no less powerful idea that human beings naturally come to regard some objects as extensions of themselves in some important sense. This idea gains its intuitive force from the way most people regard their homes, their immediate personal effects, and other material things that play a double role as part of their most immediate environment in daily life and at the same time as expressions of their personalities.[28]

Insofar as capitalism connotes a general regime of protection of private property, it enlists these still potent justifications on its side. Conversely, attacks on capitalism engender the sense of outrage that most people feel at a threat to their simple possessions and the immediate fruits of their labor. Marx and Engels realized this well when they sought to dissociate the socialist case for abolition of private property from any threat to the security of ordinary possessions:

> We communists have been reproached with the desire of abolishing the right of personally acquiring property as the fruit of a man's own labor.... Hard-won, self-acquired, self-earned property! Do you mean the

---

27 This is, roughly, Locke's theory of property. See above, n. 22. It must be noted that Locke did not confine the scope of his natural right to property to objects with which the individual mixed his labor, but argued that the invention of money justified a natural right of unlimited accumulation. See the discussion in C.B. MacPherson, *The Political Theory of Possessive Individualism: Hobbes to Locke* (London, 1962), pp. 197–220.

28 See works cited in n. 23, above; *see also* the discussion in T.H. Green, *Lectures on the Principles of Political Obligation*, reprinted in C.B. MacPherson, ed, *Property: Mainstream and Critical Positions* (Toronto, 1978), pp. 103–17.

> property of the petty artisan and of the small peasant, a form of property that preceded the bourgeois form? There is no need to abolish that; the development of industry has to a great extent already destroyed it, and is destroying it daily.[29]

I have argued in this essay that we no longer have any coherent concept of property encompassing both simple thing-ownership, on the one hand, and the variety of legal entitlements that are generally called property rights on the other. If correct, this argument means that the forceful intuitions behind the moral arguments for simple thing-ownership can no longer be as readily transferred to the legal institutions of the capitalist economy, as they could when private property was a clearly comprehended unitary concept.[30]

Of course, the legitimacy of capitalism does not rest solely, or perhaps even predominantly anymore, on the notion of intrinsic moral rights to private property. Especially among the professionals and intellectuals for whom the breakdown of the concept of property is most likely to be apparent, the moral basis of capitalist institutions is likely to be found in other, more instrumental, values. Thus, capitalism is more commonly defended today on the basis of its capacity to produce material well-being and its tendency to protect personal liberty.

However, the belief that capitalist economic organization is especially protective of personal liberty is itself linked in a subtle way to the traditional conception of property. The connection is suggested by the theory of capitalist private law offered by the Austrian legal sociologist Karl Renner.[31] Renner described the fundamental structure of the capitalist legal order as made up of two basic elements: the right of ownership and the right of personal liberty. Ownership defines the relationship between man and nature, which consists of the control by separate individuals of separate parcels of the material world.

---

29 Marx and Engels, *The Communist Manifesto*, trans. Moore (Chicago, 1969), pp. 41–42.

30 Compare the interesting passage in Joseph Schumpeter, *Capitalism, Socialism and Democracy*, 3d ed. (New York, 1950), p. 142:

> "The capitalist process, by substituting a mere parcel of shares for the walls of and the machines in a factory, takes the life out of the idea of property. It loosens the grip that once was so strong—the grip in the sense of the legal right and the actual ability to do as one pleases with one's own.... Dematerialized, defunctionalized and absentee ownership does not impress and call forth moral allegiance as the vital form of property did."

31 What follows is a quite free interpretation of the argument of Renner's *The Institutions of Private Law and their Social Functions*, ed. O. Kahn-Freund, trans. A. Schwarzschild (London, 1949). Renner's discussion at pp. 81–95 captures the main thrust of his theory.

The right of personal liberty defines the relations between persons—a relation of independent equality, in which each person is free to do as he likes, consistent with respect for the rights of others. The interaction of the two rights creates a structure in which atomistic individuals stand, on the one hand, in a vertical relation of domination to the things they own, and on the other hand, in a horizontal relation of mutual independence to all other individuals. The only legal relations among the individuals, then, are those created by their voluntary agreements.[32]

The ideological significance of this simple and compelling picture of civil society is that it masks the existence of private economic power. The only relation of domination it recognizes is the relation of *dominium* or ownership over things. The danger of domination over persons—infringement of liberty—arises only when the state and public law are introduced, creating the power of sovereignty, or *imperium*. Thus, liberty can be threatened only by the state, and by the state only in its public law role, not in its role as neutral enforcer of the private law relations of ownership and contract.

This structure depends for its plausibility upon the obsolete thing-ownership conception of property. Acceptance of the bundle-of-rights conception breaks the main institutions of capitalist private law free from the metaphor of ownership as control over things by individuals. Mature capitalist property must be seen as a web of state-enforced relations of entitlement and duty *between persons*, some assumed voluntarily and some not.

Given this conceptual shift, the neutrality of the state as enforcer of private law evaporates; state protection of property rights is more easily seen as the use of collective force on behalf of the haves against the have-nots. It then becomes a matter for debate whether the private power centers of the unregulated capitalist economy, on the one hand, or the augmented state machinery of a socialist or mixed system, on the other, pose the more serious threat to personal liberty. The conflict between capitalism and socialism can no longer be articulated as a clash between liberty on the one side and equality on the other; both systems must be seen as protective against different threats to human freedom.

32 See the interestingly similar interpretation of Locke's *Second Treatise* in Louis Dumont, *From Mandeville to Marx: The Genesis and Triumph of Economic Ideology* (Chicago and London, 1977), chap. 4. C.B. MacPherson, n. 27 above, has argued persuasively that in early liberal theory the category of "equal individuals" was confined to property owners.

V

The breakdown of the traditional conception of property serves at the same time to undermine traditional Marxism, and to suggest that the natural development of industrial capitalism is toward a mixed economy. To put the point briefly: private property need not be *abolished* by revolution if it tends to *dissolve* with the development of mature capitalism.

Marxists have tended to view the transition from capitalism to socialism as necessarily a convulsive, qualitative transfer of ownership of the means of production from the bourgeoisie to the proletariat—a revolution. This revolution might under certain historical circumstances take place peacefully,[33] but the end of capitalism cannot, on a Marxist view, be gradual or partial.[34] There can be no compromise or halfway house between forms of social system; people live either under capitalism or under socialism.

This world view is strongly compatible with a thing-ownership conception of property—indeed, perhaps influenced and reinforced by such a conception. Marxist definitions of the forms of social system tend to focus on who owns the means of production.[35] Marxists sometimes note that this does not necessarily mean formal or juridical ownership, but rather real or economic

---

33 For a discussion of Marx's view that socialism might be achieved without violence in some advanced capitalist countries, see Shlomo Avineri, *The Social and Political Thought of Karl Marx* (Cambridge, 1968), pp. 211–20.

34 The classic Marxist account of the transition to socialism is the celebrated passaged from *Capital*, vol. 1, trans. Moore and Aveling (London, 1887), pp. 788–89:

> "Along with the constantly diminishing number of magnates of capital, who usurp and monopolise all advantages of this process of transformation, grows the mass of misery, oppression, slavery, degradation, exploitation; but with this too grows the revolt of the working-class, a class always increasing in numbers, and disciplined, united, organized by the very mechanism of the process of capitalist production itself. The monopoly of capital becomes a fetter upon the mode of production, which has sprung up and flourished along with, and under it. Centralisation of the means of production and socialisation of labor at last reach a point where they become incompatible with their capitalist integument. This integument is burst asunder. The knell of capitalist private property sounds. The expropriators are expropriated."

35 See, for example, the definition of advanced capitalist countries in Ralph Miliband, *The State in Capitalist Society* (New York, 1969), p. 7: "They have in common two crucial characteristics; the first is that they are all highly industrialized countries; and the second is that the largest part of their means of economic activity is under private ownership and control."

ownership.[36] Nevertheless both real and formal ownership have in common an all-or-nothing character. Something owned is either mine or thine, but not a little bit of each.

The Marxist approach is then substantially undermined by the demonstration that the category of all-or-nothing ownership has become increasingly unimportant as a form of legal thought in modern capitalist economies, where legal control over resources is increasingly fragmented into particularized entitlements. This fragmentation of property is most strikingly evident with respect to the large publicly held corporations that control the chief means of production. I am not speaking here primarily of the much-debated "separation of ownership and control."[37] The growth of power of non-shareholding management is only one aspect of the more general phenomenon of the dispersion of lawful power over the resources involved in a modern corporation. Not only managers and common shareholders, but also other classes of shareholders, directors, bondholders, other creditors, large suppliers and customers (through contractual arrangements), insurers, government regulators, tax authorities, and labor unions—all may have some of the legal powers that would be concentrated in the single ideal thing-owner of classical property theory.

There are clear structural similarities between this multiple institutional control and the mechanisms often suggested for controlling socialist enterprises—workers' councils, hired expert managers, central planners, suppliers, and buyers, each with influence, none with anything that might be called total power. Once the perspective of ownership is abandoned and the focus of inquiry shifts to particular legal rights and duties, on the one hand, and actual practical control, on the other, it seems natural to suppose that under any social system a variety of individuals, institutions, and interests are likely to share both the legal and the actual power over anything so complex as a major productive enterprise.[38]

On this view, capitalism and socialism become, not mutually exclusive forms of social organization, but tendencies that can be blended in various

36 *See, e.g.*, Nicos Poulantzas, *Political Power and Social Classes*, trans. T. O'Hagan (London, 1973), pp. 26–28.

37 In their classic account, *The Modern Corporation and Private Property*, rev. ed. (New York, 1967), p. 66, Berle and Means do suggest the important fragmenting and disintegrating effect of the recognition that "ownership" has become a formal and largely meaningless conception with respect to the modern corporation: "Control divorced from ownership is not . . . a familiar concept. . . . Like sovereignty, its counterpart in the political field, it is an elusive concept, for power can rarely be sharply segregated or clearly defined."

38 See the argument to this effect in C.A.R. Crosland, *The Future of Socialism* (New York, 1963), pp. 35–42.

proportions.[39] Important differences between profit-oriented market exchange and political collective decision as methods of organizing and operating enterprises remain. But the idea that natural necessity somehow imposes a stark choice between organizing an economy according to one or the other mode becomes less plausible, once the single-owner presupposition is dropped.

I do not want to overstate the extent to which the breakdown of classical property theory undercuts Marxist socialism. The central theoretical feature of Marxism remains the view that capitalist society is fundamentally divided into two sharply distinct and irreconcilably opposed classes, the bourgeoisie and the proletariat. Once this picture of society is accepted, it becomes a matter of detail that economic resources are controlled through complex and overlapping legal forms. As long as all rights of ownership are held within a compact and identifiable bourgeois class, it makes sense to characterize capitalism as ownership of the means of production by the bourgeois class as a whole. What analysis of the disintegration of property does is to indicate how totally Marxism depends upon the dubious reifications of its theory of class division and class struggle.

VI

The substitution of a bundle-of-rights for a thing-ownership conception of property has the ultimate consequence that property ceases to be an important category in legal and political theory. This in turn has political implications, which I have explored in the last two parts of this chapter. I believe that history confirms the centrist political tendency of the attack upon traditional conceptions of property. The legal realists who developed the bundle-of-rights notion were on the whole supporters of the regulatory and welfare state, and in the writings that develop the bundle-of-rights conception, a purpose to remove the sanctity that had traditionally attached to the rights of property can often be discerned.[40]

---

39 This approach to questions of economic organization has recently been given perhaps its most impressive and systematic treatment in Charles E. Lindblom, *Politics and Markets: The World's Political-Economic Systems* (New York, 1977).

40 The "bundle-of-rights" conception of property appears in well-articulated form for the first time (insofar as I have discovered) in Wesley Hohfeld, "Some Fundamental Legal Conceptions as Applied injudicial Reasoning," 23 *Yale Law Journal* 16 (1913). Thereafter, it became part of the conceptual stock-in-trade of the legal realist movement, often with a

The same point is illustrated by the most influential recent theoretical work on questions of economic justice, John Rawls's *A Theory of Justice*. The concept of property rights plays only the most minor role in that monumental treatise, which on the whole displays a welfare-state liberal orientation toward questions of the organization of economic life.[41]

I would want to deny, however, that the account and explanation of the breakdown of the concept of property offered here is in the last analysis ideological, in the pejorative sense of a mystifying or false apologetic. The development of a largely capitalist market economy toward industrialism objectively demands formulation of its emergent system of economic entitlements in something like the bundle-of-rights form, which in turn must lead to the decline of property as a central category of legal and political thought.

---

strong implication that "private" and "public" property were not as different as traditional property theory would suggest. *See, e.g.*, Cohen, op. cit., n. 4 above, pp. 357–59.

41 *See* John Rawls, *A Theory of Justice* (Cambridge, 1971), pp. 265–74. This is the place for a recantation. Some years ago I criticized Rawls for failing to treat property (in the classic thing-ownership sense) as a fundamental category within his theory of social justice. Thomas Grey, "Property and Need: The Welfare State and Theories of Distributive Justice," 28 *Stanford Law Review* 880–84 (May 1976). I now think that I was wrong, for the reasons implicit in this entire essay.

Langdell's Orthodoxy

Thomas C. Grey

It seems natural to begin the history of modern American legal thought in 1870. In that year, Oliver Wendell Holmes, Jr., in the first words of his first major essay, wrote "It is the merit of the common law that it decides the case first, and determines the principle afterwards."[1] In the same year, Christopher Columbus Langdell joined the faculty and became the first Dean of the Harvard Law School. Teaching his first class in Contracts, he began not with the customary introductory lecture, but by asking "Mr. Fox, will you state the facts in the case of *Payne v. Cave?*"[2]

Holmes' words broke with orthodoxy and anticipated legal realism by finding merit in intuitive case-by-case adjudication. But what did Langdell's twin debut as Dean and teacher have to do with the beginning of modern legal thought? Two connections are fairly obvious. First, the method of teaching that Langdell launched in his first Contracts class, by shifting the focus of legal instruction from abstract principles to cases, ended up promoting the same

* This article originally appeared in *University of Pittsburgh Law Review*, Vol. 45:1 (1983–1984) pp. 1–53.

** Professor of Law, Stanford University. This is a much-expanded version of the Mellon Lecture delivered at the University of Pittsburgh School of Law on October 28, 1982. Financial support for the research was provided by the Stanford Legal Research Fund, made possible by a bequest from the Estate of Ira S. Lillick and by gifts from Roderick M. and Carla A. Hills and other friends of the Stanford Law School. I am grateful for the research assistance of Carl Ruggiero and Walter Johnson and for the typing and retyping of Ann Babb. My thanks to the colleagues and friends—too many to name—who made helpful comments on earlier drafts, and extra thanks to those whose criticisms got me to make substantial changes: Barbara Babcock, John Ely and Bob Gordon. Due to the specialized nature of the sources used, the author has certified to the University of Pittsburgh Law Review the accuracy of a substantial amount of the bibliographical information.

1 Holmes, *Codes, and the Arrangement of the Law*, 5 AM. L. REV. 1, *reprinted in* 44 HARV. L. REV. 725 (1931).

2 Langdell was named Dane Professor in January, 1870, and taught courses in Negotiable Paper and Partnerships in the spring of that year, apparently by the traditional lecture method. 2 C. WARREN, HISTORY OF THE HARVARD LAW SCHOOL 359, 363 (1908). He was named first Dean in September, *id.* at 370–71; and gave the first case-method class that fall, *id.* at 372–73.

© KONINKLIJKE BRILL NV, LEIDEN, 2014 | DOI 10.1163/9789004272897_005

modern case-centered view of adjudication that Holmes had stated.[3] Second, during his Deanship, Langdell created at Harvard the model for the standard American three-year graduate law school staffed by a career faculty committed to research that has since been the institutional basis for the development of modern legal thought.[4]

The third connection between Langdell's debut and the beginning of the modern era is more obscure. As Langdell taught his course in Contracts, and later as he and his many colleagues and disciples carried on all their teaching and writing,[5] they promulgated a distinctive system of legal thought that I call classical orthodoxy.[6] But what is modern about this classical orthodox system? Is it not the very antithesis of modernity in legal thought?

---

3 This was a common observation of later critics who traced the Legal Realist "jurisprudence of the hunch" back to the pedagogy of the case. *See, e.g.*, Dickinson, *Legal Rules: Their Function in the Process of Decision*, 79 U. PA. L. REV. 833, 846 (1931); Lucey, *Natural Law and American Legal Realism*, 30 GEO. L.J. 493, 526 n. 67 (1942). Marcia Speziale has imaginatively expanded on the point while reversing the perspective, treating Langdell as a proto-Realist hero, in Speziale, *Langdell's Concept of Law as Science: The Beginnings of Anti-Formalism in American Legal Theory*, 5 VT. L. REV. 1 (1980). One must avoid identifying Langdell's pedagogic innovations with his jurisprudence; the two were independent, in the sense that articulate critics of the latter were at the same time defenders and practitioners of the former. *See* O. HOLMES, COLLECTED LEGAL PAPERS 42–43 (1920) [hereinafter cited as HOLMES, COLLECTED PAPERS]; Gray, *Methods of Legal Education*, 1 YALE L.J. 159 (1891); and *see infra* text accompanying note 83.

4 On the establishment of Langdell's model at Harvard, see 2 C. WARREN, *supra* note 2, at 354–418, 428–53. Chase, *The Birth of the Modern Law School*, 23 AM. J. LEGAL HIST. 329 (1979) stresses the large role that Langdell's patron, Harvard president Charles Eliot, played in the process. For Eliot's own account, see Eliot, *Langdell and the Law School*, 33 HARV. L. REV. 518 (1920).

On the spread of the Langdellian model of the law school beyond Harvard, see, for a general account, Stevens, *Two Cheers for 1870: The American Law School*, in 5 PERSPECTIVES IN AMERICAN HISTORY 405, 426–35 (D. Fleming & B. Bailyn eds. 1971); and for case-studies, J. GOEBEL, FOUNDATION FOR RESEARCH IN LEGAL HISTORY, A HISTORY OF THE SCHOOL OF LAW, COLUMBIA UNIVERSITY 131–58 (1955), and W. JOHNSON, SCHOOLED LAWYERS (1978).

5 James Barr Ames, Joseph Beale and Samuel Williston, junior colleagues of Langdell at Harvard, were the most important of his disciples in classical orthodoxy.

6 "Orthodoxy" refers loosely to the view, held more or less and in different forms by lawyers at all times, that legal judgments are made by applying pre-existing law to facts. I take the term "classical" (and much more than the term, *see infra* note 176) from D. Kennedy, The Rise and Fall of Classical Legal Thought, 1850–1940 (1975) (unpublished). *See also* Kennedy, *Toward an Historical Understanding of Legal Consciousness: The Case of Classical Legal Thought in America, 1850–1940*, 3 RESEARCH IN LAW AND SOCIOLOGY 3 (1980); and Kennedy, *Form and Substance in Private Law Adjudication*, 89 HARV. L. REV. 1685, 1728–31 (1976). Kennedy's line between "classical" and "pre-classical" legal thought roughly corresponds to Llewellyn's

Rather, classical orthodoxy is the thesis to which modern American legal thought has been the antithesis. This relation between them was manifested very early. Just a decade after the year of their common debut, Langdell's most Langdellian book provoked Holmes, who was reviewing it, to formulate the central slogan of legal modernism: "The life of the law has not been logic; it has been experience."[7] Thereafter, as Langdell's book stood to Holmes' aphorism, so stood classical orthodoxy to modern legal thought generally: the indispensable foil, the parental dogma that shapes the heretical growth of a rebellious offspring.

Langdell was mainly a doctrinal writer rather than a philosopher, and to get a sense of his legal theory it is best to begin by looking at his treatment of a doctrinal problem. When someone accepts a contractual offer by mail, does the contract become binding when the acceptance is mailed or when it is received? There are practical arguments on both sides of the question, but most modern writers have agreed that the balance of convenience favors making the acceptance binding when mailed—the so-called "mailbox rule." And modern writers, thinking it more important to have the question settled than to worry endlessly over whether it is settled right, have agreed to treat the mailbox rule as established law.[8]

---

familiar distinction between the "Formal" and the "Grand" Style, *see* K. LLEWELLYN, THE COMMON LAW TRADITION—DECIDING APPEALS 35–45 (1960); I reserve the term "formal" to describe one of the traits of classical legal thought, *see infra* text accompanying note 26.

A particularly helpful treatment of classical thought is Gordon, *Legal Thought and Legal Practice in the Age of American Enterprise, 1870–1920* in PROFESSIONS AND PROFESSIONAL IDEOLOGIES IN AMERICA, 1730–1940 (L. Stone & G. Geison eds. 1983). Other useful discussions are W. TWINING, KARL LLEWELLYN AND THE REALIST MOVEMENT 10–25 (1973); and White, *The Impact of Legal Science on Tort Law, 1880–1910*, 78 COLUM. L. REV. 213, 214–32 (1978).

7 Holmes, Book Review, 14 AM. L. REV. 233, 234 (1880). Langdell's book was his SUMMARY OF THE LAW OF CONTRACTS (1880) [hereinafter SUMMARY]. An earlier version of this work was appended to the second edition of Langdell's contracts casebook in 1879; it was itself the descendant of a much shorter doctrinal summary appended to the first edition, C. LANGDELL, CASES ON CONTRACTS (1st ed. 1871; 2d ed. 1879). [Hereinafter citations to the casebook are to the second edition.]

Holmes repeated the line about logic and experience in the first lecture of his series on the common law given at the Lowell Institute in late 1880, possibly in Langdell's presence. M. HOWE, JUSTICE OLIVER WENDELL HOLMES: THE PROVING YEARS, 1870–1882 157 (1963). It then appeared as the third sentence of the book derived from those lectures, O. HOLMES, THE COMMON LAW 5 (M. Howe ed. 1963; orig. 1881) [hereinafter THE COMMON LAW] and has since passed into the common idiom of English-speaking lawyers.

8 1 CORBIN ON CONTRACTS § 78 (1963). For more extensive discussion of the practicalities, see Llewellyn, *On Our Case-Law of Contract: Offer and Acceptance, II*, 48 YALE L.J. 779 (1939).

When Langdell confronted it, the question had not yet been settled. The courts of England and New York had adopted the mailbox rule, but those of Massachusetts had rejected it.[9] According to Langdell, the issue between the alternatives was not merely a practical one. In his view, fundamental principles dictated that the acceptance must be received before the contract could be formed. This followed from the doctrine that a promise could not be binding unless it was supported by consideration. The consideration for the offer was the offeree's return promise. But a promise by its nature is not complete until communicated; a "promise" into the air is no promise at all. Since there was no promise, there was no consideration and could be no contract, until the letter of acceptance was received and read. The mailbox rule could not be good law.[10]

Langdell took note of the argument that the mailbox rule would best serve "the purposes of substantial justice, and the interests of the contracting parties, as understood by themselves," and responded that this was "irrelevant"[11]—a claim that has ever since been taken to express the wretched essence of his kind of legal thinking. It was in dismay at these very words that Holmes called Langdell a "legal theologian" and wrote that law is not logic but experience.[12]

For all his rejection of the idea, Holmes himself well understood what it meant to conceive of law chiefly as "logic." The first great critic of classical orthodoxy, he thoroughly grasped its premises, many of which he shared.[13]

---

9 Adams v. Lindsell, 1 B. and Ald. 681 (England, 1818); Mactier's Admin, v. Frith, 6 Wend. 101 (New York, 1830); McCulloch v. Eagle Ins. Co., 18 Mass. (1 Pick.) 278 (1822).

10 SUMMARY, *supra* note 7, at 1–2, 12–15. It is worth noting from the first cited passage that Langdell's argument is based squarely on the doctrine of consideration, not on "the nature of an acceptance." He thought acceptance of a gift, for example, could become effective as soon as there was any manifestation of consent to the gift by the donee, whether or not communicated to the donor. But an acceptance could not become a return promise until it was communicated.

11 *Id.* at 20–21. The statement was an intentional jurisprudential flourish; Langdell went on to say "but, assuming it to be relevant…" and supplied some perfunctory practical and policy arguments for his position.

12 *See* Holmes, *supra* note 7.

13 There has been a recent scholarly tendency to find contradictions between the formalist elements in Holmes' doctrinal writing and his famous realist jurisprudential aphorisms. *See* Gordon, *Holmes' Common Law as Legal and Social Science*, 10 HOFSTRA L. REV. 719, 727 n. 60 (1982). For my view on this subject, see *infra* notes 162–63 and accompanying text.

Holmes' ambivalence toward Langdell's work appears in his review of the SUMMARY, *supra* note 7. Holmes did say that law was not logic but experience, and called Langdell "the greatest living legal theologian," *id.* at 234, but at the same time praised his talents: 'There cannot be found in the legal literature of this country, such a *tour de force* of patient and profound intellect working out original theory though a mass of detail…." *Id.* at

By contrast, our view of the old system is less clear, obscured by nearly a century of polemics against "mechanical jurisprudence," "Bealism," "transcendental nonsense" and similar targets set up for summary demolition.[14] But as we should guess from the very persistence and intensity of the polemical assault on classical orthodoxy, when taken as a whole, it was a powerful and appealing legal theory, not the feeble dogma portrayed in the critics' parodies.

The heart of the theory was the view that law is a science. Langdell believed that through scientific method lawyers could derive correct legal judgments from a few fundamental principles and concepts, which it was the task of the scholar-scientist like himself to discover.[15] The view had considerable continuity with aspirations toward legal science that Anglo-American lawyers had stated in the past.[16] But Langdell and his followers took the view of law as science seriously and carried it out programmatically in a way that had no precedent in the common law world,[17] erecting a vast discursive structure that

---

233–34. Holmes' later comment on the SUMMARY in a letter to Pollock expressed the same ambivalence:

> "A more misspent piece of marvelous ingenuity I never read, yet it is most suggestive and instructive. I have referred to Langdell several times in dealing with contracts because to my mind he represents the powers of darkness. He is all for logic and hates any reference to anything outside of it, and his explanations and reconciliations of the cases would have astonished the judges who decided them. But he is a noble old swell whose knowledge, ability and idealist devotion to his work I revere and love."

1 HOLMES-POLLOCK LETTERS 17 (M. Howe ed. 1941) (letter of April 10, 1881) [hereinafter cited as HOLMES-POLLOCK LETTERS]. *Cf.* Holmes' later letter, *id.* at 140.

14 J. FRANK, LAW AND THE MODERN MIND 53–61 (2d ed. 1949); Cohen, *Transcendental Nonsense and the Functional Approach*, 35 COLUM. L. REV. 809 (1935); Pound, *Mechanical Jurisprudence*, 8 COLUM. L. REV. 605 (1908).

15 *See infra* text accompanying note 42. By way of contrast, *see* Holmes, *supra* note 1, at 728: "Law is not a science, but is essentially empirical. Hence, although the general arrangement should be philosophical, even at the expense of disturbing prejudices, compromises with practical convenience are highly proper."

16 For earlier Anglo-American expressions of the ideal of legal science, see the inaugural lectures of Blackstone and Story as, respectively, Vinerian Professor at Oxford in 1758, and Dane Professor at Harvard in 1829. 1 W. BLACKSTONE, COMMENTARIES *3–37; J. STORY, MISCELLANEOUS WRITINGS 440–76 (1835). For discussions of ante-bellum American ideas of legal science, *see* M. HORWITZ, THE TRANSFORMATION OF AMERICAN LAW 1780–1860, 253–66 (1977); P. MILLER, THE LIFE OF THE MIND IN AMERICA 117–85 (1965). For still earlier antecedents, see Shapiro, *Law and Science in Seventeenth Century England*, 21 STAN. L. REV. 727 (1969).

17 "Legal Science" of a type closely related to Anglo-American classical orthodoxy has been the dominant enterprise of legal writers in Europe since the beginning of the nineteenth century, and remains so to this day. The prototype is F. VON SAVIGNY, POSSESSION (E. Perry

came to dominate legal education and to greatly influence the practical work of lawyers and judges. It is my purpose to reconstruct the premises of this classical orthodox system of thought; to explain its central concept, legal science, and to account for its rise and fall as a dominant legal ideology.

I

Classical orthodoxy was a particular kind of legal theory—a set of ideas to be put to work from *inside* by those who operate legal institutions, not a set of ideas about those institutions reflecting an *outside* perspective, whether a sociological, historical or economic explanation of legal phenomena. This inside-outside distinction is not quite the same as the familiar distinction between normative and descriptive theories. Inside as well as outside theories purport to represent legal institutions accurately, and many outside theories have normative as well as descriptive force.

An ideal inside theory would contain an accurate account of legal institutions, a method for operating them, a creed for llegal professionals, and a justification of the institutions for outsiders, all combined in a single comprehensive and coherent formulation. An inside theory is thus an *ideology* in the sense of that term that excludes the pejorative connotation of a mystifying apologetic for bad institutions.[18] Even the best imaginable set of legal institutions needs an ideology, and a good ideology does not falsely represent its sponsoring institutions.

The following analytic scheme is meant to allow a somewhat more precise description of Langdell's classical orthodoxy than has been usual, and one that permits us to compare it with other legal theories. According to this scheme, legal theories are defined by the relations they establish among five possible goals of legal systems: comprehensiveness, completeness, formality, conceptual order and acceptability.[19]

---

trans. 1st ed. 1848; German orig., 1806); a methodological exposition is K. Gareis, The Science of Law (A. Kocourek trans. 1911). For accounts aimed at the Anglo-American reader, *see* M. Cappelletti, J. Merryman, J. Perillo, The Italian Legal System 164–96 (1967); Schmidt, *The German Abstract Approach to Law* 1965 Scandinavian Studies in Law 131. Historical accounts are A. Watson, The Making of the Civil Law (1981) and J. Dawson, The Oracles of the Law (1968).

18 For the different senses of "ideology," *see* R. Geuss, The Idea of a Critical Theory 1–26 (1981); G. Lichtheim, The Concept of Ideology 3–46 (1967).

19 Sources I have drawn on in formulating this scheme include C. Alchourron & E. Bulygin, Normative Systems 61–64 and *passim* (1971); A. Kronman, Max Weber 72–95 (1983);

Comprehensiveness. A legal system is fully *comprehensive* if it provides an institutional mechanism for the unique resolution of every case within its jurisdiction. A system can fail to be comprehensive through procedural gaps or procedural overlaps. There would be a procedural *gap* if courts could decline to decide a case because they found that substantive law provided no clear right answer.[20] There would be a procedural *overlap* if two courts had jurisdiction of the same dispute, and power to issue conflicting relief, without any institutional mechanism for resolving the conflict.[21] Almost all legal systems purport to be fully comprehensive, and legal theory generally takes this requirement as a given—itself an important fact, which highlights the centrality of the dispute-resolving role of the law.[22]

Completeness. A legal system is *complete* if its substantive norms provide a uniquely correct solution—a "right answer"—for every case that can arise under it. A system can be incomplete by containing either substantive *gaps*—factual situations to which no existing norms apply—or *inconsistencies* between overlapping norms.[23] Most modern legal theorists believe that com-

---

R. Unger, Law in Modern Society 48–58 (1976); M. Weber, On Law in Economy and Society 61–64 (M. Rheinstein ed., E. Shils & M. Rheinstein trans. 1969); Friedman, *On Legalistic Reasoning—A Footnote to Weber*, 1966 Wisc. L. Rev. 148; and Kennedy, *Form and Substance in Private Law Adjudication*, *supra* note 6, at 1687–1701.

20 As with the celebrated (because exotic in legal history) *référé* established by the French revolutionary organic act of 16 August 1790, allowing courts to refer cases to the legislature where existing law was unclear; the procedure was rejected and comprehensiveness restored to French law by Article 4 of the Napoleonic Code, which provides: "A judge who refuses to decide a case, under pretext of the silence, obscurity or insufficiency of the law, may be prosecuted as being guilty of a denial of justice." See the discussion in F. Geny, Method of Interpretation and Sources in Positive Private Law 49–59 (J. Mayda trans. 1954).

21 For example, conflicting judgments were issued by common law and equity courts in the dispute between Coke and Ellesmere, until James I resolved the dispute in favor of equity. 1 W. Holdsworth, History of English Law 248–51 (1903).

22 On my formulation, a legal system is complete if there is a procedurally unique resolution of every *case*. A stronger formulation would require unique resolution of every *dispute*, defining a case as a dispute over which the law takes jurisdiction. The two versions can be partly harmonized by treating disputes over which the law does not take jurisdiction as resolved in favor of the *status quo*, though the equivalence does not hold to the extent it is unclear what the *status quo* is.

23 Alchourron and Bulygin analyze and further subcategorize gaps and inconsistences. Alchourron & Bulygin, *supra* note 19, at 31–34, 61–64, 145–48, and 170–75. They treat a distinction between "consistency" (no contradictions) and "completeness" (no gaps) as of major significance. I believe the distinction is not as important in law as it is in more theo-

pleteness cannot be achieved, though comprehensiveness can; if every case must be decided, there will inevitably be some for which the norms of the system provide no answer, or provide inconsistent answers. In these cases, modern theory says the judge must exercise discretion, either to create a new norm or to choose between the conflicting norms.[24] Recently a number of theorists, headed by Ronald Dworkin, have disagreed with this; Dworkin, for example, asserts, in his claim that even hard cases have "right answers," the orthodox view that our legal system is complete.[25]

Formality. A legal system is *formal* to the extent that its outcomes are dictated by demonstrative (rationally compelling) reasoning. The universal formality of a system is a *sufficient* condition to guarantee its completeness; necessarily, if every case can be decided by uncontroversial reasoning then every case has a right answer. It was a central goal of classical orthodoxy to achieve completeness through formality. But universal formality is not a *necessary* condition for completeness; Dworkin, for example, claims completeness for our legal system without universal formality. In his view, there is a right answer for every case, but no demonstrative reasoning to the answers in hard cases.[26]

---

retical domains, which unlike the law work under no requirement of comprehensiveness. Any legal inconsistency can be treated as a gap—that is, a gap in the system of metanorms that are provided to settle clashes between inconsistent lower level norms.

24 Many post-classical civil law codes give general instructions on how such decisions are to be made, the best-known of which is Article 1 of the Swiss Civil Code: "In the absence of an applicable legal provision, the judge pronounces in accordance with customary law and, in the absence of a custom, according to the rules that he would establish if he had to act as legislator." A. WATSON, *supra* note 17, at 169. *See* J. MAYDA, FRANCOIS GENY AND MODERN JURISPRUDENCE 31–64 (1978) for an analysis of the Swiss courts' experience under Article 1. Geny's notice of "free objective search" (*libre recherche scientifique*), expounded in F. GENY, *supra* note 20, at 352–431, has been particularly influential in modern civil law treatment of the "gap" problem.

25 R. DWORKIN, TAKING RIGHTS SERIOUSLY (paperback ed. 1978) [hereinafter cited as TAKING RIGHTS SERIOUSLY]; *see also* R. SARTORIUS, INDIVIDUAL CONDUCT AND SOCIAL NORMS 181–210 (1975). Alchourron and Bulygin distinguish between the Ideal and the Postulate of Completeness: the former takes completeness as a goal, while the latter states that it has been achieved within a legal system. The confusion of Ideal and Postulate, which they attribute to Dworkin, they call the "rationalist illusion." C. ALCHOURRON & E. BULYGIN, *supra* note 19, at 175–80.

26 R. DWORKIN, *supra* note 25; *see also* R. SARTORIUS, *supra* note 25. Both Dworkin and Sartorius believe that the "right answers" in hard cases derive from the applications of decisional standards that have "weight" and hence lend themselves to being "balanced." For criticism of the use of the metaphor of weighing or balancing when there exists no

Conceptual Order. A legal system is conceptually ordered to the extent that its substantive bottom-level rules can be derived from a small number of relatively abstract principles and concepts, which themselves form a coherent system. The conceptual ordering is formal where the derivation of the decisive rules of the system from its more general principles and concepts is demonstrative; the derivation can also take some less rigorous form, producing an informal but ordered system.[27] Among the concepts of an ordered legal system, one can distinguish the classificatory *categories* that demarcate bodies of law (e.g., tort, contract, crime) from the operative *concepts* used in the principles from which decisive rules are derived (e.g., consideration, proximate cause, malice).[28]

---

procedure by which people can either measure the attributes in question or serially order actions or states of affairs with respect to them, *see* A. DONAGAN, THE THEORY OF MORALITY 23–24 (1977). For an interesting formalization of "balancing" see Nozick, *Moral Complications and Moral Structures*, 13 NAT. L. FOR. 1 (1968).

27 Thus, a legal theory may pursue conceptual order, without any assumption that general principles can lead by formal reasoning to decisions. Such an approach was characteristic of American judges before the Civil War, working in what Llewellyn called "the Grand Style," *see* K. LLEWELLYN, *supra* note 6, at 38; they sought guidance, but not dictation, from general principles. A classic statement was Chief Justice Shaw's:

> "It is one of the great merits and advantages of the common law, that, instead of a series of detailed practical rules, established by positive provisions, and adapted to the precise circumstances of particular cases, which would become obsolete and fail, when the practice and course of business, to which they apply, should cease or change, the common law consists of a few broad and comprehensive principles founded on reason, natural justice, and enlightened public policy *modified and adapted to the circumstances of all the particular cases which fall within it.*"

Norway Plains Co. v. Boston & Maine R.R. Co., 67 Mass. 263, 267 (1854) (emphasis added).

For a contemporary natural law philosopher's statement of the notion of informal (nondemonstrative) reasoning from the most general moral principles down to intermediate moral rules *see*, A. DONAGAN, *supra* note 26, at 66–74. Ronald Dworkin likewise illustrates informal conceptualism in his treatment of reasoning from "concepts" to more concrete "conceptions," *see* R. DWORKIN, *supra* note 25, at 101–05, 134–37. However, Dworkin disparages what I here call "conceptual ordering." *Id.* at 44, 344. He apparently believes principles and general concepts play a large role in legal reasoning, but thinks their arrangement and systematization not worthwhile. Finally, Holmes was a master and devotee of legal conceptual ordering, but believed it could not greatly contribute to the formality of the law (a goal he also pursued, but through different means); *see infra* notes 162–63 and accompanying text.

28 The distinction, though not a sharp one, is useful. The operative concepts will be seen by modern lawyers as result-determining in most instances; typically it affects the result whether there was "acceptance," or "assumption of the risk," or "possession" (to add three examples to those in the text). By contrast, except in rare cases (such as those turning on

The notions of completeness, formality and conceptual order—which we may group together as the values of legality—allow us to give a relatively clear meaning to otherwise vague terms commonly used in debates about legal theory. Thus, a "discovery" or "declaratory" theory of adjudication asserts the goal (or claims the achievement) of completeness for a legal system; right answers are *there*, to be discovered and declared. "Formalism" describes legal theories that stress the importance of rationally uncontroversial reasoning in legal decision, whether from highly particular rules or quite abstract principles.[29] "Conceptualism" describes legal theories that place a high value on the creation (or discovery) of a few fundamental principles and concepts at the heart of a system, whether reasoning from them is formal or informal.[30] One could give a purely descriptive sense to the term "mechanical jurisprudence" by applying it to a system which achieved comprehensive completeness through a defined decision procedure guaranteed to produce a correct judgment in every case.[31]

Acceptability. A legal system is *acceptable* to the extent that it fulfills the ideals and desires of those under its jurisdiction.[32] Putting the point another way:

---

which statute of limitations applies) the classification of a case as one of tort, contract, property, business regulation or the like will not directly affect how the case comes out.

The indirect effect of category-assignments and the ideological importance of legal categorical schemes have been neglected both by advocates and by legal scholars. For a rare full-scale study, *see* Kennedy, *The Structure of Blackstone's Categories*, 28 BUFFALO L. REV. 205 (1979) and for an application of the approach, *see* Rabin, *The Historical Development of the Fault Principle: A Reinterpretation*, 15 GA. L. REV. 925, 948–54 (1981).

29 Non-conceptualist formalism is a common attitude among lawyers; they want clear rules, but place little importance on more abstract doctrinal formulations. Holmes detached his formalism from his conceptualism; *see infra* notes 162–63 and accompanying text.

30 *See supra* note 27.

31 To expand on this somewhat cryptic formulation: A system is comprehensive if there is a definite institutional sequence for deciding every case; it is complete if there is a substantive correct answer for every case. Obviously, the established procedure might not achieve the correct answer. (Suppose it takes great moral sensitivity to reach the right answer in many cases, but the judges given jurisdiction over these cases are a bunch of clods.) This incongruence can be escaped if the correct answers are such that they can be reached by applying an essentially mechanical decision procedure to the case. Then, by analogy to the theory of formal systems, the system would be not only consistent and complete but also, in the logicians' term, "decidable." In such a system, all cases (once properly coded) could be decided by a computer, which would make the term "mechanical jurisprudence" quite apt.

32 In speaking of ideals and desires, I mean to distinguish between "ideal interests" and "material interests," both of which are distinct from ideas. ("Not ideas, but material and ideal interests, directly govern men's conduct." M. WEBER, *The Social Psychology of the*

we aspire that our legal systems fulfill extra-legal values. But this latter way of speaking begs controversial questions in legal philosophy; there is an old debate between those who think the values encompassed under "acceptability" are to be viewed as extra-legal considerations, and those who regard these values as themselves part of the law.[33]

A further point must be made about the goal of acceptability. Social values are already implicit in the internal goals of the legal system, the goals of legality. In particular, the aspiration toward completeness through formality rests in part on the practical social demand that official action be reasonably predictable, so that people may plan their lives. At the same time formality is often linked to the ideal goal of personal liberty by the slogan "a government of laws and not of men." Legality may also intrinsically involve values additional to these. When I speak of acceptability, as distinguished from other goals of legal systems, I thus refer to values apart from those already implicit in the goals of legality.[34]

II

In the terms of the analytic scheme just sketched, the heart of classical theory was its aspiration that the legal system be made complete through universal formality, and universally formal through conceptual order. A few basic top-level categories and principles formed a conceptually ordered system above a large number of bottom-level rules. The rules themselves were, ideally, the holdings of established precedents, which upon analysis could be seen to be

---

World Religions, FROM MAX WEBER: ESSAYS IN SOCIOLOGY 267, 280 (H. GERTH & C. MILLS eds. 1946)). The distinction appears in social theory in various guises; for example, Habermas distinguishes between "value" (the material) and "meaning" (the ideal) as the chief alternative sources of legitimation. J. HABERMAS, LEGITIMATION CRISIS 93 (T. McCarthy trans. 1973).

33 *Compare* H.L.A. Hart, *Positivism and the Separation of Law and Morals*, 71 HARV. L. REV. 593, 627–29 (1958) *with* Fuller, *Positivism and Fidelity to Law: A Reply to Professor Hart*, 71 HARV. L. REV. 630 (1958), *and both with* B. CARDOZO, THE NATURE OF THE JUDICIAL PROCESS 133 (1921) (debates between treating considerations of policy as part of the law or as a legitimate source of judge-made law are mere "verbal disputations" which "do not greatly interest me").

34 Lon Fuller's notion of an "inner morality of law" might correspond to those aspects of acceptability implicit in the goals of legality. L. FULLER, THE MORALITY OF LAW 33–94 (1964).

derivable from the principles.[35] When a new case arose to which no existing rule applied, it could be categorized and the correct rule for it could be inferred by use of the general concepts and principles; the rule could then be applied to the facts to dictate the unique correct decision in the case.

The system was doubly formal. First, the specific rules were framed in such terms that decisions followed from them uncontroversially when they were applied to readily ascertainable facts. Thus, classical orthodoxy sought objective tests, and avoided vague standards, or rules that required determinations of state of mind.[36] Second, at the next level up one could derive the rules themselves analytically from the principles.[37]

For example, reconstructing Langdell's argument against the mailbox rule, we start with the top-level principle, based on authority,[38] that a contract cannot be formed until there is bargained-for consideration, which is either

---

35 The lack of correspondence between the explicit holdings of judicial decisions and the "real rules" that in his view justified the results in those cases was one of the most remarkable features of Langdell's doctrinal writing. A good example of his style is the passage at SUMMARY, *supra* note 7, at 16–18, in which he manages to reduce all judicial affirmations of the mailbox rule, but one, to dicta, and then condemns the sole survivor of the massacre on the ground that it had rested on the authority of a slain predecessor. *See* Holmes' comment on this practice in his letter to Pollock, HOLMES-POLLOCK LETTERS *supra* note 13, at 140, and J.C. Gray's criticism, quoted *infra* note 70. A more moderate classical approach to case law is lucidly described in E. WAMBAUGH, THE STUDY OF CASES 8–29 and *passim* (1894). In a curious way, Langdell's practice anticipated the theory later adopted by the Legal Realists, according to which the only authoritative parts of a judicial opinion were the facts (the stimulus) and the result (the response). Oliphant, *A Return to Stare Decisis*, 6 AM. L. SCH. REV. 215 (1927).

36 This aspect of classical theory is best illustrated in the work of Williston; *see* G. GILMORE, THE DEATH OF CONTRACT 35–44 (1974). Holmes was the strongest advocate of objective and formal tests, but in my view he was not proceeding from classical premises. *See infra* note 163. Among the classical writers, Ames was least insistent on objectivity and formality; *see infra* note 102. Langdell fell between Williston and Ames on this score; he retained vestiges of the pre-classical "meeting of the minds" view of contract formation, but would invariably substitute objective tests by way of presumption whenever state of mind could not be clearly shown. *See* SUMMARY, *supra* note 7, at 193–94, 243–44.

37 "Analytically" is a better term than "deductively" here, as it avoids the latter term's connotations of purely formal inference. A more specific rule follows "analytically" from a more general principle, if its content can be derived from the principle by "conceptual analysis" or "from the meaning" of the terms used in the principle. (Philosophy of language buffs will recognize the difficulties raised by the scare-quoted terms; *see* Moore, *The Semantics of Judging*, 54 S. CAL. L. REV. 151, 180–246 (1981).)

38 For Langdell's view on the basis of the consideration doctrine, *see infra* notes 81–87 and accompanying text.

promise or performance (definition). In a bilateral contract case, there is no performance, and the only promise is contained in the offeree's acceptance (definition). But a promise requires communication of its content to its promisee (analytic truth). And when the promise is by letter, the content is not communicated until the letter is received and read (analytic truth). Therefore, the contract is not formed until the letter is received and read. The reasoning has been formal down to the bottom-level rule, which is itself framed in such terms as to be formally applicable to objectively ascertainable facts. Thus, if the bottom-level rule were, for example, that the acceptance letter had to be received, read *and understood*, the requirement of rule-formality would not be met.

It was crucial to the completeness of the system that it be conceptually ordered, and that its fundamental principles and their constitutive concepts be sufficiently abstract to cover the whole range of possible cases. Bottom-level rules, specific as they were, could not be available in advance to deal with all new fact situations; if the law were only a collection of specific rules it would not be complete.[39] But though the concepts should be abstract, they could not be vague or ambiguous. Unless they were precise as well as abstract, the derivations of the rules from them could not be formal, and judges would have arbitrary power. Can norms be both abstract and precise? Consider the axioms and postulates of geometry.

All this was aspiration; the actual state of the common law was such as to leave the legal scientists a great deal to do. Judges often did not accurately state the rules on which they decided cases.[40] Further, the basic principles had not been properly formulated and arranged. The law consisted of a mass of haphazardly arranged cases: a "chaos with a full index."[41] Langdell himself concisely stated the project of classical legal science in a poignantly optimistic passage:

> Law, considered as a science, consists of certain principles or doctrines. To have such mastery of these as to be able to apply them with constant facility and certainty to the ever-tangled skein of human affairs, is what

39 This view is implicit in Langdell's famous description of legal science, *infra* text accompanying note 42. Williston made it explicit and articulately defended it late in his life, after the Legal Realists had made it part of their program to break law into "narrower categories," *infra* note 177. *See also* S. WILLISTON, LIFE AND LAW 208–09, 213–14 (1940). *See also* the discussion of "generality" in Kennedy, *Form and Substance in Private Law Adjudication*, *supra* note 6, at 1689–90.

40 *See supra* note 35.

41 T.E. Holland wrote that "the old-fashioned English lawyer's idea of a satisfactory body of law was a chaos with a full index." Quoted in Holmes, *Book Review*, 5 AM. L. REV. 114 (1870).

> constitutes a true lawyer.... The number of fundamental legal doctrines is much less than is commonly supposed; the many different guises in which the same doctrine is constantly making its appearance, and the great extent to which legal treatises are a repetition of each other, being the cause of much misapprehension. If these doctrines could be so classified and arranged that each should be found in its proper place, and nowhere else, they would cease to be formidable in their number.[42]

Now we come to the omitted factor: what was the role of acceptability in the classical orthodox system? One can easily be misled by Langdell's notorious claim that substantial justice and the interests of the parties were *irrelevant* to the validity of the mailbox rule.[43] Did this mean that considerations of acceptability played no role in doctrinal reasoning? Examination of Langdell's work shows that he held no such view.

Throughout his work, Langdell appealed to considerations of justice or policy.[44] Thus, he wrote that equitable defenses are imposed where "the substantive law ... is inadequate to the purposes of justice."[45] He said that the law adopts fictions "only ... to promote justice, i.e., in order to prevent some injustice or some inconvenience which would otherwise arise."[46] Where contractual covenants are to be performed on the same day, the law "does perfect justice" by "raising a presumption ... that they are to be performed at the same moment, and concurrently." This constructive dependency "is founded upon equality, which is justice" and so "is regarded by the law with favor."[47] The law presumes mental consent from the physical act of promising; but this presumption is "only for purposes of justice and convenience;" thus, the presumption is not made and the offer lapses when actual consent would be impossible, as in the case of the offeror's death or insanity.[48] The common law gives an

---

42 C. LANGDELL, *supra* note 7, at viii–ix.

43 *See supra* text accompanying note 11.

44 In one of his rare jurisprudential essays, Langdell distinguished between "obligations" and "duties." The former were created by the acts of individuals and enforced by the State, whose only object in merely enforcing them was "to see that all persons within its jurisdiction act justly towards others." By contrast, duties "originate in commands of the State," commands based on "motives of policy." Abstractly, then, justice and policy were the whole basis of law for him. C. LANGDELL, A BRIEF SURVEY OF EQUITY JURISDICTION 224 (1908) [hereinafter cited as SURVEY].

45 SURVEY, *id.* at 253.

46 SUMMARY, *supra* note 7, at 8.

47 *Id.* at 170.

48 *Id.* at 224.

inventor no property right to his invention, because the consequences would be "intolerable," but does protect an author's work, because such a right "clashes with the interest of only one class of persons, namely, those who desire to reap where others have sown."[49]

It is fair to say that these arguments of justice and policy do not bulk large in the Langdellian corpus.[50] Langdell's most common form of doctrinal discourse was simple dogmatic pronouncement, and when he went beyond that, his more usual appeal was to authority or to "principle" (that is, doctrinal coherence). But he clearly regarded the appeal to "justice or convenience" (acceptability) as legitimate in at least some circumstances. Why then did Langdell insist that such an appeal was "irrelevant" to the validity of the mailbox rule, an issue on which authority was divided?

The answer will emerge more clearly after we look at what Langdell said when he rejected concerns of acceptability in sponsoring another famously unattractive doctrinal position. In unilateral contract cases, where the offeror promises something in exchange for performance by the offeree rather than for a return promise (offers of rewards are an example), Langdell argued that there was no consideration and hence could be no contract until the performance was actually completed. Offers were always revocable until the contract was formed.[51] Thus in a hypothetical case familiar to generations of law students, A offers B one hundred dollars if he will touch the top of the flagpole; B then laboriously climbs the pole, and just as he is about to touch the top, A shouts, "I revoke." On Langdellian doctrine, A owes B nothing.

As Langdell freely admitted, this doctrine "may cause great hardship and practical injustice," and as a result, "ingenious attempts have been made to show that the offer becomes irrevocable as soon as performance of the consid-

49 Langdell, *Patent Rights and Copy Rights*, 12 Harv. L. Rev. 553, 554 (1899).

50 For other examples of appeal to justice or policy, see Summary, *supra* note 7, at 11, 177, 202–03, 209–10; Survey, *supra* note 44, at 16, 46, 101. Langdell was much more apt to explain and justify rules of pleading and procedure on instrumental grounds than doctrines of substantive law, as illustrated throughout C. Langdell, Summary of Equity Pleading (2d ed. 1883). As a classical legal scientist he regarded procedure as instrumental to the enforcement of substantive, scientifically ascertained rights; procedure was thus a kind of technology in the service of legal science. *Cf. infra* text accompanying note 173.

51 Summary, *supra* note 7, at 3. For the same reason, an offer for a bilateral contract that by its terms stipulated that it would remain open for a time (a "firm offer") was nevertheless revocable at the will of the offeror. *Id.* at 240.

eration begins."[52] But in his view, well-intentioned as such arguments were, they could not prevail because they "have no principle to rest upon."[53]

This argument captures the essence of Langdell's view of the place of acceptability in legal doctrine. Considerations of justice and convenience were relevant, but only insofar as they were embodied in *principles*—abstract yet precise norms that were consistent with the other fundamental principles of the system. To let considerations of acceptability directly justify a bottom-level rule or individual decision would violate the requirement of conceptual order, on which the universal formality and completeness of the system depended. In classical orthodox thought, acceptability was to influence decision only subject to the constraint of universally formal conceptual order.[54]

What explains the strict primacy of formal conceptual order in classical theory? The short answer is that it was necessary to justify the claim that law was a science. To grasp what this meant, we must understand the conception of science that was involved. Then we can see better why the classical theorists thought it so important that the law be a science of that kind.

III

On first encounter, the very idea of "legal science" held by Langdell and his followers is baffling. Everyone understands the idea of empirical scientific study of legal institutions. There are also two recognized normative approaches to law that are thought scientific in some sense: a Benthamite legal policy science on the one hand, or a deductive natural law system based on self-evident moral axioms on the other. But Langdell's kind of theory fits none of these patterns. It claims to be empirical and yet its practice is highly conceptual; it delivers normative judgments, yet proclaims the positivist autonomy of law from morals. This seems to be an incomprehensible jumble of induction with deduction and of norm with fact.[55]

Behind the apparent jumble is a theory that can be made intelligible, if not ultimately satisfying. The core notion of classical legal science can be grasped through the analogy to geometry, as that subject was understood in the late nineteenth century. The geometric analogy can then be twice qualified in an

---

52 *Id.* at 4.

53 *Id.*

54 *See supra* note 39 and accompanying text.

55 For a lucid statement of the standard critique, *see* Dickinson, *The Law Behind Law, I & II*, 29 Colum. L. Rev. 113, 141–46; 285–96 (1929).

attempt to make it more applicable to law, once to take account of the role of legal precedent, and a second time to allow for the historical and progressive claims of classical legal thought. Let me first develop the primary analogy, and then introduce the qualifications.

Geometry

The aspiration of classical orthodoxy toward a conceptually ordered and universally formal legal system readily suggests a structural analogy with Euclidean geometry. The axioms and postulates of Euclid stand to his theorems as the principles of classical law stood to its rules. The application of legal rules to individual fact situations in the decision of cases was then like the application of geometric theorems to solve practical problems of measurement.

Of course, I have not invented the analogy between legal science and geometry. The geometric ideal pervades the literature of the whole rationalist movement to create exact sciences of ethics, politics and law that dominated European thought from Grotius to Kant, and that still remains strong in European legal scholarship today.[56] In England, more than on the Continent, that movement struggled against a politically potent pre-Enlightenment common law tradition. Blackstone's *Commentaries*, with their blend of rationalist principle and Gothic tradition—"science" and "mystery" in Daniel Boorstin's words—illustrate the characteristic English compromise.[57] But major English figures also spoke for pure Enlightenment and science, proclaiming the undiluted geometric ideal. Thus, Locke spoke of replacing the rhetorician and the common lawyer with the moral geometer,[58] and later John Austin, founder of legal science in England, urged his followers to "imitate the methods so successfully pursued by geometers."[59] That the geometric ideal is still alive today

---

56 Characteristic exponents of the geometric method were Spinoza, Leibniz, Pufendorf and Wolff; for a summary account of their application of the method to law *see* C. FRIEDRICH, THE PHILOSOPHY OF LAW IN HISTORICAL PERSPECTIVE 110–21 (1958). The passage from Descartes, quoted *infra* note 62, is a classic statement of the rationalist faith that the method of geometry could conquer the whole field of human knowledge. *See supra* note 17 on European legal science.

57 *See* D. BOORSTIN, THE MYSTERIOUS SCIENCE OF THE LAW 11–30 (1941).

58 "[I]f Men would in the same method, and with the same indifferency, search after moral, as they do mathematical Truths, they would find them to have a stronger Connection one with another, and a more necessary Consequence from our clear and distinct Ideas, and to come nearer perfect Demonstration, than is commonly imagined." J. LOCKE, AN ESSAY CONCERNING HUMAN UNDERSTANDING 552 (P. Nidditch ed. 1975).

59 J. AUSTIN, THE PROVINCE OF JURISPRUDENCE DETERMINED 77–78 (H.L.A. Hart, ed. 1954; orig. 1832).

in moral and political theory, though much chastened in the immediacy of its ambitions, is evident when John Rawls writes: "We should strive for a kind of moral geometry with all the rigor which this name connotes. Unhappily the reasoning I shall give will fall short of this.... Yet it is essential to have in mind the ideal one would like to achieve."[60]

To capture the parallel between classical legal science and geometry, we must lay aside the modern school-taught view that Euclidean geometry, like other mathematical theories, is simply an uninterpreted formal system of terms and inference rules. We must go back to the view people held for over two thousand years, and which all of us who are not specialists in relativity theory or philosophers of mathematics still intuitively accept. We believe that Euclid's axioms are not merely human constructs, but rather obvious and indubitable physical truths about the structure of space, from which nonobvious truths (like the Pythagorean theorem) can be proved by sequences of indubitable deductive steps.[61] It is the breathtaking nature of this movement from truisms to new knowledge about the world through pure thought that has made Euclidean geometry the great paradigm of the power of reason throughout the history of the West.[62]

---

60 J. Rawls, A Theory of Justice 121 (1971).

61 The traditional and modern views, respectively, are summarized in P. Davis & R. Hersh, The Mathematical Experience 322–30, 339–44 (1981). Relativity theory has joined with mathematical formalism in our century to dethrone Euclidean geometry by showing that "space is Riemannian."

62 The magic of geometric demonstration has its classic illustration in Socrates' dialogue with the slave in Plato's *Meno*, The Dialogues of Plato 82b–85b. A wonderful example of the seductive power of Euclid's method of proof appears in John Aubrey's life of Hobbes:

> "He was 40 yeares old before he looked on Geometry; which happened accidentally. Being in a Gentleman's Library, Euclid's Elements lay open, and 'twas the 47 *El. libri* I [Euclid's proof of the Pythagorean theorem]. He read the proposition. By G—, sayd he (he would now and then sweare an emphaticall Oath by way of emphasis) *this is impossible*—So he reads the Demonstration of it, which referred him back to such a Proposition; which proposition he read. That referred him back to another, which he also read. *Et sic deincips* [and so on] that at last he was demonstratively convinced of that trueth. This made him in love with Geometry."

1 J. Aubrey, Brief Lives 332 (A. Clark, 1898).

Compare Descartes' formulation of the geometric ideal in the *Discourse on Method:*

"Those long chains of perfectly simple and easy reasonings by means of which geometers are accustomed to carry out their most difficult demonstrations had led me to fancy that everything that can fall under human knowledge forms a similar sequence; and that so long as we avoid accepting as true what is not so, and always preserve the

But how can the geometric analogy capture the claim of classical legal science to be experimental and inductive? To understand this, we must make a further assumption about geometry that departs from both traditional rationalism and modern conventionalism. We must see the geometric axioms neither as rationally self-evident intuitions, nor as stipulated formal definitions, but rather as especially well-confirmed inductive generalizations about the physical world. This was a standard view of geometry in the late nineteenth century, reflecting the treatment of the subject in the bible of Victorian philosophy of science, J.S. Mill's *System of Logic.*[63]

In Mill's view, we learn the geometric axioms by observing over and over again that, for instance, two straight lines never enclose a space.[64] If we observed an apparent violation of this general law, we would know that our senses or our measurement techniques were deceiving us. Though not a truth of logic, the axiom is so well-confirmed by prior experience that no inconsistent observation could rationally overthrow it, just as, according to Hume, no miraculous claim could rationally be accepted.[65]

> right order for deduction of one thing from another, there can be nothing too remote to be reached in the end, or too well hidden to be discovered."

R. DESCARTES, PHILOSOPHICAL WRITINGS 21 (E. Anscombe & P. Geach ed. and trans., 1964).

63 "It remains to inquire, what is the ground of our belief in axioms—what is the evidence on which they rest? I answer, they are experimental truths; generalizations from observation. The proposition, two straight lines cannot enclose a space... is an induction from the evidence of our senses." J. MILL, A SYSTEM OF LOGIC 151–52 (People's Edition 1889) [hereinafter SYSTEM OF LOGIC]. *See generally* Mill's discussion of mathematical knowledge, *id.* at 141–64, and his preceding discussion of deductive reasoning, *id.* at 119–41. The other view of geometry current among educated Anglo-Americans during the classical orthodox period was the Kantian position—that geometric axioms are synthetic *a priori* truths constituting the necessary forms of human experience of space—particularly as expounded in 1 W. WHEWELL, PHILOSOPHY OF THE INDUCTIVE SCIENCES 19–21, 91–111 (London 1840).

The modern idea of Euclidean geometry as conventional or purely formal was not generally current in the late 19th century, though the non-Euclidean geometries had been discovered earlier in the century. Thus, the leading British geometer Arthur Cayley could still assert in 1883 that Euclid's parallel axiom (which the non-Euclidean geometries dispense with) "does not need demonstration, but is part of our notion of space." *Quoted in* M. KLINE, MATHEMATICS: THE LOSS OF CERTAINTY 95 (1980).

64 SYSTEM OF LOGIC, *supra* note 63, at 151–52.

65 *See id.* at 153–55 for Mill's explanation of the illusion of the self-evidence of geometric truth, and *see id.* at 407–18 for his discussion of Hume's argument. Mill's view of mathematical knowledge as at base empirical, long wholly rejected, has staged a contemporary

Mill, the great empiricist, himself strongly urged the importance of deductive systematization of theory in natural science. As he pointed out, observations inductively supporting a generalization transfer their confirming power undiminished to any proposition that logically follows from that generalization. At the same time, the derived proposition transfers its own independent inductive support back to the generalization, since the logical derivation has shown it to be within that generalization's scope. The arrangement of inductively derived generalizations into a deductive system thus vastly extends our use of the resources of experience, by spreading the confirming force of observations undiminished even through long and difficult chains of deductive inference. Geometry provides the clearest example of this method, but it was exemplified in classical physics as well.[66]

When this structure—induction of axioms, deduction of theorems—is applied to law, it helps clarify the otherwise baffling talk of observation, experiment and the like that appeared in Langdellian literature, while the legal scientists so extensively devoted themselves to pure conceptual reasoning in their doctrinal work.[67] For them, the fundamental principles of the common law were discerned by induction from cases; rules of law were then derived from principles conceptually; and finally, cases were decided, also conceptually, from rules.

For legal science, the universe of data was not the totality of sense experience of the physical world, but rather the restricted set of reported common law decisions—hence Langdell's often-reviled remark that all the materials of legal science were to be found in printed books.[68] The legal scientist inductively generalized legal principles from the cases. As with Mill's treatment of inductive evidence, the better existing case-law confirmed a principle, the more proper it was to disregard as a mistake any single judicial decision inconsistent with the principle.[69]

To illustrate: in geometry, the Pythagorean theorem, for which we have no direct inductive confirmation, draws to itself the great mass of experience

---

comeback. *See* Lakatos, *A Renaissance of Empiricism in the Recent Philosophy of Mathematics?*, in PROBLEMS IN THE PHILOSOPHY OF MATHEMATICS 199 (I. Lakatos ed. 1967).

66 SYSTEM OF LOGIC, *supra* note 63, at 141–43, 209–11.

67 *See infra* note 104.

68 Langdell, Speech (Nov. 5, 1886), 3 LAW Q. REV. 123, 124 (1887).

69 Sir Frederick Pollock made explicit the analogy between the deviant precedent and the wayward observation in his unusually sophisticated statement of classical legal-scientific method, Pollock, *The Science of Case Law*, ESSAYS IN JURISPRUDENCE AND ETHICS 237, 246–49 (1882).

supporting the Euclidean axioms as soon as it is shown to follow from them as a matter of logic. Similarly, in legal science, the rule that an acceptance by mail must be received to be effective—a doctrine for which there was little common law authority—took on all the precedential support underlying the principle of consideration once Langdell "demonstrated" that the rule followed logically from the general principle. Once the logic of Langdell's substantive derivation was granted, there was then nothing unscientific about his dismissal of the New York and English decisions endorsing the mailbox rule, any more than there would be in treating as clearly mistaken a recorded observation that the sides of a right triangle were of lengths 3, 4 and 6.[70]

Circularity

The analogy between legal science and Mill's conception of geometry seems to fail at an important point. Our observations, which (in Mill's view) support the geometric axioms, themselves draw their force from our general trust in the direct evidence of our senses. They thus have an authority independent of the theory they support.

In orthodox legal science, by contrast, there is no obvious analog to sense-perception as a validating basis for judicial decisions. Decisions are thought authoritative in orthodox legal theory because they follow from the rules and principles that constitute the law; but in the classical conception of legal science, the rules and principles constituting the common law are themselves inductively derived from the cases.[71] The enterprise thus seems to be circular in a way Mill's conception of geometry is not.

There are two general lines of response the legal scientist might make to this point. One would be to admit that legal science is circular, while insisting that natural science is circular in the same way and none the worse for it. The other

70 For the criticism of Langdell as unscientific on this account, note his colleague John Chipman Gray's letter to President Eliot:

> "In law the opinions of judges and lawyers as to what the law is, *are* the law, and it is in any true sense of the word as unscientific to turn from them, as Mr. Langdell does, with contempt because they are 'low and unscientific,' as for a scientific man to decline to take cognizance of oxygen or gravitation because it was low or unscientific."

Letter from John Chipman Gray to President Eliot (January 8, 1883), *quoted in* M. Howe, Justice Oliver Wendell Holmes: The Proving Years, 1870–1882, at 158 (1963).

71 It would be wrong to reconstruct classical orthodoxy as requiring that the cases must determine a *unique* set of principles. To say that would deny any role for considerations of acceptability in the discovery of principles, but as shown, *supra* notes 43–54 and accompanying text, even Langdell conceded acceptability a place in doctrine as long as it was brought to play only at the level of principle.

would be to break out of the circle by finding a source of validity for judicial decisions that was independent of the rules and principles.

Though the first or "confession and avoidance" approach was not historically available to the classical legal scientists, we can, in the spirit of rational reconstruction, sketch the argument. Writers in contemporary philosophy of science and epistemology argue that science cannot rest firmly, as positivist theory insists it should, on the evidence of the senses; natural science itself is in important respects circular. Thus, Kuhn and others have shown that every successful scientific theory coexists with significant counter-instances and anomalies. An established theory is not killed by observations or even by a "crucial experiment" alone, but only by a rival theory that the scientific community of the day finds more attractive and illuminating.[72] Further, the old clarity has been taken from the very distinction between observed fact and theory on which traditional empiricism rests. Not only philosophy of science but experimental psychology now teaches us that there is no pure and pre-theoretical sense experience, no innocent eye; all our data are "theory laden."[73]

As Einstein said, "It is the theory which decides that we can observe";[74] the philosopher Nelson Goodman has said more recently that "facts are small theories, and true theories are big facts."[75] Quine tells us that our belief-system faces "the tribunal of experience" as "a corporate body," and does not naturally divide into discrete propositions that can be tested for their correspondence to discrete facts.[76] Taken together and pushed hard, these ideas can make the relation between data and theory in natural science seem almost as circular as

---

72 T. KUHN, THE STRUCTURE OF SCIENTIFIC REVOLUTIONS 77–91 and *passim* (2d ed. 1970). *See also* N. HANSON, PATTERNS OF DISCOVERY (1958); T. KUHN, THE ESSENTIAL TENSION 266–92, 320–39 (1977); L. LAUDAN, PROGRESS AND ITS PROBLEMS (1977); M. POLANYI, PERSONAL KNOWLEDGE 18–48 (1958). *Compare* Lakatos, *Falsification and the Methodology of Scientific Research Programmes*, CRITICISM AND THE GROWTH OF KNOWLEDGE 91–196 (I. Lakatos & A. Musgrave eds. 1970).

73 *See* E. GOMBRICH, ART AND ILLUSION, 291–329; N. Hanson, *supra* note 72, Chapter 1; J. Hochberg, Perception 105–57 (2d ed. 1977); T. KUHN, THE STRUCTURE OF SCIENTIFIC REVOLUTIONS, *supra* note 72, at 111–35.

74 Or so Heisenberg reported him to have said, in a book of reminiscences written many years after the event. W. HEISENBERG, PHYSICS AND BEYOND 63 (1971). Heisenberg recalls that it was rumination on this remark of Einstein's that led him to his Uncertainty Principle. *Id.* at 77–78.

75 N. GOODMAN, WAYS OF WORLDMAKING 97 (1978). *See also* N. GOODMAN, LANGUAGES OF ART 68 (2d ed. 1976) ("Is a metaphor, then, simply a juvenile fact, and a fact a senile metaphor?").

76 W. QUINE, *Two Dogmas of Empiricism*, FROM A LOGICAL POINT OF VIEW 20, 41 (2d ed. 1961).

the relation between cases and principles in classical legal theory. Contemporary "neo-orthodox" legal theorists have seen and exploited the point.[77]

But these modern ideas would have been alien to the world of the classical legal scientists. Their natural response to a charge of circularity would not be to concede then justify it, but to deny the circle by identifying an extra-theoretical source of validation for judicial decisions, comparable to sense-perception in the case of natural science.[78] Two candidates suggest themselves to serve as such an alternative source of validity: intuition and the doctrine of precedent.

Take intuition first. Just as the data of natural science are validated by sense-perception, so individual judicial decisions might be thought validated by a "sixth sense" that permits direct decision of cases from the facts, without the mediation of general norms. We can distinguish three separate versions of such a sixth sense: first, there might be a "moral sense," a supposed universal human faculty for the direct intuition of right and wrong in concrete situations; second, there might be a "common sense," or generally shared tacit knowledge of the conventional morality of a particular society; and finally, there might be a "trained intuition," a specialized professional skill developed by lawyers in the course of their apprenticeship and practice, which allows them to make legal judgments peculiar to their own system.[79]

---

77 *See, e.g.*, Fried, *The Laws of Change: The Cunning of Reason in Moral and Legal History*, 9 J. LEGAL STUD. 335, 343–44 (1980). Compare this to Ronald Dworkin's more complex discussion, distinguishing legal from natural scientific reasoning, while claiming close resemblance between the two, in TAKING RIGHTS SERIOUSLY, *supra* note 25, at 159–68.

78 The Victorian positivist-empiricist account of science received its classic statement in Mill's SYSTEM OF LOGIC, *supra* note 63; a view nearer the modern one appeared in W. WHEWELL, *supra* note 63.

79 The notions of "moral sense" and "moral sentiment" dominated eighteenth century British moral philosophy; see the summary in A. MACINTYRE, A SHORT HISTORY OF ETHICS 157–77 (1966), and the detailed analytic treatment in Broad, *Some Reflections on Moral Sense Theories in Ethics*, READINGS IN ETHICAL THEORY 363 (W. Sellars & J. Hospers eds. 1952).

The idea of "common sense" as I use it here stresses the origin of the common law in shared community morality. For an expression of this view, see J. REDLICH, THE COMMON LAW AND THE CASE METHOD 37 (1914):

> "In the common law country, the law appears in the national thought as a quality which to a certain extent comes of itself to men and to the relations which bind men together; as something that is always there and for that reason is known and understood by every one of the people themselves."

The notion that experienced judges have an often inarticulate "trained intuition" that leads them to right decisions is commonplace among case-law theorists; *see, e.g.*, R. POUND, INTRODUCTION TO THE PHILOSOPHY OF LAW 54 (1922).

Some version of a sixth sense theory is presupposed by the common legal argumentative technique of *reductio ad absurdum*, under which a putative legal principle is refuted by deriving from it a judgment in a particular case, real or hypothetical, that is intuitively seen to be unacceptable. Reliance on such intuitions in formal legal argument necessarily grants that they have legally authoritative force. Similarly, the "Socratic" method of pedagogy uses the *reductio*. The student's offer of a putative rule is tested by the teacher's statement of a hypothetical case in which the rule would produce an unacceptable result, as all can see—and here the shared intuitions of even novice students are taken as decisive. Since beginning students cannot have developed any peculiarly legal "trained intuition," reliance on the *reductio* in elementary teaching seems to presuppose a latent legal "common sense" in the lay mind, the content of which can be elicited by supplying appropriate cases for judgment.[80]

But the classical scientists, proponents of the pedagogic case-method though they were, stated no "sixth sense" view of case-decision, and for good reason. Any such approach accepts intuitions of the acceptability of particular results in individual cases as legitimate building blocks for legal doctrine. But such "khadi justice" intuitionism would violate the cardinal classical tenet that correct legal judgments must be principled—that is, formally derivable from general principles.[81] In the classical synthesis, as I have argued, considerations of acceptability could properly be taken into account only at the level of general principle.[82] The case-method was thus in contradiction with classical orthodox theory—a contradiction manifested in practice by the historical paradox that Langdell's own educational innovations did help to undermine his approach to legal doctrine.[83]

Apart from a theoretically unacceptable "sixth sense," the other independent source of authority for case-decisions—and the one reluctantly adopted

---

A "sixth sense" theory could of course combine the three kinds of intuition in various mixtures to justify case decisions, apart from their consistency with doctrine. No actual "sixth sense" theory proclaims intuition, trained or otherwise, to be infallible; even the strongest intuitionistic legal theories retain some notion that individual judgments should be checked against rules and principles. *See, e.g.*, J. FRANK, LAW AND THE MODERN MIND 140–141 (2d ed. 1949).

80 As the linguist elicits judgments of "grammaticality" by appealing to the tacit knowledge of the grammar of his language possessed by every native speaker. For a development of the linguistics analogy, *see infra* note 98.

81 *See supra* text accompanying notes 36–37.

82 *See supra* text accompanying note 54.

83 *See supra* note 3 and accompanying text.

by classical legal theory to break out of its logical circle—was the doctrine of *stare decisis.* Recall the vicious circle again: the source of common law principles was the cases, the standard for correct case decision was consistency with the principles. Breaking out required a source for the legal validity of decisions independent of the principles—an analog to the fallible but independent authority of sense-perception in supporting the observation-statements that supply the data of natural science.

Precedent

Let me approach the use of *stare decisis* as an independent source of legal validity in a somewhat roundabout way. The classical scientist accepted that a legal system must be comprehensive, as well as having the logical virtues of completeness, formality and conceptual order. To recall what this means, consider that to the classical scientist, a judicial decision, unlike the hypothetical legal judgment of a lawyer or a scholar, could be evaluated along two separate dimensions. First, one could ask if the decision was substantively correct, derived logically from the right legal rules and principles. Second, one could ask of a judicial decision whether it was jurisdictionally and procedurally correct; that is, did it issue from the designated court, and according to the prescribed forms. The legal system would achieve comprehensiveness if every decision satisfied this second dimension of evaluation.[84]

In the practice of natural science, there is no analog to the requirement of comprehensiveness for a legal system. Scientists, unlike judges, have no professional obligation to decide every "case" within their "jurisdiction." Quite consistently with the premises of their enterprise, they can admit that there are things science cannot explain. Thus, science sets its own jurisdiction, which it defines by the scope of its substantive theories.[85] Indeed, the pronouncement of a "scientific solution" that is not backed by the theoretical scientific wherewithal constitutes pseudo-science, one of the chief sins against the scientific ethic.

By contrast, a judge must decide a case over which he has jurisdiction, whether or not he is satisfied that his decision is scientifically correct.[86] Where the procedurally final court decides "incorrectly", it has still produced a judg-

84 *See supra* notes 20–22 and accompanying text, and note 31.

85 Scientists commonly hold the article of faith (or working rule of method) that all events are "in principle" subject to scientific explanation. This is very different from being subject to a professional obligation to give scientific explanations for events defined by "jurisdictional" rules that are separate from substantive scientific theories.

86 *See supra* notes 20–22, *infra* note 153 and accompanying text.

ment terminating the case. The legal system gives such a judgment binding authority over the parties by the principle of *res judicata*; as to them, it is the law's last word.

Further—coming finally to the main point—the common law doctrine of *stare decisis* gives a decided case authoritative force with respect to future decisions in other cases, whether or not the case is later thought to have been decided correctly in the light of principle. This precedential force is traditionally justified mainly on the ground that people will rely on even "scientifically incorrect" official precedents in ordering their affairs.[87] Under the classical view of precedent, a decision or two that is out of whack with "principle" might be set aside as "not good authority," though never entirely dismissed from consideration until overruled. But an established line of precedent, however inconsistent with "principle" in its inception, becomes binding law, and the seamless web of doctrine must somehow be rearranged to accommodate it.[88]

Stare decisis thus provided the outside source of validity for decided cases that was necessary to save the classical science of law from vicious circularity. But it could do so only at the price of compromising the classical orthodox aspiration toward universally formal conceptual order. The partial authority of even "incorrect" decisions meant that *stare decisis* jostled against what Williston called *stare principiis*, without any formal higher level principle to decide between them.[89] In law, unlike science, error, if persisted in, at some point

87 Other justifications are given for *stare decisis*—the convenience of relying on the wisdom of the past, the unfairness of not treating like cases alike (apart from considerations of notice)—but it is the reliance argument that supports giving precedential force to "wrong" past decisions.

88 *See* Pollock, *supra* note 69. *Compare* Langdell's treatment of the mailbox rule precedents, *supra* note 9 and accompanying text, *with* his treatment of the doctrine of consideration itself, *infra* notes 91–97 and accompanying text.

89 S. Williston, *supra* note 39, at 205. "*Stare decisis*, or follow the precedents, was the old legal maxim. In effect for this Langdell's followers substituted *stare principiis*, follow the principles, even if they overthrow some decisions." *Id.* Some—but classical theory had no formal way to decide how many.

A difference, greater in theory than in practice, between legal science in England and the United States during the classical period, was that English judges purported to be absolutely bound by precedent; the distinction was blurred by manipulation of the distinction between holding and dictum. And see the assessment of American doctrine in E. Wambaugh, *supra* note 35, at 108: "We live under a system of *stare decisis*, tempered slightly by a power to overrule."

became truth; and where that point lay could only be determined according to considerations of acceptability that were never satisfactorily formalized.[90]

Langdell himself reluctantly accepted this unformalizable tension among principle, precedent and acceptability; it is well illustrated in his discussion of the doctrine of consideration. Langdell did not regard that doctrine as essential to a rational system of contract law. He recognized, for example, that European civil law enforced promises lacking consideration, and that the common law itself required no consideration for promises under seal.[91] He also recognized the unhappy results that flowed from the consideration doctrine; it was the villain of the piece in the flagpole problem, where Langdell conceded that it produced "hardship and injustice."[92] Further, he believed that the original adoption of the doctrine had not been logically required by pre-existing law—indeed, going the other way might have been "the more rational course."[93] "But," Langdell went on, "whatever may have been the merits of the question originally, it was long since conclusively settled" in favor of the consideration doctrine.[94] That being so, the courts could not, consistent with their proper role, abandon the doctrine; and it must be enforced with full rigor within its logical scope, as in the flagpole situation.

On the other hand, Langdell argued, some courts had carried the doctrine beyond its logically proper area by applying it to various contracts governed by mercantile law; that certain merchant promisors should not properly be held to the requirement of consideration was in his view "very clear upon principle."[95] However, "it must be confessed … that the generally received opinion among lawyers is otherwise."[96] What does the legal scientist do with a line of existing decisions that follow received opinion, but are contrary to principle, and extend a doctrine better never adopted in the first place? Langdell's response to this conflict of precedent with principle and acceptability was to

---

90 Considerations of acceptability as used at the level of principle, *see supra* notes 43–54 and accompanying text, were presumably themselves not formal; but one of the points of allowing them to be invoked only at the level of principle was to insulate the normal workings of the system from their effect, thus preserving its general formality. *Stare decisis* meant that whenever there was a clash between "principle" and "authority," formality was lost; hence the frantic efforts of classical scientists to reconcile apparently inconsistent cases, *see supra* note 35.

91 SUMMARY, *supra* note 7, at 58, 100.

92 *See supra* note 52.

93 SUMMARY, *supra* note 7 at 60–61.

94 *Id.* at 61.

95 *Id.* at 63.

96 *Id.*

say, with uncharacteristic equivocation, that these decisions, "if they cannot be pronounced erroneous, must at least be deemed anomalous."[97] Thus was the geometric structure of law's universally formal conceptual order caught in the ever-tangled skein of human affairs.[98]

---

97 *Id.* Langdell's more philosophical colleague Beale later stated, "The law of a given time must be taken to be the *body of principles* which is accepted by the legal profession, whatever that profession may be. . . ." J. BEALE, TREATISE ON THE CONFLICT OF LAWS 150 (1916) (emphasis added). This did not resolve the Langdellian dilemma; only those received professional opinions that fitted into a "body of principles" constituted the law for Beale. *Cf. infra* note 109.

Langdell's view of the relative importance of principle and precedent is perhaps best expressed in his discussion of Lord Mansfield's view that a promise to do what the promisor was under a pre-existing moral obligation to do was binding. He noted two theories that might be given for such a view; 1) that the moral obligation was sufficient consideration, and 2) that in such cases, no consideration was required. As between these theories, the second

> "would have been less untenable, and less mischievous in its tendency. It would indeed have been liable to the serious objection of involving judicial legislation, but the theory of moral consideration was liable to the much greater objection, at least from the scientific point of view, that it could only succeed at the expense of involving a fundamental legal doctrine in infinite confusion."

SUMMARY, *supra* note 7, at 89.

98 Langdell's dilemma was comparable to that of the prescriptive grammarian trying to establish when "bad but common" usage has become "correct," while necessarily conceding that the grammar of a language has its only source in the usage of its native speakers. The analogy between a people's law and its language is an old one; indeed it was the foundation metaphor of the historical school of jurisprudence, *see* F. VON SAVIGNY, THE VOCATION OF OUR AGE FOR LEGISLATION AND JURISPRUDENCE 24–31 (1st ed. London, A. Hayward trans. 1831. German orig. 1814). But the analogy has not been exploited since the rise of modern scientific linguistics. It seems an extraordinarily illuminating one, both where it holds and where it does not; perhaps a full development of the analogy would count as a "structuralist" legal theory, in the one fairly clear sense of that term. For example, Saussure's distinctions between *langue* (language, treated as an abstract object) and *parole* (its application); and between diachronic (historical) and synchronic (present time-slice) study of language both cast useful light on "legal science." *See* F. DE SAUSSURE, COURSE IN GENERAL LINGUISTICS 13–14, 80–85 (W. Baskin trans. 1974). Chomsky's distinction between "competence" and "performance," and the use he makes of intuitions of "grammaticality" are suggestive in thinking about intuitionistic theories of case law of the sort sketched in *supra* text accompanying notes 79–80. N. CHOMSKY, ASPECTS OF THE THEORY OF SYNTAX, Chapter 1 (1965). Finally, both law and language have aspects of the "conventional" in the rigorous sense of that term developed in D. LEWIS, CONVENTION (1969), following T. SCHELLING, THE STRATEGY OF CONFLICT (1960); for some exploration

Progress

Viewed on a larger scale, the problem of the place of precedent in classical orthodoxy became the problem of the place to be given to history and change in legal theory. Did the fundamental principles of the law change, and if so how? Under the geometric analogy, legal principles should be universal and eternal; history would be simply the record of their gradual discovery. This was indeed the view held by natural law theorists.[99] But it was a position the classical legal scientists firmly rejected. They accepted the nineteenth-century evolutionary idea that law, even in its fundamentals, was not unchanging but progressively evolving; as Sir Henry Maine had argued, the legal order grew from the primitive to the advanced, from a regime based on status to one based on contract.[100]

Thus, Langdell wrote in the Preface to his *Cases on Contracts* that each basic legal doctrine "has arrived at its present state by slow degrees; in other words, it is a growth, extending in many cases through centuries."[101] His disciple, Ames, wrote of the gradual evolution of legal norms from the formal and amoral rules of primitive law toward a closer coincidence of the principles of law and morals.[102] And Beale, the most self-consciously philosophical expo-

---

of the connections, *see* Johnson, *On Deciding and Setting Precedent for the Reasonable Man*, 62 ARCHIV FUR RECHTS-UND-SOZI-ALPHILOSOPHIE 161 (1976).

99 And given contemporary exposition by Charles Fried, *supra* note 77 at 349–50, where Fried amusingly, and *almost* dead-pan, analogizes the history of legal thought to the history of logic or mathematics. Fried has more recently, and with apparent solemnity, announced "doubts" about his earlier view on the ground that "a priori moral reflection on rights seems inadequate to yield the necessary richness of our legal system" so that after all perhaps law cannot be fully reduced to "a branch of moral philosophy." Fried, *The Artificial Reason of the Law or: What Lawyers Know*, 60 TEX. L. REV. 35, 37 (1981).

The classical legal scientists unanimously rejected natural law jurisprudence—some of them in a mild tone, as in the case of Langdell, *see supra* note 49, or in the case of Beale, *see infra* note 108 and accompanying text. On the other hand there was Sir Frederick Pollock, who wrote thus after reading an exposition of natural law theory:

> "I had long known of *Naturrecht* as a thing existing in German books, but it had never come in my way to any serious extent.... We have to thank Professor Lorimer for revealing the mystery in as good English as the nature of the subject admits. As I came to the last page I said to myself with a mental gasp and shiver 'Ugh—Ugh—now I know what *Naturrecht* is.' "

F. POLLOCK, *The Nature of Jurisprudence*, *supra* note 68, at 1, 20.

100 H. MAINE, ANCIENT LAW 170 (9th ed. 1883); P. STEIN, LEGAL EVOLUTION (1980).

101 C. LANGDELL, *supra* note 42, at viii.

102 J. AMES, *Law and Morals*, in LECTURES ON LEGAL HISTORY (1913). Ames was much more the practicing historian than the other classical orthodox scholars; he tended to find doc-

nent of classical orthodoxy, wrote that "the common law changes.... The law of today must of course be better than that of seven centuries ago, more in accordance with the general principles of justice, more in accordance with the needs of the present age, more humane, more flexible and more complex."[103]

Langdell's reference to legal doctrine as a "growth extending through centuries" also suggests an analogy between classical legal science and evolutionary biology—one thinks of legal categories as species and genera, and of cases as specimens.[104] To the extent that biological taxonomy involves the development of an ordered conceptual hierarchy, the biological and geometrical analogies were not in conflict. And insofar as biology suggests a changing rather than a static subject matter, with the scientist seen as the rational classifier of slowly evolving categories of natural phenomena, it actually does come closer than geometry to the classical orthodox conception of legal science. But the biological metaphor cannot supplant the geometric, because law, like geometry, but unlike taxonomic biology, uses its ordered intellectual system not only to classify specimens but to solve problems.[105]

Langdell's evolutionary language likewise suggests the connection between classical legal science and the historical school of jurisprudence, whose central

---

trines evolving, through a kind of inner logic, in a progressive direction. He was also much more given to moralism and a spirit of reform than was Langdell. For example, against the spirit of formalism, he answered the question raised by the title of his essay *How Far an Act May Be a Tort Because of the Wrongful Motive of the Actor?*, *id.* at 399, by saying: quite far. On other occasions, his work reflected the purest formalist spirit, as illustrated by his essays *The Nature of Ownership*, *id.* at 192, and *Can a Murderer Acquire Title by his Crime and Keep It?*, *id.* at 310.

103 J. BEALE, *supra* note 97, at 149. Beale was the philosopher of classical orthodoxy; the cited work (an early-published fragment of his full TREATISE ON THE CONFLICT OF LAWS (1935)) at 114–89, contained the fullest published expression of his jurisprudential views. *See also*, *Notes by Robert Lee Hale from Jurisprudence Lectures given by Joseph Henry Beale, Harvard Law School, 1909*, 29 U. MIAMI L. REV. 281–333 (1975) (hereinafter *Jurisprudence Lectures*).

104 Cf. Langdell, *supra* note 67, at 124: "We have also constantly inculcated the idea that the library is the proper workshop of professors and students alike; that it is to us all that the laboratories of the university are to the chemists and physicists, the museum of natural history to the zoologists, the botanical garden to the botanists." In fact, like Langdell in this passage, when classical orthodox writers drew their frequent analogies between legal and experimental science, they seem to have referred quite at random to the various natural sciences. *See, e.g.*, Keener, *The Inductive Study of Law*, 28 AM. L. REV. 713 (1894) (physics); W. KEENER, CASES ON QUASI-CONTRACT, Preface (1888) (geology); LIEBER'S HERMENEUTICS 329 (W. Hammond ed. 1880) (astronomy).

105 That is, biological taxonomies are systems of categories; legal systems, like geometry, combine categories with operative concepts. *See supra* note 28.

thesis was that a nation's law is necessarily rooted in the contingent and evolving traditions and customary practices of its people.[106] But it would be a mistake to identify classical orthodoxy too closely with the historical school, which was represented in America particularly by Langdell's contemporary, James Coolidge Carter.[107] Langdell and his followers placed more emphasis than did Carter on principle and reason as against precedent and custom; the classical view thus straddled the natural law and historical schools.

According to classical legal science, history did provide the necessary raw material—the cases—on which reason operated in extracting legal principles. The classical writers thus viewed traditional natural law theories that lacked this positive basis as philosophical speculation rather than legal science.[108] But classical scientists did not identify legal principles with customs; thus Beale wrote, "the common law from its inception has been based upon principles, not upon custom."[109]

If law was not a body of eternal truths but rather a set of evolving principles, and yet these principles were not identified with custom, what was the vehicle for legal change in classical theory? Of course, there was legislation, but the classical writers saw statutes as haphazard and anomalous incursions into the body of common law, not fit for scientific study.[110] Precedent too could bring change in the law; a decision not originally supported by existing principles could, if adhered to, eventually establish itself as authoritative doctrine.[111] But such a decision was in the first instance an error, from the classical perspective. If error that managed to entrench itself was the only mechanism of change, how did the law progress?

106 *See, e.g.*, F. VON SAVIGNY, *supra* note 98.

107 J. CARTER, THE PROVINCES OF THE WRITTEN AND THE UNWRITTEN LAW (1889); J. CARTER, LAW, ITS ORIGIN, GROWTH AND FUNCTION (1907).

108 J. BEALE, *supra* note 97, at 143. He pressed the same charge, with more acerbity, against the project of Benthamite codification in Beale, *The Development of Jurisprudence During the Past Century*, 18 HARV. L. REV. 271, 282–83 (1905). In the latter piece, Beale praised Savigny and the other scholars of the historical school for their "great work" in correcting the abstract errors both of Benthamism, and of what he oddly called "the subjective and deductive philosophy of the middle ages." *Id.* at 283.

109 Beale, *Book Review*, 20 HARV. L. REV. 164 (1906) (signed "J.H.B."); and see *Jurisprudence Lectures*, *supra* note 103, at 291–92. Elsewhere, Beale insisted that "the one most important feature of law" is "that it is not a mere collection of arbitrary rules, but a body of scientific principle." J. BEALE, *supra* note 97, at 135.

110 *See infra* note 171 and accompanying text.

111 *See, e.g.*, Langdell's discussion of the consideration doctrine, *supra* notes 91–97, and accompanying text.

Recalling the biological metaphor, one can imagine a Darwinian explanation.[112] But classical orthodoxy instead provided an idealist account of the progress of the common law, one that gave a central role to the legal scientist.[113] Progress occurred when the scholar (or the great judge or lawyer) discovered a previously unrecognized principle, one that provided a simple and satisfying explanation for existing decisions, and that at the same time reflected the slowly changing needs and conditions of society. Such a principle, because immanent in decided cases, was already the law, so that its articulation was an act of discovery, not one of illegitimate legislation. On the other hand, once discovered it would produce different, better decisions than had the older, less scientific formulation of doctrine and hence would contribute to the progress of the law.

A famous example of this sort of classical law reform was Brandeis' and Warren's extraction of a right to privacy from a scattering of older cases previously regarded as unrelated.[114] Brandeis, a master of Langdellian technique, artfully argued that these cases were better explained by a general principle of protection of privacy than by the grounds given by the judges who had decided them.[115] But at the same time as he rooted it in a principle that elegantly reconciled the cases, Brandeis explicitly justified the new right on forward-looking grounds of policy, arguing that it was required by changed social conditions such as mass literacy, the rise of a popular press, the crowded conditions of modern life, and the increased personal sensitivity that supposedly accompanied higher general standards of education.[116]

Because Brandeis' attention to these considerations of policy supported his doctrine at the level of general principle, it was consistent with the tenets of classical orthodoxy.[117] But in the stress he gave to policy as against logic in

---

112 That is, there could be a process of essentially random judicial deviation from established law, and those judicial "errors" that turned out to be socially useful would survive while the rest were forgotten. For such an argument *see* Priest, *The Common Law and the Selection of Efficient Rules*, 6 J. LEGAL STUD. 65 (1977).

113 This view of the role of the legal scientist may be implicit in Langdell's reference to the scientific law teacher as analogous to "the Roman jurisconsult," LANGDELL, *supra* note 67, at 124. It becomes explicit in Ames, *The Vocation of the Law Professor*, *supra* note 92, 354, 364–67. Beale *supra* note 97, at 150, positively trumpets it where he speaks of the influence of law teachers on the growth of the law "comparable in degree" to that of judges and "likely to increase in the future more rapidly than that of judges."

114 Brandeis & Warren, *The Right to Privacy*, 4 HARV. L. REV. 193 (1890).

115 *Id.* at 198–214.

116 *Id* at 195–96.

117 *See supra* text accompanying note 54.

carrying the burden of his argument, he was straining the spirit of orthodoxy and anticipating the direction of post-classical legal theory. Brandeis' argument showed that Langdellian techniques could serve the cause of conscious law reform. But the classical system could not in the end make too much of a virtue of its flexibility without undermining its promise of determinate geometric order.

IV

What was the special appeal of classical orthodoxy in late nineteenth century America? The natural place to start is with its promise of universal formality—"every case an easy case." The legal system was to be so arranged that it resolved hard disputes by indubitable (even if complex) reasoning, as Euclidean geometry resolves intuitively problematic spatial questions. The system would be predictable; people could know in which circumstances they would get the aid and in which they would face the opposition of state power. Further, people would be free from public force exerted for the arbitrary personal ends of its guardians. Other things being equal, these would be gains for everyone. But businessmen, the ascendant group in late nineteenth century America, had special needs for legal predictability, and were particularly drawn to the associated "rule of law" conception of freedom.[118]

Though legal realists were later to question it, the classical link between conceptual order and formality seemed clear in 1900.[119] So modern-minded an observer as Max Weber believed that classical legal science—he focused on its German Pandectist rather than its American Langdellian version—enhanced the kind of practical legal predictability that businessmen care about.[120] He even carried this acceptance of classical assumptions to the point of being puzzled at how capitalism could have developed and flourished in England, which with its common law writ system and absence of university legal scholarship lacked a proper conceptually formal system.[121]

Beyond its promise of predictability, a more directly political explanation of the appeal of classical legal science was the ideological support it provided for

118 *See* Trubek, *Max Weber on Law and the Rise of Capitalism*, 1972 Wis. L. Rev. 720, 739–46.

119 On the Realist challenge, *see infra* notes 162–69 and accompanying text.

120 For Weber's association of "formal legal rationality" with Pandectist legal science, *see* M. Weber, On Law in Economy and Society, *supra* note 19, at 64.

121 *See, e.g.*, *id.* at 353; Weber's various and contradictory remarks on "the England Problem" are collected in Trubek, *supra* note 118, at 746–48.

business through its treatment of economic power relations as neutral, scientifically derived private law rights. The progressive proponents of social legislation certainly saw this ideological connection; all the early critiques of legal classicism linked it with political conservatism.[122]

Nor was the point confined to critics of legal science. John Austin had earlier made an unusually candid pitch for the geometric method in law and ethics on the ground that its impersonal certainty could fortify existing institutions against popular unrest.[123] And nearly a century after Austin, the sponsors of the American Law Institute and its Restatement project were still promising that sound legal science could quell popular discontent by convincing people that judicial protection of the private law status quo was neutrally scientific rather than political.[124]

It is more doubtful whether classical legal science actually influenced the course of judicial decision in a pro-business direction. During the period from 1870 to 1940, the most important political issues in the legal system were questions of public law: how the Populist-Progressive-New Deal legislative program was to be received by legal professionals.[125] The conservative position was that the important common law private rights were constitutionally protected against collective interference unless the legislation could be shown to be closely related to the accepted police power goals of health, safety or morals.[126] For conservative judges, legislation that passed the constitutional hurdle still faced the canon that statutes in derogation of the common law were to be strictly construed.[127]

Neither of these conservative doctrines was particularly congenial to classical orthodoxy. The classicists did not regard public law, including constitutional law, as amenable to scientific study at all. Thus, Langdell's Harvard colleagues and disciples Beale and Ames threatened to withdraw their offer to help the new University of Chicago Law School get started because its organizers proposed to teach a substantial number of public law courses, thus violating the Harvard curricular dogma that students must be exposed only to

---

122 *See, e.g.*, HOLMES, COLLECTED PAPERS, *supra* note 3; R. Pound, *supra* note 14.

123 J. AUSTIN, *supra* note 59, at 79; *cf. id.* at 67–70.

124 1 A.L.I. PROC. 8 (1923) (uncertainty and complexity of law create disrespect for law and consequent unrest); *id.* at 10 ("lack of agreement among lawyers concerning the fundamental principles of the common law is the most potent cause of uncertainty").

125 As compared with the ante-bellum period, where a good case can be made for the greater importance of private law; this is a central thesis of M. HORWITZ, *supra* note 16.

126 C. TIEDEMAN, LIMITATIONS OF POLICE POWER (1886).

127 Pound, *Common Law and Legislation*, 21 HARV. L. REV. 383 (1908).

scientific "pure law" courses.[128] Constitutional law was unscientific because hopelessly vague, as typified by the police power doctrine; the question whether a statute was "reasonably related to safety, health or morals" could not be treated formally. To the legal science mentality such open-ended questions were political, not legal, and the courts abandoned any scientific role in trying to answer them. On the rare occasions when the classicists discussed constitutional questions, they thus tended to follow the line laid down by James Bradley Thayer (himself not a classicist)[129]—deference to the legislature unless there was clear violation of a positive constitutional command.[130]

The legal scientists were likewise not much attracted to the problems of statutory interpretation; they believed that the haphazard law laid down in the statute books did not lend itself to conceptual ordering.[131] When they did confront statutory problems they did not tend to rely on the canon about statutes in derogation of the common law. Their formalism rather pointed them toward literal readings that avoided both narrowing and expansive purposive interpretation.[132]

---

128 F. ELLSWORTH, LAW ON THE MIDWAY 67 (1977).

129 Thayer, *The Origin and Scope of the American Doctrine of Constitutional Law*, 7 HARV. L. REV. 129 (1893). For Thayer's generally pragmatic and unclassical approach to law, see his essay *The Present and Future of the Law of Evidence*, 12 HARV. L. REV. 71 (1898).

130 *See, e.g.*, Langdell, *The Status of Our New Territories*, 12 HARV. L. REV. 365 (1898) (the Constitution places no restraint on administration of territories annexed from Spain); Williston, *Freedom of Contract*, 6 CORNELL L. REV. 365, 375–80 (1921) (constitutional decisions enforcing "liberty of contract" disapproved).

131 *See Jurisprudence Lectures*, *supra* note 103, at 297–301. Beale distinguishes between the rare successful statute, which is "capable of having its corners rubbed off, and of being assimilated by the common law," *id.* at 298 (there are only "a very narrow range" of such statutes, *id.* at 300); and the typical statute which is "done by haphazard legislation by a legislature chosen not primarily for wisdom," often at the insistence of a lawyer who has lost a case and drafts a statute to correct the injustice but who "is not wise enough to foresee its effects other than the particular injustice in mind." *Id.* at 300–01.

Reviewing Dicey's LAW AND PUBLIC OPINION IN ENGLAND, Langdell complained that the title was misleading; Dicey used the word "law" but wrote about "legislation." Clearly in Langdell's mind the two were separate. Langdell, *Dominant Opinions in England During the Nineteenth Century in Relation to Legislation as Illustrated by English Legislation, or the Absence of It, During that Period*, 19 HARV. L. REV. 151 (1906).

132 A good example is Ames' discussion of the famous case of *Riggs v. Palmer* in *Can a Murderer Acquire Title by his Crime and Keep It?*, *supra* note 102, at 310. The New York statute of wills made no provision for the case where the devisee murdered the testator in order to acquire his property. The court interpreted the statute to deprive the murderer of his ill-gotten gains, a view Ames found "impossible to justify" because of its conflict with

It would have been surprising if the classical scientists had been enthusiastic supporters of late nineteenth century big business. They were men of a scholastic bent, generally drawn from an old commercial and professional class that was being pushed from its place in the hierarchy of power by the new industrial and transportation tycoons. The natural political orientation for people of their type was to the Mugwumps, and later to the right wing of the Progressive movement. They were believers in science, traditional virtue and apolitical expertise, favoring sound currency, free trade, civil service reform and clean municipal government.[133]

Classical legal thought thus took only a moderately conservative stance in the political struggles of its time. On the one hand, the classical scientists drew a sharp line between neutral law and partisan politics, placing the fundamentals and many of the details of the market and private property system on the legal rather than the political side of the line. On the other hand, they accepted, however reluctantly, the legitimate power of the legislative majority to step across that line in pursuit of goals too vague for legal-scientific definition.[134]

Such was the relation of classical orthodoxy to Americans' material interests; how did it appeal to their ideal interests, their urge to find meaning in life? During the post-Civil War period, many Americans experienced at once the complication and the disenchantment of their world. The security of living in a coherent and cognizable life-world—the "island community" of Robert Wiebe's phrase—was destroyed for many by a communications and transportation revolution that left people experiencing their lives as newly controlled

---

the literal terms of the statute. *Id.* at 312. *See also* Langdell, *The Northern Securities Case and the Sherman Anti-trust Act,* 16 HARV. L. REV. 538, 551 (1903).

133 *See generally* G. BLODGETT, THE GENTLE REFORMERS 19–47 (1966); R. HOFSTADTER, THE AGE OF REFORM 131–73 (especially 157–58) (1955).

134 In this respect, I disagree with Duncan Kennedy's claim that decisions such as Lochner v. New York, 198 U.S. 45 (1905), were representative of the classical mode. Kennedy, *Toward an Historical Understanding of Legal Consciousness: The Case of Classical Legal Thought in America, 1850–1940, supra* note 6. *Lochner* represented rather the pre-classical and relatively "political" constitutionalism that received its most striking exposition in the famous preface to C. TIEDEMAN, *supra* note 126, at vi–viii. *See also* the thunderous rhetoric of J. DILLON, THE LAWS OF ENGLAND AND AMERICA 203–15 (1894). For the authentic classical approach, *see supra* note 130 and accompanying text. Dillon and Tiedeman looked back to Story, Webster, Rufus Choate and the spirit of Whig constitutionalism, under which the judges were seen as guardians of order, virtue and property against the passions of the mob.

by distant and invisible forces.[135] At the same time, the consolations of both traditional religion and liberal humanist self-esteem were assaulted by Darwinism, with its implication that human as well as physical nature could be fully explained in terms of blind and purposeless mechanism.[136]

Against this background, the dry geometry of classical legal orthodoxy had a certain paradoxical quasi-religious appeal to the educated elite. Legal science promised a complete and universally formal system of norms, and so offered determinate answers in an increasingly incomprehensible world. As traditional religion lost its capacity to supply an underlying order to moral and political life (for portions of the elite), legal orthodoxy promised just such an order in the form of the "few fundamental principles" of the common law. In these few simple principles, the individual could comprehend the fundamentals of the whole law, and the society that had come to seem inconceivably vast, unmanageably complex and mechanistically amoral could be seen as having a set of established norms at its center.[137]

More concretely, the legal science movement supplied an ideological background for the emerging national bar. The bar, despite all its growth and new wealth, passed through a crisis of institutional self-doubt during the last third of the nineteenth century, even as it was first organizing into a cohesive nationwide professional group. It is hardly possible to read a speech given at a bar association meeting during that period without finding either lamentation for the lost independence of the American lawyer, newly in servitude to business, or defensive bluster against charges that the profession had been commercialized and degraded.[138]

During the same period, secular science and the new major universities where science was practiced were in the ascendancy of their prestige, replac-

---

135 *See* T. Haskell, The Emergence of Professional Social Science 24–47 (1977); R. Wiebe, The Search for Order, 1877–1920 11–75 (1967).

136 P. Boller, American Thought in Transition: The Impact of Evolutionary Naturalism, 1865–1900 22–46 (1969); Meyer, *American Intellectuals and the Victorian Crisis of Faith*, Victorian America 59–77 (D. Howe ed. 1976).

137 The religious dimension of the quest for legal certainty is evoked in Cardozo's words:

> "I was much troubled in spirit, in my first years upon the bench, to find how trackless was the ocean on which I had embarked. I sought for certainty. I was oppressed and disheartened when I found that the quest for it was futile. I was trying to reach land, the solid land of fixed and settled rules, the paradise of a justice that would declare itself by tokens plainer and more commanding than its pale and glimmering reflections in my own vacillating mind and conscience."

B. Cardozo, *supra* note 33, at 166.

138 *See* R. Hofstadter, *supra* note 133, at 158–61 and sources by him.

ing the church in the minds of the social and intellectual vanguard as the locus of higher, spiritual value in otherwise materialist America.[139] Lawyers who saw themselves in that vanguard were happy to hear Holmes, for example, say that law is "an enterprise for the thinker" in which "a man may live greatly."[140] Holmes, the first great critic of classical orthodoxy, was also drawn by his own philosophic ambitions to the classical enterprise of conceptual ordering.[141] While he recognized that "general principles do not decide concrete cases,"[142] he practiced and revered conceptual jurisprudence, which for him raised law above mere commerce, as he celebrated in words that have adorned many law school graduation speeches since:

> Happiness ... cannot be won simply by being counsel to great corporations and having an income of fifty thousand dollars.... The remoter and more general aspects of the law are those which give it universal interest. It is through them that you not only become a great master in your calling, but connect your subject with the universe and catch an echo of the infinite, a glimpse of its unfathomable process, a hint of the universal law.[143]

At a still more concrete level, legal science built a bridge between lawyers' urge to feel that they practiced a learned profession, and the need of the new universities for an alliance with the rich and influential bar. The university's pretensions to be the seat of pure learning stood in the way of this alliance as long as the study of law was seen as the mere craft-training that Veblen, for instance, said it was.[144] The idea of legal science met this difficulty, as Langdell spelled out:

> If law be not a science, a university will consult its own dignity in declining to teach it. If law be not a science, it is a species of handicraft, and may best be learned by serving an apprenticeship to one who practices it. If it be a science, it will scarcely be disputed that it is one of the greatest and

---

139 L. Veysey, The Emergence of the American University 121–79 (1965).

140 Holmes, Collected Papers, *supra* note 3, at 29–30.

141 *See infra* notes 162–63.

142 Lochner v. New York, 198 U.S. 45, 76 (1905).

143 Holmes, Collected Papers, *supra* note 3, at 202.

144 T. Veblen, The Higher Learning in America 211 (1918). ("the law school belongs in the modern university no more than a school of fencing or dancing.")

> most difficult of sciences, and that it needs all the light that the most enlightened seat of learning can throw upon it.[145]

It is impossible to believe that Langdell was cynical or manipulative in what he said, or that there was not genuine passion behind Holmes' eloquence. For them, and for a handful of their contemporaries, legal scholarship was an end in itself.[146]

Apart from disinterested love of scholarship, the classical scientists in their work as law teachers necessarily had to carry out the organization and simplification of the mass of legal materials that is prerequisite to successful teaching. Earlier, Blackstone, Kent and Story had found their vocation as legal system-builders when they agreed to teach law to beginners.[147] So, in their time, Langdell's followers—the first full-time American legal professoriate—faced with the need to make outlines and summaries of their subjects for pedagogic purposes, perhaps were especially inclined to confer a high value on the task of conceptual ordering, thus making a virtue out of necessity.

Pulling these strands together, we can see a converging network of demands—political, spiritual, professional and educational—that defined the situation of late nineteenth century American legal thinkers. It would be an exercise in the old historical game of hindsight determinism to say that this situation necessarily produced classical orthodoxy. What can fairly be said is that Langdell's system did nicely meet this particular group of demands, at least for a brief moment in time.

---

145 Langdell, *supra* note 67, at 124.

146 On Langdell's idealism (and Holmes' own), see Holmes' letter to Pollock quoted in *supra* note 13.

147 The connection between university law teaching and conceptual, systematic legal thought was one of Weber's central themes; M. WEBER, *supra* note 19, at 216–17, 274–78. It is significant that German legal science was intimately linked to university legal education from its origins early in the nineteenth century. Similarly, the English legal science movement, closely related to American classical orthodoxy, arose with the development of serious university-based law study at Oxford during the 1870's and 1880's. *See* F. LAWSON, THE OXFORD LAW SCHOOL, 1850–1965 69–85 (1968). On the other hand, not all university-based law teachers were classical in their approach; there were also Whig throwbacks, like Tiedeman and Baldwin, and precursors of modernity, like Gray and Thayer.

V

Though classical orthodoxy haunts us still, it did fall from its position of explicit dominance, for reasons that are worth recalling. One reason was certainly political; Progressive and later New Deal lawyers saw classical orthodoxy as a form of conservative ideology. In part this was a confusion of Langdellian legal science with the laissez-faire constitutional doctrines epitomized by the *Lochner* decision. But it was also in part a realistic assessment. Classical orthodoxy did claim to discover politically neutral private law principles by rigorous scientific methods, and thus reinforced the view of the common law contract and property system as a "brooding omnipresence in the sky" rather than as a contingent allocation of power and resources.[148]

Apart from its perceived political bias, classical theory, with its vision of the law as determined by a few relatively fixed and fundamental principles, was not readily adapted to a period of rapid social change. The very factors that made classicism reassuring to people frightened by change—its suggestion that there were stable fundamentals under a chaotic surface—made it seem hopelessly unrealistic to those who felt the need to confront the turmoil. In this sense, the turn against classical orthodoxy was part of that "revolt against formalism" that characterized much American social thought during the early years of the twentieth century.[149] The point is related to the prior one; most of the rebels against formalism were political reformers too. But the tendencies are separable; for example Holmes, no reformer, was a leader of the anti-formalist revolt; he captured its spirit when he denigrated the "human longing for certainty and repose" that is flattered by "logical method and form" while hiding from the reality that "certainty generally is illusion and repose is not the destiny of man."[150]

---

148 For Holmes' famous "brooding omnipresence" phrase *see* Southern Pacific Co. v. Jensen, 244 U.S. 205, 222 (1917). The notion captured by the familiar phrase that there was a general law of private rights, common to the Anglo-American world, toward which the actual decisional law of the various common law jurisdictions should ideally converge was a central doctrine of classicism. It is most clearly articulated and defended in J. BEALE, *supra* note 97, at 138–39, 144–50. Beale proved the existence of such a body of law by a kind of transcendental deduction, thus: "To say that the Common Law in the broader sense is not truly law would logically lead to the abolition of every law school of more than local importance and the transfer of its students to the faculty of philosophy." *Id.* at 139. The general common law was a "condition of possibility" for the existence of the Harvard Law School.

149 M. WHITE, SOCIAL THOUGHT IN AMERICA: THE REVOLT AGAINST FORMALISM (1947).

150 HOLMES, COLLECTED PAPERS, *supra* note 3, at 181.

As these familiar explanations of the fall of classical orthodoxy suggest, it was, like any significant ideology, not a closed system of ideas, but rather continuous with the life around it. But for purposes of study, I have abstracted the ideas of classical orthodoxy into an intellectual system. Thus abstracted, its fall is best represented, though with some artificiality, not by recounting the interests or motives of its critics but by stating the content of their critique.[151] Let me now translate that critique into the terms that I originally used to describe the classical system itself.

First, recall the outlines of classical orthodoxy. The uniquely correct judgments required so that the legal system could be *complete* were supplied by an array of bottom-level rules, stated in precise and objective (*formal*) terms, only one of which would properly apply to any fact situation. The rules were deducible from the top-level fundamental principles, themselves inductively extracted according to scientific canons from the mass of prior decisions. The principles had to be relatively few and consistent among themselves (*conceptually ordered*), independently appealing (*acceptable*) and had to reconcile most decided cases (*stare decisis*). Where a situation occurred for which no existing rule was available, the appropriate rule had to be derivable from the existing principles, which by their abstract formulation provided gapless and unambiguous coverage of all potential cases. Direct appeal to acceptability in deciding a new case by itself, or in formulating a bottom-level rule to cover it, was precluded by the requirement of conceptual ordering, which in turn was necessary to guarantee completeness. Ideally, every decision was correct "in principle"; that is, its decisive rule followed by analytical reasoning from abstract norms that were themselves immanent in the existing case law of the system.

Holmes, Pound and others attacked this classical structure with a two-part critique. They began by pressing the question *why* considerations of acceptability should not be considered in formulating bottom-level rules and in deciding individual cases. The classical response was that to allow *ad hoc* practical judgment meant abandoning legal science, which meant abandoning the certainty, predictability and accountability of legal decision generally. The

151 Thus, I remain in the domain of systematic description (or "interpretation," which sounds fancier), and duck what to many is the crucial question: the relative causal significance of the interests and the ideas. I do think causal questions in social theory meaningful and potentially answerable, even if we will never have scientific laws in this area. But I do not know enough to answer this one—except to point back to my text, and to say that I would not be so interested in the ideas if I did not think they had some significant causal force.

critics then mounted their decisive denial of the success and indeed the possibility of the central classical project of formal conceptual ordering.

Let me spell out these points in more detail; the presentation takes the form of a rational reconstruction, not purporting to fit exactly the argument of any one critic, but trying to capture the essence of their common position. The critique begins by stressing the practical function of the courts. Adjudication is first of all an instrument for the peaceful and orderly resolution of disputes.[152] This point draws support from the requirement of comprehensiveness to which all legal systems adhere. Judges must decide cases within their jurisdiction; they cannot refuse to decide because no clear answer is supplied by the law. There is a live dispute that must be resolved whether or not it is covered by a rule. The requirement of comprehensiveness is not suspended to achieve completeness, or conceptual order, as might be expected if the primary goal of the legal system were to develop or maintain a harmonious body of substantive law.[153]

Further, once disputes are settled in a procedurally final way, they generally are left alone by the law, even if later shown to have been decided incorrectly. This is the force of the familiar legal principle of *res judicata*, which has no counterpart in science. In addition, unresolved jurisdictional conflicts—threats to comprehensiveness—within the legal system are perceived as serious crises.[154] Perceived substantive anomalies in legal doctrine arise constantly and create no similar sense of crisis.

Our views of courts primarily as dispute-settlers rather than scientific authorities likewise appears in our tendency to discourage them from ruling on hypothetical or abstract questions of law. Where there is a dispute, the court must rule; where there is no dispute the court should not.

Given the essentially practical *function* revealed by these features of the courts, is it not natural to judge their work by the practical *standard*, the

---

152 It would be an interesting bit of intellectual history to trace the idea of adjudication as primarily "dispute resolution." The notion is implicit in Holmes' early remark that it is the merit of the common law to decide the case first. *See supra* note 1. It is given the first explicit statement I have found by Gray: "The function of a judge is not mainly to declare the law, but to maintain the peace by deciding controversies." J. GRAY, THE NATURE AND SOURCES OF THE LAW 100 (1921).

153 *See supra* notes 20–21 and accompanying text.

154 As with the Coke-Ellesmere dispute, *supra* note 21; or as with President Nixon's equivocation over whether he would consider himself bound by a Supreme Court ruling that he must surrender his tapes to the Watergate prosecutor.

standard of acceptability?[155] Of course, we do not simply direct courts to decide every dispute in the most acceptable way, but that is because to do so would vest in these powerful institutions a degree of discretion that would itself be unacceptable. The values of legality—completeness, formality and conceptual ordering—have their place, but each invocation of these values must be subject to the ultimate test of acceptability. Why should unacceptable results be imposed—as in the flagpole case—when there is available a rule that produces more satisfactory and fairer resolutions of real disputes?

The classical response to this was that rigorous adherence to principle both allowed the law as a whole to be understood[156] and allowed courts, by derivation of correct rules from established principles, to decide new and previously unanticipated cases.[157] It was at this point that the critics mounted their second and decisive assault—their challenge to the scientific pretensions of classical theory.

The classical scientists had been bold enough to set out a concrete test for the success of their enterprise, implying that failure to achieve it would amount to a refutation of their claims. The test was stated in Langdell's statement quoted earlier: "The number of fundamental legal doctrines is much less than is commonly supposed.... If these doctrines could be so classified and arranged that each should be found in its proper place, and nowhere else, they would cease to be formidable in their number."[158]

Langdell and his followers set out to realize this program with impressive ability and energy. They wrote articles, organized cases into structured casebooks, and composed huge treatises.[159] Finally, they inspired the Restatement project whose purpose was to establish a grand consensus, enlightened by legal science, on the fundamental principles of the common law.[160] As the Restatements appeared toward the end of the '20s, the failure of the great

155 A point is typically made by saying that case-decisions inevitably *are* influenced by considerations of acceptability, whether this is officially admitted or not; thus Holmes: "Behind the logical form lies a judgment as to the relative worth and importance of competing legislative grounds, often an inarticulate and unconscious judgment, it is true, and yet the very root and nerve of the whole proceeding." HOLMES, COLLECTED PAPERS, *supra* note 3, at 181.

156 S. WILLISTON, *supra* note 39, at 213–14.

157 Hence Langdell's reference to mastery of "the ever-tangled skein of human affairs," *supra* text accompanying note 42.

158 *See supra* note 42.

159 G. GILMORE, *supra* note 36, at 57–60.

160 "The restatement here described, if adequately done, will do more to improve the law than anything the legal profession can undertake. It will operate to produce agreement on

classical project to attain Langdell's goal of discovering the few simple principles that underlie the mass of cases became wholly obvious. Thurman Arnold wittily summarized the situation:

> [T]he Restatement... has become another book which must be consulted, while the cases and texts pour out as before. No sooner is the Restatement of Trusts completed than Bogert produces seven volumes on trusts in place of his one volume work, backed by 22,000 cases.... No sooner is the Restatement of Contracts off the press than lawyers find a new edition of Williston, increased in size from four volumes to eight.... Are students relieved of their labors? The answer is found in any great law office.... [M]emoranda are carefully preserved... but their indexing is so difficult and their quantity so formidable that it is easier to start afresh with the digests.... Are the professors' labors relieved? The answer is found in the fact that the number of legal articles written by members of his craft which the brethren are supposed to read... are increasing daily.... All this has advanced the art of advocacy since the time of Daniel Webster in the same manner as the inflation of the German mark advanced business in Germany.[161]

Thus were the boldest claims of classical orthodoxy empirically undermined. But its critics had been convinced long before on analytical grounds that the enterprise was unsound. The basic flaw was the failure of the link between conceptual order and formality. Practical predictability of judicial decision can often be obtained by the framing of formal and objective bottom-level rules to govern decision. A will, for example, is valid if it is attested by two witnesses, not if it is "adequately" or "reasonably" attested. But rules of this sort have to be manufactured by arbitrary acts of human will; they cannot be deduced from the kind of high-level abstract principles classical science sought to discover.

Holmes, who himself valued both conceptual order and formality, insisted on the disjunction between them when he observed that "general principles do not decide concrete cases."[162] Easy cases were those settled by unambiguously

---

the fundamental principles of the common law, give precision to use of legal terms, and make the law more uniform throughout the country." 1 A.L.I. PROC., *supra* note 124, at 18.

161 Arnold, *Institute Priests and Yale Observers—A Reply to Dean Goodrich*, 84 U. PA. L. REV. 811, 820 (1936).

162 Lochner v. New York, 198 U.S. 45, 76 (1905). The "general principle" that Holmes referred to was his own: "a constitution is not intended to embody a particular economic theory." Having said that the principle could not by itself decide the case he went on "But I think

applicable specific rules. In hard cases, where no single clear rule was applicable, plausible deductions from general principles could always be constructed on both sides. The actual decision of such cases required drawing a line, arbitrarily, on a continuum between competing concepts.

Holmes believed that judges could establish rules in such situations by observing the clustering of decided cases and then imposing artificially sharp boundaries around the fuzzy clusters formed. These rules, arbitrary as they were, could provide useful predictability if followed uniformly by judges in later cases. But rules of this kind could not be logically derived from the principles, whose abstract character guaranteed that they would be indeterminate at the edges.

For the more moderate critics of classical orthodoxy like Holmes, the formulation and conceptual ordering of the legal principles was far from useless to the decision process; that principles did not by themselves decide concrete cases was not to say that the cases could be as well decided without them. The principles focused attention on the competing considerations relevant to the decision, providing guidance by confining the range of argument. But in hard cases this guidance ran out before the decision was reached.[163]

---

that the proposition just stated, if it is accepted, will carry us far toward the end." As always with Holmes, the correct general principle was useful in directing the mind toward the appropriate considerations for decision, though it could not dictate decision by itself. *See generally infra* note 163.

163 Throughout his career, Holmes consistently adhered to the view of the relation between general principles and specific rules stated in the text. He believed, early and late, that it was important to arrange and conceptually arrange the law "philosophically"—that is, according to an appropriate set of abstract and legally autonomous concepts. *See supra* note 15; HOLMES, THE COMMON LAW, *supra* note 7, at 104 (doctrine should be reduced to "a philosophically continuous series"); HOLMES, COLLECTED PAPERS, *supra* note 3 at 195–97 (jurisprudence as a valuable study; law should be analyzed into "philosophical" categories like contract and tort, rather than "empirical" ones like shipping and telegraphs). He believed that such abstractions did not decide hard cases; it was a fallacy to suppose that "a given system, ours for instance, can be worked out like mathematics from some general axioms of conduct." *Id.* at 180. But a sound conceptual scheme and accurately stated general principles could guide and aid decision; *supra* note 162.

At the fuzzy periphery of even the best general concepts and principles indeterminate cases would arise, and for this, the remedy was the imposition of arbitrary rules in the interest of legal predictability. *See* Baltimore and Ohio R.R. v. Goodman, 275 U.S. 66 (1927); HOLMES, THE COMMON LAW, *supra* note 7, at 88–103; HOLMES, COLLECTED PAPERS, *supra* note 3, at 232–38. Holmes stated his view of the relation between principles and rules in a way he was never to improve on or significantly alter in his essay *The Theory of Torts*, 7 AM. L. REV. 652 (1873), *reprinted in* 44 HARV. L. REV. 773, 775 (1931):

Other Realists showed that formality itself did not always produce predictability, the virtue it was supposed to serve, giving as evidence some of Holmes' own unsuccessful efforts to impose clear rules on intrinsically variable situations.[164] Judges and juries would respond to direct considerations of acceptability whether they should or not. When clear and objective rules produced injustice or inconvenience in application, some courts would continue to apply them according to their terms while others would find ways to wriggle out and reach the sensible result. Thereby was predictability, the reason for imposing the rule in the first place, lost. In many situations decisions would be both more predictable and more acceptable if the ruling norm were a vague standard that allowed judges or juries to apply their intuitive sense of fairness case-by-case, rather than a clear rule that was sporadically and covertly evaded.[165]

Similar difficulties inevitably arose from the effort actually to stick to more abstract principles. Sometimes accepted principles *did* point strongly to one result rather than another, but the indicated result conflicted with established practice, or with widely shared views of acceptability. In these situations some courts would evade the implications of principle and reach the results suggested by policy or custom, while others would conscientiously and woodenly follow principle. A lawyer could not tell a client in advance how a court would come out.

Several elements of the Realists' critique of classical orthodoxy are drawn together in their treatment of an aspect of the doctrinal problem we started with: when does contract acceptance by mail become effective? Even though Langdell had demonstrated the unprincipled nature of the mailbox rule, it had become uniformly accepted by doctrinal writers. Williston, the orthodox scientist of contract law, pronounced the rule to be binding, though with some

---

"The growth of law is apt to take place in this way: Two widely different cases suggest a general distinction which is a clear one when stated broadly. But as new cases cluster around the opposite poles, and begin to approach each other, the distinction becomes more difficult to trace; the determinations are made one way or the other on a very slight preponderance of feeling, rather than articulate reason; and at last a mathematical line is arrived at by the contact of contrary decisions, which is so far arbitrary that it might equally well have been drawn a little further the one side or the other. The distinction between the groups, however, is philosophical, and it is better to have a line drawn somewhere in the penumbra between darkness and light, than to remain in uncertainty."

164 *See, e.g.*, Pokora v. Wabash Railway Co., 292 U.S. 98 (1934) (Cardozo, J.).

165 Fuller, *American Legal Realism*, 82 U. PA. L. REV. 429, 432–38 (1934).

regret given its lack of sound basis in "principle."[166] It did not occur to him that the actual decisions might reveal a still more particularized (hence unprincipled) pattern. But Realist contract scholars noticed that courts were frequently holding certain contracts to have been formed even *before* the acceptance was mailed. In cases involving life insurance policies, where applicants (offerors) submitted applications subject to approval by the central office of the company, and then died after the central office approved the application but before the signed policy (the acceptance) was mailed, courts often held that the policy had gone into effect and the benefits must be paid.[167]

Here was a special rule for life insurance cases, not announced by the courts because it conflicted with orthodox "established law," but based on a sensible bias toward compensating survivors and a feeling that no injustice was done once the insurer had decided to issue the policy. Williston did not so much disapprove this pattern of decisions as fail even to notice it. He cited some of these cases in a footnote to his treatise, identifying them only as anomalous departures from the general doctrine;[168] he could not even conceive that there might be rules governing acceptance still more particularized than what he saw as the already too *ad hoc* mailbox rule. Thus the pursuit of generality of principle that was the hallmark of the classical scientists led them to miss altogether lines of doctrine that were acceptable and that could produce predictable results once recognized, but that, to recall Langdell's words, "had no principle to support them."[169]

For the critics, conceptual ordering was not, as in classical orthodoxy, a form of scientific discovery, but rather a pragmatic enterprise, to be judged by its success in achieving its practical ends. High-level generalization of legal doctrine in the form of principles might give some rough guidance in the process of judicial decision and can serve as a kind of information storage and retrieval indexing system for lawyers. Its main importance, however, is pedagogic: a newcomer to the law needs an overview of its main doctrines, stated in oversimplified but readily comprehensible form.[170]

But in the eyes of sophisticated modern lawyers, using the general formulas devised for these pedagogic and indexing purposes to deduce legal judgments is the mark of a tyro, a black letter lawyer. The real law is seen as an intricate

166 1 S. Williston & G. Thompson, Contracts 234 (1936).

167 Patterson, *The Delivery of a Life Insurance Policy*, 33 Harv. L. Rev. 198, 203–05 (1919).

168 1 S. Williston & G. Thompson, *supra* note 166, at 204 n.4.

169 The lesson just summarized was drawn in Cook, *Williston on Contracts*, 33 Ill. L. Rev. 497, 511–14 (1939).

170 *See, e.g.*, Pound, *Classification of Law*, 37 Harv. L. Rev. 933, 938–40 (1924).

filigree formed by the interaction of social policies with the specific, detailed fact-patterns of worldly practice. The exemplars of legal craft in post-classical doctrinal technique are thus the scholar Corbin and the judge Cardozo, both renowned for their refusal to accept dictation from general principles and for their masterfully attentive use of the facts of particular cases.[171]

VI

The modern critics' denigration of conceptual ordering meant that even in its fall classical orthodoxy achieved a secret triumph. The classical scientists had purported to do no more than make precise and scientific what had always been implicit in the substance of the common law and the methods of common lawyers. But in their pursuit of logical order Langdell and his colleagues had actually created a largely new conceptual structure that effectively replaced the older Blackstonian outline of the law in the discourse of the profession.[172]

The classical scheme was based on an interlocking set of hierarchial distinctions, each of which served to focus lawyers' attention on what was thought primary and essential, and what merely peripheral, in the body of legal materials. Thus, the classical scientists drew a basic line between substantive law on the one hand and procedure and remedies on the other, with the former treated as primary and the latter as merely instrumental.[173] Applying that distinction, they treated the distinction between law and equity, potentially an ideologically charged clash of governance by rule with judicial discretion, only as an aspect of the peripheral law of remedies.[174] Within substantive law, they

171 *See, e.g.*, G. Gilmore, *supra* note 36, at 74–81. A leading expression of this contemporary viewpoint is Llewellyn's semi-mystical notion of "situation sense." K. Llewellyn, *supra* note 6, at 121–22.

172 The oddity, from our perspective, of the pre-classical scheme is the theme of Kennedy, *supra* note 28.

173 *See supra* note 50. For an analysis and effective ironical reversal of this classical ordering, see Arnold, *The Role of Substantive Law and Procedure in the Legal Process*, 45 Harv. L. Rev. 617 (1932).

174 For a statement of the core of the Langdell-Ames theory of equity, *see* Ames, *Christopher Columbus Langdell*, *supra* note 102, at 476; for a summary statement of the theory *see* C. Langdell, Summary of Equity Pleading, *supra* note 50, at 27–40. The implications of the traditional view of equity are drawn out in Hohfeld, *The Relations Between Equity and Law*, 11 Mich. L. Rev. 537 (1913); Pound, *The Decadence of Equity*, 5 Colum. L. Rev. 20 (1905).

distinguished public law from private, treating private law as the core and public law as the peripheral and anomalous hybrid of law and politics.[175] Within private law, their fundamental subcategories were contract and tort, which corresponded respectively, in the classical image of society, to a broad realm of freedom governed by the principle of the mutual consent of individuals and a narrow realm of collective control governed by a principle of liability for injury wrongly done. They extruded the "collectivist" principle of unjust enrichment from contract without receiving it into tort, and hence left it in a secondary doctrinal position. Finally, they isolated the law of property as the doctrinal dumping ground for the anomalous survivals of the pre-liberal family and land-based legal order.[176]

I have stated the classical categorical scheme in deliberately political terms in order to show that it implied value judgments that most modern lawyers would not accept—for instance, its assignment of peripheral roles to procedure and to public law. But the classical scientists never put these judgments forward as potentially controversial claims. They rather treated their conceptual scheme as a neutral system of categories within which all legal controversy would take place. Within this scheme, the classical scientists made further and obviously controversial assumptions, the most general of which was that abstract legal concepts such as contract and tort had essences, in which scholars could discover principles that in turn could dictate determinate legal judgments.

It was this essentialist approach to legal argument that the post-classical critics assaulted and overthrew, along with much of the lower-level doctrine derived through it. These Realist writers focused their intellectual energy on the task of critique. Most of them, in their constructive moments, also pursued the enterprise of creating a legal policy science. Those Realist critics who did not believe in policy science tended to confine their constructive work to the problems of fact-finding, and to discern those highly particular bottom-level rules and practices that they believed directly affected legal decision. Their

175 *See supra* notes 128–32 and 134 and accompanying text. I believe it was this ordering, rather than any attempted integration of public and private law, that was most characteristic of classical orthodoxy. *Compare* Kennedy, *Toward an Historical Understanding of Legal Consciousness: The Case of Classical Legal Thought in America, 1850–1940*, *supra* note 6, for the "integration" thesis.

176 I owe this overall picture of the classical private law ordering mostly to the pathbreaking analysis in Duncan Kennedy's unpublished manuscript on classical legal thought, D. Kennedy, The Rise and Fall of Classical Legal Thought, 1850–1940, *supra* note 6.

characteristic project was the replacement of general and abstract legal categories by narrow and concrete ones.[177]

Almost all modern theorists, after forcefully rejecting the classical belief that this or that legal rule is "inherent" in this or that legal concept, have gone on to suppose that if general conceptual schemes cannot supply decisive major premises for legal judgments, they can have no importance at all. The roles of such schemes in elementary pedagogy and in indexing legal materials seem relatively trivial. Thus, scholars generally no longer treat what Holmes called "the arrangement of the law," the architecture of its concepts, as worth their serious attention.[178]

But categorical schemes have a power that is greatest when it is least noticed. They channel the attention of those who use them, structuring experience into

---

177 The "narrow-category" idea differentiated Legal Realist writers like Radin, Green, Arnold and Llewellyn from earlier critics of classical thought like Holmes and Pound. The earlier critics had continued to pursue the ordering of the law into "philosophical" abstract concepts, while abandoning the classical ideal of formal reasoning from these concepts to case-decisions. For characteristic statements of the "narrow category" idea, *see* Llewellyn, *Some Realism About Realism*, 44 HARV. L. REV. 1222, 1237 (1931); Radin, *The Theory of Judicial Decision, or: How Judges Think*, 11 A.B.A. J. 357 (1925). For applications, see K. LLEWELLYN, CASES AND MATERIALS ON SALES 561 (1931) (note on "title"); Arnold, *Criminal Attempts—The Rise and Fall of an Abstraction*, 40 YALE L.J. 53 (1930); Cook, *supra* note 169.

Apart from the "narrow category" approach to legal doctrine, the two other distinctive features of Legal Realism were the iconoclasm of most Realists and the serious interest some of them took in quantitative and behaviorist study of legal institutions. *See* Schlegel, *American Legal Realism and Empirical Social Science: From the Yale Experience*, 28 BUFFALO L. REV. 459 (1980).

178 There have been occasional moments of realization that the Langdellian structuring of the first-year legal curriculum decisively shapes the legal consciousness of students, with subsequent unsuccessful flurries of effort at designing the curriculum along "functional" lines; *see* R. Stevens, *supra* note 4, at 471–75, 511–15. The occasional direct challenges to the classic private law ordering have left the placid hegemony of the classical ordering unshaken. *See, e.g.*, L. FRIEDMAN, CONTRACT LAW IN AMERICA (1965), G. GILMORE, *supra* note 36.

A more significant change in legal consciousness was represented by the Legal Process movement of the 1950's, as authoritatively expounded in H. Hart & A. Sacks, The Legal Process (1958) (unpublished). The Legal Process school integrated procedure, public law and administrative process into a general theoretic framework for the legal system based on the organizing concept of "institutional competence." But Legal Process theory did not challenge either the classical private law ordering based on tort and contract, or the ultimate primacy of private law and of judicial decision within the legal system ("private ordering," "principled adjudication").

the focal and the peripheral. In so doing, they influence judgment much as the agenda for a meeting influences the results of its deliberations. Heedless of this power of categories, modern legal theorists have not supplanted the classical ordering but have left it to half-survive in the back of lawyers' minds and the front of the law school curriculum, where it can shape our thinking through its unspoken judgments—Langdell's secret triumph.

VII

Many of the post-classical critics wished to replace the classical science of legal principles with a Benthamite policy science. In this, they followed Holmes' advice that "the true science of the law" lay not in "logical development as in mathematics" but rather in "the establishment of its postulates . . . upon accurately measured social desires."[179]

But it is striking how little progress (if progress is the right word) has been made toward basing law on the accurate measurement of desires. The main accomplishment of decades of earnest preachment on behalf of policy science seems to have been that in recent years lawyers and judges sometimes (law teachers and scholars more often) have come to invoke the comforting metaphor of "balancing" when they discuss choices that involve the conflict of incommensurable values—the choices that less comforting modernist discourses call "political" or "existential."[180]

Apart from the balancing idiom, legal discourse largely retains its orthodox form. On official occasions, lawyers and judges still mostly talk in terms of rules and principles, presupposing right answers even to hard questions of law and disfavoring explicit arguments of policy. The contemporary school of thought led by Ronald Dworkin argues that this orthodox discourse is too durable to be treated in legal realist fashion as mere myth and rhetoric, and has

---

179 Holmes, Collected Papers, *supra* note 3, 225–26.

180 For a critique of the use of "weighing" and "balancing" metaphors where agreed methods of measurement or ordering are patently lacking, *see* A. Donagan, *supra* note 26. Holmes often spoke of line-drawing along a continuum to express the judicial function in hard cases, a metaphor that does away with the implication that the judge has access to a set of scales that will do his work for him. His opinion in Pennsylvania Coal Co. v. Mahon, 260 U.S. 393 (1922), for example, points to the competing considerations thought relevant to decision without anywhere suggesting that they have pre-existing "weights."

tried to formulate a legal theory that is consistent with orthodox premises and yet escapes the standard modern critique of classical orthodoxy.[181]

A movement in legal theory that has closer links to the Benthamite dream of policy science is the school of law and economics. But, on closer inspection, that school turns out to be neo-orthodox too. Its leader, Richard Posner, says that economic analysis cannot supplant, but only predict and criticize, a course of legal decision carried on case-by-case according to orthodox methods. And Posner finds "efficiency," with all the connotation of approval that term carries in his theory, in the content as well as the methods of Langdellian private law.[182]

With all their differences, these neo-orthodoxies have in common their response to a current nostalgia for classical legal theory. To understand what is more than crudely political in this nostalgia, one must recall and try again to feel the pull of the simple tenets of Langdell's creed: law is a science; its materials are all in law books; behind the mass of those materials are a few simple principles; and discovery of those principles will allow us to "master the ever-tangled skein of human affairs." These tenets may have the appeal they do to many legal scholars because, if classical orthodoxy was only a pseudo-science, at least it was an occasionally elegant one that allowed a certain ingenuity in its application, as compared to the pseudo-science of balancing and policy

181 "The 'myth' that there is one right answer in a hard case is both recalcitrant and successful. Its recalcitrance and success count as arguments that it is no myth." TAKING RIGHTS SERIOUSLY, *supra* note 25, at 290. As noted, *supra* note 27, Dworkin has disparaged efforts at classical-style conceptual ordering, for reasons that are not clear given his general approach. Other contemporary writers in the same vein have enthusiastically revived the search for a structure of general principles behind the law. *See, e.g.*, C. FRIED, CONTRACT AS PROMISE (1981); R. EPSTEIN, A THEORY OF STRICT LIABILITY: TOWARD A REFORMULATION OF TORT LAW (1980); G. FLETCHER, RETHINKING CRIMINAL LAW (1977).

182 The efficiency of late nineteenth century private law is a pervasive theme of Posner's work; *see, e.g.*, Posner, *A Theory of Negligence*, 1 J. LEGAL STUD. 29 (1972). His preference for autonomous and traditional legal method over direct application of economic analysis by lawyers and judges emerges from Posner, *Some Uses and Abuses of Economics in Law*, 46 U. CHI. L. REV. 281, 284–87, 297–301 (1979); Posner, *The Present Situation in Legal Scholarship*, 90 YALE L.J. 1113, 1113–119 (1981). A quick look at the first published opinions of Posner, J., confirms the traditionalism of his method; they are classical in their austerity, brevity, absence of footnotes, and absence of interdisciplinary apparatus of any kind. Thus even an antitrust case evokes no economic analysis beyond the minimum required by precedent. *See* Products Liability Ins. v. Crum & Forster Ins., 682 F.2d 660 (7th Cir. 1982). The style aspires to the elegant directness of Holmes and Hand—aphorisms and all. *See* Muscare v. Quinn, 680 F.2d 42, 45 (7th Cir. 1982) ("Three appeals in a case about a goatee are enough.").

that succeeded it. Law students must be tired of hearing how Policy X balanced against Policy Y produces Legal Rule Z—the Papa Bear, Mama Bear, Baby Bear fable of our contemporary classrooms and more advanced upper courts.[183]

The neo-orthodoxies drawn from economics and moral philosophy resemble classical legal science in their capacity to promote structured puzzle-solving of a sometimes interesting kind. But, in contrast to the classical theory, they dilute the autonomy of law (and hence, potentially, the status of the profession) by shifting research outside the law library; this compromises their appeal to lawyers and confines them even within legal academia largely to the ghetto of courses designated as peripheral by titles beginning "Law and. . . ."[184] For this reason, they have little chance to succeed as our ruling legal ideology the still-dominant hybrid of Legal Process theory and the remnants of classical orthodoxy. They will probably never supply a scheme of categories and concepts that actually shape legal argument and judgment, though they no doubt

---

183 Connoisseurs of this form of discourse will have their favorite examples. As a teacher of Constitutional Law, I am inclined to vote for the argot surrounding the "levels of scrutiny" in present-day equal protection jurisprudence. On the other hand, when I teach Torts, I am drawn to the California Supreme Court's often-repeated statement that in deciding what duty to impose in negligence cases it will consider: "the foreseeability of harm to the plaintiff, the degree of certainty that the plaintiff suffered injury, the closeness of the connection between the defendant's conduct and the injury suffered, the policy of preventing future harm, the extent of the burden to the defendant and consequences to the community of imposing a duty to exercise care with resulting liability for breach, and the availability, cost and prevalence of insurance for the risk involved." Rowland v. Christian, 69 Cal. 2d 108, 443 P.2d 561, 70 Cal. Rptr. 97 (1968). Here, the banal domesticity of Mama and Papa Bear is replaced by an ill-assorted menagerie in unseemly orgy. This is not the "Grand Style" reborn.

184 Charles Fried sees and attempts to forestall this threat in the essay cited *supra* note 99; Richard Epstein, *see supra* note 181, has always attempted to sustain a genuinely autonomous legal discourse in his doctrinal work, at the cost of an element of the arbitrary in his conclusions. Posner's judicial style, *supra* note 182, reflects his sense of the importance of legal autonomy. *Compare* Arnold, *Judge Jerome Frank*, 24 U. Chi. L. Rev. 633, 633–34 (1957):

> "As a judge he had only one disqualification. He lacked that narrowness of purpose, that preoccupation with the law as a separate discipline, that exclusion of social and economic considerations, which removes the "Law" from the everyday world and thus makes it such an impressive and important symbol. . . . Certainly it is true that the idea of federal judges roaming the stormy fields of economics, sociology, psychiatry and anthropology, their black robes flapping in the winds of controversy, is a disquieting one, even to the writer."

can play the humbler role of reducing the gap between legal scholarship and the rest of the intellectual world.

Apart from their conceptual ordering of the law, the classical scientists' main achievement was to articulate better than have any other Anglo-American lawyers the curious second-best utopia that animates the legalist mind. They left behind them a memorable and illuminating elaboration of the coolly seductive fantasy that, even in the absence of genuine communal solidarity, an industrial society might nonetheless be held together by a structure of legal doctrine that, conceived in the pure spirit of science and possessed of its elegant rigor, transcends the ugly partisan struggles of politics, and at the same time defines the boundaries of the sovereign self in a way sufficiently practical to resolve real human disputes.

Holmes and Legal Pragmatism

Thomas C. Grey

Oliver Wendell Holmes is the great oracle of American legal thought, but as with other oracles his message is subject to much dispute. His admiring readers have mainly stressed Holmes the critic of Langdellian legal formalism, who said the life of the law was not logic but experience.[1] Others, generally less admiring, have focused on Holmes the Social Darwinist, who celebrated the struggle for existence, or Holmes the amoral positivist, who analyzed law from the perspective of a "bad man."[2] In recent years, still others have emphasized yet another Holmes, one whose main achievement as a legal thinker, apart from a few memorable anti-formalistic jurisprudential slogans, was a body of surprisingly abstract and conceptual doctrinal writing.[3] One of the few points

* This article originally appeared in *Stanford Law Review*, Vol. 41, No. 4 (Apr., 1989), pp. 787–870.

** Professor of Law, Stanford Law School. My thanks to Robert Gordon, David Hollinger, William Simon, Robin West, and Steven Winter for their valuable comments, and to Richard Klingler and Henry Bemporad for their useful research assistance. Barbara Babcock has as usual provided especially careful and searching editing, and every other kind of support as well. My sister Alison Anderson unwittingly started me on this project many years ago when she gave me two volumes of Holmes' correspondence, and she has inspired me by her example in many ways since; this article is for her.

1 Among the most enthusiastic expressions of this perspective are the various essays in the collection edited by Felix Frankfurter, especially those by Morris Cohen, John Dewey, Frankfurter himself, and Harold Laski. MR. JUSTICE HOLMES (F. Frankfurter ed. 1931). For a contemporary expression of the same view, *see* the chapter *Mr. Justice Oliver Wendell Holmes, the Completely Adult Jurist*, in JEROME FRANK, LAW AND THE MODERN MIND 253–60 (1930). A more sophisticated appreciation of Holmes which treats his critique of formalism as central to his work is MORTON WHITE, SOCIAL THOUGHT IN AMERICA: THE REVOLT AGAINST FORMALISM 59–75 (2d ed. 1957).

2 *See, e.g.*, LON L. FULLER, THE LAW IN QUEST OF ITSELF 62–63, 92–95 (1940); Henry M. Hart, *Holmes' Positivism—An Addendum*, 64 HARV. L. REV. 929 (1951); Yosal Rogat, *The Judge as Spectator*, 31 U. CHI. L. REV. 213 (1964).

3 Grant Gilmore particularly stressed this aspect of Holmes. *See* GRANT GILMORE, THE DEATH OF CONTRACT 13–53 (1974); GRANT GILMORE, THE AGES OF AMERICAN LAW 48–56 (1977). Robert W. Gordon has pursued the theme as well. *See* Gordon, *Holmes'* Common Law *as Social and Legal Science*, 10 HOFSTRA L. REV. 719, 726–29 (1982).

© KONINKLIJKE BRILL NV, LEIDEN, 2014 | DOI 10.1163/9789004272897_006

on which all commentators agree is Holmes' greatness as a prose stylist.[4] But when combined with the range of competing interpretations of his work, even the brilliance of his prose suggests another unflattering account—Holmes the eclectic aphorist, whose purely literary talent for glittering phrases conceals a muddle of mutually inconsistent ideas.[5]

My thesis is that while there are indeed multiple and apparently clashing strands in Holmes' thought, most of them weave together reasonably well when seen as the jurisprudential development of certain central tenets of American pragmatism. Conflicts do remain when Holmes' work is interpreted from this perspective, but they can be explained by a characteristic paradox—the man was disabled by temperament, by experience, and by the historical context in which he found himself from adequately practicing the pragmatism he so eloquently preached.

Holmes as legal pragmatist is hardly a new idea. His associations with Charles Sanders Peirce and William James, as well as his admiration for John Dewey, have led a number of intellectual historians to count him as an adherent and even a founder of the pragmatist movement.[6] At the same time, legal theorists have associated both his generally empirical and instrumental approach to law, and his specific account of legal rules as predictions of judicial decisions, with familiar pragmatist teachings.[7] But there are serious problems with these standard positions. On the biographical side, while Holmes did express admiration for Dewey, he never made clear what it was that he admired. And his more specific remarks about pragmatism and the other well-known pragmatists were critical, often harshly so. He condemned James'

---

4 The agreement is not confined to the parochial world of lawyers; even so demanding a literary critic as Edmund Wilson judged Holmes' style to be "perfect." EDMUND WILSON, PATRIOTIC GORE 781 (1962).

5 *See* Saul Touster, *Holmes a Hundred Years Ago:* The Common Law *and Legal Theory*, 10 HOFSTRA L. REV. 673, 707 (1982) (characterizing Holmes as an unsystematic "utterer of 'smart things' ").

6 *See, e.g.*, MAX H. FISCH, *Justice Holmes, the Prediction Theory of Law, and Pragmatism*, in PEIRCE, SEMEIOTIC, AND PRAGMATISM: ESSAYS BY MAX FISCH 6 (K. Ketner & C. Kloesel eds. 1986) reprinting Max H. Fisch, *Justice Holmes, the Prediction Theory of Law, and Pragmatism*, 39 J. PHIL. 85 (1942)); PHILIP P. WIENER, EVOLUTION AND THE FOUNDERS OF PRAGMATISM 172–89 (1965).

7 On instrumentalism, *see* Benjamin Cardozo, *Mr. Justice Holmes*, in MR. JUSTICE HOLMES, *supra* note 1, at 1, 6–7; ROBERT S. SUMMERS, INSTRUMENTALISM AND AMERICAN LEGAL THEORY 20–34 (1982). On the pragmatic aspects of the prediction theory, *see* Fisch, *supra* note 6; *see also* Frederic Rogers Kellogg, *The Making of an American Legal Philosophy*, in THE FORMATIVE ESSAYS OF JUSTICE HOLMES 1, 50–57 (F. Kellogg ed. 1984) [hereinafter FORMATIVE ESSAYS].

version of pragmatism as "humbug";[8] and while he apparently knew little of Peirce's ideas, he did not think highly of what he knew. In the end, what Holmes said directly about pragmatism and its exponents does not by itself support placing him in the pragmatist camp.[9]

When we turn from Holmes' direct statements about pragmatism and the pragmatists to his legal thought itself, the difficulty is to identify anything *distinctively* pragmatist in his writings. He did treat law as a utilitarian instrument for the satisfaction of human desires, but as he said himself, "the judging of law by its effects and results did not have to wait for W[illiam] J[ames]."[10] The English analytical positivists who followed Bentham and Austin had made the instrumental approach to law prominent long before American pragmatism came on the scene. Holmes was certainly one of the important American exponents of English analytical positivism, and his prediction theory is a significant elaboration of that approach to law. But if this were all there were to Holmes, we would add little by calling him a pragmatist.[11]

My suggestion is that we can understand the distinctively pragmatist cast to Holmes' legal thought if we take account of the recent revival and reinterpretation of pragmatism within Anglo-American philosophy.[12] The "neo-pragmatists"

---

8 1 HOLMES-POLLOCK LETTERS 139 (M. Howe ed. 1941) (letter dated June 17, 1908).

9 I review the evidence on Holmes' views of the leading pragmatists in an appendix to this article. *See* text accompanying notes 368–421 *infra.*

10 1 HOLMES-LASKI LETTERS 20 (M. Howe ed. 1953) (letter dated Sept. 15, 1916).

11 H.L. Pohlman argues that Holmes is best seen as continuing the tradition of Bentham and Austin, *see* H.L. POHLMAN, JUSTICE OLIVER WENDELL HOLMES AND UTILITARIAN JURISPRUDENCE (1984), and concludes that nothing is gained by characterizing him as a pragmatist. *Id.* at 163–64. In my view, Pohlman significantly understates the importance of historicist social theory in Holmes' legal thought. *See* text accompanying notes 74–81, 90–91 *infra.*

12 Richard Rorty has been the best-known promoter of the pragmatist revival. *See* RICHARD RORTY, PHILOSOPHY AND THE MIRROR OF NATURE (1979); RICHARD RORTY, CONSEQUENCES OF PRAGMATISM (1982). Rorty's introductory essay to the latter volume, *Introduction: Pragmatism and Philosophy,* is a good summary of the new interpretation of pragmatism. *Id.* at xiii–xlvii. For a sample of the many other recent philosophical works that take neo-pragmatist positions, though without adopting the pragmatist label, *see* RICHARD J. BERNSTEIN, BEYOND OBJECTIVISM AND RELATIVISM: SCIENCE, HERMENEUTICS, AND PRAXIS (1985); NELSON GOODMAN, WAYS OF WORLDMAKING (1978); SAUL KRIPKE, WITTGENSTEIN ON RULES AND PRIVATE LANGUAGE (1982); HILARY PUTNAM, REASON, TRUTH AND HISTORY (1981); P.F. STRAWSON, SKEPTICISM AND NATURALISM (1985). Kripke and Strawson both stress the influence of Hume and the later Wittgenstein on their formulations. Another important influence on the neo-pragmatist revival has been the modern historicist reconception of natural science associated with Thomas Kuhn. *See*

reject the long-standing treatment of pragmatism as simply a minor element in the triumphant advance of scientific positivism.[13] In this traditional view, the pragmatists were merely thinkers who anticipated and stated in a confused way some of the ideas later worked out more rigorously by the logical positivists and their successors in the philosophy of science. A parallel view of pragmatism in legal theory would see Holmes, Roscoe Pound, and its other exponents as relatively primitive and confused precursors of the more rigorous and sophisticated form of scientific instrumentalist jurisprudence represented by contemporary law and economics, cost-benefit analysis, and public choice theory.

By contrast, the new philosophical interpretation of pragmatism stresses certain ways in which it departs from and indeed undermines orthodox scientific empiricism, particularly in its focus on human inquiry as a culturally situated form of activity. Much as William James' original formulation of pragmatism sought to mediate between "tough-minded" devotees of science and "tender-minded" religious believers,[14] the neo-pragmatists seek a bridge across the divide that has separated Anglo-American from European philosophy in this century. On one side of this divide, English speakers (and some Austrian helpers) have tended to conceive of philosophy as an enterprise dedicated to exploring the foundations of knowledge through a rigorous account of natural scientific method, with the ultimate aim of extending that method to all areas of human inquiry.[15] On the other side, European philosophy has long stood in an adversary relation to natural science and technology, pursuing the (often quasi-religious) search for meaning, sometimes culminating in a discovery of meaninglessness, through the exploration of culture and lived experience.[16]

THOMAS S. KUHN, THE STRUCTURE OF SCIENTIFIC REVOLUTIONS (2d ed. 1970); THOMAS S. KUHN, THE ESSENTIAL TENSION (1977).

13 *See, e.g.*, A.J. AYER, THE QRIGINS OF PRAGMATISM (1968); W.V. Quine, *The Pragmatists' Place in Empiricism*, in PRAGMATISM: ITS SOURCES AND PROSPECTS 21 (R. Mulvaney & P. Zeltner eds. 1981). Quine, who downplays the historicist aspects of pragmatism stressed by Rorty and others, argues that the term "pragmatism" fails to usefully distinguish itself from "empiricism," and hence "draws a pragmatic blank." *Id.* at 23.

14 WILLIAM JAMES, PRAGMATISM: A NEW NAME FOR SOME OLD WAYS OF THINKING 3–40 (1907) [hereinafter W. JAMES, PRAGMATISM].

15 This ambition runs throughout the work of the Logical Positivists, a representative selection of whose writings can be found in LOGICAL POSITIVISM (A.J. Ayer ed. 1959).

16 This generalization is meant to characterize the main line of European philosophy since Kant's critiques overthrew the tradition of Cartesian foundational rationalism; the line

This schism matters to legal scholars because it extends beyond philosophy to divide students and theorists of social phenomena more generally, including those who focus upon law. The positivist project of developing "social sciences" modeled on physics, chemistry, and biology has dominated Anglo-American social theory, while the European tendency has been to study society and culture interpretively, as text-analogues to be understood rather than as natural phenomena to be explained. The extension of the European style of theorizing into American intellectual life in recent years has produced sharp divisions between the traditionally dominant positivist approach, and a newer movement toward "hermeneutic" and "post-modernist" modes of thought. This division is evident within legal thought as well, where jurisprudential approaches based upon the economic paradigm of rational choice remain dominant, but are increasingly subject to challenge from approaches that stress the centrality of culture, history, language, ideology, and rhetoric.

The neo-pragmatists' pluralistic conception of inquiry challenges the dominance of natural science in the intellectual life of the English-speaking world, and some traditional positivists see their work as a nihilistic challenge to reason itself. But when compared with other post-modernist thinkers, the new pragmatists can be seen as still working within the scientific empiricist tradition broadly conceived. They tend to reject both the pervasive relativism and the oppositional stance toward natural science that many European philosophers and social thinkers have adopted, and they accept the spirit of scientific inquiry, in which theory is tested against experience by a reflective and critical community of inquirers. Pragmatists see even natural-scientific inquiry as having unavoidably interpretive and culturally conditioned aspects; at the same time they believe that humanistic and explicitly evaluative inquiry can be pursued rationally and with the reasonable hope of progress. In social theory generally, and legal theory more particularly, the pragmatist tendency is to promote trade rather than warfare between normative and descriptive theorists, storytellers and model-builders, interpreters and causal explainers.[17]

---

begins with Hegel, runs through Kierkegaard, Nietzsche, and Dilthey, and encompasses such disparate modern thinkers as Heidegger, Sartre, Gadamer, Ricoeur, and Derrida.

17 For some philosophical applications of "the new pragmatism" to social thought, *see* Richard Rorty, *Method, Social Science, and Sodal Hope*, in Consequences of Pragmatism, *supra* note 12, at 191, 203–08 (contrasting the progressive and optimistic John Dewey with the relativistic and pessimistic European post-modernist Michel Foucault); and Hilary Putnam, Meaning and the Moral Sciences 66–77 (1978). For a political theorist's work in a pragmatist vein, *see* Don Herzog, Without Foundations (1985). The reach of pragmatism beyond philosophy to social thought and practical politics is nothing new; David Hollinger has shown that in the heyday of Dewey's

Finally, in interpreting the history of pragmatism, the neo-pragmatists have departed from their predecessors by emphasizing Dewey over Peirce and James as the central figure in the movement.[18] Dewey's own focus was not so much on the methods of the natural sciences (as with Peirce) or on the life-situation of the individual (as with James), but more on issues of social theory, politics, and law. It was Dewey who particularly developed the pragmatist critique of the traditional philosophical "quest for certainty", Dewey who particularly undermined the positivist dualisms of subject and object, mind and matter, fact and value, and Dewey who particularly stressed the shaping effect of cultural and historical context on human inquiry. And these are the aspects of pragmatism that have dominated the recent revival.

In what follows, I spell out my own version of the recent reinterpretation of pragmatism, and then look at Holmes' legal theory from the perspective it provides, with special emphasis on the elements common to the thought of Holmes and Dewey. I was moved to my study by the strongest single piece of direct evidence linking Holmes to pragmatism: when late in life he read Dewey's *Experience and Nature*, Holmes wrote that its "view of the universe ... came home to me closer than any other that I know."[19] As one for whom Dewey's masterpiece also comes very close to home, I was particularly struck by this remark, especially in view of the great differences in social and political outlook between the two men. Could there perhaps be some deeper unity that

influence, his version of pragmatism provided a significant framework for the general thinking of educated Americans on social questions, and hence was influential in arenas well beyond the philosophy department. *See* DAVID A. HOLLINGER, *The Problem of Pragmatism in American History*, in IN THE AMERICAN PROVINCE 23 (1985).

The point is made most impressively in JAMES KLOPPENBERG, UNCERTAIN VICTORY: SOCIAL DEMOCRACY AND PROGRESSIVISM IN EUROPEAN AND AMERICAN THOUGHT, 1870–1920 (1986). This book, which I discovered just as this article was going to press, gives an account of pragmatism strongly parallel to my own.

18 At the same time, both James and Peirce have themselves been persuasively reinterpreted along "neo-pragmatist" lines. On James, *see* David A. Hollinger, *William James and the Culture of Inquiry*, in IN THE AMERICAN PROVINCE, *supra* note 17, at 3. And in a study that parallels this one in many ways, Catharine Hantzis brings out elements in Holmes' legal theory that depart from the conventional legal positivism so often attributed to him by noting the similarities between his ideas and the pragmatism of Peirce. Catharine Hantzis, *Legal Innovation Within the Wider Intellectual Tradition: The Pragmatism of Oliver Wendell Holmes, Jr.*, 82 NW U.L. REV. 541 (1988).

19 2 HOLMES-POLLOCK LETTERS, *supra* note 8, at 272 (letter dated July 26, 1930). Dewey expressed similar intellectual kinship with Holmes. *See* John Dewey, *Justice Holmes and the Liberal Mind*, in MR. JUSTICE HOLMES, *supra* note 1 [hereinafter Dewey, *Justice Holmes*]; JOHN DEWEY, EXPERIENCE AND NATURE 417–19 (2d ed. 1929).

explained the sense of intellectual kinship they shared? That question started me in search of a Holmesian theory of law that fit with Dewey's kind of pragmatism.[20]

Such a study responds to two motives, and I can only hope that I have somehow managed to negotiate the conflicts between them. First, in common with many American lawyers, I am fascinated by Holmes, a fascination compounded of repulsion and attraction. It is easy to list the man's repulsive aspects: his naive attraction to pseudo-scientific eugenics, his fatalism, his indifference to human suffering, his egotism and vanity, his near-worship of force and obedience. But even when all that is taken into account, I am drawn on by Holmes' charms of person and of style, charms enhanced for the interpretive suitor by the complexities and paradoxes that shroud his character and thought. And the substance of his most famous teaching, the primacy of experience over logic, still seems to me the central, if obscure, truth of American legal thought; as Cardozo wrote, "Here is the text to be unfolded. All that is to come will be development and commentary."[21]

That conviction introduces my second motive, which is the wish to have my own present say in furtherance of a neo-pragmatist approach to legal theory. It has been common to promote legal theories by enlisting Holmes among their sponsors, but the precedents are not all auspicious. One who attempts to combine in a single study a commentary on Holmes and a contribution to contemporary legal theory risks doing neither well. While incurring this risk, I take some comfort from the words of Chauncey Wright, an early influence on Holmes, who wrote that "[t]he most profitable discussion is, after all, a study of other minds—seeing how others see, rather than the dissection of mere propositions."[22] The personal is the theoretical. Such, at least, is my justifica-

---

20 I should say a word about my sources. Holmes' published extra-judicial writings are not voluminous, and I have read them all—his essays, speeches, letters, and his one book, *The Common Law.* I have not reviewed the mass of his judicial opinions as exhaustively, nor drawn on them as much in my argument, but my knowledge of the familiar among them, along with a sampling of the less familiar, confirms that they do not add new elements to the body of his general legal thought. He had only so many things to say, a mid-sized stock of basic insights and aphorisms. The interpretive problem is to show how a set of familiar elements fit together, if they do at all.

For my account of pragmatism, I have drawn inspiration from the neo-pragmatist writers already cited, and material mainly from the writings of Dewey, supplemented by references to Peirce and James.

21 Benjamin Cardozo, *Mr. Justice Holmes*, in MR. JUSTICE HOLMES, *supra* note 1, at 3.

22 Quoted in P. WIENER, *supra* note 6, at 30.

tion for this binocular effort to present pragmatism through the lens of Holmes while at the same time presenting Holmes through the lens of pragmatism.

The study is a long one, and a sketch in advance may be helpful. In Part I, I spell out my version of what distinguishes American pragmatism from the scientific empiricism out of which it grew, its doubly practical account of inquiry as at once situated in existing practice and instrumental to practical ends. In Part II, I summarize the core of Holmes' application of this perspective to law, his conception of "law as experience," a conception synthesizing the apparently conflicting historical and analytical schools of jurisprudence. In Parts III and IV, I consider aspects of Holmes' legal thought often believed to conflict with his experiential account of law—respectively, the conceptualism discernible in his treatment of legal doctrine, and the apparently narrow positivism of his emphasis on the prediction of judicial action. I argue that when properly understood, both Holmes' conceptualism ("law as logic") and his positivism ("law as prediction") are consistent with his pragmatist account of law as experience. In Part V, I turn to a real and serious practical contradiction in Holmes' work, the conflict between his spectatorial detachment from his own society on the one hand, and his commitment to a life of active participation in its government by law on the other. Finally, in Part VI, I argue that in the course of Holmes' unsuccessful struggle with this contradiction, he came to understand and articulate his own version of the important concept that Dewey called "the end-means continuum," a concept that is essential if legal pragmatism is to differentiate itself from the more reductive forms of legal instrumentalism.

I The Priority of Practice

Those who would make Holmes a pragmatist have usually had in mind his conception of law as the coercive use of state power through the courts, aimed at the promotion of public welfare or the satisfaction of collective wants. The conception is thought pragmatic because it is at once empirical and instrumental. Descriptively, for Holmes, the law is "what the courts ... do in fact," and it draws its content largely from "[t]he felt necessities of the time."[23] Prescriptively, legal principles are to be derived from "accurately measured social desires," with these to be approximated, in the absence of a better

23 Oliver Wendell Holmes, *The Path of the Law* (1897), in Collected Legal Papers 161, 173 (1920) [hereinafter *The Path of the Law*]; Oliver Wendell Holmes, The Common Law 5 (M. Howe ed. 1963) (originally published 1881) [hereinafter The Common Law].

measuring stick, by "conformity to the wishes of the dominant power" in the community.[24]

While nothing in such a conception of law is inconsistent with pragmatism, the difficulty, mentioned already, is seeing anything *distinctively* pragmatist in it. As Holmes himself was quite aware, the view of law as regularized coercion and as a means to an end was not new either with him or with those we think of as pragmatists.[25] Beginning more than a century before pragmatism was first heard of, and continuing throughout a long and immensely influential career, Jeremy Bentham had promoted the idea that law was the use of collective force as a means to human happiness. In this, he was followed by his disciple John Austin, whose theory became the orthodoxy of English analytical jurisprudence while Holmes was a law student.[26] Holmes was a member of the first generation of American lawyers to be much influenced by the utilitarian positivism of the analytical jurists; only in a later generation would such views become dominant, as, in a sense, they remain to this day. Yet there was nothing original to America, nothing derived from James or Peirce, nothing peculiar to pragmatism, in Holmes' often reiterated application of Benthamite slogans to law.

Bentham's instrumentalism applied the post-Enlightenment spirit of scientific positivism to law and politics. Central to this spirit was the conviction that,

---

24 OLIVER WENDELL HOLMES, *Law in Science and Science in Law* (1899), in COLLECTED LEGAL PAPERS 210, 226 (1920) [hereinafter *Law in Science*]; OLIVER WENDELL HOLMES, *Montesqueieu* (19), in COLLECTED LEGAL PAPERS 250, 258; *see also* THE COMMON LAW, *supra* note 23 at 36.

25 *See* note 10 *supra* and accompanying text. The point that there is nothing uniquely pragmatic in a utilitarian, instrumental conception of law is forcefully made throughout H. POHLMAN, *supra* note 11.

26 The publication of a second edition of Austin's *Province of Jurisprudence Determined* in 1861 rescued the work from the obscurity into which it had sunk after its original publication in 1832. Sarah Austin's edition of his *Lectures on Jurisprudence*, reconstructed from his manuscripts, appeared in 1863. For this bibliographic history, *see* H.L.A. Hart, *Introduction* to JOHN AUSTIN, THE PROVINCE OF JURISPRUDENCE DETERMINED AND THE USES OF THE STUDY OF JURISPRUDENCE at vii, ix (1954) (originally published 1832) [hereinafter J. AUSTIN, THE PROVINCE OF JURISPRUDENCE]. Holmes checked Austin's *Lectures* out of the library some five times between 1863 and 1871. MARK DE WOLFE HOWE, JUSTICE OLIVER WENDELL HOLMES: THE SHAPING YEARS, 1841–1870, at 194 & noted (1957) [hereinafter M. HOWE, THE SHAPING YEARS]. Peter King unfortunately omits any consideration of Holmes in his otherwise useful study of the transmission of analytical positivism to America. *See* PETER S. KING, UTILITARIAN JURISPRUDENCE IN AMERICA: THE INFLUENCE OF BENTHAM AND AUSTIN ON AMERICAN LEGAL THOUGHT IN THE NINETEENTH CENTURY (1986).

as Richard Rorty has put it, "natural science—facts about how spatio-temporal things worked—was all the Truth there was."[27] Applied to law, the positivist spirit required that if legal propositions were to have scientific standing, they must be reducible to factual claims. Accordingly Austin, following Bentham's lead, analyzed legal rights and duties in terms of two straightforwardly factual questions: what person or group in society is habitually obeyed, and what has he, she, or it commanded?[28] Under this conception, the determination of what the law is requires no value judgment; the lawyer needs only to identify behavioral regularities and consult the plain meanings of words.

For positivists of the Benthamite persuasion, moral and political evaluation could proceed rationally only if evaluative discourse itself could be reduced to factual terms. Otherwise it was pure rhetoric, "simple nonsense," or "nonsense upon stilts."[29] The only empirical realities available as plausible sources of value judgements were human desires and sensations of pleasure or pain. Thus utilitarianism became the prescriptive corollary of positivism. An action or a law was right to the extent it promoted pleasure or satisfaction, and prevented pain or frustration. Given this starting point, moral questions became in principle issues of fact, which, it was hoped, technical progress would one day reduce to mere matters of measurement. But this day was not yet at hand, and the still immature science of utilitarian ethics or "censorial jurisprudence"—the study of what the law should be—had to be kept strictly separate from "expository jurisprudence," the identification of the positive law that was actually in force.[30]

Much of Holmes' legal thought can be explained in terms of this Victorian scientific positivism—what Holmes himself called "the scientific way of looking at the world."[31] From this outlook followed his legal positivism and a version of utilitarianism tempered by skepticism about the practical possibilities of measuring utility. Not only his functional account of law generally, but also

---

27 RICHARD RORTY, *Introduction: Pragmatism and Philosophy*, in CONSEQUENCES OF PRAGMATISM, *supra* note 12, at xiii, xv.

28 *See* J. AUSTIN, THE PROVINCE OF JURISPRUDENCE, *supra* note 26, at 9–33; JEREMY BENTHAM, OF LAWS IN GENERAL, 1, 18–19 (H.L.A. Hart ed. 1970) (originally completed 1782).

29 JEREMY BENTHAM, *Anarchical Fallacies*, (n.d.), in 2 THE WORKS OF JEREMY BENTHAM 489, 501 (1962) (J. Bowring ed. 1838–1843) [hereinafter WORKS OF BENTHAM].

30 JEREMY BENTHAM, *An Introduction to the Principles of Morals and Legislation* (1780), in 1 WORKS OF BENTHAM, *supra* note 29, at 1, 148; *see also* J. AUSTIN, THE PROVINCE OF JURISPRUDENCE, *supra* note 26, at 184–91.

31 *The Holmes-Cohen Correspondence*, in PORTRAIT OF A PHILOSOPHER: MORRIS R. COHEN IN LIFE AND LETTERS 313, 321 (L. Rosenfield ed. 1962) (letter dated Feb. 5, 1919) [hereinafter *Holmes-Cohen Correspondence*].

his analysis of lawyer's law as prediction, his promotion of an external standard of liability, and his critique of the use of moral terms in legal discourse, all were consistent with a program of reducing vague and value-laden questions to clear and factual ones. These aspects of Holmes' legal thought fit in with the utilitarian analytical jurisprudence of Bentham and Austin—the legal branch of nineteenth-century scientific positivism. But while ideas such as these are consistent with pragmatism, they are in no way distinctive to it.

The founding pragmatists managed to break away from the standard brand of scientific positivism. At the same time, and in an analogous way, Holmes' work in legal theory came to surpass that of his positivist predecessors. The differences between pragmatist and positivist theories of knowledge are, in fact, the background against which one can show that Holmes took legal thought beyond analytical positivism, in a distinctively pragmatist direction.

We can best begin our account where the pragmatists themselves did, with their naturalistic account of human mind and mental activity—"inquiry," in Dewey's encompassing term. The pragmatist view of inquiry represented a major departure from long-standing views of human knowledge. British empiricism and its traditional rival, European rationalism, had implicitly shared a dualistic conception of the human being as a spiritual or immaterial mind somehow lodged in a material body. In its origin, this conception of the mind as metaphysically distinct from the body traces back in Western thought at least to Plato, and over time it became fused with the "soul" of Christian theology. Carrying its multiple philosophical and religious origins with it, the notion of the immaterial but substantial mind-soul or spirit was implanted in the foundations of the developing Western scientific world view by both the rationalist Descartes and the empiricist Locke in the seventeenth century. Through the period of the Enlightenment, Western philosophers, however oriented they were toward science, did not root it out. Even in the work of a nineteenth-century philosophical positivist who came as close to pragmatism as did John Stuart Mill, we find an implicitly dualistic account separating mind from matter, in which human knowledge of an objective, material and external world must somehow be built up from subjective and immaterial impressions and ideas occurring in an internal and intangible mental medium.[32] How this is to be done is the "problem of knowledge," to be solved by the special philosophical sub-discipline of "epistemology"; epistemology in turn is built upon

32 John Stuart Mill, A System of Logic Ratiocinative and Inductive, in 7 Collected Works of John Stuart Mill 1, 56–64, 74 (J.M. Robson ed. 1973).

an ontology that divides the world into mind and matter, Descartes' *res cogitans* and *res extensa*.[33]

The pragmatist departure from this traditional concept of the mental world seems in large part traceable to the influence of nineteenth-century evolutionary thinking.[34] By locating mankind firmly within the animal kingdom, Darwin made it plausible to treat human mental capacities as evolved functions of natural organisms, arising from simpler forms of animal behavior as a result of their survival-promoting tendencies. As this perspective took hold, the distinction between spirit and nature, or mind and matter, came to seem increasingly arbitrary. If the human being was a biological organism, "mind" and "the mental" could only refer to those workings of the organism that rose above whatever level of complexity had come to be defined as "merely animal."

It is a mistake, however, to overemphasize the place of evolutionary biology in the origins of pragmatism; certain characteristic elements of nineteenth-century social thought were equally important. In reaction to the ahistorical rationalism of the Enlightenment, a wide range of social theorists emphasized and developed the importance in human affairs of cultural evolution, or History with a capital "H." This tendency in social thought, which we may loosely label "historicism," stressed the fundamental character of historical change and cultural variation, and thereby undermined the philosophical search for a single definite set of faculties and categories that constituted "the human understanding."[35]

The collectivist bias of emerging historical, linguistic, and anthropological studies helped undermine the notion of the human being as an individual who, by virtue of the imprisonment of his or her spirit in a carnal body, was a little lower than the angels. In its place arose the idea of humanity as a species that, by virtue of its collective capacity to generate, transmit, and adapt culture by means of language, was a little higher than the apes. This concern with cultural as well as biological evolution provided the pragmatists with an essential safeguard against materialist reductionism, or behaviorism, which attempts to escape the "mind-body problem" by simply reducing to the physical, or even denying the reality of, phenomena traditionally classified as mental or cultural.

33 René Descartes, *Meditations on First Philosophy* (1642), in Descartes: Philosophical Writings 114–15 (E. Anscombe & P. Geach eds. 1964).

34 *See generally* P. Wiener, *supra* note 6.

35 For the importance of historical and cultural themes in the development of nineteenth-century British evolutionary thought, and their relative independence from Darwinian theory, *see* generally J.W. Burrow, Evolution and Society (1966).

These developments in biological and social theory focused philosophers' attention on some of the fundamental difficulties with the traditional accounts of mind. How can a ghostly mind be linked to the material world through the bodily machine that it somehow haunts? How can we have reliable knowledge of an outer physical world if all our experience is made up of mental impressions and ideas projected in some inner and immaterial theater? The acute debates over these questions during the previous two centuries had preoccupied philosophers with what John Dewey called "[t]he alleged discipline of epistemology."[36]

The pragmatist breakthrough was to reject all mind-body dualisms and treat thought or "inquiry" as a mode of the human organism's activity, an adaptive product of biological and cultural evolution. Peirce, the founder of pragmatism, described a belief as a "habit of mind" that enables the organism to cope with some aspect of its environment.[37] When action on a habitual belief does not produce the expected result, the believer experiences the "irritation of doubt." "Inquiry," which Peirce described as "a struggle to attain a state of belief" or "settlement of opinion," is supposed to resolve the irritation of doubt in favor of some belief that can once again reliably guide the believer's action.[38] Of course, this new belief, when acted upon, might itself lead to new doubt, thus requiring new inquiry.[39]

Though there were important differences among the leading pragmatists, all of them endorsed this Darwinist-historicist account of human inquiry.[40] They treated "the mind" as an evolved mode for coping with the environment, a set of biologically based powers that included the crucial capacity to learn language. Linguistic capacity allowed human mental powers to be vastly aug-

---

36 JOHN DEWEY, ESSAYS IN EXPERIMENTAL LOGIC 264 (1916) [hereinafter J. DEWEY, EXPERIMENTAL LOGIC].

37 CHARLES SANDERS PEIRCE, *The Fixation of Belief*, in 5 COLLECTED PAPERS OF CHARLES SANDERS PEIRCE paras. 358, 367 (C. Hartshorne & P. Weiss eds. 1934).

38 *Id.* paras. 374–375.

39 Peirce's earliest pragmatist essay was a taxonomy of the methods of settling opinion, among which he included "tenacity" (resisting doubt), "authority" (accepting the opinions of leaders), and "inspiration" (reasoning a priori, as in philosophical rationalism). But better than any of these, according to Peirce, is the method of science—hypothesis and experiment—because its practice is self-confirming and its achievements progressive. *Id.* paras. 377–387; *see also* JOHN DEWEY, THE QUEST FOR CERTAINTY 227–28 (1929).

40 *See, e.g.*, J. DEWEY, EXPERIMENTAL LOGIC, *supra* note 36, at 183–219; JOHN DEWEY, HUMAN NATURE AND CONDUCT 172–80 (1922); J. DEWEY, THE QUEST FOR CERTAINTY, *supra* note 39, at 224–28; JOHN DEWEY, LOGIC: THE THEORY OF INQUIRY 7–10, 12–14 (1938) [hereinafter J. DEWEY, THE THEORY OF INQUIRY]. W. JAMES, PRAGMATISM, *supra* note 14, at 59–66.

mented and modified along many different paths of cultural development.[41] The pragmatists thus provided an escape from the philosophical paradoxes inherent in the confused conception of the Platonic-Christian-Cartesian-Lockean mind-soul, that hybrid entity with its many and conflicting roles: the locus of personal identity and moral being, the active organ of decision, the seat of creativity and imagination, the passive theater of perception, the storehouse of memory, and the immaterial and indestructible survivor of the body's mortality.

The pragmatists' account of the mind and inquiry was thus thoroughly *practical,* in two related senses. First, on the side that derived from historicist social thought, they treated thinking as contextual and situated; it came always embodied in *practices*—habits and patterns of perceiving and conceiving that had developed out of and served to guide activity. Some of these habits and patterns were instinctive, some were learned individually, but those most distinctively human resulted from the capacity for language; they were products of culture, collectively developed and transmitted. Second, on the side that derived from Darwinism, the pragmatists regarded thinking as an adaptive function of an organism, practical in the sense that it was *instrumental.* It had evolved as a problem-solving capacity, oriented toward survival. In its most developed form, thinking functioned to help resolve, by means of conscious reflection and experimental revision, the real problems and live doubts that arose in the course of acting on unreflective and habitual practices. Holmes himself provided a characteristically compact summary of these two tenets: "all thought," he said, is at once "social" and "on its way to action."[42]

Whereas older accounts of pragmatism emphasized its instrumentalism, the distinctive feature of recent reinterpretations of pragmatism is to give equal significance to its contextualist thesis—the idea that thought is essentially embedded in a context of social practice. Not only is contextualism no less fundamental to the pragmatists' thought than instrumentalism; it is what most sharply distinguishes them from orthodox scientific positivists. Indeed, development of the contextualist thesis led the pragmatists to their most profound philosophical innovation: the rejection of philosophical "foundationalism."

---

41 *See* J. DEWEY, EXPERIMENTAL LOGIC, *supra* note 36, at 331–32. Dewey's best general statement of the importance he placed upon language as an independent force in the development of culture is the chapter *Nature, Communication, and Meaning,* in J. DEWEY, EXPERIENCE AND NATURE, *supra* note 19, at 166–207.

42 OLIVER WENDELL HOLMES, *John Marshall* (1901), in COLLECTED LEGAL PAPERS 266, 270 (1920) [hereinafter *John Marshall*].

Foundationalism is a long name for the age-old philosopher's dream that knowledge might be grounded in a set of fundamental and indubitable beliefs. For the rationalist tradition descended from Descartes, the cornerstones of knowledge are those rational intuitions that survive as clear and distinct ideas in the face of the thinker's effort at universal doubt. For the empiricist tradition running from Bacon, Hobbes, and Locke to the logical positivism of this century, the foundations of factual knowledge are the bare uninterpreted data delivered to the mind by the senses. The tradition of modern Western epistemology, both rationalist and empiricist, has imagined that knowledge can be securely based only if the inquirer strips away all habitual and conventional ways of thought, and builds a purified structure based on valid inferences from indubitable premises.

The pragmatists' first thesis—that knowledge is essentially contextual, situated in habit and practice—holds that no such zero-based method of inquiry is possible. Peirce stated the point forcefully: No one, he said, can set out to think either by "doubting everything" or by "observing 'the first impressions of sense.' " Rather:

> [T]here is but one state of mind from which you can "set out," namely, the very state of mind in which you actually find yourself at the time you do "set out"—a state in which you are laden with an immense mass of cognition already formed, of which you cannot divest yourself if you would; and who knows whether, if you could, you would not have made all knowledge impossible to yourself?[43]

In a similar vein, James stressed that the individual always begins with "a stock of old opinions."[44] When these are put under strain by some incongruous perception or desire, the individual seeks to escape from the "inward trouble" thus generated by "modifying his previous mass of opinions."[45] But "[h]e saves as much of it as he can, for in this matter of belief we are all extreme conservatives.... The most violent revolutions in an individual's beliefs leave most of his old order standing."[46] Similarly, Dewey stressed the beginning of thought in

---

43 Charles Sanders Peirce, *What Pragmatism Is* (1905), in 5 Collected Papers of Charles Sanders Peirce, *supra* note 37, paras. 411, 416; *see also* Charles Sanders Peirce, *Some Consequences of Four Incapacities* (1868), in *id.* at paras. 264, 265 [hereinafter C.S. Peirce, *Four Incapacities*].

44 W. James, Pragmatism, *supra* note 14, at 59.

45 *Id.* at 59–60; *see also id.* at 64.

46 *Id.* at 60; *see also id.* at 224–25.

habit; the human being is in the first instance a creature of habit, not of reason.[47] Only when habit and practice become problematic is there occasion for inquiry, the application of conscious intelligence to a situation. The task of inquiry is not the impossible one of building a purified structure of truths from the ground up, but rather the practical one of making such modifications in the existing body of knowledge as will solve the difficulty at hand. This remains as true for the most abstract theoretical puzzle in mathematics or speculative philosophy as it does for those ordinary problems of daily life in which conscious deliberation originates.[48]

Practices are not only habitual and largely unconscious; they are mainly collective in origin. The pragmatists emphasized the *social* origins of the great mass of settled belief from which inquiry proceeds. We see that practices are collective, when we consider that they are mediated by language, the conventional, collectively constituted, spontaneously evolved, complex communicative structure of meaningful signs that underlies all reflective or conscious thought. Language supplies not only the forms in which thought is represented and conveyed, but much of the stuff of thought itself.[49] Thus, Peirce argued that thought was essentially carried on by means of signs, of which the most important were the conventional signs that constitute language.[50] In fact, in emphasizing the role of language and the collective notion of inquiry, Peirce went so far as to hold that reality itself is simply the object on which the representations of a community of inquirers are destined in the long run to converge.[51]

---

47 *See* J. DEWEY, HUMAN NATURE AND CONDUCT, *supra* note 36, at 172–80; J. DEWEY, EXPERIMENTAL LOGIC, *supra* note 40, at 184–88.

48 *See* J. DEWEY, THE QUEST FOR CERTAINTY, *supra* note 39, at 186–87; *cf.* J. DEWEY, EXPERIENCE AND NATURE, *supra* note 19, at viii–ix ("We cannot lay hold of the new, we cannot even keep it before our minds, much less understand it, save by the use of ideas and knowledge we already possess.").

49 *See* J. DEWEY, EXPERIENCE AND NATURE, *supra* note 19, at 166–207; J. DEWEY, THE THEORY OF INQUIRY, *supra* note 40, at 45–47. George Herbert Mead's contribution to pragmatism was to work out in far more detail than Dewey or James the role that language and communication play in establishing selfhood and social cooperation—that is, to work out a pragmatic social philosophy. *See* H.S. THAYER, MEANING AND ACTION: A CRITICAL HISTORY OF PRAGMATISM 232–68 (1981).

50 *See* C.S. PEIRCE, *Four Incapacities*, *supra* note 43, para. 283; C.S. PEIRCE, *What Pragmatism Is*, *supra* note 43, para. 421.

51 *See* C.S. PEIRCE, *Four Incapacities*, *supra* note 43, para. 311; *see also* H.S. THAYER, *supra* note 49, at 235–36.

The pragmatists thus broke not only with the foundationalism of the empiricist tradition, but also with its methodological individualism. They did not regard society as a construct built up out of elementary individuals, each possessing a rich array of pre-social qualities. Rather, they argued, the individual person, the knowing, willing subject of Enlightenment epistemology and political philosophy, is only the late and sophisticated product of a complex cultural development.[52]

This first thesis of pragmatism—the situated, historical, practice-constituted character of human life and thought—is not unique to the pragmatists. It has been a central theme for all those modern philosophers who have broken from the foundationalist tradition in Western thought. The erstwhile logical positivist Otto Neurath captured the essence of anti-foundationalism in a famous metaphor, when he described human inquirers as sailors on a boat that can never come to drydock for repair, so that they must maintain and reconstruct it as they sail, using its own material and what flotsam they come upon.[53] In his later work, Wittgenstein often stressed the social, habitual, and practical basis of all reasoning: "What has to be accepted, the given, is . . . *forms of life*."[54] And Heidegger held that all beliefs presuppose prejudices—judgments already made, implicit in practice, prior to reflection, largely historical and collective in origin, tacitly accepted, and for the moment unquestioned.[55]

Even before pragmatism as such came on the scene, the concept of human inquiry as essentially situated and historically conditioned was one of the central themes of nineteenth-century social thought. It appears in Hegel, from whom it was taken in a revolutionary direction by Marx. But it was most conspicuous in the Burkean-romantic brand of conservative social theory that in the English-speaking world drew inspiration from the traditional ideology of

---

52 *See* J. DEWEY, EXPERIENCE AND NATURE, *supra* note 19, at 208–11; C.S. PEIRCE, *What Pragmatism Is*, *supra* note 43, para. 421; *see also* H.S. THAYER, *supra* note 49, at 232–34 (discussing Mead's views). James is often said to have neglected the cultural and linguistic bases of thought, but David Hollinger argues persuasively to the contrary. *See* D. HOLLINGER, *supra* note 17, at 9–10, 20–22.

53 Otto Neurath, *Protocol Sentences*, in LOGICAL POSITIVISM, *supra* note 15, at 199, 201.

54 LUDWIG WITTGENSTEIN, PHILOSOPHICAL INVESTIGATIONS pt. 2, at 226e (G.E.M. Anscombe trans. 3d ed. 1968). For similar late-Wittgensteinian remarks, *see*, for example, *id.* pt. 1, paras. 19, 23, 217, 240–242; LUDWIG WITTGENSTEIN, ON CERTAINTY paras. 166, 189, 204 (G.E.M. Anscombe & D. Paul trans. 1969); LUDWIG WITTGENSTEIN, REMARKS ON THE FOUNDATIONS OF MATHEMATICS pt. 1, paras. 113–116 (G.E.M. Anscombe trans, rev. ed. 1978).

55 *See* MARTIN HEIDEGGER, BEING AND TIME 188–203 (J. Macquarrie & E. Robinson trans. 1962).

the common law, and found theoretical expression in Friedrich von Savigny, Sir Henry Maine, James Coolidge Carter, and the other proponents of the historical school of jurisprudence.[56] The leading pragmatists, however, did not share the Burkean conservatism common among so many thinkers who stress the centrality of history and context to human social life. Their analysis grants no special authority to unconscious habit and slowly evolved custom; self-conscious reflection and innovative reason are equally central to their account of inquiry. The pragmatist thesis is that human thought always and necessarily arises in a situated complex of beliefs; on any given occasion, the great mass of these beliefs must be left tacit and simply used, not made explicit and subject to doubt, if thought is to proceed at all. But from this the pragmatists draw no inference that any particular idea or belief should be treated as even presumptively immune from questioning.

Rather, pragmatists treat critical reflection as a natural aspect of thought, an aspect as natural, if not as easy, as following habit. Conscious inquiry arises naturally whenever a person enters a problematic situation, a case in which habitual and unconscious belief produces trouble.[57] And this happens all the time, romantic conservatism notwithstanding. Here we come to the second and more familiar pragmatist thesis: Thought or inquiry is instrumental as well as situated in practice. Reflective, deliberative, even contemplative thinking originates in the practical need to solve real problems.

The pragmatists were not, of course, the first to situate thinking within the experience of everyday life; this insight goes back at least to Aristotle.[58] Their innovation was to move the category of the practical from the periphery to the

---

56 Among the best studies of historicist evolutionary thought are J. BURROW, *supra* note 35, and PETER STEIN, LEGAL EVOLUTION (1980) (focusing on legal thought). An important background figure in the development of historicist social thought, neglected by these writers, was David Hume. On the striking extent to which Hume's ideas anticipate the historicist aspects of pragmatism sketched here, *see* DONALD W. LIVINGSTON, HUME'S PHILOSOPHY OF COMMON LIFE 24, *passim*, (1984). For the legal significance of Hume's social thought, *see* GERALD J. POSTEMA, BENTHAM AND THE COMMON-LAW TRADITION 81–143 (1986).

57 *See* J. DEWEY, EXPERIMENTAL LOGIC, *supra* note 36, at 225; *see also* J. DEWEY, THE QUEST FOR CERTAINTY, *supra* note 39, at 244–45.

58 Dewey explicitly makes the connection to Aristotle in J. DEWEY, EXPERIMENTAL LOGIC, *supra* note 36, at 331–34. The pragmatist thesis that thought is always situated in a social context could likewise be traced to the Aristotelian thesis that human beings are essentially social animals. For works of a neo-pragmatist tendency that stress their Aristotelian roots, *see* ALISDAIR MACINTYRE, AFTER VIRTUE (1981); MARTHA C. NUSSBAUM, THE FRAGILITY OF GOODNESS (1986).

center in their account of human reason. This reversed the familiar Platonic and Aristotelian ordering in which speculation or theory is the primary and highest form of reason. For pragmatists, the capacity for reason is best suited to practical concerns because it arises from our efforts to deal with those concerns.[59]

Both the traditional ordering of the practical and theoretical, and the pragmatist reversal of that ordering, are illustrated in the origin of the term "pragmatism" itself. Peirce took the word from Kant, who had defined "pragmatic" beliefs as those that were "contingent only," supplying "a ground for the actual employment of means to certain actions" even though "another might form a better judgment."[60] The strength of a pragmatic belief was measured by the believer's willingness to bet on it: "Sometimes it turns out that a man has persuasion sufficient to be valued at one ducat, but not at ten.... Thus pragmatic belief admits of degrees which, according to the difference of the interests at stake, may be large or small."[61]

In Kant's view, this merely contingent and relative pragmatic type of belief was different in kind from genuine knowledge. Through science, human beings could gain true knowledge of the spatio-temporal natural world of cause and effect; and through reflection on their capacity for deliberation about what to do, they could gain true practical knowledge of the moral realm. But the assessment of the likelihood of attaining an end through given means must remain in the lower category of the pragmatic—mere guesswork. In a transvaluative flip worthy of Nietzsche, Peirce reversed the Kantian hierarchy, and assimilated all human science, speculative philosophy, and moral inquiry into the category of the pragmatic.[62] All judgments—scientific and moral as well as prudential and technical—were contingent, probabilistic, relative to a situation and to the interests of an agent or a community of agents. Thought was no

59 Contemplative and theoretical reason gained its traditional privilege in Western thought, Dewey argued, by virtue of the pervasive class-divided form of social organization that associates work and practical concerns with menial status, and the leisure for contemplation and theory with high status. *See* J. DEWEY, THE QUEST FOR CERTAINTY, *supra* note 39, at 4–5; J. DEWEY, EXPERIENCE AND NATURE, *supra* note 19, at 93–94.

60 IMMANUEL KANT, CRITIQUE OF PURE REASON 661 (F. Muller trans. 2d ed. 1896) (originally published 1781).

61 *Id.* at 661–62. Compare Holmes' view: "I describe myself as a *bet*tabilitarian. I believe that we can *bet* on the behavior of the universe in its contact with us. We bet we can know what it will be." 2 HOLMES-POLLOCK LETTERS, *supra* note 8, at 252 (letter dated Aug. 30, 1929).

62 *See* C.S. PEIRCE, *What Pragmatism Is*, *supra* note 43, para. 412.

longer to be conceived as something distinct from practice, but rather it simply *was* practice, or activity, in its deliberative or reflective aspect.[63]

In making this assimilation, the pragmatists took a decisive step beyond orthodox nineteenth-century positivism. Following a tradition as firmly lodged in British empiricism as in European rationalism, positivists had treated philosophy and science not as forms of problem-solving practical reason, but as autonomous, distinctively "mental" activities prior to and independent of practice, aimed at providing an accurate representation of an objective external reality. Rejecting this dualism, the pragmatists applied the utilitarian test of consequences to theories, as well as to rules for action, on the ground that all beliefs were, directly or indirectly, action-guiding and, accordingly, should be judged by their efficacy in leading the agent through experience successfully.[64]

The notion of making beliefs, thoughts, or propositions accurately represent external reality played no essential part in the pragmatic account of inquiry. The "externality" of "the world" was the other side of the coin to the "internality" of "the mind"; having rejected the one, the pragmatists had no need for the other.[65] They believed that it sometimes made sense to speak of ideas or propositions as copying or representing facts, but representational accuracy

---

63 Dewey makes the point best in the chapter *Nature, Life and Body-Mind*, in J. DEWEY, EXPERIENCE AND NATURE, *supra* note 19, at 248–97. *See also* 2 WILLIAM JAMES, THE WORKS OF WILLIAM JAMES: THE PRINCIPLES OF PSYCHOLOGY 1136–93 (F. Burkhardt ed. 1981) (originally published 1890).

64 Peirce once described pragmatism as "scarce more than a corollary" of the English psychologist Alexander Bain's definition of a belief as " 'that upon which a man is prepared to act.' " C.S. PEIRCE, *Historical Affinities and Genesis* (1906), in 5 COLLECTED PAPERS OF CHARLES SANDERS PEIRCE, *supra* note 37, para. 912. Peirce learned of Bain's definition from Holmes' friend, the young Boston lawyer Nicholas St. John Green, whom Peirce called "the grandfather of pragmatism." *Id.* On Bain's influence, *see* M. FISCH, *Alexander Bain and the Genealogy of Pragmatism*, in PEIRCE, SEMEIOTIC, AND PRAGMATISM, *supra* note 6, at 79. Holmes himself evidently learned of Bain's conception of belief indirectly, through the writings of James Fitzjames Stephen. *See* M. HOWE, THE SHAPING YEARS, *supra* note 26, at 267–70. On Green's contributions to pragmatism, *see* P. WIENER, *supra* note 6, at 152–71; on his apparent anticipation of some of Holmes' own ideas, *see* Jerome Frank, *A Conflict with Oblivion: Some Observations on the Founders of Legal Pragmatism*, 9 RUTGERS L. REV. 425, 434–44 (1954).

65 For a pragmatist, the materialist and behaviorist theories that deny the reality of the mental simply rehearse the standard Cartesian error of dividing the world into *res extensa* and *res cogitans*. *See* text accompanying note 32 *supra*. Such views accept the Cartesian categories, only to assert that one of them is empty. Pragmatists, instead, reject the basic metaphysical views on which the "spirit-matter" distinction rests. As Holmes wrote, "I don't perceive why there is any more right to think away consciousness than there is to

was not a *general* criterion for evaluating either ordinary beliefs or scientific theories. The general criterion was success in helping people cope with the world.[66]

Holmes understood this feature of pragmatism and appreciated its originality; in one of his few bits of grudging praise for James' version of pragmatism, he acknowledged that his old friend had "made a valuable contribution in pointing out that ideas were not necessarily faint pictures of original experience…."[67] He himself often invoked this pragmatist insight into the instrumental character of thought, most notably in the words of his *Gitlow* dissent: "Every idea is an incitement. It offers itself for belief and if believed it is acted on…."[68]

A corollary of pragmatism, derived from the tenets that thought is always both situated and instrumental, is a kind of perspectivism. Because new beliefs emerge out of a complex of already existing beliefs that can never be made fully conscious and explicit, all useful beliefs may not ultimately prove commensurable with each other. Furthermore, because inquiry is at root an instrument to guide action (including the action of further inquiry), its products are subject to revision as the ends sought in action change. This double relativity of situation and purpose implies a tentative attitude toward all beliefs, including especially those "theoretical" and "fundamental" ones to which we are most likely to attribute permanent and universal validity. The pragmatist rec-

---

think away nerve tissue—the total is the datum." *Holmes-Cohen Correspondence, supra* note 31, at 325 (letter dated July 21, 1920).

66 James promoted the so-called "pragmatic theory of truth," which equated true beliefs with those that are on the whole advantageous to hold. *See* W. James, Pragmatism, *supra* note 14, at 197–236. This has long drawn the fire of critics who argue that we have independent standards of truth and falsity at least for some beliefs, such as those for which a "correspondence" account of truth is apt, and that there is no guarantee that beliefs true in the correspondence sense will always prove expedient, even in the long run, for those who hold them. *See* Bertrand Russell, *William James's Conception of Truth*, in Philosophical Essays 112, 125–26, *passim* (rev. ed. 1966). Dewey corrected James on this point. *See* J. Dewey, Experimental Logic, *supra* note 36, at 318–20. A solution to the problem, consistent with Dewey's approach, and reasonably congruent with ordinary usage, would be to confine judgments of truth or falsity to those claims or beliefs that are in principle subject to assessment in terms of representational accuracy.

67 1 Holmes-Pollock Letters, *supra* note 8, at 191 (letter dated Apr. 26, 1912).

68 Gitlow v. New York, 268 U.S. 652, 673 (1925); *cf. John Marshall, supra* note 42, at 270 ("all thought is social, is on its way to action"); Oliver Wendell Holmes, *Introduction to the General Survey by European Authors in the Continental Legal Historical Series* (1913), in Collected Legal Papers 298, 298 (1920) ("The philosophers teach us that an idea is the first step toward an act.") [hereinafter *Introduction to the General Survey*].

ognizes that the best account of a phenomenon (such as law) from one angle, for one purpose, at one time, might not serve as well from another perspective, rooted in another temporal context, and aimed at different goals. In its mature version, as Dewey stated it, pragmatism rejects the assumption that there must exist a comprehensive and final account of "reality" that, if attained, would bring the process of scientific and philosophical inquiry to a close.[69]

A pragmatic legal theorist will embed questions about law in a context and address them for a purpose, and so may reach different and apparently inconsistent answers as context and purpose vary. The point of view of the judge, the legal commentator, the counselor, and the legal historian or anthropologist might produce analyses of the concept of law that seem mutually inconsistent. There is no reason to assume in advance that these alternative accounts, directed as they are to different purposes, are, like the different perceptions the blind men had of the elephant, to be reconciled in some all-comprehending meta-account, though a wise pragmatist will also accept as legitimate the "philosophical" human need to generate such unifying accounts. This perspectival pluralism turns out to be particularly important to understanding Holmes' pragmatist jurisprudence, with its apparently conflicting accounts of the legal elephant as experience, logic, and prediction. To these accounts we now turn.

II Law as Experience

To apply the central pragmatic tenets to law means to treat it as a practical enterprise in two senses. First, law is constituted of practices—contextual, situated, rooted in custom and shared expectations. Second, it is instrumental,

---

69 For an example of Dewey's perspectivism, see his comments on the aims of education:

> "[T]he *statement* of aim is a matter of emphasis at a given time. And we do not emphasize things which do not require emphasis—that is, such things as are taking care of themselves fairly well. We tend rather to frame ... our explicit aims in terms of some alteration to be brought about. It is, then, no paradox requiring explanation that a given epoch or generation tends to emphasize in its conscious projections just the things which it has least of in actual fact. A time of domination by authority will call out as response the desirability of great individual freedom; one of disorganized individual activities the need of social control as an educational aim."

John Dewey, Democracy and Education 111–12 (1916). Nelson Goodman has provided an excellent contemporary version of perspectivism in N. Goodman, *supra* note 12, at 1–21, 91–140. For a clear account of the perspectivism of Nietzsche, a contemporary of the American pragmatists, and a thinker whose views on this subject paralleled theirs in important ways, *see* Alexander Nehamas, Nietzsche: Life as Literature 42–73 (1985).

a means for achieving socially desired ends, and available to be adapted to their service. The first point, about practice and context, suggests the perspective of the historical school of jurisprudence; the second or instrumental point suggests Benthamite utilitarian positivism. Standard nineteenth-century jurisprudence regarded these theories as rivals. A central innovation of legal pragmatism was to comprehend that each of them expresses a partial truth about law, the one reflecting its situated and the other its instrumental character. An adequate theory should synthesize them rather than choose between them.[70] It is to Holmes that we owe the first clear statement of such a synthesis.

John Dewey stated the same synthesis when he came, late in life, to attempt a brief summary statement of his "philosophy of law."[71] With the historical jurists, he argued that the main source of law was custom, the network of interaction and expectation that gave structure to social life. At the same time, with the utilitarian positivists, he held that law's end or criterion of evaluation was the extent to which it produced desired practical consequences in application.[72]

In this synthesis, Dewey followed Holmes, with whose dictum that "the life of the law is not logic but experience" he was certainly familiar.[73] The well-known words that follow "experience" in the opening passage of *The Common Law* elaborate Holmes' conception of the sources of law:

---

70 Holmes indicated his ambition to synthesize the analytic and historical schools in OLIVER WENDELL HOLMES, *Science of Legal Judgment*, in JUSTICE OLIVER WENDELL HOLMES: HIS BOOK NOTICES AND UNCOLLECTED LETTERS AND PAPERS 5 (H. Shriver ed. 1936) [hereinafter BOOK NOTICES] (reprinting Book Notice, 6 AM. L. REV. 134 (1871)):

> "A treatise on the sources of the law which shall strike half way between the somewhat latitudinary theorizing of Savigny and the too narrow exclusiveness of Austin, will form a chapter of jurisprudence which is not yet written, and which it is worthy of the ambition of an aspiring mind to write."

Id. at 5–6.

John Stuart Mill had contrasted the Bentham-Austin analytical approach to Sir Henry Maine's historical jurisprudence, but without suggesting any synthesis of them, in his review essay on Austin's *Lectures on Jurisprudence*. JOHN STUART MILL, *Austin on Jurisprudence* (1863), in DISSERTATIONS AND DISCUSSIONS 157, 161–71 (1873). Holmes read this essay of Mill's. *See* Patrick Kelley, *Oliver Wendell Holmes, Utilitarian Jurisprudence, and the Positivism of John Stuart Mill*, 30 AM. J. JURIS. 189, 199 (1985).

71 John Dewey, in My Philosophy of Law 73 (Julius Rosenthal Foundation ed. 1941).

72 *See id.; see also* John Dewey, *Logical Method and Law*, 10 CORNELL L.Q. 17 (1924); JOHN DEWEY, THE PUBLIC AND ITS PROBLEMS 51–57 (2d ed. 1954); John Dewey, *The Historic Background of Corporate Legal Personality*, 35 YALE L.J. 655 (1926).

73 *See* Dewey's extensive quotation from Holmes' works in Dewey, *Justice Holmes supra* note 19, at 33.

> The felt necessities of the time, the prevalent moral and political theories, intuitions of public policy, avowed or unconscious, even the prejudices which judges share with their fellow-men, have had a good deal more to do than the syllogism in determining how men should be governed.[74]

On the one hand, law is situated: It draws on *felt* necessities; *unconscious* intuitions; *prejudices*—the tacit patterns of thought inherited from the past. It cannot be treated as a pure logical system because it "embodies the story of a nation's development through many centuries."[75] On the other hand law is instrumental: It responds to moral and political *theories; avowed* intuitions of public policy—the products of future-directed deliberation. To identify what law is, one must attend both to "what it has been" and to "what it tends to become."[76] The jurist must both remember and imagine, "alternately consult[ing] history and existing theories of legislation."[77] Law is "a reaction between tradition on the one side and the changing desires and needs of a community on the other."[78] To identify law with experience is to treat it as "policy coupled with tradition."[79]

Given that legal "experience" has both past-embedded (customary) and forward-looking (deliberative) aspects, what relation should these elements bear to each other for the judges and commentators who state and shape the law? Holmes answers, as usual, with an aphorism: "[C]ontinuity with the past is only a necessity and not a duty."[80] On the one hand, continuity with the past *is* a necessity—which is merely to repeat that law is always situated. No working system of practice can be built by reasoning from the bare ground of human nature alone. If we leave out all the institutions, practices, and beliefs that exist now only because they existed in the past, we will have insufficient resources to build with—no culture, no shared values, no language (hence no collective deliberation), and indeed no recognizably human individuals. Custom, the

74 THE COMMON LAW, *supra* note 23, at 5.

75 *Id.*

76 *Id.*

77 *Id.*

78 OLIVER WENDELL HOLMES, *Twenty Years in Retrospect* (1902) [hereinafter *Twenty Years in Retrospect*], in THE OCCASIONAL SPEECHES OF JUSTICE OLIVER WENDELL HOLMES 154, 155 (M. Howe ed. 1962) [hereinafter OCCASIONAL SPEECHES].

79 THE COMMON LAW, *supra* note 23, at 123.

80 *Law in Science, supra* note 24, at 211; *see also* OLIVER WENDELL HOLMES, *Learning and Science* (1895), in COLLECTED LEGAL PAPERS 138, 139 (1920) [hereinafter *Learning and Science*].

accretion of situated experience, "limits the possibilities of our imagination, and settles the terms in which we shall be compelled to think."[81]

On the other hand, continuity with the past is no categorical imperative—law is a functional instrument meant to meet present and future human needs. To show that a legal rule has a customary basis is not to justify that rule, though it may suggest expectations that impose legitimate claims. But the main practical point of historical research on law is to stress the contingent and variable character of practices that historically unsophisticated practical lawyers may regard as inevitable and rationally necessary. Historical inquiry aims toward reform. Rather than blindly follow a rule for no better reason than that "so it was laid down in the time of Henry IV,"[82] the judge and commentator should recognize that "the present has a right to govern itself so far as it can" and engage in "scrutiny and revision" guided by "considerations of social advantage."[83]

It is worth reviewing the debate between the schools of legal theory that supplied the context for Holmes' aphorism about continuity with the past. On the one side, English utilitarian positivists and European rationalist codifiers stood for the spirit of the Enlightenment, the spirit summarized by Kant in the slogan "think for yourself!"[84] For all their differences, Kant, the philosopher behind German legal science, and Bentham, the founder of English analytical positivism, shared a commitment to liberate the human mind from its state of "tutelage"—the tutelage of the past, with its weight of customs, traditions, and inherited texts.

Nowhere did the Enlightened feel the weight of the past more than in the law. They responded with the thought-experiment of stripping away the tutelage of the past in imagination, preliminary to a similar defoliation in actual social practice. Thus Bentham sought to clear away the tangle of customary English common law and construct in its place a code designed on the Principle of Utility, every provision of which was rationally aimed at attaining the greatest happiness of the greatest number.[85] His enemy was a jungle of irrational custom, prejudice, and superstition, hidden behind a false front of pretended reason. The enemy was epitomized by the *Commentaries* of Sir William

81 *Law in Science, supra* note 24, at 211; *cf.* THE COMMON LAW, *supra* note 23, at 5 n.a.

82 *The Path of the Law, supra* note 23, at 187.

83 *Learning and Science, supra* note 80, at 139; THE COMMON LAW, *supra* note 23, at 33; *The Path of the Law, supra* note 23, at 184.

84 *"Sapere Aude!"*—literally, "Dare to know!" IMMANUEL KANT, *What is Enlightenment?* (1784), in KANT ON HISTORY 3 & n. 1 (L. Beck ed. 1963).

85 J. BENTHAM, *An Introduction to the Principles of Morals and Legislation, supra* note 30, at 2.

Blackstone, which culminated the long common law tradition while domesticating its inherited irrationalities in the smooth rhetoric of the Age of Reason.[86]

Against the codifying jurisprudence of the Enlightenment there arose a romantic and conservative reaction based upon faith in the virtues of tradition, organic solidarity, and cultural particularity, and upon distrust of innovation and abstract reason. In Europe, this reaction found its vehicle in the formation of the historical school of jurisprudence. The historicists argued that the basis of all law is custom, the set of evolved norms that give a society its identity. According to their central metaphor, a community's law is like its language, a collective product, peculiar to its people and their history, gradually developed, a structure of contingent elements and rules, and yet one so deeply rooted in practice as to be almost entirely resistant to conscious modification. Because law had this character, to reform it through codification was impossible and where attempted harmful—as misguided as the attempt to impose a constructed artificial language on a people.[87]

Though the historical school had an important English spokesman in Sir Henry Maine, it never found as large a following in the English-speaking countries as it did in Germany.[88] This was not because it failed to touch a sympathetic nerve but rather because it said nothing that was in substance new to English and American lawyers. Historical jurists only restated the conventional wisdom of the "the common law tradition" as it had been articulated over the centuries by Coke, Hale, and Blackstone and translated into the language of political theory by David Hume and Edmund Burke. The commonplaces of that tradition included the conception of law as custom, adapted to circumstances through a gradual process of case-by-case decision by judges each of

86 *See generally* Jeremy Bentham, *A Fragment on Government; or a Comment on the Commentaries* (1776), in 1 Works of Bentham, *supra* note 29, at 221 [hereinafter J. Bentham, *A Fragment on Government*].

87 The classic statement of the historical school position is Friedrich Karl von Savigny, Of the Vocation of Our Age for Legislation and Jurisprudence (reprint ed. 1975) (A. Hayward trans. 2d. ed. 1831).

88 Sir Henry Maine's best known works applied historicist social theory to law but did not take the polemical position in favor of customary law and against codification and reformist legislation characteristic of von Savigny and his American disciple James Coolidge Carter. *See, e.g.*, Henry Maine, Ancient Law (2d ed. 1863). But in his later work, Maine revealed his full commitment to the standard Burkean legal conservatism of the historical jurists. See, for example, his praise of "historical Constitutions, Constitutions gradually developed through the accumulation of experience" as compared to "*a priori* Constitutions, Constitutions founded on speculative assumptions remote from experience." Henry Maine, Popular Government 176 (1885).

whom felt bound to discover a law implicit in the body of prior precedents. This process, in its collective wisdom, was thought more impressive than the conscious intelligence of any individual could possibly be; the law that emerged from it was said to be the perfection of reason, but an admittedly artificial reason, to be learned only through apprenticeship and experience.[89]

The two schools of jurisprudence thus shared the factual premise that the law up to the present had largely been the product of custom. At that point they diverged—the Enlightened argued that the only proper way to remove the law's haphazard excrescences was to start from scratch (at least in imagination) and build up a new body of law by rational inference from first principles; the historical jurists responded that workable law must always be based in custom, and that no good could possibly come from conscious and instrumental law reform.

Holmes' maxim that "continuity with the past is no duty but only a necessity" synthesized these two schools and provided a reconciliation of their main tenets. On the one hand, the historicists were importantly right. The Benthamite project of clearing away and building anew was the social and institutional analogue of the Cartesian epistemological project of submitting all inherited belief to doubt, so as to rebuild knowledge from the ground up upon indubitable foundations. And the pragmatic response was the same one Peirce had made to Descartes: In remaking a society or its law there was no ground zero to set out from; the only starting point was where you actually found yourself, "laden with an immense mass of cognition already formed, of which you cannot divest yourself if you would; and who knows whether, if you could, you would not have made all knowledge impossible to yourself?"[90] As Holmes put the same point in the legal context,

89 For "the artificial reason of the law," see Prohibitions del Roy, 12 Coke's Reports 63, 65 (1608); for the connection between Burkean political philosophy and the common law tradition, *see* J.G.A. POCOCK, *Burke and the Ancient Constitution: A Problem in the History of Ideas*, in POLITICS, LANGUAGE AND TIME 202 (1973); for Hume's place in that tradition, *see* G. POSTEMA, *supra* note 56, at 110–43; and for a modern conservative political philosopher's restatement of the common law tradition, see the chapter *The Changing Concept of Law*, in FRIEDRICH AUGUST VON HAYEK, LAW, LEGISLATION AND LIBERTY: RULES AND ORDER 72–93 (1973).

90 C.S. PEIRCE, *What Pragmatism Is*, *supra* note 43, para. 416.

> [o]ne fancies that one could invent a different code under which men would have been as well off as they are now, if they had happened to adopt it. But that *if* is a very great one. The tree has grown as we know it. The practical question is what is to be the next organic step.[91]

On the other hand, Holmes' view of law also embodied utilitarian reformism, because recognition of law as customary and situated did not necessarily have conservative implications. No one could discard all customary beliefs and practices at once, but this did not immunize any subset of those beliefs and practices from "scrutiny and revision."[92] As Holmes said, just because "we all are compelled to take on faith at second hand most of the rules on which we base our action and our thought," it does not follow "that each of us may not try to set some corner of his world in the order of reason, or that all of us collectively should not aspire to carry reason as far as it will go throughout the whole domain."[93] In the short run we may be ruled by our habits and unreflective desires; in the longer run we have "every reason ... for trying to make our desires intelligent."[94]

This is the framework of Holmes' mature pragmatic conception of law. In thus describing it, I do not mean to deny that Holmes himself did indeed hold many conservative political and legal views. In fact, he began his career quite close to the orthodoxy of the common law tradition. In his first essay in legal theory, *Codes, and the Arrangement of the Law*,[95] Holmes debated in fairly conventional terms the standard topic of codification. He argued that the strength of the common law was its flexibility and adaptability. The source of this strength was the tacit practical wisdom of the common law judge, who "decides the case first and determines the principle afterwards."[96] Legal principles gradually emerged out of lines of precedent, so that a "well settled legal doctrine embodies the work of many minds, and has been tested in form as well as substance by trained critics whose practical interest it is to resist it at every

91 Oliver Wendell Holmes, *Holdsworth's English Law* (1909), in Collected Legal Papers 285, 289 (1920) [hereinafter *Holdsworth's English Law*].

92 The Common Law, *supra* note 23, at 33.

93 *The Path of the Law, supra* note 23, at 185.

94 Oliver Wendell Holmes, *ideals and Doubts* (1915), in Collected Legal Papers 303, 305 (1920) [hereinafter *Ideals and Doubts*].

95 Oliver Wendell Holmes, *Codes, and the Arrangement of the Law*, in Formative Essays, *supra* note 7, at 77, 77 (reprinting *Codes, and the Arrangement of the Law*, 5 Am. L. Rev. 1 (1870) [hereinafter *Codes, and the Arrangement of the Law*].

96 *Id.*

step."[97] No individual's "faculty of generalization, however brilliant," could supply these advantages, which would be lost if a code were adopted as binding law.[98]

But even in his early writings, Holmes came to deviate significantly from conservative common law orthodoxy. He soon recognized that the traditional viewpoint presupposed the existence of a unified community, bound by shared values and interests. Yet he saw before him an industrial society rapidly dividing along class lines at the same time that it was becoming more economically interdependent.[99] And he became increasingly skeptical about the rationally adaptive character of the process of case-by-case decision. Borrowing a concept from the anthropologists, Holmes came to believe that "in large and important branches of the law the various grounds of policy on which the various rules have been justified are later inventions to account for what are in fact *survivals* from more primitive times."[100] No longer did it seem so clear to him that the less conscious the process of evolution the better the product. Rather the discovery that new reasons have been invented to justify old practices that in fact survive merely by the force of social inertia should encourage lawyers to "reconsider" and "decide anew whether those reasons are satisfactory."[101]

During his years on the Massachusetts bench, Holmes became more sympathetic with Benthamite reformism—particularly toward the end of the 1890s, when he confronted the obdurately conservative response of the bench and bar to the demands of the labor movement. This experience drove him to write that it was "revolting" to retain dysfunctional rules of law supported by nothing more than "blind imitation of the past."[102] He advocated yet more strongly the practical use of legal history for "clearing away rubbish" by identifying those

97 *Id.*

98 *Id.*

99 *See* his anonymously published editorial note on the prosecution of the leaders of the British Gas Stokers' Strike. OLIVER WENDELL HOLMES, *Herbert Spencer: Legislation and Empiricism*, in BOOK NOTICES, *supra* note 70, at 104 (reprinting *Summary of Events: Great Britain*, 7 AM. L. REV. 582 (1873)).

100 THE COMMON LAW, *supra* note 23, at 33 (emphasis added). Holmes took the concept of the "survival" from the early English anthropologist Sir Edward Tylor. For a discussion of Tylor, *see* J. BURROW, *supra* note 35, at 234–59. Holmes cited Tylor's work in O.W. Holmes, *Primitive Notions in Modern Law* (pt. 1), in FORMATIVE ESSAYS, *supra* note 7, at 129, 135–36, 139 (reprinting *Primitive Notions in Modern Law*, 10 AM. L. REV. 422 (1876)).

101 THE COMMON LAW, *supra* note 23, at 33.

102 *The Path of the Law*, *supra* note 23, at 187.

rules that were "mere survivals" ripe for reform.[103] The ultimate aim was to produce a legal system in which "every rule ... is referred articulately and definitely to an end which it subserves, and ... the grounds for desiring that end are stated or are ready to be stated in words."[104] The law's postulates should ideally be established "upon accurately measured social desires instead of tradition."[105]

But these Benthamite words alone do not fully convey Holmes' views; he retained his historicist skepticism about the prospects for accurately measuring social desires. He did not believe that even with the help of "statistics and every modern appliance" there would ever be "a commonwealth in which science is everywhere supreme."[106] In practice, it was "only occasionally" possible to measure competing desires accurately; in the usual case, "the worth of the competing social ends ... cannot be reduced to number and accurately fixed."[107] On the question of the "worth" of different policies "in a more far-reaching sense than that of expressing the *de facto* will of the community for the time.... as yet no one has much to say."[108] Thus for him the notion of a code comprehensively justified on utilitarian grounds could never be more than an ideal providing inspiration for more limited changes.[109]

Holmes' attitude toward legal and political reform remained at bottom "an unconvinced conservatism."[110] "I don't believe much in anything that is," he once wrote to John Henry Wigmore, "but I believe a damned sight less in anything that isn't."[111] Precisely because he "rarely could be sure" that one rule "tends more than its opposite to the survival and welfare of the society where

---

103 *Law in Science, supra* note 24, at 225–26. Holmes thus articulated his pragmatic approach to history in a letter to Laski: "History has to be rewritten because history is the selection of those threads of causes or antecedents that we are interested in—and the interest changes in fifty years." 1 HOLMES-LASKI LETTERS, *supra* note 10, at 409 (letter dated Mar. 11, 1922).

104 *The Path of the Law, supra* note 23, at 186. Compare the similar discussion of legal classification in J. BENTHAM, *A Fragment on Government, supra* note 86, at 237.

105 *Law in Science, supra* note 24, at 225–26.

106 *Id.* at 242.

107 *Id.* at 231.

108 *Holdsworth's English Law, supra* note 91, at 288.

109 *See Law in Science, supra* note 24, at 242–43.

110 *Holdsworth's English Law, supra* note 91, at 289.

111 Letter From Oliver Wendell Holmes to John Henry Wigmore (Dec. 4, 1910), *quoted in* MARK DE WOLFE HOWE, JUSTICE OLIVER WENDELL HOLMES: THE PROVING YEARS, 1870–1882, at 198 (1963) [hereinafter M. HOWE, THE PROVING YEARS].

it is practiced,"[112] he was slow to depart from precedent. "Precisely my skepticism, my doubt as to the absolute worth of a large part of the system we administer, or of any other system, makes me very unwilling to increase the doubt as to what the court will do."[113] The only legal value that could be "assumed as certainly to be wished" was "that men should know the rules by which the game will be played."[114]

In fact, Holmes' conservatism was not always simply skeptical and "unconvinced." Alongside his pragmatic conception of the critical uses of history, he had a powerful streak of romantic antiquarianism. "I love the old," he wrote to Pollock.[115] "I feel . . . to my finger tips" a "reverence for venerable traditions," he said in a speech dedicating a memorial to the sailors of Ipswich, every sentence of which expresses his passionate attachment to the Massachusetts past.[116] The sentiment applied to law as well, where it produced some deep purple Holmesian rhetoric. The common law, growing "for near a thousand years," was "one of the vastest products of the human mind," a mighty system that had "the final title to respect that it exists, that it is not a Hegelian dream, but a part of the lives of men."[117]

As with most of his passions, Holmes had the capacity for self-critical distance from his antiquarianism. Thus he could write: "How delightful is the mixed emotion half noble, aesthetic—half fishy—that of the collector, with which one turns to ancient things . . . ."[118] He warned of the "deceptive charm" of legal history and the accompanying "pitfall of antiquarianism" into which lawyers were drawn by the "peculiar logical pleasure in making manifest the continuity between what we are doing and what has been done before."[119]

But awareness of the "peculiar" and "half fishy" pleasures of nostalgia did not always protect Holmes. His intended masterpiece, *The Common Law*, is deeply flawed by sentimental legalistic antiquarianism. His project in the book was to produce a doctrinal restatement of the common law that was guided by

---

112 O.W. HOLMES, *Twenty Years in Retrospect, supra* note 78, at 156.

113 *Id.*, *see also Law in Science, supra* note 24, at 239; *Holdsworth's English Law, supra* note 91, at 290; *cf.* Southern Pac. Co. v. Jensen, 244 U.S. 205, 221 (1917) (Holmes, J., dissenting); Stack v. New York, N.H. & Hart. R.R., 177 Mass. 155, 158–59, 58 N.E. 686, 687 (19).

114 *Holdsworth's English Law, supra* note 91, at 289.

115 2 HOLMES-POLLOCK LETTERS, *supra* note 8, at 123 (letter dated Nov. 5, 1923).

116 OLIVER WENDELL HOLMES, *Ipswich* (1902), in OCCASIONAL SPEECHES, *supra* note 78 at 136, 136.

117 *Learning and Science, supra* note 80, at 140; *The Path of the Law, supra* note 23, at 194; *see also* 1 HOLMES-POLLOCK LETTERS, *supra* note 8, at 24 (letter dated Nov. 5, 1883) (Holmes found Burke "marvelous great.").

118 1 HOLMES-LASKI LETTERS, *supra* note 10, at 64 (letter dated Feb. 27, 1917).

119 *The Path of the Law, supra* note 23, at 194; *Learning and Science, supra* note 80, at 139.

the demands of contemporary policy, using historical research primarily to identify anachronistic survivals. But Holmes' love of the old and the alluring logical pleasures of historical continuity led him repeatedly astray. The book today reads as a hodgepodge, honeycombed with passages in which ancient cases are treated not as objects of critical historical explanation, but as authoritative precedents, to which Holmes gave ingenious but tendentious lawyerly readings in support of controversial propositions of law he favored.[120]

Because Holmes' conservatism in both its skeptical and its romantic mode was so pervasive, it is important to see that it has no necessary connection with the basic pragmatist tenets that he so well articulated. Dewey, for example, welcomed Holmes as a philosophical kindred spirit even while recognizing that the two of them disagreed on many of the political questions of the day.[121] Dewey used pragmatist premises as a basis for an optimistic brand of activist liberal reformism. For him, the situated character of human belief and practice served a liberating rather than a Burkean and cautionary function; when he criticized the ascription of finality and universality to some set of local, customary, and partial principles, he conceived himself as removing an obstacle to social transformation.[122]

Others have made even more radical use of the pragmatist stress on context and situation. The point is that if theory is necessarily situated within and closely dependent upon practice, then current theory loses its claim to finality. Things now "impossible even in theory" become possible as theory adapts to changes in practice, themselves driven in part by earlier theory. That is the common-sense basis of the dialectical Marxist conception of revolutionary *praxis* and of the critique of ideology characteristic of much modern Marxism.[123] The application of this idea to law has been one of the central

120 The point was made first in 1882 in A.V. Dicey's review of *The Common Law*. *See* A.V. Dicey, *Holmes's "Common Law"*, The Spectator, Literary Supplement, June 3, 1882, at 745, *reprinted in* Touster, *supra* note 5, app. 2, at 712 [reprinted version hereinafter cited as *Dicey Review*]. For specific quotes, *see* note 258 *infra*. The point is made again, persuasively, in Gordon, *supra* note 3, at 733.

121 Dewey, *Justice Holmes and the Liberal Mind*, *supra* note 73, at 37, 43.

122 *See* John Dewey, Human Nature and Conduct, *supra* note 40, at 80–82; John Dewey, Liberalism and Social Action 48–50, *passim* (1935); J. Dewey, The Public and Its Problems, *supra* note 72, at 6–7.

123 "The materialist doctrine concerning the changing of circumstances and upbringing forgets that circumstances are changed by men and that it is essential to educate the educator himself.... The coincidence of the changing of circumstances and of human activity or self-changing can be conceived and rationally understood only as *revolutionary practice*."

themes of the Critical Legal Studies movement.[124] These radical uses are as consistent with a pragmatist framework as Dewey's liberal reformism or Holmes' skeptical conservatism.

From a certain philosophical perspective, Holmes' pragmatist theory of law is, like much pragmatist theory, essentially banal. At its most abstract level it concludes in truisms: Law is more a matter of experience than of logic, and experience is tradition interpreted with one eye on coherence and another on policy. Similarly, Peirce's critique of foundational epistemology did away with the exciting theories that had engaged great minds from Descartes to Kant and, if accepted, left nothing interesting to say at the most general level about how human beings acquire knowledge. In the same vein, almost all of Dewey's best work involved the critique of elegantly structured dualistic theories and their replacement with one version or another of his standard monistic (and monotonous) truisms: that generalizations tend to be situated instrumentalities marking temporary distinctions of degree, not absolute truths delineating sharp boundaries, and that some of them are good for some purposes in some contexts, others for other purposes in other contexts. After a pragmatist critique, the theory of the effect of separation on human relationships might come down to: sometimes "out of sight, out of mind," and sometimes "absence makes the heart grow fonder."

The payoff of pragmatist philosophy is thus often more in the critique than in the construction. This is why Dewey called philosophy "criticism" and metaphysics the "ground-map of the province of criticism."[125] Pragmatism rejects the maxim that you can only beat a theory with a better theory, when this carries with it such essentially aesthetic criteria of theory choice as elegance, rigor, and originality. No rational God guarantees in advance that important areas of practical activity will be governed by elegant theories. Certain useful theories, such as those concerning the motions of the heavenly bodies, do indeed turn out to be simple, rigorous, and altogether pleasing to the intellectual taste. On the other hand, the theories most helpful for understanding the weather are messy, complex, and unlovely, and they may always remain so.

Pragmatists thus tend to be theoreticians armed with a presumptive suspicion of neat theories; this is not because they despise neatness, but because they know how obsessively those drawn to theorizing love it. Thus, typically of

---

KARL MARX, *Theses on Feuerbach*, in THE GERMAN IDEOLOGY 121, 121 (C. Arthur ed. 1970) (discovered and originally published in 1888).

124 *See, e.g.*, Robert W. Gordon, *New Developments in Legal Theory*, in THE POLITICS OF LAW: A PROGRESSIVE CRITIQUE 281, 286 (D. Kairys ed. 1982).

125 J. DEWEY, EXPERIENCE AND NATURE, *supra* note 19, at 412–13.

pragmatist theory, Holmes' central point about judges' law was a critical one; law *isn't* "logic" in Langdell's exciting and geometrically precise sense.[126] It was partly to avoid a discursive vacuum, and partly to nudge practice roughly in the right direction, that he added the vague constructive alternative that law *is* "experience," by which he meant an indefinite mixture of habit, instrumental reason, and the search for internal coherence. Dewey used the term "experience," and his other favorite, "situation," in very much the same way, as designedly vague terms meant to give a sense of partial closure and some approximate practical remapping of the conceptual space his critique had vacated.[127]

Within the field of legal practice and ideology, the Holmesian slogan about the primacy of experience over logic serves as a guide and morale-booster to practitioners and scholars who work in a context in which Langdellian formalism retains a primeval and often unrecognized power. But from an external philosophical perspective that evaluates theories according to their intrinsic intellectual interest, the slogan has nothing much to recommend it. No doubt this is why books about legal philosophy discuss Holmes' "prediction theory" much more than his maxim about logic and experience. The idea that statements of law are no more than predictions of judicial decisions is bold, reductive, and stimulating; it is also easily discredited if treated as a general definition of law, good for all purposes. But that is not how Holmes intended it. The conception of law he recommended to judges and other authoritative interpreters is to be found in the inspired imprecision of his account of law as experience.

III Law as Logic

Before we come to consider Holmes' prediction theory, it will be helpful to take account of the role of logic in his overall approach to theory within law. As we consider this subject, we come upon an apparent Holmesian paradox. Led by the late Grant Gilmore, revisionists have recently drawn attention to the fact

126 *See* text accompanying notes 133, 147–148, 162 *infra*.

127 Rorty pushes this point further than I would and criticizes Dewey's tendency to supply vague affirmative accounts to replace the rigorous but misleading theories that were the object of his critique. RICHARD RORTY, *Dewey's Metaphysics*, in CONSEQUENCES OF PRAGMATISM, *supra* note 12, at 72. In my view, the affirmative accounts are essential; Dewey's promotion of an alternative metaphysics organized around appropriately vague (but never wholly contentless) concepts like "experience" and "the situation" responds to a widespread and entirely legitimate human need for basic concepts, ontological ultimates, an overall "groundmap" or world-picture, even in the absence of epistemological foundations.

that much of Holmes' actual work was devoted to the abstract and conceptual ordering of doctrine into a structured and coherent system[128]—in other words, the kind of doctrinal legal "logic" that Langdell specialized in and that Holmes so famously contrasted with "experience." How are we to reconcile these doctrinal labors, which mark Holmes as one of the leading practitioners of classical nineteenth-century legal science, with his own celebrated critique of that enterprise? The answer is that although Holmes was indeed a conceptualist, he viewed legal systematization as a practical aid in teaching and understanding law. Unlike Langdell, Holmes did not believe doctrinal conceptualization could produce a deductive system that would make legal reasoning formal and scientific.

The revisionist commentators have correctly pointed to an aspect of Holmes' work not sufficiently stressed before. The project behind *The Common Law* was avowedly doctrinal and conceptual: "to make known the content of the law; that is, to work upon it from within, or logically, arranging and distributing it, in order, from its *summum genus* to its *infima species*, so far as practicable."[129] Holmes sought to replace the old arrangement of Anglo-American private law, based on Blackstone and the writ system, with a new "philosophical" structure organized around the categories of contract and tort. Supplementing this recategorization, he also sought to focus private law doctrine around the generalization that legal standards, even when misleadingly phrased in terms of internal and subjective states of mind, actually tended to make liability turn on the objective question whether the actor's external conduct matched that which was to be expected of the typical member of the community, the "reasonable man." And to a large extent, in collaboration with Langdell, Ames, Wigmore, Keener, and others, Holmes succeeded: By the end of the century, the new doctrinal classification, and to a lesser degree the generalization of the "external" standard of liability, had come to dominate teaching and professional commentary in private law.[130]

---

128 G. Gilmore, The Death of Contract, *supra* note 3, at 14–53; G. Gilmore, The Ages of American Law, *supra* note 3, at 48–56; Gordon, *supra* note 3, at 726–29.

129 The Common Law, *supra* note 23, at 173.

130 The best account of this doctrinal reclassification remains Duncan Kennedy, The Rise and Fall of Classical Legal Thought 1850–1940 (Oct. 1975) (unpublished manuscript) (on file with the author). On Holmes' central role in the classical reordering of tort law, *see* G. Edward White, Tort Law in America 12–19 (1980). On his role in the development of classical contract doctrine, *see* G. Gilmore, The Death of Contract, *supra* note 3, at 14–53. For the triumph of the external standard, see Pollock's letter of 1893: "Nemesis is upon us. The reasonable man and the 'external standard' have filtered down to the common examination candidate, who is beginning to write horrible nonsense about

In his earliest theoretical work, Holmes attempted to follow Austin's lead and develop a universal scheme for the classification of legal duties. By the mid-1870s, however, he had come to doubt that the concept of legal duty was sufficiently general to serve as the basis for any such ordering. And in the process he had lost interest in universal schemes—which he later called "striving for a useless quintessence of all systems, instead of an accurate anatomy of one."[131]

But the anatomical metaphor itself suggests his continued interest in the structural treatment of legal concepts. As he wrote to James Bryce in 1879, Holmes' aim in *The Common Law* was to "analyse what seem to me the fundamental notions and principles of our substantive law, putting them in an order which is a part of or results from the fundamental conceptions."[132] This is not a project obviously different from the one Langdell stated in his much-quoted manifesto of classical legal science:

> Law, considered as a science, consists of certain principles or doctrines.... If these doctrines could be so classified and arranged that each should be found in its proper place, and nowhere else, they would cease to be formidable from their number.[133]

Nor did Holmes abandon the conceptualist enterprise after he went on the bench.[134] Almost two decades after *The Common Law*, in *The Path of the Law*, Holmes' most comprehensive statement of his mature legal theory, he restated

---

them." Letter from Frederick Pollock to Holmes (Aug. 31, 1893), *reprinted in* 1 HOLMES-POLLOCK LETTERS, *supra* note 8, at 46.

131 *The Path of the Law*, *supra* note 23, at 196–97. For an example of the idea of "general jurisprudence" which Holmes was criticizing, *see* J. AUSTIN, THE PROVINCE OF JURISPRUDENCE, *supra* note 26, at 366–69, 373.

132 Letter from Holmes to James Bryce (Aug. 1879), *quoted in* M. HOWE, THE PROVING YEARS, *supra* note 111, at 25. In another letter written in 1879, Holmes said his purpose was to "make a new and more fundamental analysis" of the "cardinal principles and conceptions of the law" so as to make "a new Jurisprudence or new first book of the law." Letter from Holmes to Arthur Sedgwick (July 12, 1879), *quoted in* Gordon, *supra* note 3, at 719.

133 1 CHRISTOPHER COLUMBUS LANGDELL, A SELECTION OF CASES ON THE LAW OF CONTRACTS viii–ix (2d ed. 1879).

134 For the contrary view that Holmes' experience as a judge led him to abandon his interest in the conceptualist "arrangement of the law," *see* Mark Tushnet, *The Logic of Experience: Oliver Wendell Holmes on the Supreme Judicial Court*, 63 VA. L. REV. 975, 1045–46 (1977); and G. Edward White, *The Integrity of Holmes' Jurisprudence*, 10 HOFSTRA L. REV. 633, 649–51 (1982).

in the strongest terms his dedication to conceptualism. The "most important" point of "every new effort of legal thought" was to "generalize [the law] into a thoroughly connected system," made up, as Langdell had insisted, of a "not unmanageably large" number of legal principles.[135] To thus systematize legal doctrine, the jurist must "look straight through all the dramatic incidents" presented by a case, analyze it in purely legal terms, and recognize the application of the broadest rules. The failure to get past the merely "dramatic" led jurists to write useless books on the law of subjects such as "Railroads or Telegraphs."[136]

The Legal Realists in their critique of conceptual jurisprudence would later seek (without much success) to reorder the law around just such "functional" and "real-world" topic headings. And ironically the Realists claimed Holmes as their chief authority in the assault upon the classical doctrinal framework of legal thought—a framework that he had helped to build.[137] In addition to his slogan about logic and experience, consider these other Holmesian taglines that served, and still serve, as battle cries in the never-ending War Against Langdell: "Law, being a practical thing, must found itself on actual forces";[138] "The important phenomenon is . . . the justice and reasonableness of a decision, not its consistency with previously held views";[139] "[T]he real justification of a rule of law, if there be one, is that it helps to bring about a social end which we desire";[140] "General propositions do not decide concrete cases."[141]

Nor did the Realists simply misconstrue the object of Holmes' critique in these famous passages. The line about logic and experience first appeared in

135 *The Path of the Law, supra* note 23, at 168–69. Holmes later repeated that his ambition was to give the law a "continuous, logical, philosophical exposition." Oliver Wendell Holmes, *Speech at Bar Dinner* (19), in Collected Legal Papers, 244, 245 (1920) [hereinafter *Speech at Bar Dinner*]. Holmes there explained that although he had not been able to realize this ambition as a judge, he would never abandon the project. Even after retiring from the Supreme Court in 1932, he spoke of "writing a little book embodying my views on the ultimates of the law." "[B]ut," he went on to say, "I have expressed them *passim* and I desire only repose. I am persuading myself that one has no duties at 91." 2 Holmes-Pollock Letters, *supra* note 8, at 307 (letter dated Apr. 5, 1932).

136 *The Path of the Law, supra* note 23, at 196.

137 *See, e.g.*, J. Frank, *supra* note 1, at 253–60.

138 The Common Law, *supra* note 23, at 168.

139 Book Notice, 14 Am. L. Rev. 233, 234 (1880) (unsigned review; for attribution to Holmes, *see* M. Howe, The Proving Years, *supra* note 111, at 155–57) [hereinafter *Langdell Review*].

140 *Law in Science, supra* note 24, at 238.

141 Lochner v. New York, 198 u.s. 45, 76 (1905) (Holmes, J., dissenting).

Holmes' unsigned review of Langdell's *Summary of Contract*,[142] where the context makes clear that Langdellian legal conceptualism was indeed the conception of "law as logic" that Holmes had in mind.[143] Later he referred to the "fallacy" that a system of law "can be worked out like mathematics from some general axioms of conduct."[144] In *The Common Law* he described two forms of the mistake of considering the law "only from its formal side": attempting "to deduce the *corpus* from *a priori* postulates," and "the humbler error of supposing the science of the law to reside in the *elegantia juris*, or logical cohesion of part with part."[145]

It is not difficult to identify the two groups of legal logicians Holmes had in mind. Those who would deduce the content of the law from *a priori* postulates were the German Pandectist legal scientists; they purported to found their universalized version of Roman law on neo-Kantian first principles of justice.[146] Closer to home were those who portrayed the law as an entirely self-contained geometric system of axioms, theorems, and proofs, generated by constructing the simplest and most elegant internally consistent set of principles that could organize and reconcile most of the cases; for Holmes, these were the Langdellians, as his review of Langdell's book confirms beyond doubt.[147]

How can we reconcile Holmes' critique of Langdell and the German Pandectists with his own highly conceptualistic doctrinal work? Holmes supplies an important partial answer in the practical conception of logic that he shared with Dewey and the pragmatists. As we shall see later, Holmes' answer is only a partial one; he loved the logical manipulation of doctrine for its own sake nearly as much as Langdell did, and this could lead him astray in practice. But he differed from Langdell in possessing a coherent and useful working conception of the point and place of doctrinal concepts and principles in the law.

Unlike many of the Legal Realists, Holmes greatly valued the role of conceptual systems in legal study, but unlike Langdell, he saw that role as a subordinate one. For Langdell, the fundamental principles of the common law, once extracted by induction from the cases, had the status of axiomatic general

142 C.C. LANGDELL, A SUMMARY OF THE LAW OF CONTRACTS (2d ed. 1880).

143 *See* M. HOWE, THE PROVING YEARS, *supra* note 111, at 155–58.

144 *The Path of the Law*, *supra* note 23, at 180.

145 THE COMMON LAW, *supra* note 23, at 32.

146 Holmes later makes clear that the German Pandectists are the target of his critique. *Id.* at 163–68.

147 *See Langdell Review*, *supra* note 139, at 233–34. For my own analysis of Langdell's geometric vision of legal thought, *see* Thomas C. Grey, *Langdell's Orthodoxy*, 45 U. PITT. L. REV. 1 (1983).

truths; they *were the law*, and individual decisions shown to conflict with them were thereby shown to have been wrongly decided.[148] Holmes, by contrast, considered the same general principles to be guidelines, rules of thumb, instruments of inquiry designed as practical aids to making sound decisions. They were not like mathematical axioms; the very generality of their terms guaranteed that their application would give rise to difficult or borderline cases, in which judges would have to exercise "the sovereign prerogative of choice."[149] In exercising that prerogative, judges would be guided, consciously or not, by "views of public policy" and "considerations of social advantage."[150] And this was as it should be, for the principles were meant only as intermediate premises designed to guide judges toward decisions in the public interest.

The contrast between Holmes' and Langdell's views can be illustrated by their respective treatment of the "mailbox rule" chestnut—the question of when a contractual proposal accepted by mail became binding. For Langdell, there was only one acceptable answer: The doctrine of consideration required that there must be a return promise before there could be a contract, and by its very nature a promise could not be complete until communicated. Hence the decisions holding that a contract became binding when the letter of acceptance was mailed were simply wrongly decided. Once it was shown that these decisions were inconsistent with established principle, any arguments that the rule they embodied was more just or more practical were simply "irrelevant."[151]

By contrast, Holmes, who accepted the same general view of the consideration doctrine as did Langdell, believed that no general principle could deductively settle such a question of legal detail. He criticized Langdell's treatment of this issue as that of a "legal theologian."[152] On a question at the borderline of an established legal principle, "[i]f convenience preponderates in favor of either view, that is a sufficient reason for its adoption."[153] And a rigid rule prohibiting contract formation without actual communication would violate practical common sense; it would mean, most inconveniently, that "if the letter had been delivered to the promisee and was then snatched from his hands before he had read it, there would be no contract."[154]

148 *See* Grey, *supra* note 147, at 11–13, 16–20.

149 *Law in Science*, *supra* note 24, at 239.

150 The Common Law, *supra* note 23, at 32; *The Path of the Law*, *supra* note 23, at 184.

151 C. Langdell, *supra* note 142, at 15, 20–21. I discuss Langdell's approach to arguments of justice and policy in Grey, *supra* note 147, at 13–15.

152 *Langdell Review*, *supra* note 139, at 234.

153 The Common Law, *supra* note 23, at 239.

154 *Id.* at 240; *cf. id.* at 167 (on the propriety of the "sacrifice of principle to convenience").

Holmes' attitude toward the place of principles in legal reasoning is likewise illustrated when we put his slogan "[g]eneral propositions do not decide concrete cases" back into its context within his *Lochner* dissent.[155] The general principle Holmes referred to was one he had just stated and relied on himself: "[A] constitution is not intended to embody a particular economic theory."[156] He meant his famous slogan only to qualify, not to negate, the force of this general principle, a principle which would if accepted "carry us far toward the end."[157] The principle did not deductively decide *Lochner*; one might accept it and yet strike down the maximum hours law, characterizing liberty of contract not as part of a controversial and historically transient economic theory but rather as a fundamental aspect of personal liberty. Yet Holmes believed that a judge who approached the case guided by this principle would be nudged in the direction of the correct decision.

Holmes first clearly articulated his view of general doctrines as guidelines and legal distinctions as matters of degree early in his career. There was no single idea about law that he repeated so often or was so proud of:

> The growth of the law is very apt to take place in this way: Two widely different cases suggest a general distinction, which is a clear one when stated broadly. But as new cases cluster around the opposite poles, and begin to approach one another, the distinction becomes more difficult to trace; the determinations are made one way or the other on a very slight preponderance of feeling, rather than articulate reason; and at last a mathematical line is arrived at by the contact of contrary decisions, which is so far arbitrary that it might equally well have been drawn a little further to the one side or to the other. The distinction between the groups, however, is philosophical, and it is better to have a line drawn somewhere

155 Lochner v. New York, 198 U.S. 45, 76 (1905) (Holmes, J., dissenting). The line was a Holmesian "chestnut," often repeated in various forms. *See, e.g.*, Otis v. Parker, 187 U.S. 606, 608 (1903); Vegelahn v. Guntner, 167 Mass. 92, 106, 44 N.E. 1077, 1080 (1896) (Holmes, J., dissenting); *See also* 1 HOLMES-LASKI LETTERS, *supra* note 10, at 243 (letter dated Feb. 19, 1920) ("I always say in conference that no case can be settled by general propositions, that I will admit any general proposition you like and decide the case either way."); *id.* at 390 (letter dated Dec. 22, 1921) (virtually identical statement).

156 *Lochner*, 198 U.S. at 75 (Holmes, J., dissenting).

157 *Id.* at 76 (Holmes, J., dissenting). Similarly, Holmes concluded an essay setting forth general principles of tort law with the words "my object is not to decide cases, but to make a little clearer the method to be followed in deciding them." OLIVER WENDELL HOLMES, *Privilege, Malice and Intent* (1894), in COLLECTED LEGAL PAPERS 117, 137 (1920) [hereinafter *Privilege, Malice and Intent*].

> in the penumbra between darkness and light, than to remain in uncertainty.[158]

When Holmes says that the distinctions between legal categories are "philosophical," he means (among other things) that the concepts defining and structuring those distinctions are fundamental in a practical sense, superior to alternative frames of analysis for purposes of decision.[159] He does not mean, however, that legal decisions follow deductively from "the very nature" of legal categories like contract or tort, or legal concepts like consideration or proximate cause.[160] To paraphrase Holmes' view, a fundamental legal concept, necessarily general and imprecise, applies with decreasing certainty to fact situations as they diverge from its paradigm instance.[161] In the area where neighboring concepts overlap, legal decision must assign disputed particular cases to one or another on grounds not deducible from the internal structure of the concepts.

To fix the contrast between Holmes' and Langdell's views of the place of legal principles, it is useful to distinguish between conceptualism and formalism. Conceptualism is the project of structuring law into a system of classification made up of relatively abstract principles and categories; formalism is the project of making law certain by making legal reasoning deductive. Both

---

158 Holmes, *The Theory of Torts* (1873), in FORMATIVE ESSAYS, *supra* note 7, at 117, 119 (reprinting *The Theory of Torts*, 7 AM. L. REV. 652 (1873)) [hereinafter *The Theory of Torts*]. For a few among the many repetitions of the point, *see*, for example, THE COMMON LAW, *supra* note 23, at 101; *Law in Science*, *supra* note 24, at 232. Chief Justice Charles Doe of New Hampshire repeated the gist of the idea in his opinion in Stewart v. Emerson, 52 N.H. 301, 314 (1872). With characteristic jealousy, Holmes resented Doe's failure to give him credit; he later characterized Doe, in many ways a better judge than he, as "second-rate." The controversy is explored by Doe's biographer John Philip Reid in Reid, *Brandy in His Water: Correspondence Between Doe, Holmes and Wigmore*, 57 NW. U.L. REV. 522 (1962). Ironically, Holmes seems to have picked up the idea he was so proud of from Nicholas St. John Green. *See* NICHOLAS ST. JOHN GREEN, *Insanity in Criminal Law*, in ESSAYS AND NOTES ON THE LAW OF TORT AND CRIME, 161, 166–67 (1933) (reprinting Book Notice, 5 AM. L. REV. 704 (1871)).

159 There was more to what Holmes meant by "philosophical" than this. *See* text accompanying notes 259–263, 265–268 *infra*.

160 Holmes describes the demand for a doctrine of property based upon "internal juristic necessity drawn from the nature of possession itself" as expressing "a characteristic yearning of the German mind." THE COMMON LAW, *supra* note 23, at 164. Coming from him, this was not a compliment.

161 Compare the well-known discussion of the "open texture" of language and its significance for the law in H.L.A. HART, THE CONCEPT OF LAW 121–32 (1961).

Holmes and Langdell were conceptualists; both were formalists. But they differed in how they conceived the relation between the two projects. For Langdell, the two were integrated; formality was to be achieved through the conceptualist enterprise itself. The general principles must serve as axioms constituting a deductive system that would make legal reasoning exact and scientific.[162]

For Holmes, by contrast, the conceptualist goal of coherent order and the formalist goal of objective predictability had to be pursued by different means. The concepts that were best for classificatory purposes, by virtue of their very generality, could not be applied exactly and predictably in deciding particular cases. Their application invariably involved inexact judgments of degree. The only way to achieve certain and predictable law was to artificially fix "a mathematical line" at some relatively arbitrary point within the penumbra where opposing concepts overlapped. For example, the law started with the distinction between infancy and adulthood, and ended with a line at age twenty-one; it began with the genuinely distinct but fuzzily bounded notions of night and day, and ended with a statute drawing the line at one hour before sunrise and one hour after sunset.[163]

Langdell thought of legal categories and principles as ideal realities which the legal scientist could discover and describe and which a judge could simply follow. By contrast, Holmes' primary criterion for assessing legal concepts was instrumental; legal principles were "correct" insofar as they served a practical purpose, and that purpose was typically a heuristic one. A principle was an indexing device that guided the lawyer to relevantly similar cases, while at the same time guiding the judge to the policy considerations relevant in deciding the hard cases that fell under it. Holmes stated the heuristic aim in one of his earliest essays, claiming "the end of all classification should be to make the law *knowable*."[164] He repeated the point a quarter century later in *The Path of the Law*: The aim of conceptual arrangement was to make the law "easier to be remembered and to be understood."[165]

---

162 For a fuller discussion of conceptualism, formalism, and Langdell's combination of the two, *see* Grey, *supra* note 147, at 6–15.

163 *Law in Science*, *supra* note 24, at 232. For other examples, *see* The Common Law, *supra* note 23, at 101–02.

164 Holmes, *The Arrangement of the Law: Privity*, in Formative Essays, *supra* note 7, at 95, 96 n. 2 (reprinting *The Arrangement of the Law: Privity*, 7 Am. L. Rev. 46 (1872)) [hereinafter *The Arrangement of the Law: Privity*].

165 *The Path of the Law*, *supra* note 23, at 168.

Holmes' practical heuristic criterion made "telegraphs" an inappropriate category because grouping cases on this subject did not efficiently organize legal knowledge for the law student, the lawyer, or the judge. Courts did not decide cases according to whether telegraph companies were involved. By contrast, Holmes said, "marine insurance" was a proper subdivision of contract law because "the fact that the agreement was of that sort has attached to it further and more specific consequences, such as the implied warranty of seaworthiness, which cannot be reduced under any more general head."[166]

The efficiency of conceptual schemes cannot be determined in the abstract where the aim is a practical heuristic one. Holmes often made this point by denying Langdellian claims of *scientific* status to the activity of legal categorization. "Law is not a science, but is essentially empirical. Hence, although the general arrangement should be philosophical, even at the expense of disturbing prejudices, compromises with practical convenience are highly proper."[167] Or as he wrote in direct criticism of Langdell's treatment of the law of contract:

> As a branch of anthropology, law is an object of science; the theory of legislation is a scientific study; but the effort to reduce the concrete details of an existing system to the merely logical consequence of simple postulates is always in danger of becoming unscientific, and of leading to a misapprehension of the nature of the problem and the data.[168]

In conceptually ordering the law, Holmes thought a practical balance must be struck between the claims of habit on the one hand, and those of taxonomic efficiency on the other. He favored retaining certain legal concepts even though we would not adopt them if we were arranging the law from scratch; the costs of relearning and reindexing would outweigh the gains from added clarity. Holmes mentioned the concept of ownership and the (since generally aban-

---

166 Oliver Wendell Holmes, *Codification and Scientific Classification of the Law*, in Book Notices, *supra* note 70, at 59, 60–61 (reprinting Book Notice, 7 Am. L. Rev. 318 (1873)).

167 *Codes, and the Arrangement of the Law, supra* note 95, at 80.

168 *Langdell Review, supra* note 139, at 234. In 1925, Holmes wrote to his young friend Dr. John Wu, who had written an essay praising the German neo-Kantian legal theorist Rudolf Stammler:

> "Perhaps your phrase legal *science* indicates the beginning of our divergence... [W]hen it comes to the development of *a corpus juris* the ultimate question is what do the dominant forces of the community want and do they want it hard enough to disregard whatever inhibitions may stand in the way."

Oliver Wendell Holmes, *Letters to Dr. Wu*, in Book Notices, *supra* note 70, at 149, 187 (letter dated Aug. 26, 1926) [hereinafter *Letters to Dr. Wu*].

doned) category of the law of persons as examples of taxonomically awkward legal notions that were probably too well entrenched to be worth replacing.[169] But the benefits of conceptual efficiency and the costs of inertia were real. A quarter of a century later, still pursuing the same themes, Holmes said: "Our forms of contract, instead of being made once [and] for all, like a yacht, on lines of least resistance, are accidental relics of early notions. . . ."[170]

Since the heyday of the Realists, legal thinkers have tended to assume that legal taxonomy and conceptual doctrine-building necessarily rest on Langdellian premises. Behind this assumption often lies the instinctive nominalism, or cult of the concrete, that denies all practical importance to generalization and abstraction. Yet no pragmatist would endorse such an antipathy to generalization. All the major pragmatist figures accepted and asserted the importance of general principles and systematic thought; they insisted only that the test of abstractions must be their usefulness for action and concrete inquiry. Peirce in particular abhorred nominalism and argued for the independent reality of universals.[171] And other pragmatists who did not share his metaphysical views nevertheless agreed with him about the practical importance of coherent and systematic generalization in all fields of human thought. In a 1924 essay, Dewey applied this standard pragmatist position to legal thought:

> [L]ogical systematization with a view to the utmost generality and consistency of propositions is indispensable but is not ultimate. It is an instrumentality, not an end. It is a means of improving, facilitating, clarifying the inquiry that leads up to concrete decisions .... It is most important that rules of law should form as coherent generalized logical systems as possible.[172]

He could have been paraphrasing Holmes; indeed he probably was.

Holmes had written that "[a] generalization is empty so far as it is general. Its value depends on the number of particulars which it calls up to the speaker and the hearer."[173] He did not mean by this that generalization was useless and

169 *Codes, and the Arrangement of the Law, supra* note 95, at 80.

170 *Learning and Science, supra* note 80, at 139.

171 Charles Sanders Peirce, *Lectures on Pragmatism*, in 5 Collected Papers of Charles Sanders Peirce, *supra* note 37, paras. 93–101.

172 Dewey, *Logical Method and Law, supra* note 72, at 19.

173 *Law in Science, supra* note 24, at 240. This was another of Holmes' "chestnuts," and he repeated its substance often. *See, e.g., Letters to Dr. Wu, supra* note 168, at 167 (letter dated Sept. 20, 1923) ("[T]he only use of a pint pot is to present the beer (or whatever lawful liquid it may contain), and infinite meditation upon the pot never will give you the beer.").

should be abandoned, no more than when he wrote that he would "admit any general proposition that anyone wants to lay down and decide the case either way."[174] Though he rejected the Langdellian conception of principles as axiomatic foundations for legal decision, he found great value in a system of general legal principles which could call to mind just those rules, cases, and considerations of policy that were useful in deciding the matter at hand.[175]

Indeed, all the leading Anglo-American legal thinkers of the period from about 1870 to 1920 were conceptualists in the same sense. They all would have rejected the later Legal Realist project of breaking the general and abstract concepts of the law into narrow categories and type-situations based in extra-legal experience.[176] The legal thinkers of Holmes' generation confronted a practical historical situation that impressed upon them the need for a new and perspicuous categorical arrangement of the common law. With the demise of the writ system, the organization of cases around the traditional forms of action was breaking down.[177] Blackstone's arrangement of the common law, the basis of elementary legal education for a century, had become obsolete; its scheme had served as a transition between a feudal status-based and a liberal market-based legal system, and the period of transition was over.[178] The spread of university-based legal education had created new demand for an intelligible arrangement of curriculum and courses, and as members of a new full-time law professoriate, with the time and the incentive to do scholarship, Holmes' contemporaries saw meeting that demand as their primary task and opportunity.

---

174 1 HOLMES-LASKI LETTERS, *supra* note 10, at 390 (letter dated Dec. 22, 1921).

175 *See* THE COMMON LAW, *supra* note 23, at 173; OLIVER WENDELL HOLMES, *The Use of Law Schools* (1886), in COLLECTED LEGAL PAPERS, 35, 41–42 (1920) [hereinafter *The Use of Law Schools*]; *The Path of the Law, supra* note 23, at 168, 195–202.

176 One articulation of the Realist preference for narrow and real-world categories is Karl N. Llewellyn, *Some Realism About Realism*, 44 HARV. L. REV. 1222 (1930). Holmes, in comparison, preferred "tort" and "contract" as legal categories over "shipping" and "telegraphs." *See The Path of the Law, supra* note 23, at 196. In his memoirs, Williston focused upon the preference for narrow categories as the only idea of the Legal Realists that he wholly rejected. SAMUEL WILLISTON, LIFE AND LAW 208–09, 213–14 (1940).

177 Holmes himself emphasized the disappearance of the forms of action as one of the factors facilitating his kind of conceptual rearrangement of common law doctrine. Other factors were "[t]he philosophical habit of the day, the frequency of legislation, and the ease with which the law may be changed to meet the opinions and wishes of the public"; these contributed to a situation in which "judges as well as others should openly discuss the legislative principles upon which their decisions must always rest in the end. . . ." THE COMMON LAW, *supra* note 23, at 64.

178 *See* Duncan Kennedy, *The Structure of Blackstone's Commentaries*, 28 BUFFALO L. REV., 205, 231–34 (1979).

While conceptualism was universal during the classical period of Anglo-American legal thought, adherence to the Langdellian notion of legal science was not. Not only Holmes, but Gray, Nicholas St. John Green, Thayer, and Wigmore, and in the next generation Arthur Corbin—conceptualists all in their legal scholarship—were critics of (or at least deviants from) Langdellianism. They did not accept Langdell's insistence that legal thought could and should be autonomous and universally formal as well as conceptually ordered. They did not aspire to make common law reasoning exact and deductive by excluding considerations of justice and social policy. Conceptual system-building had a significant but subordinate place in the law for them; they treated principles, categories, and taxonomies as instruments for use in the process of legal inquiry rather than its end result.[179]

It was Holmes who best articulated the view of the place of doctrinal "logic" that these early critics of classical Langdellian legal science shared. He can be fairly criticized for preaching better than he practiced the subordination of conceptual elegance and the primacy of convenience and justice.[180] But his preachments on this subject, greatly influential when he produced them, and surviving through the years by virtue of the lasting power of his literary art, remain one of the most valuable of his legacies to American law.

IV Law as Prediction

With a sense of Holmes' instrumental approach to theorizing in mind, we are in a better position to understand what he is best known for by legal philosophers—his statement that "[t]he prophecies of what the courts will

179 For Gray's criticism of Langdell, *see* M. HOWE, THE PROVING YEARS, *supra* note 111, at 158. For Green's practical and policy-oriented approach to the law, see almost any of the pieces in N. GREEN, *supra* note 158. *Proximate and Remote Cause, id.* at 1, is the best known, but just as notable are *Contributory Negligence on the Part of an Infant, id.* at 18, 24–26, and *Married Women, id.* at 31, a powerful argument which concludes: "The law of the status of women is the last vestige of slavery." *Id.* at 48. For the pragmatism of Thayer and Wigmore, see almost any passage from their treatises on the law of evidence. *E.g.*, JAMES BRADLEY THAYER, PRELIMINARY TREATISE ON EVIDENCE AT THE COMMON LAW 484–89 (1898) (introducing the "best evidence rule"); 1 JOHN HENRY WIGMORE, A TREATISE ON THE SYSTEM OF EVIDENCE IN TRIALS AT COMMON LAW §§ 24–36 (1904) (introducing "general theory of relevancy"). No one can doubt that Corbin was a critic of Langdellianism, but his multi-volume treatise on contract law also attests to his careful attention to the conceptual structure of the subject. *See* ARTHUR LINTON CORBIN, CORBIN ON CONTRACTS: A COMPREHENSIVE TREATISE ON THE RULES OF CONTRACT LAW (1950).

180 *See* texts accompanying notes 246–271, 298–310 *infra*.

do in fact, and nothing more pretentious, are what I mean by the law."[181] This has come to be enshrined in the orthodox jurisprudence textbooks as "the prediction theory," where it competes with "right reason," "tradition and custom," "the command of the sovereign," and "the behavior of officials" to be accepted as the ultimate definition of law.[182]

Holmes developed the prediction theory during the early 1870s at the same time that he was attending the meetings of the Metaphysical Club at which the pragmatic movement was founded. For this reason especially, intellectual historians have taken a keen interest in the connection between this theory and the doctrines of pragmatism.[183] They have stressed the reductive aspects of Holmes' theory: the analysis of statements about "the law" as predictions of judges' decisions, and the analysis of the decision in terms of the remedy. These elements are indeed consistent with pragmatic analysis, particularly of the sort Peirce favored, but they equally follow from the application to law of the scientific positivism of Bentham, Austin, and Mill.

Actually, the distinctively pragmatic aspect of Holmes' approach was the practical conception of jurisprudential theory that it embodied. When Holmes defined law as the prediction of judicial action, he was theorizing in the pragmatist way, contextually and instrumentally. The context and the purposes Holmes had in mind were those defined by a limited but particularly important legal perspective, that of a private lawyer counseling a client. Once this perspectival limitation is seen, most of the standard objections against the prediction theory drop away.

Holmes divided legal thought and discourse between the categories of the theoretical and the practical in two quite different ways. First, he distinguished between treating law practically (from the inside) as a working body of rules, concepts, and techniques meant to guide private and official decisions and treating it theoretically (from the outside) as an object of historical or anthropological investigation or a stimulus to philosophical speculation.[184] Second, within the internal ("practical" in the first sense) treatment of law, he distinguished between the practical (everyday, relatively concrete) formulations

181 *The Path of the Law, supra* note 23, at 173.

182 Since Holmes was at least as much concerned to direct attention to what courts "do in fact"—that is, the remedies they grant—as he was to recast propositions of law in predictive form, "the predicted remedy theory" would better capture his double emphasis. But I will stay with the standard nomenclature.

183 *See, e.g.*, M. Fisch, *supra* note 6.

184 *See, e.g., Law in Science, supra* note 24, at 211; *Introduction to the General Survey, supra* note 68, at 300–01.

used by the working practitioner, and the theoretical (academic, relatively abstract) discourse of the teacher or doctrinal commentator. The predictive analysis of law is a theory only in the second sense; it is a relatively abstract and general formulation, but it is practical in the sense of internal to the law, rooted in the activity of legal practice, and conceived instrumentally as a means for carrying on that activity. This pragmatic conception of internal theory underlay Holmes' remarks to the effect that theory was "not to be feared as unpractical" and that "even for practical purposes" it "generally turns out the most important thing in the end."[185]

This pragmatic perspective on legal theory was not standard in Holmes' time, and even today it is by no means commonly made explicit. Typically, the kind of analytical jurisprudence pursued by Bentham, Austin, and their successors has not been seen in these practical terms, but rather as a scientific analysis of legal phenomena. Analytical jurisprudence thus presents itself as "philosophy of law"—an external account of legal phenomena purporting to be truth for truth's sake, using the apparatus of another discipline, as does "history of law" or "anthropology of law." This standard view—which treats jurisprudence as theoretical in the first or external sense described above—is implicit, for example, in T.E. Holland's statements that "an exposition of existing law is obviously quite another thing from a science of law," and that jurisprudence, in contrast to law as such, is the "formal science of those relations of mankind which are generally recognised as having legal consequences."[186]

In comparison, Holmes saw jurisprudence as internal to the legal enterprise, "simply law in its most generalized part," so that "the process [of legal thought] is one, from a lawyer's statement of a case... up to the final analyses and

---

185 *The Path of the Law, supra* note 23, at 2; OLIVER WENDELL HOLMES, *The Theory of Legal Interpretation* (1899), in COLLECTED LEGAL PAPERS 203, 209 (1920).

186 THOMAS ERSKINE HOLLAND, THE ELEMENTS OF JURISPRUDENCE 4, 8 (4th ed. 1888). Consider in this light Sarah Austin's recollection of her husband's remark that he " 'ought to have been a schoolman of the twelfth century—or a German professor.' " Sarah Austin, *Preface* to 1 J. AUSTIN, LECTURES ON JURISPRUDENCE 1, 12 (5th ed. 1885) (2d ed. 1861). For Austin, the laws were one thing—sovereign commands, backed by force, aimed at social utility. The principles of jurisprudence or legal science were quite another—discoveries, axioms and theorems, conceptual truths about the nature of things legal. Austin presents his never-ending cascade of definitions and subdefinitions, distinctions and subdistinctions, without ever saying for what purpose they are offered. His lecture, *The Uses of the Study of Jurisprudence*, in J. AUSTIN, THE PROVINCE OF JURISPRUDENCE, *supra* note 26, at 366–93, is a somewhat inept effort to list certain practical side benefits for law students of a study that Austin himself obviously regards as self-justifying.

abstract universals of theoretic jurisprudence."[187] He viewed his analyses of jurisprudential concepts such as right, duty, and law itself in the same light that he viewed his conceptual formulations of substantive legal doctrine. They were meant to be practical guides to the better working of the legal system.

Unlike Holland and most of the other analytical jurists, Holmes never spoke of internal legal theory as "legal science." Rather he saw it as recipe-making, with the proof of the pudding in the eating. Science was not so practical; it was the grander enterprise of seeking exact knowledge, typically for its own sake, at the hands of those who serve "Truth, their only queen."[188] In connection with the study of law, Holmes reserved the honorific term "science" for the external historical or anthropological study of law, sometimes adding the pious hope that the utilitarian calculus might one day produce a genuinely useful Benthamite "science of legislation."[189]

Holmes proposed his prediction theory as a useful guideline for a particular and confined heuristic purpose, not as a general scientific or conceptual truth about the nature of law. As a scientific definition—one that might, for instance, identify the essence of the distinctively legal subset of social phenomena, and hence provide a theoretical basis for the comparative study of widely varying legal systems—its inadequacies have often been noted. The prediction theory fails to capture the legal attitudes of officials and probably of most ordinary citizens, attitudes that any reasonably complete sociological account of law must consider. It leaves out the element of perceived legitimacy, which seems a necessary aspect of any serious attempt to distinguish legal from other constraints as part of a general scientific study of society.[190] Nor, for similar reasons, is it an adequate account of law from the perspective of the judge.

---

187 *The Path of the Law, supra* note 23, at 195, 168. Or as Holmes noted in another context, "jurisprudence means simply the broadest generalization of the principles and the deepest analysis of the ideas at the bottom of an actual system. It is the same process, carried further, by which the law is carried out from particular cases into general rules." Oliver Wendell Holmes, *The Bar as a Profession* (1896), in Collected Legal Papers 153, 157 (1920) [hereinafter *The Bar as a Profession*].

188 *The Use of Law Schools, supra* note 175, at 38.

189 *See Codes, and the Arrangement of the Law, supra* note 95, at 80; *Langdell Review, supra* note 139, at 234; *Letters to Dr. Wu, supra* note 168, at 187 (letter dated Aug. 26, 1926).

190 Modern legal positivists have taken account of this element in their analyses: Kelsen, with his concept of the "normativity" of law, and Hart with his requirement that some participants take an "internal" attitude. *See* Hans Kelsen, Pure Theory of Law 4–10 (1967); H.L.A. Hart, *supra* note 161, at 79–88.

Holmes began to work toward the prediction theory in his first jurisprudential essay, *Codes, and the Arrangement of the Law*.[191] His project was to develop a systematic arrangement for teaching and storing legal materials. As a preliminary step in working out such a taxonomy, it is natural to seek a working definition of the subject matter, a principle by which to identify material for arrangement. An especially useful working definition might also serve to suggest a basis for the classificatory categories themselves.

Seeking a working definition and a principle of classification in 1870, Holmes looked first to Austin, who had defined "the province of jurisprudence" as comprising the general commands of the sovereign. Austin had analyzed a command as an expression of desire backed by the threat of sanction and defined the sovereign as that determinate body habitually obeyed without itself habitually obeying anyone else. Austin had inherited from Bentham a focus on sanctions as the feature distinguishing between legal and other norms; a legal right is a claim backed by a sanction.[192]

Holmes agreed with this focus, but asked why Austin had confined the province of jurisprudence to rules laid down by a sovereign. He pointed out that there were other quite definite rules of conduct backed by reliable threats of enforcement, such as rules of "positive morality," which differed from proper laws in Austin's sense only in that the sanctions backing them were applied directly by public opinion, rather than through the courts. Holmes suggested that Austin's purpose in excluding these rules of popular morality from the province of jurisprudence must be a practical one, defined by the range of professional concerns. "Courts ... give rise to lawyers, whose only concern is with such rules as the courts enforce. Rules not enforced by them, although equally imperative, are the study of no profession. It is on this account that the province of jurisprudence has to be so carefully determined."[193]

But if the professional concerns of lawyers defined the province of law study, then Austin had been wrong to define law as the commands of a sovereign. International law, for example, fell outside this definition, but it was a subject, as Holmes said, "which lawyers do practically study"; it had "rules of conduct so definite as to be written in textbooks, and sanctioned in many cases by the certainty that a breach will be followed by war."[194] A practical definition

191 *Codes, and the Arrangement of the Law*, *supra* note 95.

192 *See* J. AUSTIN, THE PROVINCE OF JURISPRUDENCE, *supra* note 26, at 9–33; J. BENTHAM, OF LAWS IN GENERAL, *supra* note 28, at 1, 18–19.

193 *Codes, and the Arrangement of the Law*, *supra* note 95, at 81.

194 *Id.*

of law—in the sense of treating whatever concerned lawyers in their professional practice—must include rules such as these.

Moving from the issue of sovereignty to the question of how to classify the rules enforced by courts, Holmes noted that Austin had followed the approach of the Roman lawyers, arranging legal doctrines according to the rights they created in claimants—dividing them first into the broad categories of personal and property rights, and further subdividing from there. Holmes questioned whether classification on the basis of legal rights was consistent with Austin's emphasis upon the sanction as the distinguishing mark of the legal norm. Since what gave a rule legal character was that it was backed by a sanction, and sanctions operated directly on defendants, Holmes thought that a sanction-based legal taxonomy should presumably classify rules in terms of *duties* (the liabilities of defendants) rather than *rights* (the claims of those benefiting from those liabilities.)[195]

Within two years of writing *Codes, and the Arrangement of the Law*, Holmes stated the prediction theory in the course of the jurisprudence lectures he gave at the Harvard Law School, a brief summary of which he published as a book notice in 1872.[196] Now he made his pragmatic orientation explicit; the defining feature of "lawyers' law" was the fact that it was "enforced by the procedure of the courts, *and therefore [was] of practical importance to lawyers*."[197] His theory was to be the theory of a practice, the practice of law:

> The only question for the lawyer is, how will the judges act? Any motive for their action, be it constitution, statute, custom, or precedent, which can be relied upon as likely in the generality of cases to prevail, is worthy of consideration as one of the sources of law, in a treatise on jurisprudence.[198]

The professional perspective led Holmes to think in terms of prediction. For the lawyer counseling a client, law was whatever general factors might motivate a judge.[199] That perspective also produced another crucial modification of

195 *Id.* at 80. For Holmes' later thoughts on this issue, *see The Arrangement of the Law: Privity*, *supra* note 164, at 95. *See also* THE COMMON LAW, *supra* note 23, at 173; *The Path of the Law*, *supra* note 23, at 168–69, 174–75.

196 Holmes, *Book Notices*, in FORMATIVE ESSAYS, *supra* note 7, at 91 (reprinting Book Notice, 6 AM. L. REV. 723 (1872)) [hereinafter *Notice: Jurisprudential Lectures*].

197 *Id.* at 91–92 (emphasis added).

198 *Id.* at 92.

199 Holmes distinguished "general" factors from such "singular motives" as "the blandishments of the emperor's wife"; these are not lawyers' law, Holmes thought, only because their singularity renders them useless as a "ground of prediction." *Id.* at 92.

Austin's analysis, replacing the sanction with the more general concept of "judicial action," or remedy. Austin had said that every proper law was a command, creating a duty; a command was an expression of a wish backed by a sanction, or threat of unpleasant consequence. But in this formulation, Holmes argued, Austin had "looked at the law too much as a criminal lawyer."[200] Taxes are levied by law, are of concern to lawyers, and are unpleasant consequences of taxed conduct, but no one would say that a "protective tariff on iron ... create[s] a duty not to bring it into the country." Rather, the tax statute grants the person subject to it "an option at a certain price." The concept of duty only really applies to those actions that it is the legislature's "absolute wish" to prevent.[201]

Having made his point with the obvious case of the tax, Holmes went on to show its much more significant but less obvious extension to the common law's main civil remedy: compensatory money damages. In the normal case, the law only charges a defendant a price for his action, measured by the actual cost imposed on the plaintiff. Since they create merely "[liability to pay the fair price or value of an enjoyment," civil damages are "not a penalty."[202] Following the analysis developed in *Codes, and the Arrangement of the Law*, Holmes concluded that an award of only compensatory damages does not rest on a breach of a legal duty in any meaningful sense. The basic rules of private law thus do not fit Austin's definition because they create options rather than laying down commands. But nevertheless they are law for the practical reason that they are "applied by the courts and must therefore be known by professional men."[203]

The analysis of civil law in terms of remedy and liability rather than sanction and duty led Holmes directly to one of his central insights: Ordinary private law, rather than enforcing the principles of corrective justice that establish moral rights and duties among individuals, is primarily a device for distributing risk according to the variable demands of public policy. If the civil remedy of compensatory damages is not a penalty, then, contrary to what Austin thought (and contrary to the main current of nineteenth-century case law and commentary), justice does not require restricting civil liability to cases involving a breach of moral right or duty. Liability without fault simply charges the defendant the price of his activity, and might be imposed for reasons of "[p]ublic policy" alone. For instance, "it may be thought that titles should be protected against even innocent conversion," or that persons should be compensated "for injuries from extra-hazardous sources, in which case negligence

200 *Id.* at 93.

201 *Id.* at 92.

202 *Id.* at 93.

203 *Id.* at 93.

is not an element."[204] Generally, in cases of ordinary civil liability "[t]he object of the law is to accomplish an external result," and legal rules imposing civil liability, like taxes and subsidies, can vary with public needs and demands. As an example, Holmes noted that strict liability for straying cattle had been "very properly abandoned in some of the western states, where the enclosure of their vast prairies is necessarily for a long time out of the question."[205]

The literature of legal theory contains few performances of more concentrated brilliance than the thirty-one-year-old Holmes' "book notice" of scarcely a thousand words.[206] His formulations represented a breakthrough, the implications of which would not be fully absorbed for several generations. At the outset of his career as a legal theorist, he planted the germ of the whole modern analysis of tort and contract in terms of risk allocation, later embodied in such notions as loss spreading, cost internalization, and efficient breach. He went on during the 1870s to develop further the policy conception of the common law, though the results of his work must be sought amidst cryptic and dubiously relevant historical and anthropological learning in *The Common Law*.[207]

Later, Holmes learned better to separate his scientific from his doctrinal interests, and he finally came to formulate his mature jurisprudential views, most fully articulated in 1897 in *The Path of the Law*.[208] In that speech he gave both the prediction theory and its associated public policy conception of civil liability their most familiar and influential statement. The occasion was an address to law students, and from the beginning Holmes stressed more forcefully than ever before the practical professional perspective out of which his theory arose. He began by noting that "[w]hen we study law we are not studying a mystery but *a well-known profession*," or, as he put it later, a "*business*."[209] The two main aspects of this business are advocacy ("to appear before judges") and counseling ("to advise people in such a way as to keep them out of court").

---

204 *Id.*

205 *Id.* Later, Holmes claimed that general strict liability in tort should be rejected as "offending the sense of justice," and unconvincingly tried to defend the consistency of that argument with his central point that civil liability involving only compensatory damages should be allocated on grounds of policy not restrained by notions of fair punishment. *See* THE COMMON LAW, *supra* note 23, at 78, 118.

206 The essay contains yet another significant element, a trenchant criticism of Austin's concept of sovereignty. *Notice: Jurisprudence Lectures, supra* note 196, at 91.

207 For discussion of the contradictions and confusions in *The Common Law, see* Gordon, *supra* note 3; *see also* text accompanying notes 246–271 *infra*.

208 *The Path of the Law, supra* note 23.

209 *Id.* at 167, 171 (emphasis added).

Law is a profession because people, knowing that "the command of the public force is intrusted to ... judges in certain cases," are willing to pay for the advice of those who make "[t]he object of [their] study ... the prediction of the incidence of the public force through the instrumentality of the courts."[210]

One might fairly criticize this account of law practice, centered on litigation and remedies, as too narrow, both normatively and descriptively. Good lawyers should frame advice to clients with more in mind than what remedial "price" will be charged if the clients are brought into court. And lawyers do in fact advise clients, conduct negotiations, and design transactions and legal structures with more in mind than the outcome of potential litigation. This was true in Holmes' time, and is even more true today. And yet even now practitioners often speak of aspects of their work not ultimately referable to the possibility of litigation as "extra-legal." However much lawyers need to understand ethics, commerce, technology, politics, public relations, and psychology, still they have no licensed monopoly as experts in any of these fields. But lawyers alone are permitted to argue before courts and to advise clients about what courts are likely to do; in this sense, litigation does provide the distinctive and, in a way, the defining focus of their work.

Whatever its faults, Holmes' account of the counseling lawyer's work bounds the claims of the prediction theory. For one who proposes to study "the law as a business with well understood limits," Holmes says it is heuristically useful to adopt the viewpoint of a "bad man" who cares only for "material consequences."[211] Not that good lawyers must be themselves bad men; indeed he thought the practice of law "tends to make good citizens and good men."[212] Rather, the bad man's perspective focuses attention on the operative aspect of the law, the remedy—"the law and nothing else" as Holmes put it.[213] He insists on the sharp distinction between law and morals embodied in the bad man's perspective "with reference to a single end, that of learning and understanding the law."[214]

Holmes applied the "bad man" or remedial perspective to generalize his earlier critique of the concept of duty in civil cases. The official rhetoric of the law claims to attach liability to violations of legal duty: wrongs (torts) and breaches (contracts). But when we wash this rhetoric in the "cynical acid" provided by the insight that the law acts as law only through its remedies, the "duty"

210 *Id.* at 167.

211 *Id.* at 171.

212 *Id.* at 170.

213 *Id.* at 171.

214 *Id.* at 170.

element vanishes.[215] Because the only remedy normally available for an ordinary tort or contractual breach is compensatory money damages, the law really only charges the tort or contract defendant the *price* of his conduct and no more. "If you commit a tort, you are liable to pay a compensatory sum. If you commit a contract, you are liable to pay a compensatory sum unless the promised event comes to pass, and that is all the difference."[216]

Holmes here suggests a double analogy. First, he assimilates normal tort and contract liability into each other by means of the unusual locution "commit a contract." Second, he compares both of these ordinary forms of civil liability to analogous liabilities that involve no "fault" or "breach of duty" as ordinarily understood. For an example of a tort, Holmes takes statutes that allow a mill owner to flood upstream neighbors' property on condition that they be compensated for the loss in value.[217] From the bad man's remedy-centered perspective, tort liability in trespass is like the duty to compensate for lawful flooding under these Mill Acts. And contractual liabilities are all, in the remedial sense, like an insurer's obligation to indemnify the insured against covered loss, a legal requirement of compensatory payment arising without any fault or "breach." In the more typical tort and contract case, in which a compensatory damage award is predicated upon a supposed "breach of duty," the remedy is just the same as in these "no-fault" cases—payment of a money amount measured by actual loss.

Holmes' point is that from the "purely legal" (that is, remedial) point of view, the language of duty and breach is misleading in the standard instances of their use. Where we want to treat an act as a genuine legal wrong, and so express an absolute legal wish that it not be done, we have appropriate remedies: criminal penalties, punitive damages, or injunctions. Where we do not use those remedies, we show ourselves not to be serious about treating the act as legally wrong. Speaking in its true language of remedies, the law in such cases simply grants the supposed duty-bearer an option either to discharge the supposed duty or pay for the actual loss caused by not doing so. And it is the job of counsel to translate for the client the actual message of the law's working remedial language.

Analyzing private law in this way opens many possibilities, some of which Holmes noted in a remarkable passage concisely anticipating the turn toward enterprise liability that accident law would take as his risk-allocating conception of civil liability gradually took hold:

215 *Id.* at 174.
216 *Id.* at 175.
217 *Id* at 173–74.

> [T]he torts with which our courts are kept busy to-day are mainly the incidents of certain well known businesses.... The liability for them is estimated, and sooner or later goes into the price paid by the public. The public really pays the damages, and the question of liability, if pressed far enough, is really the question how far it is desirable that the public should insure the safety of those whose work it uses. It might be said that in such cases the chance of a jury finding for a defendant is merely a chance, once in a while rather arbitrarily interrupting the regular course of recovery, most likely in the case of an unusually conscientious plaintiff, and therefore better done away with.[218]

The analysis to this point has focused on the remedial aspect of Holmes' theory; what of the prediction aspect? Holmes tells us that it is useful to look at legal propositions as predictions of judicial action, distinguishing them, for example, from descriptive statements about legal rights or duties, or as commands directed toward citizens. This aspect of the theory has been repeatedly assaulted for failing to guide the judge, who cannot be helped by being told that law is what she or he likely will decide.[219]

But Holmes' limited purpose is explicit and clearly defined; he is offering a perspective on the law for those "who want to use it as the instrument of their business," where that business is "to appear before judges, or to advise people in such a way as to keep them out of court."[220] This is essentially the perspective of the practitioner who counsels private clients—certainly the predominant professional work contemplated by the law students Holmes was addressing. Without much critical inquiry into the social role of the practicing bar, Holmes accepted it; moreover he thought it the proper perspective both for legal education and for much legal commentary.

218 *Id.* at 183. With this passage, Holmes abandoned his earlier defense of the fault system as required by the "sense of justice." *See* note 205 *supra*. But in another passage in *The Path of the Law*, Holmes again strayed from his own teaching on duties. In describing a legal duty as "nothing but a prediction that if a man does or omits certain things he will be made to suffer in this or that way by judgment of the court," *The Path of the Law, supra* note 23, at 169, he contradicted his position that the award of ordinary compensatory damages does not presuppose a breach of legal duty. Holmes returned to his true doctrine later in the lecture when he said that private law rules impose "duties in an intelligible sense" only when the injunctive remedy was available, and recommended against speaking of ordinary civil liabilities in the "inappropriate terms" of duties and rights, *id.* at 175–76; *cf.* THE COMMON LAW, *supra* note 23 at 173.

219 *See, e.g.*, Rogat, *supra* note 2, at 248–49.

220 *The Path of the Law, supra* note 23, at 169, 167.

Holmes was clear that the counselor's perspective is not the only one from which to view the law. We know he believed that the law could be viewed externally and impractically, as an object of study and speculation, a "great anthropological document," and from this point of view the history of the law "is the history of the moral development of the race."[221] There are other *practical* and internal points of view toward the law, as well, perspectives which dispense with the counselor's (and bad man's) clear-cut "distinction between morality and law." Holmes drew this distinction "with reference to a single end, that of learning and understanding the law."[222] From a "wider point of view . . . the distinction between law and morals becomes of secondary or no importance"—whether that is the point of view of the scholar, the speculative thinker, or for that matter the law-abiding citizen, a point of view Holmes adopted himself in a later speech when he condemned "the unrest that seems to wonder vaguely whether law and order pay."[223]

Of course Holmes was quite aware that in applying the law a judge—especially a judge of a higher court—could not operate solely on the basis of the predictive attitude. But the predictive perspective nevertheless was one the judge should have in mind, because it was the natural attitude of legal counselors, on whose advice ordinary citizens had to depend. The counselor expects to be able to advise clients on the basis of precedents. For that reason, Holmes did not think that judges "should undertake to renovate the law" wholesale.[224]

At the same time, he also believed that the judges of his time sometimes overexerted themselves in the quest for certainty; "certainty generally is illusion, and repose is not the destiny of man."[225] In the many doubtful cases that came before them, judges were called upon to "exercise the sovereign prerogative of choice."[226] And Holmes criticized his contemporaries on the bench for failing "adequately to recognize their duty of weighing considerations of social advantage."[227] In context, it could hardly be more clear that Holmes never intended his "prediction theory" as a conception of law sufficient for a judge.[228]

---

221 *Law in Science, supra* note 24, at 212; *The Path of the Law, supra* note 23, at 170.

222 *The Path of the Law, supra* note 23, at 170.

223 *Id.* at 170; Oliver Wendell Holmes, *Law and the Court* (1913), in Collected Legal Papers 291, 292 (1920) [hereinafter *Law and the Court*].

224 *Law in Science, supra* note 24, at 239.

225 *The Path of the Law, supra* note 23, at 181.

226 *Law in Science, supra* note 24, at 239.

227 *The Path of the Law, supra* note 23, at 184.

228 One might, though, quite properly criticize Holmes for not raising the question why the counselor interpreting the law to a client had no quasi-judicial duty (as an "officer of the

Holmes did not put the strictly *predictive* aspect of his theory to work in any very significant way. As an analytical jurist his main contributions were his stress on remedies as the working instruments of the law, and, most originally, his point that not all remedies were duty-creating sanctions. He did not have to define law in predictive terms to make these points.[229] But the focus on prediction did center attention on the characteristic planning role of lawyers, and sharpened the standard jurisprudential discussions of the virtues of certainty and predictability. The larger importance of the predictive approach came later, when the Legal Realists took up the divergence between book law and the working law revealed by the effort to predict official actions. Holmes' formulation thus laid the conceptual basis for much later work.

Holmes was the first writer to base a jurisprudential theory on a perspective derived from the practice of law. In so doing, he was acting as a pragmatist, developing theory that was situated in and reflective upon practice, and that was meant to be evaluated as an instrument for serving human purposes. In criticism of Holmes' view, it is fair to say that he accepted without much critical evaluation a simple positivist conception of the bar's counseling role. Still, the view of law that Holmes derived from that doubtless incomplete conception served to bring the study of remedies to the center of legal scholarship. And the explicit adoption of the practical perspective on jurisprudential theory was itself a great advance. John Noonan has written that he "cannot understand those who write on law asking abstractly, 'What is law?' How can that question be answered without asking another—'Why do you want to know?' "[230] Holmes, unlike all his predecessors and most of his successors among legal theorists, explicitly embedded his best-known answer to the first question within an answer to the second one.

V Holmes Divided: The Spectator at the Storm Center

At this point, we can see the main outlines of Holmes' legal pragmatism: his synthesis of historical ("situated") and analytical ("instrumental") jurisprudence; his practical approach to legal "logic," or doctrinal conceptualism; and

court") to consider the public welfare in shaping that interpretation. I owe this point to my colleague Bill Simon, who elaborates just such a duty, defending it as a natural extension to the bar of the Holmesian approach to the judicial role, in William H. Simon, *Ethical Discretion in Lawyering*, 101 HARV. L. REV. 1083 (1988).

229 *See* JOHN FINNIS, NATURAL LAW AND NATURAL RIGHTS 323 (1980).

230 JOHN T. NOONAN, JR., PERSONS AND MASKS OF THE LAW ix (1976).

his account of legal reasoning, from the point of view of the counseling practitioner, as effort to predict what relief a judge will grant to a client. In presenting the story this far, I have sought to develop a general version of legal pragmatism, using Holmes as my example. Now I shift my focus more to the particularities and peculiarities of Holmes' thought and work. But even here, the Holmesian paradoxes and contradictions bear on the implications of pragmatism for law.

During Holmes' last years, his influential younger admirers promoted his reputation to truly Olympian heights; a prototypical encomium was Cardozo's characterization of the old justice as "the philosopher and the seer, the greatest of our age in the domain of jurisprudence, and one of the greatest of the ages."[231] The inevitable reaction against such extravagances—Holmes' "elevat[ion]... from deity to mortality"[232] at the hands of less starry-eyed critics—has motivated much of the best subsequent commentary on his work.[233] Having argued that Holmes' jurisprudence is more coherent than some of these critical commentators have thought, I now turn to consider a genuine Holmesian contradiction, one that pervasively flawed his work as judge and commentator, one that must be considered in assessing his relation to pragmatism.

While Dewey defined pragmatism by its contrast to what he called the "spectator theory of knowledge,"[234] Holmes was, as Yosal Rogat argued in one of the best of the revisionist studies, fundamentally a spectator in his approach to the law.[235] But he was a spectator who chose to work at "the storm centre," rather than to devote his energies to the kind of external study of law that might have benefited from his unusual capacity for detachment.[236] As Robert Gordon has noted in another fine critical study, Holmes supplied the slogans for the movement that emphasized the historically conditioned and socially embedded nature of legal institutions and ideas, but in devoting his working efforts to doctrinal commentary and adjudication, left the serious work in legal history and social science during his lifetime to others, such as Sir Henry

231 Cardozo, *supra* note 7, at 5; *cf.* J. FRANK, *supra* note 1, at 253–60; Harold Laski, *Mr. Justice Holmes*, in MR. JUSTICE HOLMES, *supra* note 1, at 138.

232 Walton H. Hamilton, *On Dating Mr. Justice Holmes*, 9 U. CHI. L. REV. 1 (1941).

233 For the fluctuations in Holmes' reputation, *see* G. Edward White, *The Rise and Fall of Justice Holmes*, 39 U. CHI. L. REV. 51 (1971).

234 J. DEWEY, THE QUEST FOR CERTAINTY, *supra* note 39, at 23.

235 Rogat, *supra* note 2. Rogat forcefully denies any important similarities between Holmes and Dewey. *Id.* at 251 n. 194.

236 "We are very quiet there [at the Supreme Court], but it is the quiet of a storm centre." *Law and the Court*, *supra* note 223, at 292.

Maine, F.W. Maitland, and Max Weber.[237] When we combine Rogat's point with Gordon's, we can see the practical contradiction within which Holmes was caught. He proceeded at perspectival cross-purposes; though drawn to the law by the external viewpoint of the observer, he worked on it from the internal viewpoint of the practitioner.

Holmes himself often noted the distinction between the perspectives of the "witness" and the "actor,"[238] and he organized his 1899 lecture *Law in Science and Science in Law* around the difference between these two viewpoints.[239] Seen from the external perspective, law was an object of study or contemplation, "a great anthropological document," providing raw material for the investigation of "the morphology and transformation of human ideas." This kind of investigation could be "science in the strictest sense," to be "pursued for the pleasure of the pursuit and of its fruits, as an end in itself."[240] From the internal perspective, on the other hand, law was an instrument of government, its study a practical enterprise meant to guide the man who must "make up [his] mind... upon a living question, for purposes of action."[241] In this latter aspect, law study could not be scientific until the distant day when its postulates were established in Benthamite fashion "upon accurately measured social desires."[242] In the meantime, practical law study would be mainly craft rather than science, eclectically combining history, doctrinal clarification, and—most important of all—the prudential legislative art required to keep the law in its application congruent with the demands of the community.[243]

In the abstract, Holmes' recognition of distinct and even incommensurate internal and external perspectives on law is neither inconsistent nor

---

237 Gordon, *supra* note 3, at 746.

238 For "witness" and "actor," *see* OLIVER WENDELL HOLMES, *The Law* (1885), in COLLECTED LEGAL PAPERS, 25, 26 (1920) [hereinafter *The Law*]. *See also Langdell Review, supra* note 139, at 234; *The Path of the Law, supra* note 23, at 201–02. Of special interest on this point is *Introduction to the General Survey, supra* note 68, at 3–01, where Holmes divided the world between "external" and "internal" types, the latter of whom think "that ideas are more interesting than things." It was clear that he saw himself as "internal." *See, e.g.*, 1 HOLMES-LASKI LETTERS, *supra* note 10, at 128 (letter dated Jan. 16, 1918). Holmes' terminology may confuse; in the context of the *type of person*, the internal person (the intellectual) is drawn to theory and the external to practice. In the context of *perspective on law*, however, the external perspective is theoretical and the internal practical.

239 *Law in Science, supra* note 24.

240 *Id.* at 211–12.

241 *Id.* at 224.

242 *Id.* at 225–26.

243 *Id.* at 225.

unpragmatic. But in fact Holmes' attitudes toward the two perspectives reflected an unresolved conflict, as his tortured rhetoric at the point of transition between the two parts of *Law in Science and Science in Law* reveals. The first part concludes with a characteristic hymn of praise to the life of the mind; Holmes tells us that he knows no "more exalted form of life than that of [the] great abstract thinker" who pursues knowledge "simply to feed the deepest hunger and to use the greatest gifts of his soul."[244] But he immediately qualifies this judgment so sharply as in effect to contradict it: "But after all the place for a man who is complete in all his powers is in the fight." The "great abstract thinker" of the previous paragraph now becomes, less flatteringly, "the professor, the man of letters" who "gives up one-half of life that his protected talent may grow and flower in peace."[245] The witness' "exalted form of life" suddenly is portrayed as incomplete, stunted, and effete, by comparison to the actor's role.

This ambivalence about the roles of actor and witness characterized Holmes' entire career in the law. Rogat has persuasively made the case for this claim with respect to his judicial work. Similarly, in his role as a legal thinker, my main concern here, Holmes was likewise caught between these external and internal perspectives. In his scholarship, he chose to write as a commentator or doctrinalist, which for him meant treating the law internally, as a working system of guidance for practical decision; legal history and anthropology had a limited role in this kind of work.[246] Yet he pursued this course as a man who

244 *Id.* at 224. Statements similar in content and (mostly) in dithyrambic tone could be multiplied almost endlessly. *See, e.g.*, OLIVER WENDELL HOLMES, *The Profession of the Law* (1886), in COLLECTED LEGAL PAPERS, 29, 30 (1920) [hereinafter *The Profession of the Law*]; OLIVER WENDELL HOLMES, *Brown University—Commencement 1897*, in *id.* at 164, 165–66 [hereinafter *Brown Commencement*]; *The Path of the Law, supra* note 23, at 202; OLIVER WENDELL HOLMES, *Address of Chief Justice Holmes* (1902), in COLLECTED LEGAL PAPERS at 272, 276–77 (1920) [hereinafter *Northwestern Address*]; OLIVER WENDELL HOLMES, *Bracton de Legibus et Constuetudinibus Angliae* (1915), in *id.* at 308, 309; OLIVER WENDELL HOLMES, *The Use of Colleges* (1891), in OCCASIONAL SPEECHES, *supra* note 78, at 62, 63 [hereinafter *The Use of Colleges*]; OLIVER WENDELL HOLMES, *A Provisional Adieu* (1902), in *id.* at 150, 152 [hereinafter *A Provisional Adieu*]; 1 HOLMES-LASKI LETTERS, *supra* note 10, at 374 (letter dated Oct. 9, 1921).

245 *Law in Science, supra* note 24, at 224; *see also* OLIVER WENDELL HOLMES, *George Otis Shattuck* (1897), in OCCASIONAL SPEECHES, *supra* note 78, at 92, 95 [hereinafter *George Otis Shattuck*]; Letter from Holmes to Felix Frankfurter (July 15, 1913), *quoted in* M. HOWE, THE PROVING YEARS, *supra* note 111, at 282.

246 For the "internal" juristic aims of *The Common Law, see* THE COMMON LAW, *supra* note 23, at 173; *see also* Letter from Holmes to A.G. Sedgwick (July 12, 1879), *quoted in* Gordon, *supra* note 3, at 719; Letter from Holmes to James Bryce (Aug. 1879), *quoted in* M. HOWE, THE PROVING YEARS, *supra* note 111, at 25; Letter from Holmes to John Norton Pomeroy

was attracted to law mainly by its interest as a spectacle and an object of contemplation. As a result *The Common Law* is, as Gordon says, "a book at war with itself."[247] So distorting is Holmes' perspectival wobble that the work, for all its nominal status as a classic, was scarcely understood and perhaps rarely read as a whole until Mark Howe devoted a masterful volume to unraveling its complexities and excavating its underpinnings in Holmes' reading and thinking during the 1870s.[248]

Howe's account allows us to trace the fault lines in *The Common Law* back to their origins. Holmes' first interest in the law was entirely external. As a young Civil War veteran his passions were science, poetry, and philosophy; his companions at the time were the young writers and intellectuals of Boston and Cambridge, William and Henry James, Chauncy Wright, and Nicholas St. John Green. He came to the law in 1865 not out of any sense of professional calling, but because he was, as he put it, "kicked," "thrown," and "shoved" into it.[249] At first he doubted whether this "ragbag of details" was "worthy of the interest of an intelligent man."[250] But he soon reconciled himself, not because of any attractions from the profession's practical side, but on the ground that "law . . . may be approached in the interests of science" and "opens a way to philosophy."[251]

What did Holmes count as "science" or "philosophy"? We know that he identified as scientific the work of both the German academic historians of ancient Roman law and the mostly American historians who were uncovering the English law's Teutonic roots.[252] What gave this work the status of science was

---

(Aug. 8, 1881), *quoted in id.* at 137. On the limited relevance of historical material in *The Common Law*, *see* Gordon, *supra* note 3, at 730–33.

247 Gordon, *supra* note 3, at 720–21.

248 M. HOWE, THE PROVING YEARS, *supra* note *III; see also* Howe, *Introduction* to THE COMMON LAW, *supra* note 23, at xi, xx.

249 Letter from Holmes to Mrs. John C. Gray (Apr. 30, 1905), *quoted in* M. HOWE, THE SHAPING YEARS, *supra* note 26, at 176; *Letters to Dr. Wu, supra* note 168, at 167 (letter dated Sept. 20, 1923); 1 HOLMES-LASKI LETTERS, *supra* note 10, at 205 (letter dated May 18, 1919).

250 *Introduction to the General Survey, supra* note 68, at 301; *see also* 1 HOLMES-LASKI LETTERS, *supra* note 10, at 430 (letter dated June 1, 1922); *A Provisional Adieu, supra* note 244 at 152.

251 Letter from Holmes to William James (Apr. 19, 1868), *quoted in* 1 RALPH BARTON PERRY, THE THOUGHT AND CHARACTER OF WILLIAM JAMES 510 (1935); Letter from Holmes to Ralph Waldo Emerson (Apr. 16, 1876), *quoted in* M. HOWE, THE SHAPING YEARS, *supra* note 26, at 203; *see also* 1 HOLMES-POLLOCK LETTERS, *supra* note 8, at 16 (letter dated Mar. 5, 1881).

252 *See The Use of Law Schools, supra* note 175, at 41–42; *see also* M. HOWE, THE PROVING YEARS, *supra* note 111, at 142–48, 153.

its objectivity and its detailed reliance on evidence drawn from original sources. "All scientific study nowadays is microscopic," Holmes wrote, "even the study of history...."[253] Holmes likewise regarded as true "scientists" the anthropologists, Tylor and others, who were during this period founding the scholarly study of primitive society and law.[254]

Early on, Holmes concluded that the enterprise of the jurist, who works "from within" the law to "make known [its] content," was "not a science."[255] Yet he aspired to the scientific (external) study of law, and in the 1870s he did extensive secondary reading and some original research in legal history and anthropology. At the same time, he committed himself to the very kind of internal juristic work to which he had denied scientific status. Unable to leave the fruits of his "scientific" labors unused, he distributed throughout *The Common Law* little essays and asides on primitive social arrangements and Roman and ancient German and English law; these asides, scattered among policy arguments and doctrinal reclassifications, contribute substantially to what Gordon rightly calls the work's "recklessly miscellaneous" quality.[256] The first chapter, for example, is an extended study of the phenomenon of animism in primitive law; how it bears on Holmes' primary doctrinal concerns is, as Howe gently remarks, not "wholly clear."[257] And Holmes' fascination with the antiquities of English legal history led him to give them too much doctrinal weight, as A.V. Dicey pointed out in his contemporary review of the book.[258]

Holmes' conceptual and expository juristic focus in *The Common Law* was blurred not only by his interest in "science," but also by his ambition to do "philosophy." For Holmes, philosophy encompassed all forms of broad and speculative thought that claimed intrinsic intellectual interest. Above all it included what we might call social theory—work involving broad generalizations about human society that rested loosely on scholarly findings, but which went

253 Book Notice, 11 AM. L. REV. 327 (1877) (for attribution of this anonymous review to Holmes, *see* M. HOWE, THE PROVING YEARS, *supra* note 106, at 148) [hereinafter *Book Notice*].

254 *See* M. HOWE, THE PROVING YEARS, *supra* note 111, at 149–50.

255 THE COMMON LAW, *supra* note 23, at 173; *Codes, and the Arrangement of the Law, supra* note 95, at 80, *see also Langdell Review, supra* note 138, at 234.

256 Gordon, *supra* note 3, at 719.

257 M. HOWE, THE PROVING YEARS, *supra* note 111, at 163.

258 As Dicey noted, Holmes' "attempt to unite the historical with the analytical method," led to an "uncertainty of aim" between stating doctrines "in conformity with the decisions to be found in the year-books" and "in conformity with the dictates of right reason, or expediency. The plain truth is that our author is too much an apologist." *Dicey Review, supra* note 120, at 713–14.

beyond them to guide further research and speculation.[259] Thus he wrote during the 1870s that the "scientific" researches of the new legal historians "prepare the ground for a true philosophic history of the law."[260] The paradigm of the kind of philosophy Holmes had in mind was Sir Henry Maine's *Ancient Law*,[261] a work too speculative to count as scientific history or anthropology, but which, as Holmes later said, "fe[d] the philosophic passion."[262] Maine contributed no original research, but rather a set of fruitful social-theoretic generalizations about the patriarchal origins of government, the communal roots of property, and the movement of progressive societies from status to contract.

The Common Law in its overall thrust shows Holmes' desire to emulate Maine's kind of "philosophy," just as its many "asides" reflect the "science" of the historians and anthropologists.[263] The book's central doctrinal thesis is that contemporary standards of civil liability are (and should be) typically "objective," determined by collective social expectations, whereas their verbal formulations often misleadingly portray them as "subjective" by making reference to a defendant's individual capacities or state of mind. But Holmes does not present his "objective theory" as a normative doctrinal thesis; rather he offers it as a historical generalization, one he obviously thinks is comparable to Maine's hypotheses of the law's tendency to move from status to contract, or from communal to individual ownership. As a historical thesis, Holmes' theory is wholly unconvincing, and his formulation of the external standard in these terms has led many readers to take *The Common Law* as a work of philosophical history or social theory comparable in purpose to *Ancient Law*.[264]

Though Holmes generally considered philosophy external to the actual discourse of law, he gave internal or practical legal writing the accolade "philosophical" when it had, or aspired to, intrinsic intellectual interest along with its

---

259 In 1913 Holmes wrote that works of legal history "provide philosophical food to philosophical minds." *Introduction to the General Survey*, *supra* note 68, at 3. And as he later wrote to Laski, "I regard philosophy as simply the broader generalizations of thought that can't lift itself by the slack of its own breeches." 1 HOLMES-LASKI LETTERS, *supra* note 10 at 706 (letter dated Feb. 7, 1925).

260 *Book Notice*, *supra* note 253, at 331.

261 H. MAINE, ANCIENT LAW, *supra* note 88.

262 1 HOLMES-LASKI LETTERS, *supra* note 10, at 429 (letter dated June 1, 1922). For Holmes' general assessment of Maine, *see* HOLMES-POLLOCK LETTERS, *supra* note 8, at 31 (letter dated Mar. 4, 1888).

263 Howe points out that the structure of *The Common Law* corresponds to that of *Ancient Law*, M. HOWE, THE PROVING YEARS, *supra* note 111, at 149 n. 31, suggesting that Holmes was more influenced by Maine than he liked to admit.

264 *See, e.g.*, *id.* at 212–13 (quoting FREDERICK POLLOCK, PRINCIPLES OF CONTRACT xi (1881)).

practical classificatory and decision-guiding use.[265] And he found ideas intrinsically interesting only when they were *general*. He "hate[d] facts" and thought the "chief end of man is to form general propositions," to which he always added the twist—meant to stress that he valued his generalities as ends in themselves, not for their utility—that "no general proposition is worth a damn."[266] The philosophy that consoled him as he lay at Ball's Bluff, thinking himself mortally wounded, was a faith in *general* ideas: "*good & universal* (or *general law*) are synonymous terms in the universe."[267] And as he often said in later years, what differentiated gossip from philosophy for him was only that the former treated a fact "as if it really stood apart" while the latter made it "a part of the whole."[268]

Holmes' conscious or unconscious striving to make his internal legal discourse "philosophical" led him to his most characteristic vice as a doctrinal writer—a pervasive and excessive generality. As John Chipman Gray observed, "Mr. H. carries his theories of simplification too far: there is too much tendency on his part to make cases come under the principle, wh[ich] cannot really

---

265 Thus Holmes wrote that an "interest in philosophical speculation" lay behind the renewed interest shown at Langdell's Harvard in "analyzing and generalizing the rules of law and the grounds on which they stand." *The Use of Law Schools, supra* note 175, at 42. And he urged that the general categorical arrangement of legal doctrine should be at the same time "philosophical" and subject to "compromises with practical convenience." *Codes, and the Arrangement of the Law, supra* note 95, at 80; *see also The Theory of Torts, supra* note 158, at 119. And if in the midst of practical commentary, there arose the chance to make a pretty, though useless, point, so much the better; thus Holmes admitted to Pollock that "in practice it does not much matter" whether his own objective or an opponent's constrained subjective theory of interpretation was adopted, but added that "theory is none the less interesting when it is outside the limits of possible proof or refutation. . . ." 1 HOLMES-POLLOCK LETTERS, *supra* note 8, at 95, 96 (letter dated July 16, 1899).

266 1 HOLMES-LASKI LETTERS, *supra* note 10, at 205 (letter dated May 18, 1919); 2 HOLMES-POLLOCK LETTERS, *supra* note 8, at 13 (letter dated May 26, 1919); *see also* OLIVER WENDELL HOLMES, *Dr. S. Weir Mitchell* (1900), in OCCASIONAL SPEECHES, *supra* note 78, at 119, 121 [hereinafter *Dr. Mitchell*]; *Holmes-Cohen Correspondence, supra* note 31, at 314 (letter dated Apr. 12, 1915).

267 OLIVER WENDELL HOLMES, JR., TOUCHED WITH FIRE: CIVIL WAR LETTERS AND DIARY OF OLIVER WENDELL HOLMES, JR., 1861–1864, at 28 (M. Howe ed. 1946) [hereinafter TOUCHED WITH FIRE].

268 *Brown Commencement, supra* note 244, at 16; *see also* OLIVER WENDELL HOLMES, *Remarks to the Essex Bar*, in OCCASIONAL SPEECHES, *supra* note 78, at 48, 49; 1 HOLMES-LASKI LETTERS, *supra* note 10, at 129 (letter dated Jan. 18, 1918); *id.* at 810 (letter dated Dec. 27, 1925).

belong there."[269] In *The Common Law*, for example, Holmes tended to leave out aspects of living tort law that focus on subjective states of mind in the service of his effort to force doctrine into "a philosophically continuous series" arranged along the dimension of objectively foreseeable probability of harm.[270] And the extension of the external standard to the criminal area led him to understate quite grossly the concern with individual moral culpability reflected in the substantive law of crimes.[271]

After finishing *The Common Law*, Holmes came to believe that "inside the body of the law" the "field for generalization... was small," so that if he was to continue to write about law "as a philosopher," he must approach it externally, through other disciplines like ethics, history, anthropology, and political economy.[272] He had every opportunity to make the change when he was offered and accepted a professorship at the Harvard Law School, where he insisted that, in addition to teaching ordinary law courses, he should be free to devote part of his working time to "studies touching the history and philosophy of law."[273] But a few months into his academic career, he unhesitatingly—some colleagues thought precipitately—accepted a seat on the Massachusetts Supreme Judicial Court.[274] He would be a judge for the remaining fifty years of his active life, thus guaranteeing that his daily work would confine his thinking "inside the body of the law," where he had said there was little room for significant generalization.

269 Lecture by John Chipman Gray, Harvard Law School (Jan. 12, 1883), *quoted in* M. HOWE, THE PROVING YEARS, *supra* note 111, at 276 (Chipman quote based on student notes of lecture).

270 *See* THE COMMON LAW, *supra* note 23, at 104. Holmes to some extent corrected the excessive focus on the objective degree of probability as the determinant of liability in *Privilege, Malice and Intent*, *supra* note 157, at 118–19.

271 *See* THE COMMON LAW, *supra* note 23, at 41–43. Holmes' failure to sufficiently distinguish criminal prohibition from civil liability was one of the (lesser) flaws of his dissent in Bailey v. Alabama, 219 U.S. 219, 245–51 (1911) (Holmes, J., dissenting).

272 Letter from Holmes to James Bryce (Dec. 31, 1882), *quoted in* M. HOWE, THE PROVING YEARS, *supra* note 111, at 280.

273 Letter from Holmes to Charles Eliot (Nov. 1, 1881), *quoted in* M. HOWE, THE PROVING YEARS, *supra* note 111, at 260.

274 For Howe's account of Holmes' decision to accept the judicial appointment, *see* M. HOWE, THE PROVING YEARS, *supra* note 111, at 265–70 (Holmes' failure to consult with his Dean or colleagues before leaving his post in the middle of the academic year left behind some bitterness against him at Harvard, though he had specified in joining the faculty that he would be free to accept a judgeship if one were offered.).

As he later described his state of mind at the time of his appointment, he was confronted by a choice between "applying [my] theories to practice and details or going into another field."[275] Why did he choose "practice and details" over "science" and "philosophy"? In a letter to James Bryce written soon after the decision, Holmes anticipated the language he later used in the *Law in Science* lecture; to reject a "share in the practical struggle of life which naturally offered itself" would be "the less manly course."[276] But many years later, after his reputation and self-esteem were finally secure and he could speak of the decision in less self-serving terms, he put the matter differently. He told his young admirer Laski that in addition to "natural fear and the need of making a living," he had thought that "(at 40) ... it would take another ten years to master a new subject," and he "couldn't bargain that my mind should remain suggestive at that age." He concluded wistfully: "I think I was right but there are many tempting themes on which it seems as if one could say something if one knew enough—I am glad on the whole that I stuck to actualities against philosophy (the interest of all actualities)."[277]

In fact, Holmes seems to have accepted the judgeship on the assumption that his creative work as a scholar and thinker was done. He had no inclination for further detailed research in legal history or anthropology, and his taste in "philosophy" ran to the artful aphorism or *aperçu*, not to systematic exposition.[278] In this, his abilities and his tastes were in harmony; few if any

275 1 HOLMES-LASKI LETTERS, *supra* note 10, at 291 (letter dated Nov. 17, 1920).

276 Letter from Holmes to James Bryce (Dec. 31, 1882), *quoted in* M. HOWE, THE PROVING YEARS, *supra* note 111, at 280–81. Years later, Holmes wrote to Frankfurter in a similar vein. *See id.* at 282; *see also George Otis Shattuck, supra* note 245, at 95–96.

277 1 HOLMES-LASKI LETTERS, *supra* note 10, at 291–92 (letter dated Nov. 17, 1920). Howe notes Holmes' persistent Puritan tendency to approve the less pleasant course, M. HOWE, THE PROVING YEARS, *supra* note 111, at 282. To this effect, *see* OLIVER WENDELL HOLMES, *Memorial Day* (1884), in OCCASIONAL SPEECHES, *supra* note 78, at 4, 11 [hereinafter *Memorial Day*] (the Puritan virtue is to choose the "most disagreeable" alternative—the context makes plain that Holmes is not being wholly ironic); OLIVER WENDELL HOLMES, *Arthur P. Bonney and Frederic T. Greenhalge* (1896), in *id.* at 87, 89 (" 'The good is one thing, the pleasant is another; the wise prefer the good.' "). Holmes described his choice to enlist in the army in 1861 in the same terms as he later described his decision to become a judge: "[A]s life is action and passion, it is required of a man that he should share the passion and action of his time at peril of being judged not to have lived." *Memorial Day, supra*, at 6–7. He wrote of the chance to serve on the United States Supreme Court in terms of preparing for battle. *See Twenty Years in Retrospect, supra* note 78, at 157.

278 For some of Holmes' many statements of preference for philosophers' *apercus* over their systems, *see* 1 HOLMES-POLLOCK LETTERS, *supra* note 8, at 261 (letter dated Mar. 1, 1918); 2 *id.* at 52 (letter dated Aug. 28, 1920); 1 HOLMES-LASKI LETTERS, *supra* note 10, at 133 (letter

writers on the law have matched his gift for compressed expression, which is seen to its best effect in letters, essays, and judicial opinions. On the other hand, his only attempt at a full-length and systematic work of "science" or "philosophy," *The Common Law*, does not represent his best work. Holmes spoke of himself, perhaps even half-consciously so, when he wrote of those "men of the world," the aphorists, whose work outlives "the greatest works of intellect"; "it is the second rate that lasts."[279]

In becoming a judge, Holmes entered a life to which, for all the scope it gave to his literary gifts, he was not wholly suited. Judging is an enterprise deeply concerned with "practice and details," and neither Holmes' talents nor his inclinations lay in this direction. Generations of law students have marveled at the simple lack of informed common sense manifested by such judgments as his pronouncement that a motorist at a rail crossing must stop, look, and listen for a train, and get out of the car if necessary to do so, on pain of being found

---

dated Feb. 7, 1918); *id.* at 277 (letter dated Aug. 30, 1920); 2 *id.* at 971–72 (letter dated Aug. 18, 1927); *Letters to Dr. Wu, supra* note 168, at 162 (letter dated Apr. 1, 1923); *id.* at 186 (letter dated Aug. 26, 1926). It is interesting to compare these statements with what he wrote of his father, the celebrated poet and essayist:

> "[H]e contented himself too much with sporadic *aperçus*—the time for which, I used to say when I wanted to be disagreeable, had gone by. If he had had the patience to concentrate all his energy on a single subject, which perhaps is saying if he had been a different man, he would have been less popular, but he might have produced a great work."

Letter from Holmes to Clara Stevens (July 26, 1914), *quoted in* M. HOWE, THE SHAPING YEARS, *supra* note 26, at 19.

The possibilities for psycho-biographical speculation here are further enriched by considering Holmes' oft-reiterated insistence on the great differences between the "thinker" (like himself) and the "poet" or "man of letters" (like Emerson, James, and his father), generally to the advantage of the former. *See The Profession of the Law, supra* note 244, at 29–31; OLIVER WENDELL HOLMES, RUDYARD KIPLING (1893), *quoted in* OCCASIONAL SPEECHES, *supra* note 78, at 71;, *Dr. Mitchell, supra* note 266, at 120; 1 HOLMES-POLLOCK LETTERS, *supra* note 8, at 96 (letter dated July 16, 1899); 1 HOLMES-LASKI LETTERS, *supra* note 10, at 474 (letter dated Jan 13, 1923); *id.* at 533 (letter dated Sept. 4, 1923); *id.* at 593 (letter dated Feb. 17, 1924). And yet Holmes conceived of philosophy in an artist's way; he sought to "see the universal in the particular," to "show the infinite in the finite." *Letters to Dr. Wu, supra* note 168, at 164 (letter dated June 16, 1923); HOLMES-SHEEHAN CORRESPONDENCE 51 (D. Burton ed. 1976) [hereinafter HOLMES-SHEEHAN CORRESPONDENCE] (letter dated Oct. 27, 1912).

279 OLIVER WENDELL HOLMES, *Montesquieu* (1900), in COLLECTED LEGAL PAPERS 250, 250 (1920). *But see Holmes-Sheehan Correspondence, supra* note 278, at 51 (letter dated Oct. 27, 1912) ("Only the first rate lasts.").

contributorily negligent.[280] By his own admission, he was "academic to the point of unreality"; he did not "read the papers or otherwise feel the pulse of the machine"; he "never [knew] any facts about anything" and was baffled whenever a visitor asked "some informal intelligent question about our institutions or the state of politics or anything else."[281]

Becoming a judge did not change his attitude toward the gritty facts of human disputation. To him lawsuits were "mannerless conflicts over often sordid interests."[282] The cases he decided dealt mostly with "trifling and transitory matters."[283] The realm of "[t]he practical" was "a mean and stony soil," the world of fact a "mass of sordid details" until transfigured by "some new generalization."[284] Then it served only as "raw material" that could "challenge your power to idealize the brute fact," and "nourish" valuable abstractions with the necessary empirical content.[285] Until the thinker's power of generalization could impart to life some "mystic spiritual tone," it was only a "roar of bargain and battle," inhabited by "men . . . like flies—here swept away by a pestilence—there multiplying unduly and paying for it."[286]

---

280 Baltimore & O.R.R. v. Goodman, 275 U.S. 66, 69–70 (1927).

281 1 HOLMES-POLLOCK LETTERS, *supra* note 8, at 116 (letter dated Jan. 10, 1904); *id.* at 124 (letter dated May 25, 1906); *id.* at 118 (letter dated Sept. 24, 1904).

282 *The Profession of the Law, supra* note 244, at 29.

283 *Speech at Bar Dinner, supra* note 135, at 245; *cf. Holmes-Cohen Correspondence, supra* note 31, at 319 (letter dated Sept. 10, 1918).

284 *Letters to Dr. Wu, supra* note 168, at 184 (letter dated Jan. 31, 1926); *id.* at 176–77 (letter dated Jan. 27, 1925).

285 *Id.* at 190 (letter dated Jan. 31, 1927); Letter from Holmes to Felix Frankfurter (July 15, 1913), *quoted in* M. HOWE, THE PROVING YEARS, *supra* note 111, at 282; *Letters to Dr. Wu, supra* note 168, at 175 (letter dated Mar. 6, 1924).

286 OLIVER WENDELL HOLMES, *The Class of '61* (1911), in OCCASIONAL SPEECHES, *supra* note 78, at 160, 162 [hereinafter *The Class of '61*]; 1 HOLMES-LASKI LETTERS, *supra* note 10, at 762 (letter dated July 23, 1925); *see also id.* at 194 (letter dated Apr. 8, 1919) ("I respect your respect for the human soul while still doubting whether to share it. The formula of life to great masses would be Feed—*F-outre* [Fuck] and Finish, and I am not sure that it won't remain so."). In interpreting statements like these, on which Rogat and others build much of their indictment of Holmes' world view, one should apply to him what he said to his fellow veterans of the 20th Massachusetts Regiment: "[A] great trial in your youth made you different." OLIVER WENDELL HOLMES, *The Fraternity of Arms* (1897), in OCCASIONAL SPEECHES, *supra* note 78, at 100, 101. He spent three of his formative years "soaked in a sea of death." OLIVER WENDELL HOLMES, *Remarks at a Meeting of the Second Army Corps Association* (1903), in *id.* at 158, 159. For the definitive account of Holmes' war experiences, *see* M. HOWE, THE SHAPING YEARS, *supra* note 26, at 80–175. Holmes wrote, only half ironically, "I lost my humanity with my abolition days in college and in the army."

In Holmes' conception, the working of the idealizing imagination upon the world of brute fact was aesthetic rather than political; it might transfigure but not transform. Like his Calvinist ancestors, Holmes saw in the sequence of events the unfolding of a predestined tale. The philosophy that consoled him at Ball's Bluff was fatalistic: "now as ever I believe that whatever shall happen is best—for it is in accordance with a general law. . . ."[287] "I see the inevitable everywhere," he wrote.[288] "I do in a sense worship the inevitable. . . ."[289] Of course "the mode in which the inevitable comes to pass is through effort," and as a practical matter "[w]e must be serious in order to get work done," but ultimately the human sense of power over events was only "the trick by which nature keeps us at our job."[290] His fatalism led him to accept "a rough equation of isness and oughtness."[291]

In its practical aspects, judging was for Holmes only a "job"; he remained drawn to the law by the same purely external interests as had first motivated

---

1 HOLMES-LASKI LETTERS, *supra* note 10, at 769 (letter dated Aug. 1, 1925). Saul Touster sensitively explores the numbing effect of the war on Holmes' capacity for emotional involvement, in Touster, *In Search of Holmes from Within*, 18 VAND. L. REV. 437 (1964), and Edmund Wilson interestingly compares Holmes' reaction to his war experience to that of Ambrose Bierce, in E. WILSON, *supra* note 4, at 621–28, 753–66. Holmes was given to skeptically sanguinary remarks about killing the other fellow when you disagree with him enough, even though his view is as good as yours. *See, e.g.*, OLIVER WENDELL HOLMES, *Natural Law* (1918), in COLLECTED LEGAL PAPERS 310, 312 (1920) [hereinafter *Natural Law*]; 2 HOLMES-LASKI LETTERS, *supra* note 10, at 862 (letter dated Aug. 5, 1926). These remarks were rooted in the personal experience of killing Confederate soldiers. For after Holmes' abolitionist idealism had been extinguished by years of slaughter, as well as by his formation of close bonds with fellow officers who were Southern sympathizers, he came to regard the Confederate soldiers as honorable men doing their duty.

287 TOUCHED WITH FIRE, *supra* note 267, at 28.

288 2 HOLMES-POLLOCK LETTERS, *supra* note 8, at 230 (letter dated Sept. 20, 1928).

289 *Holmes-Cohen Correspondence, supra* note 31, at 334 (letter dated Jan. 30, 1921); *see also* 1 HOLMES-LASKI LETTERS, *supra* note 10, at 469 (letter dated Jan. 6, 1923) (the proposition that "repressions and extinctions" are "inevitable" is "sufficiently established by their occurrence.").

290 *Ideals and Doubts, supra* note 94, at 305; *Letters to Dr. Wu, supra* note 168, at 185 (letter dated May 5, 1926); *see also Northwestern Address, supra* note 244, at 273–74; HOLMES-SHEEHAN CORRESPONDENCE, *supra* note 278, at 28 (letter dated July 17, 1909).

291 "I do accept 'a rough equation of isness and oughtness'. . . . I also would fight for some things—but instead of saying that they ought to be I merely say they are part of the kind of a world that I like—or should like." 2 HOLMES-LASKI LETTERS, *supra* note 10, at 948 (letter dated June 1, 1927).

him.[292] In 1876, writing as a young lawyer to the old philosopher Emerson, he said that what justified law to him was the path it opened to philosophy.[293] In 1915, writing as an old judge to the young philosopher Morris Cohen, he expressed his pleasure that a philosopher should be interested in the law, and added: "I hardly should be interested in it—if it did not open a wide door to philosophizing. . . ."[294] Though the lawyer's working life is a "greedy watch for clients and practice of shopkeepers' arts," still "a man may live greatly in the law" because it stimulates "the large survey of causes" where "thought may find its unity in an infinite perspective."[295] Though "artists and poets" shrink from law, still it is "human"—not because lawyers deal with human beings and their human joys and pains, but because law as "a part of man, and of one world with all the rest" teaches the "philosophical" lesson of the "continuity of the universe."[296] And the law's true fascination, he said in the Emersonian peroration to *The Path of the Law*, lies in those "remoter and more general aspects" wherein the lawyer can "catch an echo of the infinite, a glimpse of its unfathomable process, a hint of the universal law."[297]

Those who believe that questions of law should be kept sharply separate from questions of public policy might regard Holmes' kind of intellectual

---

292 On Holmes' view of "jobbism," *see* OLIVER WENDELL HOLMES, *Sidney Bartlett* (1889), in OCCASIONAL SPEECHES, *supra* note 78, at 51, 54 [hereinafter *Sidney Bartlett*]; *Speech at Bar Dinner, supra* note 135, at 247; 1 HOLMES-LASKI LETTERS, *supra* note 10, at 385 (letter dated Dec. 9, 1921); *id.* at 723 (letter dated Mar. 26, 1925); *Letters to Dr. Wu, supra* note 168, at 178 (letter dated Mar. 26, 1925). Yosal Rogat explores the roots of this stoical professionalism in Holmes' alienation from the America of the Gilded Age, comparing him to his contemporaries Henry James and Henry Adams. Rogat, *supra* note 2, at 228–43. Both Holmes' "jobbist" or professionalist ethic and his aesthetic approach to law have further (and positive) implications developed later. *See* text accompanying notes 347–366 *infra.*

293 Letter from Holmes to Ralph Waldo Emerson (Apr. 16, 1876), *quoted in* M. HOWE, THE SHAPING YEARS, *supra* note 26, at 203.

294 *Holmes-Cohen Correspondence, supra* note 31, at 314 (letter dated Apr. 12, 1915).

295 *The Profession of the Law, supra* note 244, at 29–30.

296 *Brown Commencement, supra* note 244, at 165, 166.

297 *The Path of the Law, supra* note 23, at 202; *see also Introduction to the General Survey, supra* note 68, at 300–02; 1 HOLMES-POLLOCK LETTERS, *supra* note 8, at 22 (letter dated Aug. 27, 1883). I thank Sandy Levinson for drawing my attention to the Emersonian echoes in many of Holmes' purple passages. Holmes was greatly influenced by Emerson, whom he credited with "imparting a ferment." *Letters to Dr. Wu, supra* note 168, at 176 (letter dated Jan. 27, 1925). From the sage of Concord he drew not only his sentiment of acceptance of the universe and worship of the inevitable, but also his celebration of action, vitality, and process. On the importance of Emerson in the origins of pragmatism, *see* RICHARD POIRIER, THE RENEWAL OF LITERATURE 13–14, 17–18, 192–202 (1987).

detachment as a positive qualification for a judicial career. But of course one of Holmes' chief claims to greatness as a legal thinker is his critique of any such view of the judicial process. Holmes believed that adjudication should and must be result-oriented, fundamentally legislative. For him, the formal justification of judicial decision in terms of precedent and legal principle was "the evening dress which the newcomer puts on to make itself presentable according to conventional requirements"; but "[t]he important phenomenon" was the "justice and reasonableness" of the actual decision itself.[298] In cases not settled by clear positive command, judges were to exercise their "sovereign prerogative of choice," producing interstitial legislation based on "considerations of social advantage."[299]

Sound legislative judgment was thus a primary judicial qualification, and Holmes best expressed his sense of the kind of person likely to possess this quality in the uncharacteristically unstinted praise he gave to Massachusetts' antebellum Chief Justice Lemuel Shaw. Though in "technical knowledge" many judges had surpassed Shaw, Holmes wrote, "the strength of that great judge lay in an accurate appreciation of the requirements of the community whose officer he was." Because "few have lived who were his equals" in understanding those "grounds of public policy" which are the ultimate criteria of good law, he had been "the greatest *magistrate* which this country has produced."[300]

Years later, after more than thirty years on the bench, Holmes wrote in similar terms of his colleague and good friend, United States Chief Justice Edward Douglas White: "He is always thinking what will be the practical effect of the decision (which of course is the ultimate justification or condemnation of the principle adopted.)" Holmes went on to add a revealing note of contrast between White's mode of judging and his own: "I think of [the decision's] relation to the theory and philosophy of the law—if that isn't too pretentious a way of putting it. We generally come out the same way by very different paths. But we sometimes come together head on with a whack."[301]

---

298 *Langdell Review, supra* note 139, at 234.

299 *Law in Science, supra* note 24, at 239; *The Path of the Law, supra* note 23, at 184. For other statements of this often reiterated Holmesian theme, *see* THE COMMON LAW, *supra* note 23, at 5, 32–33, 167–68, 244, 263–64; *Privilege, Malice and Intent, supra* note 157, at 120, 129–30; *Learning and Science, supra* note 80, at 139; *Law in Science, supra* note 24, at 225–26; *ideals and Doubts, supra* note 94, at 306–07.

300 THE COMMON LAW, *supra* note 23, at 85.

301 HOLMES-SHEEHAN CORRESPONDENCE, *supra* note 278, at 58 (letter dated Jan. 31, 1913). On Holmes' high opinion of White's legislative judgment, *see* also 1 HOLMES-POLLOCK LETTERS, *supra* note 8, at 170 (letter dated Sept. 24, 1910); 1 HOLMES-LASKI LETTERS, *supra* note 10, at 294 (letter dated Nov. 26, 1920).

In fact Holmes did not believe that "theory and philosophy" necessarily supplied the practical knowledge and understanding that made a good judicial legislator. As a pragmatist, and hence a believer in the situated and tacit character of belief, he thought that "successful men of affairs" operated on "premises" that though "inarticulate" were often "profound."[302] Applying the point to the judiciary, Holmes defended the appointment of politicians as judges, which had produced Marshall, Story, Taney, and Chase, along with his contemporaries Taft and White. He feared that "men... of the abstract type only exceptionally prove wise in practical affairs," adding wryly that coming from him this was obviously a "disinterested judgment."[303] Though no one could ever have mistaken Holmes for a modest man, he was able to admit his own deficiencies in practical wisdom and common understanding (at least to a fervent admirer). Thus he wrote to Laski: "[N]ot being a man of affairs and affairs being half at least of life I look up to those who have profound insights and foresights and successfully act on them."[304] And when Brandeis scolded him for ruling on labor legislation without understanding the facts of industrial life, he accepted the criticism as fair, and even read a few legislative studies of factory conditions before begging off on account of age and going back to Aristotle, Hegel, and French novels for his vacation reading.[305]

Perhaps sensing his own deficiencies as "a man of affairs," Holmes in his judicial role adopted, as a kind of surrogate for Shaw's or White's sound instinctive sense of good public policy, his well-known attitude of deference to legislative judgment.[306] His reputation as a great judge rests largely on his many

302 1 HOLMES-LASKI LETTERS, *supra* note 10, at 121 (letter dated Dec. 26, 1917).

303 *Id.* at 797 (letter dated Nov. 13, 1925).

304 *Id.* at 374 (letter dated Oct. 9, 1921).

305 *See id.* at 204–05 (letter dated May 18, 1919); *id.* at 212 (letter dated June 16, 1919); *id.* at 268 (letter dated June 11, 1920); *id.* at 430 (letter dated June 1, 1922); 2 HOLMES-POLLOCK LETTERS, *supra* note 8, at 13 (letter dated May 26, 1919); *id.* at 17–18 (letter dated June 27, 1919). For Holmes' recognition of the advantages of Brandeis' practical knowledge of affairs, *see* 1 HOLMES-LASKI LETTERS, *supra* note 10, at 485 (letter dated Mar. 1, 1923); *id.* at 810 (letter dated Dec. 27, 1925); 2 *id.* at 1135 (letter dated Feb. 22, 1929). More generally, for Holmes' admiration of Brandeis, perhaps the greatest *practicing* pragmatist American law has known, *see* 2 HOLMES-POLLOCK LETTERS, *supra* note 8, at 191 (letter dated Oct. 31, 1926). Samuel Konefsky provides a judicious comparative assessment of their practical contributions as Supreme Court justices, giving Holmes his considerable due but ranking Brandeis clearly higher. SAMUEL J. KONEFSKY, THE LEGACY OF HOLMES AND BRANDEIS 258–84 (reprint ed. 1974).

306 Holmes' conception of judicial impartiality required the judge to be "superior to class prejudices and to his own prejudices," OLIVER WENDELL HOLMES, *Despondency and Hope*

eloquent reiterations of this attitude in constitutional cases during a period of progressive legislative activity—and his reputation as a liberal statesman rests almost wholly on this basis.[307]

Of course deference to the legislature could not guide him in common law adjudication, and it is in this area, where his learning was so deep, that his judicial performance was least impressive and has had the least influence. As a judge, he was skilled at the conceptual aspect of the work ("untying knots" he called it[308]), and he could follow the wishes of his community when those wishes were given positive embodiment.[309] But his very lack of connection to that community and lack of empathy with its central concerns disabled him

---

(1902), in OCCASIONAL SPEECHES, *supra* note 78, at 146, 148 [hereinafter *Despondency and Hope*], and to remember "that what seem to him to be first principles are believed by half his fellow men to be wrong," *Law and the Court, supra* note 223, at 295. "I hope and believe that I am not influenced by my opinion that it is a foolish law," he said of the Sherman Act. 1 HOLMES-LASKI LETTERS, *supra* note 10, at 248–49 (letter dated Mar. 4, 1920). The judge was to legislate only in the interstices left by the legislature, Southern Pac. Co. v. Jensen, 244 U.S. 205, 221 (1917) (Holmes, J., dissenting), and the cultivation of an attitude of impartiality was all that could confine judicial legislation to its properly interstitial character. When Holmes criticized admired colleagues like White and Brandeis for being unjudicial, it was because he thought they lacked this attitude, and hence sometimes went beyond the interstitial in their judicial legislating. *See, e.g.*, 1 HOLMES-LASKI LETTERS, *supra* note 10, at 294 (letter to Justice White dated Nov. 26, 1920); *id.* at 556 (letter dated Nov. 5, 1923.).

307 Holmes' many illiberal views have been adequately chronicled. *See generally* Yosal Rogat, *Mr. Justice Holmes: A Dissenting Opinion* (pts. 1 & 2), 15 STAN. L. REV. 3, 254 (1962–1963). In addition to Holmes' well-known adherence to Social Darwinism, laissez-fairism, and eugenics, note also his attitudes on race, 1 HOLMES-LASKI LETTERS, *supra* note 10, at 372 (letter dated Sept. 27, 1921) ("One accepts the union of O[thello] and D[esdemona], black and white, because one has been so accustomed to it. Otherwise it would disgust most of us"), and gender, 2 *id.* at 1035 (letter dated Mar. 7, 1928) ("if I were sincere and were asked certain *whys* by a woman [I] should reply, 'Because Ma'am I am the bull.' "). On the other side are the relatively rare opinions in which he invokes the power of judicial review on the liberal side, particularly on questions of free speech and fairness in criminal procedure. Did any of Holmes' "liberal activist" opinions, other than his dissent in Frank v. Mangum, 237 U.S. 309, 345–50 (1915), predate Brandeis' joining him on the Court?

308 *See* 2 HOLMES-POLLOCK LETTERS, *supra* note 8, at 61 (letter dated Jan. 23, 1921); *Letters to Dr. Wu, supra* note 168, at 167 (letter dated Sept. 30, 1923).

309 For the kind of relatively minute legal conceptual points that especially engaged Holmes' interest as a judge, *see*, for example, 1 HOLMES-POLLOCK LETTERS, *supra* note 8, at 27 (letter dated Mar. 12, 1886); *id.* at 33 (letter dated Feb. 23, 1890); *id.* at 39–40 (letter dated July 8, 1891); *id.* at 50–51 (letter dated Apr. 2, 1894); *id.* at 243 (letter dated Feb. 18, 1917) ("We have had all manner of interesting and important cases—the two are not the

from being the kind of "great magistrate" that Lemuel Shaw had been. When, occasionally, his judgment was not distorted by jealousy or vanity, it was even a deficiency he recognized in himself.[310]

VI The End-Means Continuum and the Lawyer's Work

Holmes' predicament, then, was to be an instrumentalist without an adequate system of ends. While he conceived of law as a tool for the achievement of the good, on the question of what the good was, he thought that apart from "the *de facto* will of the community for the time ... as yet no one has much to say."[311] Nor, in the absence of formal legislative guidance, did he even have much of a sense for the temporary *de facto* collective will; he had chosen to serve a com-

same."); *id.* at 262 (letter dated Mar. 22, 1918); *id.* at 273 (letter dated Nov. 24, 1918) (a "pretty point in Sovereignty").

310 Holmes' jealous vanity appears in his snide "tribute" to John Marshall; he characterized Marshall as basically a party politician who had luckily happened on the scene at a moment when history was on his party's side. *John Marshall, supra* note 42, at 267–68. Holmes went on to say that he preferred to celebrate the "originators of transforming thought," those who see theoretical issues in "little decisions" which effect "interstitial change[s]" in the "tissue of the law." *Id.* at 269. But, he concluded sadly, "what the world pays for is judgment, not the original mind," so that centenary tributes must be paid to those (like Marshall) who decide "great questions and great cases" of the sort that involve "the Constitution or a telephone company." *Id.* Marshall's political "judgment" was, of course, exactly the quality Holmes had praised in Shaw, and would later praise in White. It was the same quality, he admitted in his better moments, that he lacked himself.

Later, after his nomination to the Supreme Court, Holmes groused to Pollock about press commentary, which naturally focused on his widely publicized pro-labor dissent in Vegelahn v. Guntner, 167 Mass. 92, 104–09, 44 N.E. 1077, 1079–82 (1896), the opinion that had led a Progressive president to appoint him. Holmes particularly resented the journalistic charge that he was "brilliant but not very sound," complaining that journalists "bully me with Shaw, Marshall and the rest." 1 HOLMES-POLLOCK LETTERS, *supra* note 8, at 106 (letter dated Feb. 23, 1902). For other gloomy reflections on his failure to get the credit he thought he deserved for his work as a state court judge, see *Despondency and Hope, supra* note 306, at 147, and *Twenty Years in Retrospect, supra* note 78, at 157.

Toward the end of his life, after Holmes' career on the U.S. Supreme Court had finally gained him the reputation he wanted, Harvard Law School hung his portrait next to Marshall's. Holmes referred to this as "the handsomest compliment that they could pay." 2 HOLMES-POLLOCK LETTERS, *supra* note 8, at 268 (letter dated June 9, 1930).

311 *Holdsworth's English Law, supra* note 91, at 288.

munity with whose values he was out of sympathy, whose opinions he did not know, whose very newspapers he did not read.

As an "internal" man who thought that "ideas are more interesting than things," Holmes was by nature a spectator or "witness," yet he chose to work within the law as an "actor."[312] He was reconciled to being a lawyer by a faith that law could "furnish philosophical food to philosophical minds."[313] But he had to struggle to square this faith, which drove him to see every case as an illustration of the "theory and philosophy of the law," with his instrumental conception of law as essentially legislative, to be judged by its "justice and reasonableness."[314] This struggle gave him a curious half-out-of-body vision, an ability to look in on the law from the outside at the same time as he operated upon it from within.

His double vision led Holmes to celebrate the value of the lawyer's work in an unusual way. The passages he composed for ceremonial legal occasions on the theme of how to "live greatly in the law" are familiar ornaments of law school deans' welcoming speeches and commencement speakers' valedictories.[315] But these passages are exceptional within the canon of the law's celebratory rhetoric for more than their stylistic qualities. They lack the usual references to law as a force for good in the community, whether as the bulwark of liberty, the refuge of the oppressed, the source of order and stability, or the guarantor of prosperity.[316] Their focus is entirely on the intrinsic joys rather than on the instrumental justifications of the lawyer's work.

312 *Introduction to the General Survey, supra* note 68, at 300–01; *The Law, supra* note 238, at 26–27.

313 *Introduction to the General Survey, supra* note 68, at 300.

314 HOLMES-SHEEHAN CORRESPONDENCE, *supra* note 278, at 58 (letter dated Jan. 31, 1913); *Langdell Review, supra* note 139, at 234.

315 As Holmes put it in the most-quoted of these passages, "I say... that a man may live greatly in the law as well as elsewhere; that there as well as elsewhere his thought may find its unity in an infinite perspective; that there as well as elsewhere he may wreak himself upon life, may drink the bitter cup of heroism, may wear his heart out after the unattainable." *The Profession of the Law, supra* note 244, at 30; *see also The Law, supra* note 238, at 26; *The Use of Law Schools, supra* note 175, at 38–39, 48; *The Bar as a Profession, supra* note 187, at 159; *The Path of the Law, supra* note 23, at 202; *Law in Science, supra* note 24, at 212, 224; *John Marshall, supra* note 42, at 270; *Northwestern Address, supra* note 244, at 276–77; *Introduction to the General Survey, supra* note 68, at 300–01 OLIVER WENDELL HOLMES, *Albert Venn Dicey* (1898), in OCCASIONAL SPEECHES, *supra* note 78, at 106, 107; *A Provisional Adieu, supra* note 244, at 152; *cf. The Bar as a Profession, supra* note 187, at 154 (discussing the possibility of great success at the bar without much education).

316 A rare counterexample, which focuses on the practical work of the bar as its main function, is *Twenty Years in Retrospect, supra* note 78, at 154–57.

The dangers of this kind of rhetoric, especially when it has behind it the force of Holmes' literary art, are evident. It renders in impressive terms lawyers' self-conception as practitioners of a demanding craft and members of a learned profession, while ignoring the immediate and material external consequences of their work on others.[317] This portrayal of legal practice flowed naturally out of Holmes' most conspicuous defect as a judge and "practical legislator"—his spectatorial detachment from his social context. Having noticed this defect in his qualities, it is now time to consider the qualities of the defect.[318] In my view, Holmes' lack of any strong vision of the social good led him to concentrate with unusual focus on the respects in which pragmatism's stress on situation and context differentiate it from simple instrumentalism.

Excessive focus on the instrumental aspects of pragmatism, especially with emphasis on its evolutionary biological roots, readily makes it into the philistine and drearily reductive philosophy portrayed by its critics. Pragmatists treat human inquiry as a means, an instrument—but an instrument to what ends? As Holmes once said, the theory of evolution seems to decree constant attention to survival, so "that man should produce food and raiment in order that he might produce yet other food and other raiment to the end of time." And yet, as he added, "who does not rebel at that conclusion?"[319] Well, not everyone does. Holmes himself associated the term "pragmatism" with the world view of those who endorse this same grimly philistine "food and raiment" creed, in which every activity is subordinated to some end external to itself, and nothing is done for its own sake—the world view of Mr. Gradgrind, Dickens' great parodic embodiment of English positivism and utilitarianism.[320]

---

317 For critique along these lines of Holmes' version of "living greatly in the law," *see* J. NOONAN, *supra* note 230, at 144–51. Noonan unflatteringly portrays Cardozo (following Holmes) as seeking to extract "great and shining truths" from "the sordid controversies of the litigants." *Id.* at 150 (quoting Cardozo). Also see Bill Simon's critique of the vision of legal practice as either a craft guided mainly by its own internal standards or a game to be played for its intrinsic pleasures. William Simon, *The Ideology of Advocacy: Procedural Justice and Professional Ethics*, 1978 WIS. L. REV. 29.

318 "[M]en may be pardoned for the defects of their qualities if they have the qualities of their defects." *The Class of '61, supra* note 286, at 161.

319 *Northwestern Address, supra* note 244, at 272; *see also Speech at Bar Dinner, supra* note 135, where Holmes, while conceding that "we all want" to "make a living and to succeed," referred to "our ulterior intellectual or spiritual interest," "the ideal part, without which we are but snails or tigers." *Id.* at 246.

320 "Now, what I want is Facts. Teach these boys and girls nothing but Facts. Facts alone are wanted in life. Plant nothing else, and root out everything else." CHARLES DICKENS, HARD TIMES 11 (1961) (originally published 1854).

Holmes vehemently and self-consciously repudiated this view. He denied that "the justification of science and philosophy is to be found in improved machinery and good conduct"; they were "themselves necessaries of life" which "civilization sufficiently accounts for itself" by producing. "[S]cience, like art," he said, was to be "pursued for the pleasure of the pursuit and of its fruits, as an end in itself."[321] It was in this spirit that Holmes praised a Cambridge mathematician's dedication to the derivation of a theorem he believed to be entirely useless.[322] The point was not confined to the abstract thinker; the same value attached to the care a stonemason lavished on a cathedral gargoyle placed where no one could see it, and to an explorer's search for the North Pole, simply because it was there. In Holmes' mind, these kinds of inquiry and activity respond to "categorical imperatives" that "hold their own against hunger and thirst" and "scorn to be classed as mere indirect supports of our bodily needs, which rather they defy."[323] The World War, he wrote to Laski, would be nothing but "a fight of swine for swill" if "we ceased to be interested in philosophy and art."[324] Holmes spoke on no theme with so much passion so often as he did on the value of activity, including intellectual activity, that in any usual sense we would find inexpedient and uneconomic. These passages make it impossible to accept the harsh universality of Yosal Rogat's judgment of Holmes as a man who in the end "simply did not care."[325]

How did Holmes reconcile his romantic celebration of the impractical, especially the impractical life of the mind, with the pragmatic account, which he accepted, of the place of thought in life? Pragmatic instrumentalism, after all, holds that beliefs are instruments for coping with life, treating (in Holmes' own words) "all thought" as "on its way to action."[326] How then to explain, much less justify, the delight of the mathematician at his useless theorem, not to mention the explorer's life-risking quest for the Pole? If "mind" is the name for a set of animal capacities and dispositions naturally selected, like other such capacities and dispositions, for their survival value, why should anyone pursue an end that ignores or even defies the drive to survive and reproduce? And why should anyone think such conduct praiseworthy?

---

321 *Holmes-Cohen Correspondence, supra* note 31, at 326 (letter dated July 21, 1920) (quoting *The Use of Colleges, supra* note 244, at 63); *Law in Science, supra* note 24, at 211–12.

322 *Law in Science, supra* note 24, at 211.

323 *Northwestern Address, supra* note 244, at 273–74.

324 1 Holmes-Laski Letters, *supra* note 10, at 111 (letter dated Nov. 22, 1917).

325 Rogat, *supra* note 2, at 255.

326 *John Marshall, supra* note 42, at 270.

These questions created a genuine paradox for Holmes, and he spent considerable reflection upon them. Perhaps he put his thoughts best in a letter to Cohen:

> Man is like a strawberry plant, the shoots that he throws out take root and become independent centres. And one illustration of the tendency is *the transformation of means into ends*. A man begins a pursuit as a means of keeping alive—he ends by following it at the cost of life. A miser is an example—but so is the man who makes righteousness his end. Morality is simply another means of living but the saints make it an end in itself. Until just now it never occurred to me I think that the same is true of philosophy or art. Philosophy as a fellow once said to me is only thinking. Thinking is an instrument of adjustment to the conditions of life—but it becomes an end in itself. So . . . we can see how man is inevitably an idealist of some sort . . . .[327]

This idea of Holmes'—"the transformation of means into ends"— closely parallels an important theme in Dewey's work. Holmes' first notion—that philosophy is "only thinking," and that thinking is, or begins as, "an instrument of adjustment to the conditions of life,"—reflects the instrumental side of Deweyan pragmatism. The second notion, that thinking "becomes an end in itself," is equally Deweyan, though it reflects a less well-known aspect of his work. Holmes' point is that the human capacity for generalizing is indeed a useful aid to survival; but the development of this capacity then makes its exercise intrinsically rewarding; and so the chief end of life, for some, becomes "framing generalizations" which are not (in terms of survival) "worth a damn."[328]

At the center of both Dewey's account of human action and his theory of value is the concept of the continuum of ends and means. This is one of his most important ideas, and it sharply differentiates him from other "instrumentalist" thinkers, such as Bentham and Hobbes, who understand that human action is always directed toward certain fixed ends, whether the avoidance of death or the attainment of pleasure. For Dewey, the second pragmatist tenet, the culturally situated and contextual aspect of all human inquiry and deliberation, undercuts any idea that all human activity is aimed at some limited set of fixed ends, just as it undercuts the concept that the moral life should be

327 *Holmes-Cohen Correspondence, supra* note 31, at 329–30 (letter dated Sept. 6, 1920) (emphasis added); *see also Sidney Bartlett, supra* note 292, at 54.

328 *See* note 266 *supra*.

directed by fixed rules or principles formulated and applied without regard for context and consequence. The dualism of ends and means is, for Dewey, no more tenable than any other, when it is taken to divide experience into mutually exclusive categories.[329]

As Dewey understands human conduct, individuals make plans, setting provisional goals at varying levels of abstraction, and selecting among the alternative courses of conduct that might lead to the goals.[330] But the goals that give structure to human plans are never "final"; they are at best momentary resting points whose attainment has further foreseeable consequences desirable or undesirable; hence they must themselves be evaluated as means relative to those consequences. Nor can alternative plans of action be evaluated only on the basis of their efficacy in achieving their (provisional) ends; activities, however instrumentally conceived, are to be evaluated by their intrinsic satisfactions or frustrations as well as by their consequences.[331]

Dewey's conception of the end-means continuum challenges another of the standard dualisms of Western thought: the economist's division of human activity into distinct categories of production and consumption. For Dewey, these concepts as commonly understood denote pathological rather than paradigm cases, and are of little use in characterizing normal human activity, which integrates instrumental or productive aspects with those that are final or consummatory. The concept of pure production—activity valued purely as a means of attaining external results—may approximate the reality of, for example, the most mindless and degrading forms of industrial labor. But this simply confirms that such labor is a pathological rather than a normal form of human activity.[332]

---

329 These aspects of both Dewey's and Holmes' versions of instrumentalism can be seen as developments of the Emersonian elements in the origins of pragmatism. *See* note 297 *supra*.

330 *See*, for example, Dewey's discussion of the movement between ends and means in the process of building a house in J. DEWEY, HUMAN NATURE AND CONDUCT, *supra* note 40 at 268–69.

331 Dewey's works contain numerous discussions of the end-means continuum, as well as other, related critiques of the concept of fixed human ends. *See, e.g.*, JOHN DEWEY, RECONSTRUCTION IN PHILOSOPHY 161–86 (2d ed. 1948); J. DEWEY, HUMAN NATURE AND CONDUCT, *supra* note 40, at 199–277; J. DEWEY, EXPERIENCE AND NATURE, *supra* note 19, at 354–437; J. DEWEY, THE QUEST FOR CERTAINTY, *supra* note 39, at 258–64; JOHN DEWEY, ART AS EXPERIENCE 35–57 (1934); JOHN DEWEY, THEORY OF VALUATION 40–50 (1939).

332 J. DEWEY, RECONSTRUCTION IN PHILOSOPHY, *supra* note 331, at 181; J. DEWEY, ART AS EXPERIENCE, *supra* note 331, at 341.

Similarly, pure consumption, behavior carried on entirely for its immediate reward, with no further purpose whatever, scarcely qualifies as human activity for Dewey. The economist's account of consumption might describe a kitten's play with a ball, but such purely "consummatory" conduct lacks the purposefulness which is the characteristic feature of normal human action. Even the play of very young children, Dewey noted, has this characteristic; the most initially aimless play tends to become an improvised game or drama, in which "purpose becomes a thread that runs through a succession of acts."[333] Purposefulness and enjoyment are thus not antagonists, as in the economist's account of production and consumption, but complements.

Play often involves not only an ordering of activities, as in a game, but also an "ordering of materials";[334] in such cases it merges imperceptibly into artistic creation. For Dewey, the making of art, in its organic integration of the instrumental and consummatory aspects of conduct, is the prototype of authentic human activity. Though art, like play, has its own immediate rewards, it is not pursued purely for its own sake; as with play, a thread of purpose, ulterior motive, gives unity to the process. The artist aims in the first instance at the production of the work of art itself. But the thread of purpose is not cut with the completion of the art object; the object too is an instrument for use, just as are more evidently utilitarian products. For Dewey, art is "peculiarly instrumental in quality ... a device in experimentation ... a new training of modes of perception." Works of art are tools for learning, insight, and communication; like "microscopes and microphones" they "open new objects to be observed and enjoyed."[335]

Any human activity informed by purpose and shaped by structure falls upon the end-means continuum and can be seen to resemble not only art but also work, "provided work is not identified with toil or labor."[336] For Dewey, "[w]ork which remains permeated with the play attitude *is* art."[337] And the aesthetic dimension properly pervades workaday life.[338] The social separation of activi-

333 J. Dewey, Art as Experience, *supra* note 331, at 278.

334 *Id.*

335 J. Dewey, Experience and Nature, *supra* note 19, at 392.

336 J. Dewey, Art as Experience, *supra* note 331, at 278.

337 J. Dewey, Democracy and Education, *supra* note 69, at 206.

338 In one of his best passages, Dewey insisted that an understanding of art must begin with "the events and scenes that hold the attentive eye and ear of man, arousing his interest and affording him enjoyment as he looks and listens: the sights that hold the crowd—the fire-engine rushing by; the machines excavating enormous holes in the earth; the human-fly climbing the steeple-side; the men perched high in air on girders, throwing and catching red-hot bolts. The sources of art in human experience will be learned by

ties into those pursued for their own sake and those merely instrumental, consumption and production, is, on Dewey's account, a piece of ideology reflecting and defending the class-based association of material production with menial status and leisure with privilege.[339]

Thus Dewey's psychology of action, his aesthetics, and his social philosophy are linked together around the central concept of the end-means continuum. From his account of normal human action as an integration of instrumental and consummatory aspects emerges a critique that blurs the common distinctions between work and play, on the one hand, and between play and art on the other. The consequence is a commitment to ensuring meaningful work—playful, artful, and "unalienated"—as one of the central goals of social organization. This commitment is what gives to Dewey's social philosophy its radically critical bite. Though he considered himself a liberal democrat, and rejected many aspects of Marxism, he did believe that capitalist economic organization as he knew it had failed to fulfill the goal of meaningful work for all and that classical liberal political theory and political economy had failed even to articulate this goal as one of its ideals.[340]

Now we must return our attention to Holmes, who of course was no radical, scarcely even a liberal, and who had no faith at all in the advancement of human happiness by the economic reorganization of society. These are real and irreducible differences between him and Dewey. Yet alongside these differences, we can now see the important similarities. Holmes' conception of "living greatly in the law" projected—at least for lawyers—a Deweyan vision of work as uniting means enjoyed for their own sake, and ends produced for use: work-play-art.

That Holmes had himself arrived at something like Dewey's conception of the ends-means continuum is evident in the "strawberry plant" passage already quoted, with its account of the transformation of the purely instrumental into the intrinsically valuable.[341] In one speech, Holmes applied the insight to that

> him who sees how the tense grace of the ball-player infects the onlooking crowd; who notes the delight of the housewife in tending her plants, and the intent interest of her goodman in tending the patch of green in front of the house; the zest of the spectator in poking the wood burning on the hearth and in watching the darting flames and crumbling coals."

J. Dewey, Art as Experience, *supra* note 331, at 4–5.

339 J. Dewey, Experience and Nature, *supra* note 19, at 368; J. Dewey, Art as Experience, *supra* note 331, at 4–10.

340 J. Dewey, Art as Experience, *supra* note 331, at 343–44; J. Dewey, Liberalism and Social Action, *supra* note 122, at 87–90.

341 *See* text accompanying note 327 *supra*.

most instrumental of activities, industrial production, when he said that the "chief worth of civilization" is not that it produces more goods but that it "makes the means of living more complex" and thereby "calls for great and combined intellectual efforts ... in order that the crowd may be fed and housed and moved from place to place." The "more complex and intense intellectual efforts" called forth by industrial society "mean a fuller and richer life. They mean more life. Life is an end in itself. ..."[342] This passage strikingly juxtaposes the bitter and the sweet in Holmes—on the one hand, his remoteness from the "crowd" of ordinary people, whose real material needs for decent food and housing scarcely concern him; on the other, the genuine and uncommon insight into the intrinsic value arising out of a realm of material production usually conceived entirely in instrumental terms.

Holmes' infusion of the workaday world with intrinsic value, value conceived in aesthetic terms, was a remnant he always retained from his early Emersonian romanticism. He spoke in this spirit when he told his Harvard classmates that "[l]ife is painting a picture, not doing a sum,"[343] and when, writing to his young friend Wu, he quoted Croce to the effect that "all experience is art." As he elaborated Croce's point, he noted the creatively selective quality of both art and ordinary perceptual experience: "all art is caricature, that is, it emphasizes what the artist wants to call attention to at the expense of other elements. ..." The kind of "insight" that guides this selection of the telling detail, Holmes called "the great human gift."[344] Holmes describes the philosopher in terms usually reserved for the artist as one who can "see the universal in the particular" and "show the infinite in the finite."[345]

But unlike his mentor Emerson, Holmes conceived of the "universal" and "infinite" not in Platonic terms as discoverable objects of rational inquiry; rather his conception was a genuinely pragmatic and perspectival one. For him, the idealist is one who seeks to "make—I do not say find—his world ideal," in part by adopting "an infinite *perspective*," accepting that "the universe has more in it than we understand."[346] Similarly, the Holmesian "universal"

342 *Speech at Bar Dinner, supra* note 135, at 248.

343 *The Class of '61, supra* note 286, at 161.

344 *Letters to Dr. Wu, supra* note 168, at 156–57 (letter dated Dec. 2, 1922).

345 *Id.* at 164 (letter dated June 16, 1923); HOLMES-SHEEHAN CORRESPONDENCE, *supra* note 278, at 51 (letter dated Oct. 27, 1912).

346 *The Profession of the Law, supra* note 244, at 29, 30 (emphasis added); *Natural Law, supra* note 286, at 315.

involves the connection of the particulars of ordinary experience to each other by the transfiguring vision of the imaginative eye.[347]

For the purpose of seeing the infinite and the universal, "*every* particular is as good as any other," subject to "only the qualification, that some can see it in one, some in another matter more readily, according to their faculties."[348] Everyday work thus opened the door to both art and philosophy for Holmes, and he spoke in these terms of his own work: "Life having thrown me into the law, I must try to put my feeling of the infinite into that, to exhibit the detail with such a hint of a vista as I can, to show in it the great line of the universal."[349]

Focus on the similarity between Dewey's and Holmes' thoughts on art and work risks distortion without the offsetting reminder of the very important differences. Dewey, as a temperamental activist and a convinced democrat, clearly meant his conception of work as play and art to apply to everyone, recognizing that for this to be achieved the whole system of industrial labor would have to be transformed. With Holmes, a detached skeptic whose commitment to democracy was at best ambivalent,[350] there is more doubt whether he

---

347 In his essay, *Natural Law*, Holmes identifies himself as one who "sees no reason for believing that significance, consciousness and ideals are more than marks of the finite," *Natural Law, supra* note 286, at 315, and added that "[i]f we think of our existence not as that of a little god outside, but as that of a ganglion within, we have the infinite behind us. It gives us our only but our adequate significance." *Id.* at 316. All that is required is an "imagination... strong enough to accept the vision of ourselves as parts inseverable from the rest...." *Id.*

348 *Letters to Dr. Wu, supra* note 168, at 164–65 (letter dated June 16, 1923).

349 *Id.* at 167 (letter dated Sept. 30, 1923). Holmes was presumably alluding to the Emersonian origins of his ideas about the "infinite" and "universal" when he wrote to Cohen that "early associations affect my emotional attitude toward the mystery of the world." *Holmes-Cohen Correspondence, supra* note 31, at 334 (letter dated Jan. 30, 1921).

350 Holmes' ambivalence about democracy was lifelong. As a Civil War officer he wrote: "While I'm living *en aristocrat* I'm an out-and-outer of a democrat in theory, but for contact, except at the polls, I loath the thick-fingered clowns we call the people...." Letter from Holmes to Amelia Holmes (Nov. 16, 1862), *reprinted in* TOUCHED WITH FIRE, *supra* note 267, at 71. Also, recall Holmes' comments on the mass of men as suited only for "Feed—*F-outre* and Finish." *See* note 286 *supra*. On the other side, he once said in a speech that "the deepest cause we have to love our country" was its "democratic spirit"—"that instinct, that spark that makes the American unable to meet his fellow man otherwise than simply as a man...." OLIVER WENDELL HOLMES, *The Puritan* (1886), in OCCASIONAL SPEECHES, *supra* note 78, at 25. And he wrote of Jane Addams as

> "a big woman who knows at least the facts and gives me more insights into the point of view of the working man and the poor than I had before. How excellent her discrimination between doing good *to* them and doing good *with* them. I believe with her

thought the ideal of work as partaking of art and philosophy could be extended beyond learned professionals to ordinary people.

On the one hand, Holmes did present his ethic of professionalism or "jobbism"—" 'Whatsoever thy hand findeth to do, do it with thy might' "—as a value of potentially universal application.[351] In this vein, he quoted George Herbert's lines on the infusion of the divine into the most humble work: "Who sweeps a room as for Thy laws,/ Makes that and th' action fine"[352]—a reference that Dewey noted favorably in his own essay on Holmes.[353] Holmes often showed appreciation of the intrinsic pleasures of basic human activity.[354] And he said that "[e]very calling is great when greatly pursued."[355]

On the other hand, by "greatly pursued" Holmes seems generally to have meant pursued with learning and with a bent toward abstract speculation. Sweeping a room might be "fine" but not "great"—it is hard to imagine Holmes trying it out for the challenge. He conceived of intellectual pursuits as naturally reserved for the few. Thus he celebrated the special virtues of the little band of professionals or "specialists," including lawyers, who set high intellectual standards for their work. At the same time he deplored the "effervescence

---

> that we need more democratic feeling—I like to multiply my scepticisms—for in administering constitutional law one cannot realize too clearly the possibility of different points of view for all of which there ought to be room to assist themselves if the constitution is not to be a Procrustean bed."

Benjamin G. Rader and Barbara K. Rader, *The Ely-Holmes Friendship, 1901–1914*, 10 AM. J.T. LEGAL HIST. 128, 137 (1966).

351 *Speech at Bar Dinner, supra* note 135, at 247. Characteristically, Holmes described the commitment to doing one's job well as "infinitely more important than the vain attempt to love one's neighbor as one's self." *Id.* He made explicit the link between "jobbism" or professionalism and the transformation of means into ends in *Sidney Bartlett, supra* note 292:

> "It seems to me further that the rule for serving our fellow men ... is to do one's task with one's might. If we do that, I think we find that our motives take care of themselves. *We find that what may have been begun as a means becomes an end in itself*; that self-seeking is forgotten in labors which are the best contribution that we can make to mankind; that our personality is swallowed up in working to ends outside ourselves."

Id. at 54 (emphasis added).

352 *The Bar as a Profession, supra* note 187, at 159.

353 Dewey, *Justice Holmes, supra* note 19, at 36.

354 "[A]n adequate vitality would say daily: 'God—what a good sleep I've had.' 'My eye, that was dinner.' 'Now for a rattling walk—' in short realize life as an end in itself. Functioning is all there is. ..." 2 HOLMES-POLLOCK LETTERS, *supra* note 8, at 22 (letter dated Aug. 21, 1919).

355 *The Law, supra* note 238, at 26.

of democratic negation" that "attacks the lines of Nature which establish orders and degrees among the souls of men."[356]

At this point one might ask what present use less ambivalent democrats than Holmes might make of his version of professionalism. As a beginning, his insistence on the intrinsic rewards of law practice as a craft, an art, and a goad to speculative thought reminds us of a valued partial ideal of professional life. If his words on how to "live greatly in the law" are balanced by some stress on the external and political consequences of professional activity, they do still belong in those deans' remarks and commencement speeches. Further, Holmes' rhetoric can be generalized along the lines Dewey suggests and thus can serve to articulate the broader social ideal of universal access to intrinsically satisfying work. Following Dewey, one might say what Holmes would not: It is false that "every calling" as presently constituted can be "greatly pursued." But it should be true, and its falsity stands as a continuing rebuke to the present social constitution of work.

Finally, Holmes' account of "the transformation of means into ends" responds to the most common objection to pragmatism—that it is the soulless philosophy of Mr. Gradgrind, promoting a mean and reductive approach both to life and to law. On this score, it is instructive to compare Holmes' version of the ideal the lawyer should pursue with that stated by Roscoe Pound, who was probably the first significant American legal thinker to label himself a "pragmatist."[357] Expounding his conception of "sociological jurisprudence," Pound wrote that legal scholarship should dedicate itself to a "great task … of social engineering," aimed at the creation of a system of law rationally designed with an eye to "precluding friction and eliminating waste."[358] Pound's "social engineer" would study the law scientifically, accumulating information so as to assess the machinery of the law in terms of the efficient production and distribution of material goods. This purely instrumental conception of law was not all there was to Pound's jurisprudence, but it was certainly its most prominent strand.[359] It was a view entirely consistent with Bentham's conception of law

356 *The Use of Law Schools, supra* note 175, at 37–38.

357 *See* Roscoe Pound, *A Practical Program of Procedural Reform*, 1910 PROC. ILL. ST. B.A. 373, 375. On Pound's pragmatism, *see* generally DAVID WIGDOR, ROSCOE POUND 183–205 (1974).

358 ROSCOE POUND, THE SPIRIT OF THE COMMON LAW 195–96 (1921); *see also* Roscoe Pound, *The Theory of Judicial Decision* (pt. 3), 36 HARV. L. REV. 940, 954–56 (1923).

359 Pound later leavened the "social engineering" picture with the claim that the judge requires imaginative "trained intuition" as well as calculative instrumental reason, at least for certain classes of cases. *See* Pound, *The Theory of Judicial Decision, supra* note 358, at 951.

as an instrument for the satisfaction of certain fixed human desires and the assuagement of certain fixed fears.[360]

There is much of value in Pound's engineering conception of law, especially by way of compensation for the spectatorial defects in Holmes' statement of the professional ideal. Pound rightly emphasizes the social consequences of legal practice and thus properly reinforces the sense that professional privileges carry with them social obligations. But for all this, his model of the lawyer as social engineer has defects that have become more evident over the years. For one thing, the engineering metaphor creates false hopes for the technical solution of social problems by experts, wrongly suggesting that injustice is always better redescribed as "friction" and "waste."[361] Further, it presupposes that so important an element in social life as law can remain simply a dependent variable, a means for achieving external ends. Holmes' and Dewey's concept of the ends-means continuum reminds us that law, even if it begins as an instrument for the attainment of basic ends like "food and raiment," can generate its own intrinsic values, both positive (due process, legality, the Rule of Law) and negative (legalism). Dewey well understood this; he wrote that a good system of law was partly constitutive of, not merely instrumental to, a good society.[362] Legal pragmatism thus understood is receptive to the classical republican conception both of law as a constitutive element in political life, and of politics itself as an activity of intrinsic as well as instrumental value. Together, these ideas suggest a model of lawyer as republican civil servant rather than as social engineer.[363]

---

360 For Bentham's view of the four fixed goals to be pursued by a legal system—subsistence, abundance, security, and equality—*see* J. BENTHAM, *Principles of the Civil Code*, in 1 WORKS OF BENTHAM, *supra* note 29, at 297, 302.

361 Dewey's writing is also laden with Progressive imagery suggesting scientistic and technocratic cures for social ills; but in his case, the "social laboratory" rhetoric is offset by a strong democratic sense for the importance of broad public participation in government and a recognition of the historically conditioned, political, and aesthetic dimensions of science.

362 "A good political constitution, honest police-system, and competent judiciary, are means of the prosperous life of the community because they are integrated portions of that life." J. DEWEY, EXPERIENCE AND NATURE, *supra* note 19, at 367.

363 For a modern account of legal practice as a constitutive aspect of American government, which explicitly draws on classical republican ideas, *see* Robert W. Gordon, *The Independence of Lawyers*, 68 B.U.L REV. 1, 14–30 (1988). Any such account must go significantly beyond Holmes' implicit view of the private counselor as purely the predictor of judicial action in the service of the private interests of clients. *See* text accompanying notes 181–230 *supra*.

The concept of the end-means continuum has another implication for law study: Dewey's and Holmes' ideas on the relations among art, play, and work remind us that law has a pervasive aesthetic dimension. Legal practice is inevitably an art and a craft, even a game, carried on partly for its own sake. Legal thinkers have rarely taken this point seriously. Some have recognized that a certain aesthetic sensibility supports the geometric conception of law as a closed logical system—thus the Romans' phrase *elegantia juris*. But fewer have seen that any critique of geometric formalism carries with it some aesthetic of its own, implicit if not explicit. Influenced by Holmes on this point, Karl Llewellyn was one of the few American legal thinkers really to attend to the aesthetic and rhetorical dimension of law. This appears most memorably in his treatment of jurisprudential approaches as "styles," grand and formal, rather than as "theories"; less well known is his use of the (Holmesian) analogy of law to architecture, which allowed him to formulate the aesthetic of the legal grand style as form in the service of function.[364]

But Llewellyn scarcely began the study of law as an art or craft. His most significant hint of the direction he might have followed came in a footnote written at the end of his life in which he spoke of the relation between legal aesthetics and justice, "the beautiful" and "the good" in law.[365] He suggested that justice, partly a surrogate for efficiency, is in part also an aesthetic ideal, and none the worse for it. The just is quite appropriately conceived of as the "fitting." Recent legal scholarship has begun to develop the themes anticipated by Llewellyn's hint, focusing on the place in law of literary technique, visual imagery, and religious symbolism. Particularly notable in this development have been feminist writers on law, whose own practical and contextual approach to law indicates important parallels between pragmatism and contemporary feminist thought.[366]

---

364 *See* Karl N. Llewellyn, *On the Good, the True, the Beautiful, in Law*, 9 U. Chi. L. Rev. 224 (1942), *reprinted in* Karl N. Llewellyn, Jurisprudence: Realism in Theory and Practice 167, 174–96 (1962). Holmes suggested the analogy of the legal theorist to the architect in *The Path of the Law*, *supra* note 23, at 200.

365 Llewellyn, *supra* note 364, at 224 & n.*.

366 *See* Robert M. Cover, *Foreword*: Nomos *and Narrative*, 97 Harv. L. Rev. 4 (1982); Robin West, *Jurisprudence as Narrative: An Aesthetic Analysis of Modern Legal Theory*, 60 N.Y.U. L. Rev. 145 (1985); *see also* Dennis E. Curtis & Judith Resnik, *Images of Justice*, 96 Yale LJ. 1727 (1987). Curtis and Resnick explore the iconography of justice, an issue on which Llewellyn said:

> "I am rather clear that in a fuller presentation, there would have to be included under 'The Good,' a study of 'Justice, Efficiency, and Warmth,' developing not only the problem of finding the first, and of weaving the three together, but also that of finding a

Of course Holmes was even less of a feminist than he was a radical economic reformer. And while he often contrasted scientific with literary approaches to inquiry, he did so invariably to the disadvantage of the literary.[367] But taken all in all, his version of legal pragmatism supports those who would study the place in law of narrative, metaphor, and the aesthetics of conceptual architecture. And, inevitably, he will be enlisted to supply epigraphic and aphoristic inspiration for this approach to law study—a role that might seem trivial, but only because the approach has not yet taken sufficient root. If scholarship does establish the aesthetic and rhetorical element in law as intrinsic rather than merely decorative, we will better appreciate, though still with justified suspicion, the power that a legal theorist armed with the skills of a great literary artist can wield.

It is important, finally, for those of us susceptible to Holmes' charms to recall once more the need for that suspicion. Holmes never did resolve the contradiction between the work of an actor and the perspective of a witness. His resulting ideal vision of legal practice does indeed emphasize the important and neglected "philosophical" (or aesthetic) values that bear on the lawyer's working life. But this emphasis comes at the expense of the aspects of lawyering that make it both a political and a service profession, one with special access to the levers of power, to be judged primarily by how its exercise of that power affects the lives of those subject to it. If we insistently force ourselves to make this correction in the law's image as it appears through the lens Holmes' thought provides, those of us who cannot bury him need not rest content with simply praising him. Following his own best teachings, we can properly re-situate him, and put him yet again to good use.

> symbol for law of very different character from that of a large, cold, figure, distant, blind, and carrying a sword—a symbol earth-rooted and friendly as an oak."

Llewellyn, *supra* note 364, at 224 n.*.

For more on the striking analogies between pragmatist and feminist thought, compare the formulations of the distinction between the "tough-minded" and "tender-minded" in W. James, Pragmatism, *supra* note 14, at 3–40, and the distinction between "separate" and "connected" approaches to knowledge in Mary Field Belenky, Blythe McVicker Clinchy, Nancy Rule Goldberger, & Jill Mattuck Tarule, Women's Ways of Knowing 100–30 (1986).

367 *See* note 278 *supra*.

Appendix: Holmes and the Pragmatists

Pragmatism was not only a theory; it was also an important movement, originating with Charles Sanders Peirce, later led by William James, and then by John Dewey. It used to be said that Holmes was part of this movement, indeed an important founder of it.[368] But the evidence for Holmes as a founder of pragmatism is weak, and he said much that casts doubt on whether he thought of himself as a pragmatist at all. Still, there are enough complexities on the issue to make it impossible to ascribe any simple view to Holmes.

When James introduced pragmatism by name to the world in 1898, he attributed both the word and the idea behind it to Peirce,[369] who had first articulated the idea, though without the name, in a series of articles published in *Popular Science Monthly* twenty years before.[370] Peirce's basic thesis was that general concepts get their meanings not from their antecedents in sensation, as traditional empiricism had it, but from their practical consequences in action.[371] Pragmatism, he said, followed as "scarce more than a corollary" from Alexander Bain's definition of a belief as " 'that upon which a man is prepared to act.' "[372] He first stated the thesis, and used the name "pragmatism," in a paper delivered in 1872 to a meeting of the Metaphysical Club, a small discussion group that met in Cambridge during the years after the Civil War.[373] Holmes was one of the original Metaphysicians, along with Peirce, Chauncey Wright, Nicholas St. John Green, and James.[374]

---

368 *See* M. Fisch, *supra* note 6; P. Wiener, *supra* note 6, at 172–89.

369 William James, *Philosophical Conceptions and Practical Results* (1898), in Collected Essays and Reviews 406, 410 (1920).

370 C.S. Peirce, *The Fixation of Belief, supra* note 37; Charles Sanders Peirce, *How to Make Our Ideas Clear* (1878), in 5 Collected Papers of Charles Sanders Peirce, *supra* note 37, para. 388.

371 "Consider what effects, that might conceivably have practical bearings, we conceive the object of our conception to have. Then, our conception of these effects is the whole of our conception of the object." C.S. Peirce, *How to Make Our Ideas Clear, supra* note 370, para. 402.

372 C.S. Peirce, *Historical Affinities and Genesis, supra* note 64, para. 12.

373 *Id.* para. 13; *see also* Letter from William James to Henry James (Nov. 24, 1872), *quoted in* 1 R. Perry, *supra* note 251, at 332.

374 *See* C.S. Peirce, *Historical Affinities and Genesis, supra* note 64, paras. 12–13; Letter from William James to Holmes (Jan. 3, 1868), *quoted in* 1 R. Perry, *supra* note 251, at 507. On the Metaphysical Club, *see* P. Wiener, *supra* note 6, at 18–30, and the authoritative account appearing in Max H. Fisch, *Was There a Metaphysical Club m Cambridge?*, in Studies in the Philosophy of Charles Sanders Peirce 3 (E. Moore & R. Robin eds. 1964).

On the basis of these ties, Max Fisch argued that Holmes should be regarded as one of the principal founders of pragmatism.[375] Fisch argued that Holmes' prediction theory of law, which he first publicly articulated in jurisprudence lectures he gave at the Harvard Law School in 1872,[376] was a straightforward application of the basic pragmatic maxim that Peirce had first presented to the Metaphysical Club in his paper of that year. Fisch inferred that Holmes' theory had been formulated along with Peirce's maxim and even speculated that Peirce might have derived the maxim by generalizing from the prediction theory.[377]

In fact, whatever is distinctively pragmatist in the prediction theory is not likely to have emerged from the discussions of the Metaphysical Club. As Fisch's own later research showed, Holmes' connection with the Club was very tenuous.[378] Holmes later wrote that he had not heard of pragmatism before the 1890s[379] and that he had seen Peirce "very little" during the Metaphysical Club period, because "in those days I was studying law and I soon dropped out of the band"; what benefit he had from the Club was derived from Wright and Green rather than Peirce, whom Holmes regarded as a self-important bore.[380]

Holmes apparently became aware of the term "pragmatism" only some time after James introduced it to the public in 1898.[381] Thereafter, he spoke of it several times in his letters, always critically. Holmes saw pragmatism as entirely James' creation, and his criticisms of the doctrine must be seen in the context of the complex relations between the two men. In their youth they were intense discussion partners and friends; Holmes could address James without any irony as "Oh! Bill, my beloved,"[382] while James called him in reply "my

375 M. FISCH, *supra* note 6.

376 Holmes first published the gist of the prediction theory in *Notice: Jurisprudential Lectures, supra* note 196.

377 M. FISCH, *supra* note 6, at 11–12.

378 Fisch, *supra* note 374, at 22.

379 *Holmes-Cohen Correspondence, supra* note 31, at 326 (letter dated July 21, 1920).

380 Letter from Holmes to Charles Hartshorne (Aug. 25, 1927), *quoted in* Fisch, *supra* note 374, at 11.

381 Holmes' first mention of the term is in a 1907 letter to James. *See* Letter from Holmes to William James (Mar. 24, 1907), *quoted in* 2 R. PERRY, *supra* note 251, at 459–61. Holmes had written to James over a decade before in response to the latter's essay *The Will to Believe*, which had, without using the term "pragmatism," deployed what James later treated as a central aspect of the idea. *See* Letter from Holmes to William James (May 24, 1896), *quoted in id.* at 458.

382 Letter from Holmes to William James (Dec. 15, 1867), *quoted in* 1 *id.* at 506.

Wendly boy."[383] But they were friends always conscious of serious differences. Thus in 1868 James wrote to Holmes that when they were together "I put myself involuntarily into a position of self-defense, as if you threatened to overrun my territory and injure my own proprietorship."[384] A year later James wrote to his brother Henry of the "cold-blooded, conscious egotism and conceit" by which "[a]ll the noble qualities of Wendell Holmes . . . are poisoned."[385] As late as 1876 James was still close enough to Holmes to visit him and his wife on Cape Cod, where, as he wrote to Henry, he saw Holmes' "virtues and faults . . . thrown into singular relief by the lonesomeness of the shore"; against that background Holmes appeared to James as "a powerful battery, formed like a planing machine to gouge a deep self-beneficial groove through life."[386]

Though these temperamental differences finally put an end to their active friendship, James continued to send Holmes his writings. But the breach colored all of Holmes' responses. In 1896, after reading *The Will to Believe*, Holmes commented that James' demands on the universe "are too nearly the Christian demands without the scheme of salvation. . . . This you will recognize as my ever recurring view ever since we have known each other."[387] A decade later, Holmes responded even more negatively to James' *Pragmatism* lectures. Holmes called the name itself "pedantic"[388] and declared his own adherence to one of the two warring factions—the "tough" and the "tender"—between which James wished his new philosophy to meditate:[389] "You would say that I am too hard or tough-minded. . . ."[390]

To others, Holmes used harsher terms. Thus he wrote to Sir Frederick Pollock: "*I* think pragmatism an amusing humbug—like most of William James's speculations . . . ,"[391] James, he said, was not strong in "logic" or "abstract

383 Letter from William James to Holmes (Jan. 3, 1868), *quoted in* 1 *id.* at 508.

384 Letter from William James to Holmes (May 15, 1868), *quoted in* 1 *id.* at 514.

385 Letter from William James to Henry James (Oct. 2, 1869), *quoted in* 1 *id.* at 307.

386 Letter from William James to Henry James (July 5, 1876), *quoted in* 1 *id.* at 371. For Perry's analysis of the James-Holmes relation, *see* 1 *id.* at 504–19.

387 Letter from Holmes to William James (May 24, 1896), *quoted in* 2 *id.* at 459.

388 Letter from Holmes to William James (Oct. 13, 1907), *quoted in* 2 *id.* at 462.

389 W. JAMES, PRAGMATISM, *supra* note 14, at 12, 32–33.

390 Letter from Holmes to William James (Mar. 24, 1907), *quoted in* 1 R. PERRY, *supra* note 251, at 301.

391 1 HOLMES-POLLOCK LETTERS, *supra* note 8, at 138–39 (letter dated June 17, 1908).

thinking";[392] his talent was for "art and *belles lettres*" rather than "philosophy";[393] he had taken positions "fitted to please free thinking Unitarian parsons and the ladies."[394] When James died, Holmes wrote to Pollock that it was his "little sympathy" with James' "demi spiritualism and pragmatism" that had finally driven them apart.[395]

Writing to Harold Laski, Holmes crudely parodied pragmatism: "I never could make anything out of [James'] or his friends' advocacy of his nostrum except either that in motives depending upon human conduct effort affects the result—which we have heard—or that by yearning we can modify the multiplication table, which I doubt."[396] And, with more justice, he objected to Laski's fashionable use of the term "pragmatic" to describe Benthamite legal ideas: "[T]he judging of law by its effects and results did not have to wait for W.J. or Pound for its existence. . . ."[397]

While Holmes spoke of James' psychological insight and personal charm,[398] qualities he attributed to the latter's "essential Irishness,"[399] only once did he praise one of his old friend's ideas; he conceded that James might have "made a valuable contribution in pointing out that ideas were not necessarily faint pictures of original experience."[400] Though isolated, the remark is significant, for it reveals Holmes' recognition, however grudging, of one of the basic pragmatist innovations upon orthodox empiricism.

Holmes extended his rejection of James' ideas to those of Peirce as well. After Peirce finally came to public attention in the 1920s, Holmes wrote that he

---

392 *Id.* at 192 (letter dated Apr. 26, 1912). James' own characterization reflects some agreement with Holmes' view: "You have a far more logical and orderly mode of thinking than I. . . ." Letter from William James to Holmes (May 15, 1868), *quoted in* 1 R. PERRY, *supra* note 251, at 513.

393 1 HOLMES-POLLOCK LETTERS, *supra* note 8, at 78 (letter dated Aug. 11, 1897).

394 *Id.* at 139 (letter dated June 17, 1908); *see also Holmes-Cohen Correspondence, supra* note 31, at 350 (letter dated Feb. 16, 1925).

395 1 HOLMES-POLLOCK LETTERS, *supra* note 8, at 167 (letter dated Sept. 1, 1910).

396 1 HOLMES-LASKI LETTERS, *supra* note 10, at 70 (letter dated Mar. 29, 1917). In another letter, Holmes reports his "glee" that F.H. Bradley "falls foul of Pragmatism and chops it into mincemeat"; he feared he "had missed something until I was confirmed in my criticisms by him." *Id.* at 705 (letter dated Feb. 1, 1925).

397 *Id.* at 20 (letter dated Sept. 15, 1916).

398 1 HOLMES-POLLOCK LETTERS, *supra* note 8, at 192 (letter dated Apr. 26, 1912).

399 *Id.* at 78 (letter dated Aug. 11, 1897); *see also Holmes-Cohen Correspondence, supra* note 31, at 325 (letter dated July 21, 1920). The connotations of "Irishness" for a Brahmin like Holmes were not likely to be strongly favorable.

400 1 HOLMES-POLLOCK LETTERS, *supra* note 8, at 191 (letter dated Apr. 26, 1912).

was "overrated,"[401] observing that "his reasoning in the direction of religion &c seems to me to reflect what he wants to believe."[402] This reference to religion suggests an important factor common to Holmes' rejection of the ideas of both James and Peirce: "As to pragmatism.... I now see... that the aim and end of the whole business is religious."[403] This offended against one of Holmes' own deepest intellectual commitments: the religious skepticism that he had formed as a young student before the Civil War, and that he had held to in the most testing moment of his life, when he lay wounded, mortally he thought, after the battle of Ball's Bluff.[404] In Holmes' view, James and Peirce had succumbed to wishful thinking when they made room for God in their otherwise scientific views of the universe. He could befriend and admire the Irish Catholic priest Canon Sheehan,[405] but he detested softness toward religion from within the camp of science. To Holmes, James' thesis that "we are warranted in choosing what seems to us the most effective and helpful view in cases where we have no proof either way" was "fishy" and unacceptable "for us hard-headed ones," because it created an "alliance of philosophy with religion" and allowed the religious to "bully *nous autres*" from a new "dogmatic foothold."[406] Holmes felt that in wanting "a warm God... that loves and admires us,"[407] James had given in to temptation by creating a theory that allowed him to believe in one: "His

---

401 1 HOLMES-LASKI LETTERS, *supra* note 10, at 565 (letter dated Nov. 29, 1923).

402 *Holmes-Cohen Correspondence, supra* note 31, at 341 (letter dated Sept. 14, 1923). Holmes went on to question Peirce's claims to originality: "That we could not assert necessity of the order of the universe I learned to believe from Chauncey Wright long ago. I suspect C.S.P. got it from the same source." *Id.*

403 1 HOLMES-POLLOCK LETTERS, *supra* note 8, at 140 (letter dated July 6, 1908).

404

> "Of course when I thought I was dying the reflection that the majority vote of the civilized world declared that with my opinions I was *en route* for Hell came up with painful distinctness—Perhaps the first impulse was tremulous—but then I said—by Jove, I die like a soldier anyhow—I was shot in the breast doing my duty up to the hub—afraid? No, I am proud—then I thought I couldn't be guilty of a deathbed recantation—father and I had talked of that and were agreed that it generally meant nothing but a cowardly giving way to fear—Besides, thought I, can I recant if I want to, has the approach of death changed my beliefs much? & to this I answered—No."

TOUCHED WITH FIRE, *supra* note 267, at 27–28; *cf.* M. HOWE, THE SHAPING YEARS, *supra* note 26, at 11.

405 *See* HOLMES-SHEEHAN CORRESPONDENCE, *supra* note 278, at 12 (letter dated Feb. 1904); *id.* at 28 (letter dated July 17, 1909). Holmes' admiration for Sheehan is evident throughout their correspondence.

406 1 HOLMES-POLLOCK LETTERS, *supra* note 8, at 191–92 (letter dated Apr. 26, 1912).

407 *Id.* at 140 (letter dated July 6, 1908).

reason made him sceptical and his wishes led him to turn down the lights so as to give miracle a chance."[408]

Holmes criticized the pragmatists not only for softness toward religion, but also for philistinism. In commenting on pragmatism to Cohen, he quoted an old speech in which he had said that the "justification of science and philosophy" was not to be found in "improved machinery and good conduct." Rather "[s]cience and philosophy are themselves necessaries of life. By producing them civilization sufficiently accounts for itself...." Holmes did admit that the "pragmatic utilitarian tests" were "more exquisite" than his words—"improved machinery and good conduct"—had indicated.[409] Holmes knew that he was invoking a popular canard against the pragmatists, but perhaps he felt a connection between their softness toward God and the philistine conception of progress popularly attributed to them.

But Holmes did not reject the ideas of all the leading pragmatists. Late in his life, he praised in the highest terms the work of John Dewey, who, unlike James and Peirce, did not combine pragmatism with theism. With Dewey, as with James, personal factors complicate any assessment of the significance of Holmes' judgment. In 1922, Holmes appraised Dewey's *Human Nature and Conduct* in mixed terms: it was "like shavings of jade—subtle—sometimes epigrammatic...an immense advance on any book there was when I was younger—yet somehow not quite seeming to arrive anywhere—and not feeling to me quite as new as it is civilized."[410] He disliked Dewey's reformist politics nearly as much as James' and Peirce's religiosity, noting that Dewey "talks of the exploitation of man by man—which always rather gets my hair up."[411] And three years later, his opinion was even less positive; on hearing that Laski found Dewey unreadable and that Bertrand Russell did not admire him, Holmes reported himself "pleased at what you say about John Dewey—whom I have supposed myself bound to revere, and have revered, but have not read—except in matters of no great moment or impressiveness."[412]

Then in 1926, when Holmes was 85, his young friend John Wu recommended that he read Dewey's new book *Experience and Nature*. Holmes agreed to try it, even though he had previously found Dewey "excellent but uninspired."[413] But

---

408 *Id.* at 167 (letter dated Sept. 1, 1910).

409 *Holmes-Cohen Correspondence, supra* note 31, at 326 (letter dated July 21, 1920) (quoting *The Use of Colleges, supra* note 244, at 63).

410 1 Holmes-Laski Letters, *supra* note 10, at 431 (letter dated June 14, 1922).

411 *Id.*

412 *Id.* at 803 (letter dated Dec. 5, 1925).

413 *Letters to Dr. Wu, supra* note 168, at 189 (letter dated Nov. 23, 1916).

the new work transformed his opinion; he wrote at once to Laski, "I thought [it] truly a great book."[414]

Holmes' praise for *Experience and Nature* may not have been motivated entirely by admiration for Dewey's views. Immediately after praising Dewey's book, Holmes added: "I mention that he quotes me in it as one of our great American philosophers, and pleased me thereby no little, only to say that that was not why I read it and is not why I think it great."[415] The protesting addition may protest too much; it casts some doubt on the source of the transformation of Holmes' opinion of Dewey. One is reminded of a bit of revealing self-deprecation he put in a letter to Pollock: "as Hohfeld used to crack me up naturally I thought well of him."[416] From his own testimony, we know that Holmes valued above all other things the praise of those few whom he regarded as experts.[417]

---

414 2 HOLMES-LASKI LETTERS, *supra* note 10, at 904 (letter dated Dec. 15, 1926); *see also id.* at 901 (letter dated Dec. 4, 1926); *Letters to Dr. Wu, supra* note 168, at 287 (letter dated Jan. 30, 1928); 2 HOLMES-POLLOCK LETTERS, *supra* note 8, at 287 (letter dated May 15, 1931); *id.* at 272 (letter dated July 26, 1930) ("[Dewey's] view of the universe came home to me closer than any other that I know.").

415 2 HOLMES-LASKI LETTERS, *supra* note 10, at 904–05 (letter dated Dec. 15, 1926). Dewey had written, before quoting for two full pages from Holmes' essays *Ideals and Doubts, see* note 94 *supra*, and *Natural Law, see* note 286 *supra*: "I gladly borrow the glowing words of one of our greatest American philosophers; with their poetry they may succeed in conveying where dry prose fails." J. DEWEY, EXPERIENCE AND NATURE, *supra* note 41, at 417; *see also id.* at 417–19 (quoting Holmes).

416 2 HOLMES-POLLOCK LETTERS, *supra* note 8, at 64 (letter dated Feb. 9, 1921).

417 *See Letters to Dr. Wu, supra* note 168, at 200 (letter dated Nov. 2, 1928) ("the only thing that gives one real happiness is when one whose judgment one respects says the few words that are the laurel crown"); HOLMES-SHEEHAN CORRESPONDENCE, *supra* note 278, at 58 (letter dated Jan. 31, 1913) ("I like to have the Bar think well of me, but the only thing I care much for is what a few masters scattered here and there say."); 2 HOLMES-POLLOCK LETTERS, *supra* note 8, at 71 (letter dated June 20, 1921) (Holmes lived "solely" for the favorable judgments of the "few competent like you"); *id.* at 92 (letter dated Mar. 29, 1922) ("I have had some letters and one or two notices in the papers that have touched me deeply. They have said what I longed to hear said and would almost willingly have died to hear twenty years ago."); *id.* at 260–61 (letter dated Apr. 6, 1930) (to Pollock's criticism—"The butter's spread too thick"—of an effusive tribute by Laski, Holmes wrote that he "was so touched and moved by the note of affection and made so shy by the praise that I hardly like to speak about it and could not criticize."); *Letters to Dr. Wu, supra* note 168, at 201 (letter dated July 1, 1929) (of Cardozo: "I . . . owe to him some praise that I regard as one of the chief rewards of my life."); 2 HOLMES-LASKI LETTERS, *supra* note 10, at 1272 (letter dated Aug. 9, 1930) (likewise of Cardozo: "He is one of the few who have said in print and private the things that make my life seem worth having been lived.").

Of course we should not simply discount Holmes' insistence that Dewey's praise was "not why I think [the book] great." But when he came to say why he thought *Experience and Nature* a great book, Holmes was uncharacteristically inarticulate; he "could not have summed up a chapter or a page" and would "find it hard to give any intelligible account" of the work.[418] Yet, he concluded, despite "defects of expression," Dewey seemed "to hold more of existence in his hand and more honestly to see behind all the current philosophers than any book I can think of on such themes."[419] Elsewhere, Holmes spoke of the book's "symphonic" quality and said that it reminded him of Walt Whitman.[420] Yet nowhere did he say anything specific about its content.

On this record I would certainly not confidently conclude that Dewey won Holmes' esteem merely by calling the old Justice a great philosopher. Much of this study has been devoted to tracing the similarities in the thought of the two men. And there are elements new to Dewey's work in *Experience and Nature* that might have especially appealed to Holmes.[421] But the very vigor and immediacy with which Holmes denied that Dewey's praise had influenced him reveals his discomfort with the coincidence that the book in which it appeared had elevated Dewey's stature in his mind from "uninspired" to "great."

The record of his direct remarks and their context simply leaves Holmes' relation to pragmatism in doubt. On the one hand, one might take his explicit rejections of pragmatism at face value. On this view, he accepted the pragmatists' basic positivism and empiricism, but thought on that score that James and Peirce had added nothing essentially new to Bentham and Mill. What he regarded as genuinely novel—James' justification of beliefs lacking evidentiary support on grounds of their good effect on morale—Holmes rejected. From this perspective, what Holmes found acceptable in Dewey's ideas was his generally naturalistic and evolutionary world view; and, since what he found more than merely acceptable he could not articulate, we must suspect that, especially at the age of 85, Holmes' judgment had been swayed by Dewey's praise of him.

On the other hand, Holmes might have rejected James' and Peirce's versions of pragmatism largely because they used it to justify religion. Holmes' critical

418 2 Holmes-Laski Letters, *supra* note 10, at 904.

419 *Id.* at 905.

420 *Letters to Dr. Wu*, *supra* note 168, at 190 (letter dated Dec. 5, 1926).

421 In particular, Dewey developed his theory of art further than he had before. *See* notes 335–339 *supra* and accompanying text. Also, compared to Dewey's other books, *Experience and Nature* has much less of the liberal reformist politics which Holmes disliked.

judgment on this issue may have been nudged along by his dislike of Peirce and his more complex antipathy toward James. The negative part of his early reaction to Dewey could then be explained by the latter's awkward prose style and reformist politics. If we see the evidence in this light, Holmes never really confronted a statement of pragmatism that was not tainted by the adventitious elements of religion, personality, or politics until he read *Experience and Nature*, at which point he finally reacted with unmediated enthusiasm. Further excavation of a narrowly biographical kind is not likely to decide between these conflicting interpretations.

Accidental Torts

Thomas C. Grey

One way to understand tort law is as a functional response to the social problem of accidental personal injury. That puts the negligence action at the center, and emphasizes the doctrinal choice between negligence and strict liability, while downplaying the intentional torts and the torts that do not involve physical injury. It also foregrounds the policy choice between tort and other means of dealing with accidents. This functional treatment is not uncontroversial today, but it is certainly orthodox.[1]

Here I propose to bring back into view some neglected aspects of the intellectual origins of the accident-centered approach to tort law. When torts was emerging as an important doctrinal category in the common-law world during the late nineteenth century, the early commentator who did the most to organize it around the problem of accidental injury was the young Oliver Wendell Holmes, Jr. The influential slant he gave to the subject turns out to have resulted

---

* This article originally appeared in Vanderbilt Law Review, Vol. 54:3 (2001), pp. 1225–1284.

** Nathan Bowman Sweitzer and Marie B. Sweitzer Professor of Law, Stanford Law School. My thanks to George Fletcher, Marc Franklin, Barbara Fried, Morton Horwitz, Judge Richard Posner, and Robert Rabin, and especially to Barbara Babcock, for editorial advice; to David Ibbetson, David Seipp, and James Whitman for sharing their learning on specialized historical matters; and to Joshua Layton-Rodin and Alexandra Walsh for valuable research help.

1 Its orthodoxy would be underscored by the ALI's adoption of Professor Schwartz's new draft of "general principles" for the *Restatement of Torts*, the occasion for this symposium. The draft purports to govern, not tort law as a whole, or even the tort of negligence as a whole, but only the action for negligent personal injury or property damage. The principles governing this action are said to be "general" despite their restricted domain because—as the perspective I mention presupposes—"the problem of accidental injury" is "the core of tort law." RESTATEMENT (THIRD) OF TORTS: GENERAL PRINCIPLES, Reporter's Introductory Note (Discussion Draft Apr. 5, 1999) [hereinafter Discussion Draft]. That the approach continues to be controversial is brought out by Professors Goldberg and Zipursky's article in the present symposium, criticizing the use of this "core" approach to justify reduced emphasis on the traditional duty element in the negligence action. John C.P. Goldberg & Benjamin C. Zipursky, *The Third Restatement and the Place of Duty in Negligence Law*, 54 VAND. L. REV. 657 (2001). By contrast, the *First* and *Second Restatements* did not begin with a treatment of accidental injury but gave the intentional torts pride of place as the first subject dealt with, following the traditional organization laid down by the first Harvard torts casebook. JAMES BARR AMES & JEREMIAH SMITH, A SELECTION OF CASES ON THE LAW OF TORTS (1875).

© KONINKLIJKE BRILL NV, LEIDEN, 2014 | DOI 10.1163/9789004272897_007

from his struggle with doubts, surprising and possibly instructive to us, about whether torts was a viable legal category at all.

Neither Holmes' doubts about torts nor the theory with which he resolved them had much to do with his views about proper social policy toward industrial accidents. He was mainly responding to the inner dynamics of a juristic debate about the taxonomic arrangement of the substantive law, a debate that had been triggered by the legislative abolition of the common-law forms of action. Jurists drawing on conceptual traditions inherited from Roman law favored adopting tort as a basic category, while those influenced by the analytical jurisprudence of Bentham and Austin pressed the other way. After first taking the Bentham-Austin side, Holmes discovered that centering tort law around the problem of accidents could justify its recognition as an important subject after all.

Coincidentally, the burst of personal injury litigation that accompanied the growth of railroads and factories in the late nineteenth century made Holmes' accident-centered formulation of tort law especially salient in practical terms, and his theory went on to gain the dominant position it holds today, at least in the United States. It thus turned out that in resolving an abstruse theoretical puzzle about the arrangement of the law in the way he did, Holmes was helping to construct an understanding of torts that is still dominant a century later, when its origins have largely been forgotten. As a final twist, we now have our own quite different doubts about torts, based more on concerns about accident policy than on views about conceptual arrangement—and the accident-centered conception that Holmes devised to justify the subject in the first place turns out to leave it especially vulnerable to these doubts.

I'll start by sketching a version of the accident-centered conception of torts as it exists today—the one I teach in my own introductory course on the subject. Then I'll show why torts was by no means certain to become a fundamental category, a subject taught in every law school, at the time our basic legal taxonomy emerged in the late nineteenth century. Next I'll trace the steps through which Holmes moved from his early rejection of torts as a category to justifying it as a body of law organized around negligence and accidental injury. Finally, I'll note the difficulties that the accident-centered conception poses for the continued survival of torts as a primary division of our substantive law today.

I What is a Tort?

Students come to law school with ideas about contracts, property, crime, and constitutions, but "tort" is a purely legal term corresponding to none of their ordinary notions or experiences. Telling them that it is a French word for "wrong" doesn't help much; a breach of contract is a civil wrong too, and they will learn that not all tort liability involves wrongdoing.

So I begin my introductory course in torts not with a definition, but with a sketch of its relation to the rest of the introductory curriculum, which I map using the distinctions between private and public, civil and criminal, and substantive and procedural law. These distinctions mark off constitutional law, criminal law and civil procedure respectively, leaving the substantive private-law subjects: torts, contracts, and property. Private civil liabilities can then be divided between those arising from agreement and those "imposed by law"—between contract and tort.[2] Cutting across this division, property law defines entitlements and regulates their acquisition, use and transfer.

The map helps locate torts, but still leaves it looking like a misshapen semi-catchall category—the substantive law governing some of the private civil liabilities that are not based on contract. The lack of a good definition can be partly offset by supplying some internal structure, and to that end I classify tort doctrines along two dimensions: the interests they protect, and the levels of culpability they require. I divide the interests into three classes: physical security of person and possessions; intangible personal interests in reputation, privacy, and emotional tranquility; and purely pecuniary assets and expectations. And crosscutting those interests are the three standard levels of culpability: serious wrongdoing (intent or malice), negligence, and strict liability.

I tell my students that rather than surveying the whole resulting three-by-three matrix, we will focus on accidental physical injury. That means omitting the intentional torts involving force and fraud; the business torts; the torts linked to land use; and the torts protecting intangible personal interests—defamation, invasion of privacy, and infliction of emotional distress. I have my excuses for each omission,[3] but still it is a lot to leave out. The justification is my judgment that accidental injury is what tort law is really all about.

---

2 This division is of course very rough. Contractual liability is "imposed by law" as much as any other kind, at least on some views. Unjust enrichment is often recognized as a third category of private common-law civil liability apart from tort and contract; and there are civil liabilities (for instance, for breach of trust) that for historical reasons get left out of the standard private-law categories. An old-fashioned but still interesting conceptual investigation of the relations of torts to other legal categories is Percy Winfield, The Province of the Law of Torts (1931).

3 Doctrine governing torts of force and fraud closely tracks the substantive criminal law; the business torts are dealt with in connection with legal regulation of the market; nuisance and trespass come in under property law; and defamation, privacy, and emotional distress are dealt with in an advanced torts course.

This is easy enough to show practically and politically, at least in the United States, where accident claims are at the heart of the "tort crisis" and the calls for "tort reform." But does this concentration obscure something important about the nature of tort law? I take the question seriously, knowing that there are thoughtful scholars who say that it does,[4] and that the first impressions I am imprinting on my students will tend to stick.

Portraying tort doctrines as responses to the accident problem means asking how well they deter unsafe conduct and help cushion shocks to injury victims, and also comparing them to alternative ways of pursuing those goals. One kind of traditional social insurance legislation, worker's compensation, was deliberately adopted to replace tort as the main legal regime for dealing with accidental injuries in the workplace, and more recently no-fault plans have partly replaced tort for automobile accidents in some jurisdictions. Cases on the pre-emption of state tort law by federal regulation show how Congress sees the personal injury suit as a regulatory weapon to be unleashed when more deterrence is wanted and withdrawn when deregulation is the order of the day.

A look abroad reveals that most advanced economies have more extensive social insurance for medical care and disability than does the United States. It is probably no coincidence that they also have less prominent tort systems. Most dramatically, New Zealand has virtually abolished tort liability for accidental injury, replacing it with expanded worker's compensation, supplemented by safety regulation and national health insurance. Tort law taught with a focus on accidents naturally translates into "tort law and alternatives," which then threatens to become "accident law"—a subject within which, as the New Zealand experience shows, torts itself might play no role at all.

The focus on accidents also shapes the sequence of topics. We start with the common law's choice of negligence over strict liability as the default regime for accidental injury, and then work through the elements of the negligence cause of action: duty (or duty limitation), breach, causation (proximate and factual), injury, the defenses, and damages. Next, we consider the pockets of strict liability for personal injury, attending to economic and other theories of enterprise liability. Finally, we take up the alternative ways of dealing with accidents, looking first at the interplay of insurance and tort, then at worker's

---

4 *See* ERNEST J. WEINRIB, THE IDEA OF PRIVATE LAW 3–8 (1995) (objecting to purposive or problem-based treatment of torts); Patrick Kelley, *Who Decides? Community Safety Conventions at the Heart of Tort Liability*, 38 CLEV. ST. L. REV. 315, 327 (1990) (arguing for the conceptual centrality of the intentional torts); Benjamin C. Zipursky, *Legal Malpractice and the Structure of Negligence Law*, 67 FORDHAM L. REV. 649 (1998) (arguing for the essential inclusion within negligence of claims for purely pecuniary loss).

compensation and auto no-fault, and concluding with the threat (or promise) of general tort abolition ("but not before the exam!") à la New Zealand.

My course thus gives tort doctrine a structure, with negligence at the center, flanked peripherally by the intentional and the strict liability torts. And it likewise gives the subject a corresponding central domain, the problem of accidental physical injury. I might teach it in another way, with different implications; this organization is chosen, not simply discovered. And it happens that its prototype was originally not so much chosen as invented, largely by Holmes, when torts was first emerging as a basic category of substantive law. I turn now to an account of the conceptual choices he faced, choices that are still mirrored in the pedagogic decisions I confront in organizing my introductory course.

II A Proper Subject?

When Holmes began his law studies at Harvard in 1864, it was still debatable whether torts would be a fundamental common-law subject. As recently as a decade before, when the prominent American legal commentator Joel Bishop had proposed a treatise on tort law, the publishers responded that "there was no call for a work on that subject, and there could be no sale for it."[5] Times were changing, however, and the first two torts treatises, Francis Hilliard's in America and Charles Addison's in England, appeared by the end of the 1850s. Though both were impressive as first efforts,[6] neither of them did much to justify tort law as a basic legal category. They proceeded *seriatim* through the recognized civil causes of action existing apart from contract, summarizing the applicable case law that had been developed under the actions for trespass, trespass on the case, and trover, but without giving their subject either a useful definition, a clear internal structure, or a distinctive substantive domain.[7]

5 Joel Prentiss Bishop, Commentaries on the Non-Contract Law 2, § 3, n. 2 (1889). Bishop had gained prominence with his treatise *Commentaries on the Law of Marriage and Divorce*, published in 1852. On the place of Bishop in nineteenth-century legal thought, see generally the splendid account in Stephen A. Siegel, *Joel Bishop's Orthodoxy*, 13 Law & Hist. Rev. 215 (1995).

6 As Brian Simpson observes, "in treatise writing, as in mountaineering, a special significance is rightly accorded to those who achieve firsts and thereby demonstrate that the feat is in fact possible." A.W.B. Simpson, *The Rise and Fall of the Legal Treatise: Legal Principles and the Forms of Legal Literature*, 48 U. Chi. L. Rev. 632, 652 (1981).

7 The list-like tables of contents in both Hilliard's and Addison's treatises evidence the lack of structure in their approaches to the subject. *See* Charles Addison, 1 A Treatise on the

One development that helped stimulate the emergence of substantive law categories such as torts was the reform of civil procedure. Starting with New York's Field Code in 1848, legislatures throughout the common-law world abolished the old writs and their offshoots in favor of the unitary "civil action," under which plaintiffs were simply to plead facts that established grounds for the relief sought.[8] The common law had long been taught and indexed under the formidably technical and notoriously unsystematic catalog of forms of action. This meant there was no need to classify law into substantive departments like property, contract, and tort.[9] In fact the term and even the concept "substantive law," conceived as the opposite of "law of procedure," was first brought to prominence by the mid-century movement to reform civil procedure.[10]

LAW OF TORTS v–xxiii (1860); FRANCIS HILLIARD, 1 THE LAW OF TORTS OR PRIVATE WRONGS xiii–xx (1861). Looking back in 1899 on his own early efforts at a systematic treatment of tort law, Holmes recalled how "Hilliard on Torts . . . proceeds by enumeration in successive chapters through assault and battery, libel and slander, nuisance, trespass, conversion, etc." Oliver Wendell Holmes, *Law in Science and Science in Law*, 12 HARV. L. REV. 443,451 (1899) [hereinafter *Law in Science*], *reprinted in* 3 THE COLLECTED WORKS OF JUSTICE HOLMES 406, 411 (Sheldon M. Novick ed., 1995) [hereinafter WORKS].

8 See the contemporaneous account of the procedural reforms in JOHN NORTON POMEROY, REMEDIES AND REMEDIAL RIGHTS (1876). By that time, twenty American states had adopted some version of the reformed procedure, following the lead given by New York's enactment of the Field Code in 1848. England, the homeland of the common law, swung into line with the adoption of the Judicature Act of 1873, following the earlier Common Law Procedure Act of 1852. The standard account of the mid-century reforms as a sudden "abolition of the writ system" is a bit misleading; evolution in the direction of a unified system of civil procedure had been going on for some time before the reform legislation of the latter half of the century.

9 Holmes wrote in 1871 that New York had been "clearly right in giving up the common-law forms of action." A system based on forms would be defensible if it matched "a form of action" to "every substantial duty," but the common-law forms were "arbitrary in character," rooted in "purely historical causes" and were "a positive hindrance to sound legal conceptions." Oliver Wendell Holmes, *Book Review*, 5 AM. L. REV. 359, 359 (1871), *reprinted in* 1 WORKS, *supra* note 7, at 239, 239.

10 It was Jeremy Bentham who made the distinction between substantive law and procedure (or substantive and adjective law) prominent, Jeremy Bentham, *Principles of Judicial Procedure with the Outlines of a Procedure Code* [hereinafter *Principles of Judicial Procedure*], *in* 2 THE WORKS OF JEREMY BENTHAM 1, 5 (John Bowring ed., 1962). Bentham's dichotomy differs from the older "right-remedy" distinction, and from the Roman-civilian distinction between "law of persons" and "law of things" on the one hand, and "law of actions" (procedure and remedies) on the other. The older conceptions included in the concept of "remedy" both the rules governing what actual relief or sanctions the law provided (injunction, compensatory damages, punitive damages, criminal penalties),

The opening given to legal theory by procedural innovation caught the attention of a new generation of legal intellectuals in England and America who wanted to make the study of law into a modern "scientific" discipline on the model of German legal scholarship. In company with others of his generation, the young Holmes eagerly took up the challenge of developing a new rational and systematic classification of substantive law.[11] He started in 1867 writing for the *American Law Review*, the new organ of advanced legal scholarship, and over the next few years, he intensely pursued the project of reclassifying the substantive law, while immersing himself in the details of established and emerging legal doctrine.[12]

It says a lot about the unsettled state of the scheme of legal categories at the time that the young Holmes—a lawyer steeped in traditional learning, and at the same time ambitious for intellectual reform—could conclude in an 1871 review that "[t]orts is not a proper subject for a law book."[13] Within two years, though, he had changed his mind, and in his 1873 essay "The Theory of Torts," he formulated a structural account of tort law very close to the one we use today. Implicit in this account was a focus on accidental injury as the primary

---

and the procedures through which disputes were litigated. The Benthamite scheme brings the former rules within the substantive law, which governs both the rights and duties of the parties, and what the law will do for or to them. The title of POMEROY, *supra* note 8, shows the persistence of the older terminology in a book entirely concerned with civil procedure, and not at all with remedies in the modern sense of what modes of relief or sanctions the law makes available.

11 G. Edward White points out that the movement for a "scientific" classification of substantive law, from which torts emerged as a primary category, was not simply an offshoot of the procedural reforms of the post-1850 period, but also had independent impetus in the rise of university-based legal education in the United States and England around the same time, and the associated interest of a new group of scholars in law as an autonomous subject inviting systematic conceptual elaboration. G. EDWARD WHITE, TORT LAW IN AMERICA: AN INTELLECTUAL HISTORY 3–19, esp. 8–11 (1985).

12 On the theoretical side, Holmes read Maine, Bentham, and Austin, and Roman and civilian sources; reviewed jurisprudential writings for the *American Law Review*; and wrote essays on the form of the law. On the practical side, he digested and reviewed the most recent volumes of case reports, also for the *American Law Review*, and undertook to edit the twelfth edition of Kent's *Commentaries*, which meant mastering essentially all the important legal developments of the previous two decades in England and the United States. For a detailed account of his intellectual development during this period, *see* MARK DE WOLFE HOWE, 1 JUSTICE OLIVER WENDELL HOLMES 264–86 (1957), and MARK DE WOLFE HOWE, 2 JUSTICE OLIVER WENDELL HOLMES 16–95 (1963).

13 Oliver Wendell Holmes, *Book Review*, 5 AM. L. REV. 340, 341 (1871), *reprinted in* 1 WORKS, *supra* note 7, at 237, 237 (reviewing C.G. ADDISON, THE LAW OF TORTS (1870)).

domain of torts—a focus that has continued to shape our view of the field ever since, while never becoming entirely uncontroversial. To get a sense of Holmes' analysis of tort law and how he arrived at it, we need to understand the intellectual and practical context from which he started. What led him to find torts "not a proper subject" in 1871?

A *In Favor of Torts*

Even by that date the odds were good that torts would emerge as a basic private law category. There were the Hilliard and Addison treatises, both successful enough to have justified further editions during their first decade. Torts was included as an elementary subject in the up-to-date curriculum recently established by the reforming Dean Langdell at Harvard Law School, the new center of legal science in the common-law world. And the subject was being taught there by one of the most innovative of the younger generation of legal scholars, Nicholas St. John Green.[14] The factors favoring acceptance of the subject included its long-standing prominence in Roman and civil law theory and commentary; its recognition by authoritative common-law commentators, pre-eminently Blackstone; and its manifestation in the actual statutory and decisional law of the common-law jurisdictions.

1 Roman and Civil Law

In his portrayal of Greek ideas about justice, Aristotle divided claims for rectification into those based on voluntary and involuntary transactions respectively,[15] and the classical law of Rome made a corresponding

14 *See id.* (describing the teaching of torts at Harvard by an unnamed instructor); CHARLES WARREN, 2 HISTORY OF THE HARVARD LAW SCHOOL AND OF EARLY LEGAL CONDITIONS IN AMERICA 375–76 (1908) (identifying St. John Green as instructor for the first torts class taught at Harvard, 1870–71). Green was one of the earliest contributors to the theory of torts. *See* Nicholas St. John Green, *Book Notice*, 4 AM. L. REV. 350 (1870) (reviewing SHEARMAN AND REDFIELD, A TREATISTE ON THE LAW OF NEGLIGENCE (1869)) [hereinafter Green, *Book Review*]; and especially his article on proximate cause, Nicholas St. John Green, *Proximate and Remote Cause*, 4 AM. L. REV. 201 (1870), *reprinted in* 9 RUTGERS L. REV. 452 (1954). Had he lived, Green might get some of the credit for the innovations in tort theory ascribed in this article to Holmes, who was notoriously stingy in acknowledging the most important sources of his own ideas. *See* Jerome Frank, *A Conflict with Oblivion: Some Observations on the Founders of Legal Pragmatism*, 9 RUTGERS L. REV. 425, 426–27 (1954) (implying Green's large role as a source of Holmes' ideas).

15 ARISTOTLE, NICHOMACHEAN ETHICS, bk. V, ch. 2 (W.D. Ross trans.), *in* THE BASIC WORKS OF ARISTOTLE 1006 (R. McKeon ed., 1941) (distinguishing claims arising out of "voluntary" transactions such as "sale, purchase, loan for consumption, pledging, loan for use,

fundamental distinction between contract and tort, legal obligations *ex contractu* and *ex delicto*. This conceptual framework was canonized by the commentators who restated Roman law into a general civil law for Europe, later was attributed to the very Law of Nature itself by the philosophical legal writers of the Enlightenment, and finally, during the eighteenth and nineteenth centuries, was enacted into the civil codes of major European nation states.

The structure originally established for Roman law by the Institutes of Gaius and Justinian, and thereafter generally followed by the writers in the civilian tradition, was roughly as follows. Public law (including criminal law) was distinguished from private law, and later came to be largely ignored by the post-medieval civilians, for whom Roman law essentially meant Roman private law.[16] Private law was then divided into three basic categories: the law of persons (status), the law of things, and the law of actions (remedies and procedure). The widest category, the law of things, was further divided into bodies of law governing property, successions, and obligations. Obligations, finally, were subdivided into those arising out of promise or agreement (*ex contractu*), and out of wrongs or torts (*ex delicto*).[17]

The natural law writers of the Enlightenment added further prestige to the Roman-civilian system by smoothing over its more parochial details, and then attributing the remaining abstract structure to the dictates of Reason itself. The philosophers of the law of nature varied in how closely they followed the standard Roman law structure, but most of them recognized some version of the civilian category of tort or delict, encompassing duties to make reparation for loss wrongfully inflicted.[18] The social contract and natural rights political

---

depositing, letting" from those arising out of "involuntary" transactions such as "theft, adultery, poisoning, procuring, enticement of slaves, assassination, false witness ... assault, imprisonment, murder, robbery with violence, mutilation, abuse, insult").

16 There is a brief account of criminal law toward the end of Justinian's Institutes, THE INSTITUTES OF JUSTINIAN, bk. IV, tit. xviii (entitled *De Publicias Judiciis*) (Thomas Collett Sandars ed. & trans., 1922), but in general the "law relating to [public or criminal or religious matters] was, as it were,'factored out of the civil law, which became synonymous with private law." PETER STEIN, ROMAN LAW IN EUROPEAN HISTORY 13 (1999).

17 BARRY NICHOLAS, AN INTRODUCTION TO ROMAN LAW 60, 98–99, 158–59 (1962); REINHARD ZIMMERMANN, LAW OF OBLIGATIONS 10–29 (1992). The categorization in Justinian's Institutes also included two minor divisions, quasi-contract (roughly our law of unjust enrichment), and quasi-delict, a category not readily understandable as based on any general principle, but conceivably embodying Roman notions of strict liability in tort.

18 On the passage of the post-reception Roman law through natural law theorizing to form the modern Civil Law, see the classic account in FRANZ WIEACKER, A HISTORY OF PRIVATE LAW IN EUROPE 199–275 (Tony Weir trans., 1995). The prototype is the treatment in HUGO

philosophy of the time readily classified private legal obligations into those imposed by law to protect the basic individual rights to life, liberty, and property, and those undertaken by the free consent of the individual—obligations of tort and contract respectively.

In the wake of the Enlightenment, civilian legal commentators like Pothier in France and Savigny in Germany further generalized and abstracted the doctrines of Roman law under the influence of natural law thought and later of Kantian philosophy. The commentators emerged with tort and contract doctrines that provided the basis for the treatment of these subjects in the French Civil Code as well as those of Austria and Prussia. During the nineteenth century, these doctrines were further refined under the influence of the historical school of jurisprudence in the great German Pandectist commentaries that would lay the basis for the ultimate monument of civilian legal science, the German Civil Code of 1900.[19]

Sophisticated English and American legal writers had long promoted the study of Roman and civil law on the ground that it supplied a more logical

---

GROTIUS, THE JURISPRUDENCE OF HOLLAND 459–87 (R.W. Lee trans., 1926) (1631), which summarized the Dutch law of delictual obligation in terms derived from Roman law, at the same time justifying the doctrine by reference to the requirements of universal Reason, *see id. See also* SAMUEL PUFENDORF, LAW OF NATURE AND NATIONS, Book III (Basil Kennett trans., 1717) (giving an account of the law of obligations as part of natural law); THOMAS RUTHERFORTH, INSTITUTES OF NATURAL LAW 200–08 (1754) (sketching an outline of tort law under the title "Of Reparation for Damage Done"). Pufendorf outlined tort law in Chapter 1 of Book III under the title, "That no Man be hurt; and if a Damage be done to any Man, that Reparation be made." He then treated contract law (the other half of "obligations") separately in Chapters 4 through 8. *Cf.* David Ibbetson, '*The Law of Business Rome': Foundations of the Anglo-American Tort of Negligence, in* 52 CURRENT LEGAL PROBLEMS 1999, 74, 85–87 (1999) (describing the contribution of the natural law writers to the development of the duty of care concept in modern negligence law).

19 See the summary account in STEIN, *supra* note 16, at 104–23, and the more comprehensive one in WIEACKER, *supra* note 18, at 279–386. The French Civil Code does not have a separate subdivision for obligations, but deals with both contract and delict as "Modes of Acquiring Property," with contract receiving its own title, while delicts and quasi-delicts are addressed in a chapter entitled "Engagements Formed without an Agreement." THE FRENCH CIVIL CODE (as amended to 1 July 1994) (John H. Crabb trans., 1995). For modern European code provisions and judicial decisions representative of the category of "delict" in civil law jurisdictions, see ARTHUR TAYLOR VON MEHREN, THE CIVIL LAW SYSTEM: CASES AND MATERIALS FOR THE COMPARATIVE STUDY OF LAW 339–464 (1957), and (a more detailed compendium) F.H. LAWSON & B.S. MARKESINIS, 2 TORTIOUS LIABILITY FOR UNINTENTIONAL HARM IN THE COMMON LAW AND THE CIVIL LAW (1982).

and elegant arrangement than the common-law writ system.[20] So when in the mid-nineteenth century the abolition of the forms of action required a new arrangement based on substantive law categories, it was natural to look to the civil law—where an impressive body of literature defined and elaborated the distinctions between property and obligations and then between contract and tort.

During the final period of transition from the writ system to the new simplified civil procedure, from about 1850 on, English and American legal writers came to agree that contracts would be one fundamental branch of the new substantive private law, and their treatment of the subject was much influenced by civilian scholarship.[21] Since the civilian tradition paired tort with contract as the two fundamental subdivisions of the law of obligations, recognition of contract as one basic category naturally suggested that tort should be another.

2 Common Law Commentary

As early as Bracton in the thirteenth century, English commentators seized on the Roman distinction between tort and contract to help classify the actions recognized by the common law.[22] The medieval writs of trespass on the one hand, and debt and covenant on the other, could be seen as roughly corresponding to the Roman tort and contract, and Bracton's treatment meant that from very early on the categories of the civilian law of obligations were available to English lawyers as a way of understanding their own law.[23]

In the eighteenth century, Blackstone, the most influential of all the English institutional writers, clearly set out the Roman/civilian distinction in Book III of his *Commentaries*. He classified the common-law "personal actions" into those on the one hand "founded on contract," comprising "all actions upon debt

---

20 Simpson, *supra* note 6, at 655–57; *see also* MICHAEL H. HOEFLICH, ROMAN AND CIVIL LAW AND THE DEVELOPMENT OF ANGLO-AMERICAN JURISPRUDENCE IN THE NINETEENTH CENTURY 16 (1997).

21 *See* DAVID IBBETSON, A HISTORICAL INTRODUCTION TO THE LAW OF OBLIGATIONS 220–44 (1999), for the influence of Pothier and Savigny on nineteenth century English contract theory. As his title suggests, Ibbetson's book is a sustained account of the history of English tort and contract law seen through the conceptual lens provided by the Roman-civilian categories.

22 HENRY DE BRACTON, 2 ON THE LAWS AND CUSTOMS OF ENGLAND 290 (Samuel E. Thorne trans., 1968).

23 *See* IBBETSON, *supra* note 21, at 11–94, for a particularly clear account of the medieval origins of what would become the modern law of tort and contract, seen from the perspective of the civilian categories.

or promises," and on the other those "founded... upon torts or wrongs... all actions for trespasses, nuisances, assaults, defamatory words, and the like."[24]

In similar terms, Holmes' own favorite basic American textbook from his law student days, Judge Timothy Walker's intelligent and down-to-earth *Introduction to American Law*, described the category of actions for "civil injury or wrong," for which, he noted, "the law commonly uses the latin word *delictum* or the French word tort, instead of our equally significant English words." Walker's linguistic nativism did not stop him from going on to mention the Roman distinction of "personal actions" into "*actions ex contractu*, or *actions of contract*, and *actions ex delicto*, or *actions of tort*." He classified the common law forms of action accordingly, placing debt, covenant, and assumpsit under contract, and trespass, trover, detinue, replevin, case, and ejectment under tort.[25]

By 1871, no serious student of English or American law could doubt that contracts was established as one of the basic categories in the newly emerging system of substantive law. Langdell's celebrated casebook had just appeared in America,[26] and over the next few years the Pollock and Anson treatises would conclude almost a century of English contract scholarship by giving the subject the familiar structure that still generally holds today—a structure much influenced by the civilian writers Pothier and Savigny.[27] With contracts thus established, could the other half of the traditional civilian dichotomy be far behind?

---

24 William Blackstone, 3 Commentaries on the Laws of England 117 (1768). By the "personal actions," Blackstone meant all private civil actions at law apart from the old proprietary "real" and "mixed" actions, which were already obsolescent in his time.

25 Timothy Walker, Introduction to American Law 549–60 (4th ed. 1860) (1837). Holmes rated this "admirable" work as "the best book we know of to explain to the student the actual bearing of legal principles upon the daily affairs of men;" it goes "to the root of the matter," asks for "the practical use of all these traditions and forms," and "those which cannot show such a use in their favor are dismissed from consideration." Oliver Wendell Holmes, *Book Review*, 3 Am. L. Rev. 357, 358 (1869), *reprinted in* 1 Works, *supra* note 7, at 204, 205. Holmes was still repeating his praise of Walker's book when he was in his eighties. *See, e.g.*, Oliver Wendell Holmes, *Introduction to the General Survey*, 1 Continental Legal History Series (1912), *reprinted in* 3 Works, *supra* note 7, at 439, 440.

26 C.C. Langdell, A Selection of Cases on the Law of Contracts (1871). *See* Holmes' favorable review of it as setting out "the whole law of contracts proper" according to a "plan... both original and instructive." Oliver Wendell Holmes, *Book Review*, 5 Am. L. Rev. 539, 540 (1871), *reprinted in* 1 Works, *supra* note 7, at 243, 243.

27 William Reynell Anson, Principles of the Law of Contract (1880); Frederick Pollock, Principles of Contract (1876). For an assessment of the influence of Savigny and particularly Pothier on Pollock and Anson, *see* Ibbetson, *supra* note 21, at 220–44.

3 Positive Law

Working lawyers might ignore the refinements of Roman and civil law, and even the categorizing efforts of their native commentators,[28] but they had to take account of statutes and case law that treated the tort-contract distinction as legally operative. In a summary of the history of the distinction in English law published in 1887, Frederick William Maitland noted four areas in which it made a practical difference in outcome whether an action was characterized as sounding in tort or in contract:[29]

- Joinder of actions. As early as 1682, English judges were pronouncing that "causes upon contract ... and causes upon tort cannot be joined."
- Survival of actions. Contract actions survived a plaintiff's death, but tort actions did not—so a 1627 case said; and the same distinction was sometimes (generally less clearly) intimated with respect to whether an action survived a defendant's death.
- Joinder of parties. Joint contractors had to all be sued jointly or the action was subject to dismissal, but tort liability was joint and several, so that any one of a group of joint tortfeasors could be sued alone for the entire damage jointly caused.
- Costs. Several of the procedural reform statutes passed in England leading up to the final abolition of the forms of action in 1873 made the availability of costs turn on whether the action sounded in tort or contract, and the language of some of these statutes assumed that every personal action was either "founded on contract" or "founded on tort."

The same distinctions could be found in American law, including the tendency of some early procedural reform legislation to assume that civil actions at law sounded either in contract or tort.[30]

---

28 Holmes noted T.E. Holland's remark that "the old-fashioned English lawyer's idea of a satisfactory body of law was a chaos with a full index." Oliver Wendell Holmes, *Book Review*, 5 AM. L. REV. 114, 114 (1870) *reprinted in* 1 WORKS, *supra* note 7, at 223, 223 (reviewing T.E. HOLLAND, ESSAYS UPON THE FORM OF THE LAW (1870)).

29 F.W. Maitland, *Historical Note on the Classification of the Forms of Personal Action*, *in* FREDERICK POLLOCK, THE LAW OF TORTS 368–70 (1887) (App. A). For other accounts of how English positive law made operative distinctions between tort and contract before the establishment of the modern categorical scheme after 1870, *see* J.H. BAKER, INTRODUCTION TO ENGLISH LEGAL HISTORY 454–55 (3d ed. 1990); IBBETSON, *supra* note 21, at 171–73; WINFIELD, *supra* note 2 at 76–79 (1931) (also noting the doctrine that punitive damages are sometimes available in tort, but generally not in contract).

30 *See, e.g.*, An Act Relating to the Proceedings, Practice, and Rules of Evidence, 1852 Mass. Acts 223, § 1 (providing separate actions and proceedings for tort and contract); *see also*

B *Against Torts*

We now know that the lawyers who made Hilliard's and Addison's treatises commercially successful were betting on a winning horse; torts did indeed eventually establish itself as one of the fundamental categories of Anglo-American law. Given the factors militating in its favor, it may seem to us that things could hardly have gone otherwise. But this is just an instance of the familiar fallacy of hindsight determinism. The reclassification triggered by the abolition of the writs did not have to end up with tort as one of the basic substantive subjects.

The point is supported by the very fact that a legal scholar as attuned to intellectual fashion as the young Holmes could reject torts as "not a proper subject" as late as 1871. And indeed at that point there was still much to be said against the case I have just summarized for accepting tort as a basic category. Roman and civilian theory, the tradition of common law commentary, and the actual positive law of England and America, taken together, still left the matter far from concluded.

1 Roman-Civil Law vs. Analytical Jurisprudence

Holmes' fundamental objection to tort as a subject rested on the analytical work of Jeremy Bentham, augmented in Holmes' law student days by the publication of the jurisprudence lectures of John Austin.[31] Bentham had provided

---

CAL. CIV. PROC. CODE ch. 3, §§ 337–40 (1872) (codifying *Statutes of 1850*, 343) (providing longer limitations period for actions sounding in contract than those sounding in tort, *e.g.*, slander and false imprisonment); MASS. REVISED STATUTES tit. V, ch. 120, §§ 1–8 (1836) (same); N.Y. REVISED STATUTES pt. III, ch. III, §§ 89–93 (same). *See generally* CHARLES M. HEPBURN, THE HISTORICAL DEVELOPMENT OF CODE PLEADING IN AMERICA AND ENGLAND esp. 116–17 (1897); Jeremiah Smith, *Tort and Absolute Liability—Suggested Changes in Classification*, 30 HARV. L. REV. 241 (1917), *reprinted in* HARVARD LAW REVIEW, SELECTED ESSAYS ON THE LAW OF TORTS 176, 177–78 (1924)).

31 Bentham and Austin were Holmes' primary masters in legal theory, supplemented by the insights of the historical school. He thought them much superior as theorists to the Romans, writing that "The Roman law is a priceless mass of materials for investigations like those of the great Germans... But for the philosophy of law [Bentham's] 'Fragment on Government' and Austin's lectures are worth the whole *Corpus*." Oliver Wendell Holmes, *Summary of Events*, 7 AM. L. REV. 578, 578 (1873), *reprinted in* 1 WORKS, *supra* note 7, at 322, 323. And even the work of the greatest of the German historicist writers, Savigny, was flawed because "the minute and constant reference to the Roman law more or less clogs and retards the free development of principles." Oliver Wendell Holmes, *Book Review*, 7 AM. L. REV. 320, 320 (1873), *reprinted in* 1 WORKS, *supra* note 7, at 322, 322 (reviewing ARCHIBALD BROWN, AN EPITOME AND ANALYSIS OF SAVIGNY'S TREATISE ON OBLIGATIONS IN ROMAN LAW (1872)). "It is not true that fundamental principles are more clearly brought out in the Roman than in the English law;" they were rather "obscured"

much of the ideological fuel for the procedural reforms that were sweeping away the writ system in the latter years of the century.[32] The same analysis that supported the abolition of the forms of action also portrayed as incoherent and indefensible the Roman/civil categories of "personal actions" and "obligations," the latter subdivided into contract and tort.

Bentham had insisted that law should be analyzed on the basis of a firm distinction between substantive law and procedure. This new conceptual distinction helped Bentham and Austin make the case that English law remained intellectually and practically incoherent because *substantive* legal rights and duties were learned and classified for practice under the jumbled array of *procedural* forms that had grown up over the centuries to enforce them. This had it backwards, Bentham insisted; procedure should be designed functionally to serve as the handmaiden of substance.[33]

Bentham's new substance-procedure distinction was crucial to the legislative reforms that replaced the writ system.[34] The Field Code in America and the English Judicature Act were premised on the idea that a single procedural form, the "civil action," could regulate the adjudication of all civil disputes, without altering either the pre-existing legal rights and duties of the parties or the relief triggered by their violation. The reforms could hardly have been adopted unless they had been backed by the guarantee that they would not change those elements of the existing legal order on which people relied in

---

by "principles of classification which have lost their significance, and by a philosophy which is no longer vital" Oliver Wendell Holmes, *Book Review*, 7 AM. L. REV. 652, 653 (1873), *reprinted in* 1 WORKS, *supra* note 7, at 321, 321 (reviewing T. WHITCOMBE GREEN, OUTLINES OF ROMAN LAW (1872)).

32 Holmes himself ascribed the procedural reforms of his day to "Bentham's ideas." Oliver Wendell Holmes, *The Theory of Torts*, 7 AM. L. REV 652, 653 (1873) [hereinafter *The Theory of Torts*], *reprinted in* 1 WORKS, *supra* note 7, at 326, 327. Austin's contribution had to wait for the publication in 1863 by his widow Sarah of the lectures on jurisprudence he had delivered at London University in the 1830s.

33 *Principles of Judicial Procedure*, *supra* note 10, at 6.

> "[T]he course of procedure ought to have in every instance, for its main and primary end at least, the accomplishment of the will manifested in the body of substantive laws ... Of the adjective branch of the law, the only defensible object, or say end in view, is the maximization of the execution and effect given to the substantive branch of law."

Id.

34 *See generally* M.I. Zagday, *Bentham on Civil Procedure*, *in* JEREMY BENTHAM AND THE LAW 68, 78 (George W. Keeton & Georg Schwarzenberger eds., 1948) (noting that Bentham's works greatly influenced the procedural reforms that took place in the last ten years of his life and that his teachings spurred Romilly, Brougham, and Denman to create Parliamentary Commissions to examine the law and recommend reforms).

their everyday lives. To give this assurance, the reformers invoked the new Benthamite concept of substantive law, the law that both established legal rights and duties and provided sanctions and redress for their violation. This substantive law was the substratum left unchanged by the purely procedural reforms, which affected only the machinations of lawyers and judges inside the system. The reforms were only intended to make the machinery of justice run with less delay and expense.[35]

The reformers also believed that the simplified procedure would create pressure for systematic reclassification of the law, which would make it easier to teach and learn and more accessible to the public. But a new arrangement of the law would not change its substance, except insofar as a better taxonomy exposed inconsistencies and anomalies to the kind of scrutiny that might lead on to substantive reform.[36] One of Austin's main contributions to the analytical enterprise was his work on classification, which combined Benthamite methods and ideas with civilian learning acquired in the Germany of Savigny.[37]

---

35 *See* POMEROY, *supra* note 8, at 38 (stating that when forms of action are abolished "the rights of action remain, and the remedies which could be recovered by the use of any particular action may still be secured by means of the civil action which the codes have substituted in place of all the previous forms"); Holmes, *supra* note 9, at 239–40.

> "Of course it would not be intended to change our rights, by a change in the form of pleading. Accordingly where the present existing law gives alternative remedies ... the plaintiff's election, signified at the common law by the action brought, would be one of the facts to be stated in the case."

Id.

36 For a good recent account of the codification movement in England and America, *see* Gunther A. Weiss, *The Enchantment of Codification in the Common-Law World*, 25 YALE J. INT'L L. 435 (2000). Some reformers (Bentham, Austin, and Sir James Stephen in England; David Dudley Field in the United States) thought the systematic rationalization of substantive law could best be carried out through codification, while many others, including Holmes, opposed substantive codification, arguing that the work of systematization was better left to the private efforts of independent jurists. *See* Oliver Wendell Holmes, *Codes, and the Arrangement of the Law*, 5 AM. L. Rev. 1, 1–3 (1870) [hereinafter *Codes, and the Arrangement of the Law*], *reprinted in* 1 WORKS, *supra* note 7, at 212, 212–14. The Field codification movement in New York produced not only the famous code of procedure enacted in 1848, but also a substantive civil code completed and promulgated in 1865, which, though rejected in its home state, was enacted elsewhere—for instance in California in 1872. CIVIL CODE, ANNOTATED, OF CALIFORNIA (1872); *see also* Weiss, *supra*, at 511–13 (describing the enactment of the Field Civil Code in Georgia, North and South Dakota, California, and Montana).

37 HOEFLICH, *supra* note 20, at 10–12.

The case against making torts a main department of law in this new arrangement was that, unlike contract and property, it did not make sense as a primary substantive category. As Holmes put it, the "objection to the title Torts ... is that it puts the cart before the horse, that legal liabilities are arranged with reference to the forms of action allowed by the common law for infringing them,—the substantive under the adjective law."[38]

According to both Bentham and Austin, the core of substantive law was made up of the rules establishing those legal rights and duties that empowered and regulated the behavior of individuals in daily life. Auxiliary to these "primary" rights and duties, but still within the substantive law, were the remedial or "sanctioning" rights that arose when primary rights were violated.[39] Austin argued that the substantive law should be classified according to an arrangement of primary rights—for example, rights to personal security, liberty of movement, reputation, property, and the like.[40] The remedial part of the substantive law should then be set out in a way that manifested its character as instrumental to the primary rights.[41]

Under this analysis, contract was a proper first-order legal category, because the rights arising from enforceable agreements formed a separate and recognizable class of primary rights, distinct from, say, property rights, and rights of bodily integrity. Torts, however, had no such distinctive primary subject matter. It was made up entirely of sanctioning rights, civil claims arising out of the

---

38 *The Theory of Torts*, *supra* note 32, at 331. Holmes' phrasing showed that he had not fully incorporated the Benthamite terminology—the objection to torts is not that it is a *procedural* ("adjective") category but that it is a *remedial* one. Remedies are part of the substantive law in the Benthamite (and our contemporary) scheme; we regard the question whether specific performance will be allowed for a class of contracts, or punitive damages for a class of torts, as part of the substantive law of contracts and torts respectively.

39 John Austin, *Outline of the Course of Lectures* [hereinafter *Outline*], *in* 1 AUSTIN'S JURISPRUDENCE 31, 43 (John Campbell ed., 5th ed. 1885) (explaining distinction between primary and sanctioning rights). Bentham had himself earlier made the same distinction; he proposed to state the primary rights and duties in a Civil Code, and the remedies or sanctioning rights and duties in a Penal Code. Jeremy Bentham, *General View of Complete Code of Laws* [hereinafter *View of Complete Code of Laws*], *in* 3 WORKS OF JEREMY BENTHAM, *supra* note 10, at 155, 160.

40 *See Outline*, *supra* note 39, at 4 (describing categorization of primary rights into Law of Things and Law of Persons, and subcategorization of the latter into specific rights); *see also* John Austin, *On Law, Considered with Reference to Its Purposes* [hereinafter *On Law*], *in* 2 AUSTIN'S JURISPRUDENCE, *supra* note 39, at 683, 773 (John Campbell ed., 5th ed. 1885) (describing the division of primary rights).

41 According to Austin, secondary or sanctioning rights are "instruments for the attainment of another right," namely a primary right. *On Law*, *supra* note 40, at 763–66.

violation of whatever primary rights, apart from those based on contract, that the law happened to protect by a private civil remedy.[42] The two bodies of law, tort and contract, thus did not form parallel categories at all, and the Roman-civilian division of obligations into those arising *ex contractu* and *ex delicto* incoherently mixed logical levels.[43]

Even if some fundamental legal categories—criminal law for example—should be identified on the basis of remedies rather than primary rights,[44] torts could not reasonably be one of them. The remedial category parallel to criminal law would be "civil wrongs," including breach of contract. But tort excluded breach of contract, while including some (though not all) of the civil protections for property and personal rights. Nor did the primary rights and duties whose violation were remedied by tort actions have any positive unifying characteristic, as was shown by the negative terminology of "apart from contract" and "other than contract" that was often used to name the category in its early days.[45]

Holmes made these points as he explained why he thought tort was "not a proper subject." Its domain, as generally understood, included everything

42 In the Benthamite codification scheme, civil injuries (including what we call both torts and breaches of contract) belonged in the Penal Code. *See View of Complete Code of Laws*, *supra* note 39, at 163–67 (identifying private offenses—acts detrimental to assignable individuals—as one category of offences in penal code and including in this category, *e.g.*, offenses against the person and reputation). Contract law (meaning the substantive law by which contractual rights and duties are determined) was in the Civil Code. *Id.* at 190–92. Similarly, Austin placed contract and quasi-contract in the category of primary rights, and torts—rights to remedy arising from delicts—in the sanctioning rights category. *See Outline*, *supra* note 39, at 53.

43 *Outline*, *supra* note 39, at 53–54.

44 For example, criminal law might be an appropriate substantive law category, not because the primary rights it protects or duties it enforces form a coherent group, but because criminal prosecution inflicts uniquely severe sanctions, which justifies both the use of separate procedures, and the control of this most fearful state power by general overarching substantive principles that are designed to guard against oppression (*e.g.* the rule of lenity, the requirement of *mens rea.*)

45 *See, e.g.*, BISHOP, *supra* note 5. For a recent attempt to justify the common law category "tort" as roughly equivalent to "civil wrong," *see* Peter Birks, *The Concept of a Civil Wrong*, *in* THE PHILOSOPHICAL FOUNDATIONS OF TORT LAW 31 (David G. Owen ed., 1995). Birks takes note of the Austinian objection, but overrides it on the practical (but conceptually question-begging) ground that it "drives us further and further from the categories of the law as we know them"—which is to say from the civilian scheme with its dichotomy of contract and tort, by now too firmly entrenched in Anglo-American legal terminology to be displaced. *Id.* at 47.

falling under the common law actions for trespass, trespass on the case, and trover. But no meaningful common feature united these actions, viewed as a grouping of primary rights (or, as Holmes preferred, primary duties.)[46] Trespass to land was a tort action, but the primary rights and duties it enforced were part of property law, and were remedied not only by tort suits but also by the old real and mixed actions, which lay outside the "law of obligations" altogether. Another tort action, assault and battery, enforced the rights and duties of bodily security, a primary category distinct from property. Another tort, deceit, addressed a third distinct set of primary duties, those involving fraud; and these duties were further enforced, entirely outside of tort law, by the equitable doctrine of promissory estoppel. Finally, the tort of seduction enforced a class of primary rights and duties that belonged "at the other end of the *corpus juris*"—as part of the law of persons, governing status and domestic relations.[47] Viewed from the perspective of the classification of primary rights or duties, the category of tort was thus entirely incoherent.

The critique of torts as a category was further strengthened by consideration of its relation to criminal law. The Roman-civilian taxonomy discouraged this comparison by making the distinction between private and public law

---

46 Holmes argued that the law should be classified by its primary duties, rather than rights, as Austin generally preferred, pointing out that there were legal duties without corresponding rights (duties of military service, or to pay taxes), but no legal rights without corresponding duties. *See Codes, and the Arrangement of the Law, supra* note 36, at 214; Oliver Wendell Holmes, *The Arrangement of the Law—Privity*, 7 AM. L. REV. 46, 46 (1872), *reprinted in* 1 WORKS, *supra* note 7, at 303. Holmes later abandoned his project of devising a universal legal taxonomy (whether of duties or rights); he decided that historical accident played so large a part in shaping even the broad outlines of each legal system that no scheme for classifying substantive doctrine across all systems could be fruitful. *See* Oliver Wendell Holmes, *The Path of the Law*, 10 HARV. L. REV. 457, 475 (1897) [hereinafter *The Path of the Law*], *reprinted in* 3 WORKS, *supra* note 7, at 391, 403 (arguing that the pursuit of a "useless quintessence of all systems" should be replaced by the more limited but practical project of achieving "an accurate anatomy of one").

47 Here Holmes was following Austin, who had argued that the civilian category "law of persons," should not head the *corpus juris* as it did in Roman law, but should be subordinated as a set of exceptions to the ordinary law ("law of things") that established the presumptively equal rights and duties of mature adults in a liberal society. *See Outline, supra* note 39, at 41–42, 364. Austin subclassified the law of things into rights *in personam*, basically contract and quasi-contract rights, which ran against assignable individuals, and rights *in rem*, the bulk of legal rights—those to property, bodily security, liberty of movement, and reputation—which ran against all the world. *See id.* at 45, 371–74. Thus the cases involving trespass to land, assault and battery, and deceit, would each come under separate subdivisions of the law of things, while seduction would belong to the law of persons.

fundamental, placing criminal law in the "public" category, and then focusing juristic science entirely upon private law.[48] Austin attacked both elements, the initial separation of public from private law, and the assignment of crimes to the public law side. This obscured the close relation between criminal and civil remedies in the enforcement of the primary individual rights to life, liberty, and property.[49] Most crimes (the ones that have victims) are also torts.

The actual law of remedies and sanctions in modern legal systems reveals every imaginable mix of public prosecution and private civil suit, along with such remedial hybrids as private prosecution, public regulatory enforcement using civil penalties, private rights to initiate public regulatory action, civil suits by private attorneys general, and the award of punitive damages in private civil suits, paid either to private plaintiffs or to the state.[50] The decision how to blend these remedies in enforcing primary rights or duties is an instrumental one to be made on shifting grounds of expediency, even if criminal punishment itself is limited in principle to serious moral wrongdoing.[51] So the line

48 Bentham grouped civil and criminal sanctions together in his Penal Code and defined primary rights of property, bodily security, and so on, in his Civil Code. *View of Complete Code of Laws*, *supra* note 39, at 160. The Roman law of delict involved an explicitly penal element that is absent in the common law of torts, though allowance of punitive damages shrinks the gap, *see* NICHOLAS, *supra* note 17, at 207–09. When modern writers have wanted to discuss crime under the Roman classificatory scheme they have often followed Sir Henry Maine, who considered "Delict and Crime" together in a single chapter of HENRY SUMNER MAINE, ANCIENT LAW 367 (1861). I am told by Professor George Fletcher that today criminal law is classified as private law in France, and as a separate category intermediate between private and public in Germany.

49 *See Outline*, *supra* note 39, at 67–69; *see also* John Austin, *Analysis of Pervading Notions*, *in* 1 AUSTIN'S JURISPRUDENCE, *supra* note 39, at 343, 404 ("All offences affect the community, and all offences affect individuals."). Austin substituted the term "political law" for the Roman-civil "public law," treating it as the creation of special status for public officials, hence classified under the law of persons, which in turn was the catch-all category of exceptions to the general law that established the rights and duties of legally equal individuals. *See Outline*, *supra* note 39, at 68. Bentham similarly gave separate treatment to the law governing the structure and powers of government in his Constitutional Code.

50 The modern American law governing when tort actions should be implied from, or preempted by, regulatory statutes gives an ongoing practical demonstration of the "mix of remedies" approach to public regulation and private action. *See generally* Richard B. Stewart & Cass R. Sunstein, *Public Programs and Private Rights*, 95 HARV. L. REV. 1193 (1982).

51 Neither Bentham nor Austin made a sharp distinction in principle between civil and criminal sanctions. *See Analysis of Pervading Notions*, *supra* note 49, at 343, 501. Bentham did distinguish between punitive and "satisfactive" remedies, see *Specimen of a Penal*

between tort and crime even regarded as remedial categories is blurred, and in any event no basis appears for treating tort as a category of substantive law.

One explanation for the confused legacy of the civilian categorical scheme was the failure of Roman jurists to develop the abstract concept of a legal right with correlative duties. As a result, they could not see tort and criminal law as providing different remedies for a largely overlapping set of rights and duties. Similarly, the failure to think in terms of rights and duties obscured the disparate nature of the substantive claims protected by delictual actions.

By contrast, the modern civilian writers well understood the idea of a legal right. For them it linked law to social-contract political theory, which appealed to the uncertainty and insecurity of individual natural rights in the state of nature to justify the establishment of a government empowered to define those rights by law and enforce them by regular sanctions and remedies. But the modern civilians generally did not escape the effects of the original Roman segregation of criminal law into the (thereafter largely ignored) category of public law. They continued to follow the Romans in portraying delict as a distinct body of obligations parallel to contract, rather than as the catch-all miscellany modern analytical jurisprudence showed it to be.[52]

Code, *in* 1 THE WORKS OF JEREMY BENTHAM, *supra* note 10, at 165, and Austin followed him in describing criminal punishment as having a purely deterrent function, while civil remedies had the dual functions of prevention and reparation. *Analysis of Pervading Notions*, *supra* note 49, at 503–04. Some contemporary functionalist writers have urged sharpening the distinction between tort and crime to maintain the admonitory uses of the criminal law. John C. Coffee, Jr., *Does "Unlawful" Mean "Criminal"?: Reflections on the Disappearing Tort/Crime Distinction in American Law*, 71 B.U.L. REV. 193, 193–04 (1991) ("Characteristically, tort law prices, while criminal law prohibits."); Henry M. Hart, Jr., *The Aims of the Criminal Law*, 23 LAW & CONTEMP. PROBS. 401, 404–05 (1958). Others have tended to treat criminal punishment and civil damages together under a unified theory of deterrent sanctions. *See, e.g.*, Richard A. Posner, *An Economic Theory of the Criminal Law*, 85 COLUM. L. REV. 1193, 1201–05 (1985); *see also* MARK KELMAN, A GUIDE TO CRITICAL LEGAL STUDIES 25–32, 88–99 (1987) (critiquing attempts to distinguish criminal punishment in principle from civil regulation).

52 "Delict," while structurally parallel to contract in civilian theory, was not an important category in practice in the civil law until the upsurge of accidental injuries associated with the Industrial Revolution—only a few pages in POTHIER, A TREATISE ON OBLIGATIONS CONSIDERED IN A MORAL AND LEGAL VIEW 73–76 (Francois Xavier Martin trans., 1999), and only five sections of the French Civil Code of 1804, *supra* note 19, at art. 1382–86, were devoted to the subject, by comparison to much richer treatments of contract.

2 Common Law Commentary

Roman and civil law aside, what to make of the place of the category "tort" in the work of common-law commentators? Writers from Bracton to Blackstone to Holmes' own favorite Judge Walker of Ohio seemed to have endorsed and sanctified the civilian distinction between contract and tort. Yet on this matter appearances were deceiving; tort was not yet really an established subject in the common law. And the civilian concepts of "personal actions" and "law of obligations," which paired tort with contract, had never become serious working categories for the leading common-law text writers. Hence the recognition of contract as a fundamental department of substantive law by 1870 did not entail the acceptance of tort as well.

While Bracton, Blackstone (and the good Judge Walker too) all stated the civilian contract-tort distinction, they did so only in passing. No common law commentator treated the distinction as a significant structural classifying device, or made tort a significant subject for independent analysis. Both tort itself, and the tort-contract distinction, were entirely absent from a number of the most important general treatises on the common law as a whole—Sir Edward Coke's *Institutes of the Law of England*, Sir Henry Finch's Law, Sir Matthew Hale's *Analysis of the Law of England*, and even (as late as the first half of the nineteenth century) James Kent's *Commentaries on American Law.*

Holmes spent several years of his early career annotating Kent, so the Chancellor's treatment is particularly worth noting in this respect. The reader searches in vain through the 2000-plus pages of his *Commentaries* looking for treatment of anything resembling our category of tort law. There are ten pages on the law of defamation, but this comes under the category-"rights of persons," subdivision "right to reputation"—and Kent treats libel indifferently as both a crime and a tort. A single sentence in the section on the personal right to bodily security can be taken as, in effect, the whole of Kent on Torts: "If violence has been actually offered, the offender is not only liable to be prosecuted and punished on behalf of the state, but he is bound to render to the party aggrieved adequate compensation in damages."[53] Kent analyzed private law in terms of what Austin would call primary rights, and as with Blackstone, his basic distinction was between personal and property rights. In such a scheme, tort finds no structural place.

In contrast to Kent, Blackstone did clearly articulate the civilian tort-contract distinction, in a passage earlier quoted.[54] But neither that distinction

53 James Kent, 2 Commentaries on American Law 15 (Oliver Wendell Holmes ed., 12th ed. 1873).

54 *See supra* note 24 and accompanying text.

nor the category "tort" itself played a structural role in his analysis. Blackstone's great influence makes it important to see this, lest we think that acceptance of tort as a basic subject naturally followed from his treatment of the subject. The point can only be understood when his discussion of tort is placed in the context of his work as a whole.

Blackstone's *Commentaries* were published in four books, entitled "Rights of Persons," "Rights of Things," "Private Wrongs," and "Public Wrongs." These headings superficially tracked the Roman categories,[55] so that it might seem that Book 4 dealt with public law, and Books 1–3 with the standard subdivisions of private law—law of persons, of things, and of actions.[56]

Below the surface level marked by the titles, however, the Blackstonian scheme departed substantially from any Roman models. Book 1 on the "Rights of Persons" did deal with topics such as husband and wife, master and servant, and guardian and ward, which as matters of ascriptive status would have fallen under the Roman law of persons. As its title suggests, however, Book 1 also contained Blackstone's formulation of the modern "absolute rights of individuals," the natural rights to life, liberty, property, and personal security, concepts that had no parallel in Roman law. Further, Blackstone placed his account of the British Constitution (public law to the Romans) in Book 1 as part of the law of persons, treating the powers of government officers as grants of a special kind of legal status.[57]

---

55 *See* ALAN WATSON, ROMAN LAW AND COMPARATIVE LAW 166–81 (1991) (noting parallels between Blackstone's structure and the similar four-book organization of Justinian's Institutes). Though Watson argues that Blackstone's structure was more influenced by Justinian's than has previously been recognized, he does not claim that Blackstone incorporated the Roman "law of obligations" with its tort-contract dichotomy into his organization. Another celebrated study of Blackstone's scheme largely ignores the influence of the Roman institutional ordering, emphasizing ideological factors—the need to mediate between liberal and pre-liberal features of eighteenth century English law. Duncan Kennedy, *The Structure of Blackstone's Commentaries*, 28 BUFF. L, REV. 205 (1979).

56 The Blackstonian title phrases "Rights of Persons" and "Rights of Things" are mistranslations of the Roman *jus personarum* and *jus rerun*, law of persons and law of things. Blackstone inherited the terminology (along with much else) from SIR MATTHEW HALE, ANALYSIS OF THE LAW OF ENGLAND 1 (1716) ("Now all Civil Rights or Interests are of Two Sorts: 1. *Jura Personarum*, or Rights of Persons. 2. *Jura Rerum*, or Rights of Things."). The Romans had no abstract concept of an individual ("subjective") right, for which the law then provided a remedy; rather the individual simply had an "action." NICHOLAS, *supra* note 17, at 100 n. 1. The dichotomy of right and remedy is post-medieval, and our familiar conceptual triad of right, remedy, and procedure dates only from the nineteenth century.

57 Austin, who rarely had a good word for Blackstone, did praise him for his insight that public law in this narrow sense (which Austin called "political law") should be classified

Book 2, "Rights of Things," contained Blackstone's detailed treatment of English property law. It can be seen to (very roughly) follow the order of the Roman subdivision of the "law of things" into subcategories of property, successions, and obligations. In the part corresponding to "obligations," Blackstone discussed "things personal, or chattels," and included a chapter devoted to contracts. He treated contract, however, not as a form of obligation parallel to tort, but as one among several modes of gaining or losing title to personal property, along with forfeiture, grant, and marriage. And there was nothing in Book 2 that corresponded to the delictual half of the Roman/civilian law of obligations.

Book 4, "Public Wrongs," was a detailed treatment of English criminal law and procedure. (Recall that by contrast the Romans treated criminal law as public law, and therefore not an important focus of juristic science.) The rest of Blackstone's quite extensive treatment of English public law, the body of law governing the structure of the state and the powers of officials, appeared, as previously noted, in Book 1.

It was in Book 3, "Private Wrongs," roughly corresponding to the Roman "law of actions," that Blackstone stated the civilian distinctions between real (proprietary) and personal actions, and then distinguished personal actions into those in tort and contract respectively.[58] Here we might expect to find an account of something like the Roman law of obligations, but in fact there is nothing of the kind. As already noted, Blackstone had already treated contract law in Book 2, as a mode of acquiring property. Book 3 was entirely organized around remedies and procedure, with nothing approximating a unified treatment of tort law. It dealt successively with modes of relief, the system of courts, the common law forms of action, and finally pleading and practice (roughly our civil procedure).

Blackstone's statement of the distinction between tort and contract came in passing as part of the discussion of the forms of action in Chapter 8, entitled "Of Wrongs and of Remedies, Respecting the Rights of Persons." The distinction

---

as a part of the law of status. *See Outline, supra* note 39, at 69; *see also supra* note 47. As Austin noted, Blackstone was here (as elsewhere) following the structure laid down in Sir Matthew Hale's *Analysis of the Law of England, supra* note 56, at 4–6. Dicey's famous notion that the Rule of Law rejects "administrative law," the grant of special legal powers to officials who are then safeguarded by immunity from personal suit, is prefigured by Austin's placement (following Blackstone and Hale) of public law under the category, suspect for its illiberal connotations, of the law of persons. A.V. Dicey, Introduction to the Study of the Law of the Constitution 120–21 (Liberty Classics ed., 1982) (1889).

58 *See supra* note 24 and accompanying text.

played no structural role even in that chapter, much less in the larger structure of Book 3 or the *Commentaries* as a whole. Blackstone organized Chapter 8 around the "absolute rights of persons" he had originally listed in Book 1. Among these, for example, was the right of personal liberty, and he listed as remedies available for its protection both the (private law) damage suit for false imprisonment and the (public law) writ of habeas corpus. Clearly Blackstone's concept of "private wrongs" was not limited to what civilians would classify under the law of obligations, or even under private law. He gave no separate consideration to delict or tort as a legal category.

Like Blackstone, Walker stated the tort-contract distinction, and classified the common law writs under its headings.[59] But also like Blackstone, he made no structural use of the distinction, nor did the concepts of "obligation" or "personal action" or "tort" do any conceptual work in his treatise. His primary divisions were constitutional law, law of persons,[60] law of property (with contracts treated as a subdivision), law of crimes, law of procedure, and international law. The tort-contract distinction made its brief appearance in a section on "classification of actions" in the division on procedure, which catalogued the traditional common-law actions.

Walker (an active procedural reformer in Ohio)[61] criticized the system of forms of action as arbitrary, and went on to redescribe the civil causes of action in substantive terms. But in doing so he did not make use of the tort-contract distinction; rather, like Blackstone, he classified causes of action by the rights they protected—bodily security, liberty, health, reputation, domestic comfort, and property. In listing remedies for these wrongs he confined himself to what we would describe as tort causes of action,[62] but he did not use the term "tort," or refer back to his earlier discussion of "obligation" or to the tort-contract distinction. He described contract actions not as forming a separate legal category, but rather as vindicating a species of "personal property," namely "things in action."[63] Finally, Walker distinguished civil from criminal law on

59 WALKER, *supra* note 25. I am using the fourth edition of Walker's book (1860), the one Holmes would have used. Its text conformed to Walker's third edition (1855); the latter was substantially revised from his first edition (1837).

60 *Id.* at 226–95. The law of persons comprised domestic relations, master and servant, and executors and administrators, tracking the Roman idea of status-based law.

61 *See id.* at 543. Note (a) (added to his third edition in 1855) describes the recently enacted procedural reforms in Ohio (which had followed New York) and other states, as well as Walker's own earlier efforts along these lines in Ohio.

62 Thus Walker did not follow Blackstone in listing habeas corpus alongside the tort suit for false imprisonment as a remedy protecting personal liberty.

63 WALKER, *supra* note 25, at 567.

the ground that wrongs "of a more atrocious character than ordinary" were "punished as crimes."[64]

Let me sum up. As of 1871, Holmes had not and could not have read any commentator on the common law as a whole, or on either English law or American law as a whole, who made any practical use of the civil law categories "law of obligations" or "personal actions." And neither in name nor in concept was "tort" or "delict" part of the working conceptual structure used by any of these writers.

3 Positive Law

I previously noted Maitland's 1886 survey of the features of late nineteenth century English statute and case law that relied on the tort-contract distinction. But I left out his conclusion, which was that the collective effect of these doctrines was so slight that "the courts of the present day are very free to consider the classification of causes of action without paying much regard" to the tort-contract dichotomy.[65] Maitland judged the recurring attempt to fit "the now obsolete forms of action" into the civilian classification as "never important or very successful" and "foredoomed to failure."[66] In his view, the rules about joinder of parties and joinder and survival of actions were neither firmly grounded nor hard and fast, and the recent statutory provisions that made awards of costs turn on whether actions sounded in tort or contract were ill-advised, but insignificant.

In addition to the factors noted by Maitland, many features of the common law as it had grown up over the centuries created difficulties for any effort to segregate its private law doctrines into the civilian categories of tort and contract. For accidental procedural reasons, the main common law action for breach of contract, assumpsit, had developed out of the writ of trespass on the case, which was also the basis of most of the tort actions.[67] The essential allegation of an "undertaking" (*super se assumpsit*) could readily be construed either as claiming a promise, which then became a binding contract with the giving of consideration, or as charging the defendant with the kind of expectation-altering causal intervention in the plaintiffs affairs that gave rise to a duty of care in tort. This left large bodies of law arbitrarily classifiable

---

64 *Id.* at 561.

65 *See* POLLOCK, *supra* note 29, at 370 (App. A).

66 *Id.*

67 An excellent retelling of this oft-told tale, incorporating the latest learning, is IBBETSON, *supra* note 21, at 126–51.

as either contract or tort.[68] The liabilities of bailees for accidental damage to property,[69] and of persons in the common callings for malpractice,[70] were likewise hard to disentangle in this respect, as were the liabilities of masters to servants for workplace injuries,[71] and the warranty liabilities of sellers of goods.[72]

There were other difficulties with classifying English law under the categories of the civilian law of obligations. What, for example, was to be done with trusts and fiduciary obligations in Equity,[73] and with other bodies of law (like Admiralty, with its concepts of salvage, and maintenance and cure) that had grown up outside the common law courts? In his own torts treatise, Pollock wrote that the attempt to classify personal actions as arising either in contract or tort could not "be defended as a scientific dichotomy" and that the civilian distinction made for "considerable perplexity" in the extensive "intersection between the two regions."[74]

To summarize, nothing in English law as Maitland reported it required lawyers and judges to adopt torts as a basic category of substantive law. And the ambiguous character of large bodies of important doctrine counseled against any program of sorting civil claims into categories of contract and tort. In neither respect was American law significantly different. As a result, Holmes was not defying well-established doctrine or deeply-rooted precedent, or ignoring practical necessity, when he concluded in 1871 that torts was "not a proper subject for a law book."

4 An Alternative Arrangement

It is one thing to reject the category of torts or the tort-contract dichotomy in theory; it is something else to supply a workable alternative scheme of categories. As I have noted, at the time Holmes rejected torts as a subject, he was

---

68 Pollock *supra* note 29, at 431–32.

69 *See generally* Robert J. Kaczorowski, *The Common-Law Background of Nineteenth-Century Tort Law*, 51 Ohio St. L.J. 1127, 1132–34 (1990).

70 Baker, *supra* note 29, at 471.

71 Thus Chief Justice Shaw's famous formulation of the fellow servant rule in *Farwell v. Boston & Worcester R.R. Corp.*, 45 Mass. 49, 53–57 (1842), was based on his characterization of the question of the master's vicarious liability for negligent personal injury to the servant as based on contract rather than on tort.

72 Ibbetson, *supra* note 21, at 223.

73 *See* Jeffrey Hackney, *More than a Trace of the Old Philosophy*, *in* The Classification of Obligations 123, 130–31 and *passim* (Peter Birks ed., 1997), who makes the point that the attempt to classify English law according to the civilian scheme of obligations means slighting the importance of the law of trusts, and other equitable doctrines.

74 Pollock, *supra* note 29, at 431–32.

himself pursuing the Bentham-Austin project of attempting to formulate a universally applicable classification of substantive law around abstract types of legal duties (those of all to all, of some to some, etc.) Yet two years later, when he came to write "The Theory of Torts," he was on the verge of deciding that the historicity (what we would call path-dependence) of systems of law meant that no general substantive classification along the lines laid down by Bentham and Austin was practicable.[75] This decision might have led Holmes to conclude that, whatever the abstract merits of the analytical critique of tort, any practical taxonomy of Anglo-American substantive law had to include it as a primary category.

But in fact, shortly before he rejected torts as a subject in 1871, Holmes had already come across a proposal that seemed to meet this practical objection. John Norton Pomeroy was, like Holmes himself, one of the younger generation of scientifically minded American legal scholars who had been inspired to take on the challenges posed by the abolition of the writ system.[76] In 1864, he produced an entirely plausible and detailed systematic taxonomy of the substantive law that treated property and contract as fundamental categories, and yet managed very well without tort.

Pomeroy's *Introduction to Municipal Law*[77] was advertised as a general textbook for high-school and university students. The book was in fact an impressively sophisticated introduction to the philosophy and history of law, to comparative law (by way of an account of Roman as compared to common law), and to the legal institutions and the main outlines of the substantive law of England and the United States. We know that Holmes read Pomeroy's

---

75 *See supra* note 46. Holmes half-heartedly continued his project of a general classification of duties in *The Theory of Torts*, *supra* note 32, at 331–34, and then abandoned it for good.

76 Pomeroy (1828–1885) had a distinguished career, most of it spent as the leading member of the faculty at the University of California's first law school, Hastings College of the Law. His writings on jurisprudence, constitutional law, water law, equity, and the reformed civil procedure, were recognized as authoritative in his day. A good analysis of his work, with a biographical sketch, is THOMAS G. BARNES, HASTINGS COLLEGE OF THE LAW: THE FIRST CENTURY 88–116 (1978). *See also* Stephen A. Siegel, *Historism in Late Nineteenth-Century Constitutional Thought*, 1990 WIS. L. REV. 1431, 1453–85; HOEFLICH, *supra* note 20, at 97–101.

77 JOHN NORTON POMEROY, AN INTRODUCTION TO MUNICIPAL LAW (1864). Pomeroy meant "municipal law" in its jurisprudential sense, as the internal law of a nation-state, to be contrasted with international law, a subject on which he wrote separately. *Id.* at 1.

book in the spring of 1871, around the time he pronounced torts to be "not a proper subject."[78]

For our purposes, the interest of Pomeroy's book resides in its last part, his systematic exposition of substantive law. He divided his analysis into three main chapters, on persons and personal rights, property, and contracts respectively.[79] The latter two chapters treated their subjects in terms that would be familiar to any present-day lawyer. Indeed, Pomeroy sealed his his claim to modernity by promoting contracts from a subdivision of the law of property (as in Blackstone, Kent, and Walker) to independent categorical status.

The ideas behind Pomeroy's first chapter, on persons and personal rights, however, are less accessible to us today. The chapter was divided into sections treating "general" and "peculiar" rights,[80] the latter dealing with status-based doctrines corresponding to the Roman category of the law of persons, such as the common law of domestic relations, and of master and servant.[81] This was the law governing the household and other feudal remnants, designated "peculiar" because it was thought to be withering away under society's progressive evolution from status to contract.[82]

It was in the first section, on the general rights of persons, that we find Pomeroy's well-concealed treatment of what we call the law of tort. He did not analyze torts as a separate body of substantive law, but included civil suits for damages along with constitutional restrictions on the legislature,[83] and bits of administrative and criminal law, as the remedies protecting the basic

---

78 Eleanor Little, *The Early Reading of Justice Oliver Wendell Holmes*, 8 HARV. LIBR. BULL. 163, 183 (1954). G. Edward White drew attention to Holmes' reading of Pomeroy's book in his biography, and speculated that Pomeroy might have influenced the jurisprudential views Holmes would express in *The Common Law* (1881). G. EDWARD WHITE, JUSTICE OLIVER WENDELL HOLMES: LAW AND THE INNER SELF 524 n.13 (1993). Both Pomeroy and Holmes exemplified the influence on younger American legal scholars of the German historical school, with its tendency to combine conceptualist jurisprudence and historical study.

79 POMEROY, *supra* note 77, at 358–544 (§§ 622–917) (Part III, entitled *Outlines of American Municipal Law*).

80 *Id.* at 358–454 (§§ 622–776) (Part III, Chapter I: *Persons and Personal Rights*) is divided into "persons generally, and [their] rights and dutie[s]," and "some particular classes of persons, and their peculiar rights and duties."

81 *Id.* at 429–54 (§§ 733–76).

82 MAINE, *supra* note 48, at 170.

83 *See, e.g.*, POMEROY, *supra* note 77, at 392 (§ 676) (describing the "right of religious belief and worship"). Pomeroy deals with the structure of legal institutions in an earlier part of his book that is entirely separate from his exposition of the substantive law. *Id.* at 28–213 (§§ 56–355).

primary rights.[84] These primary general rights were distinguished into political rights like the suffrage, and the civil rights presumptively applicable to all persons.

Pomeroy's civil rights (like Blackstone's "absolute rights" of persons in Book 1 of his *Commentaries*) were roughly the standard natural rights of liberal theory: personal security, subdivided into rights to life, body and limb, and reputation; the right to personal liberty; the rights to acquire and enjoy private property; and finally the right of religious belief and worship.[85] Under each right, Pomeroy catalogued the remedies, prominently including tort causes of action—but also constitutional immunities, and with a miscellany of self-help privileges, extraordinary writs, and criminal prohibitions[86] thrown in.[87]

Thus like Blackstone, Pomeroy treated the tort action for false imprisonment and the writ of habeas corpus together as remedies protecting the right of personal liberty.[88] Under the right of property, Pomeroy joined civil suits for damages and specific relief with constitutional limitations on taxation and eminent domain.[89] Under the right to security of "body and limb," he described the constitutional immunity against cruel and unusual punishments, the criminal prohibition of mayhem, the privilege of self-defense against attack, and the civil damages available through tort actions for trespass and trespass on the case.[90]

While this arrangement recalled Blackstone, Pomeroy's treatment was actually more consistent with the modernizing spirit of Bentham and Austin.[91]

84 *See, e.g., id.* at 367 (§ 636) (describing the right of self-defense as an aspect of the right of personal security).

85 *Id.* at 366–91 (§§ 634–75).

86 Pomeroy explicitly omitted any extensive treatment of criminal law in his book, on the ground that "its rules are generally based upon statutes, and are therefore very different in the several States." *Id.* at xv (Preface to the First Edition).

87 *See, e.g., id.* at 377–82 (§ 653–58) (describing how the right of personal liberty may be enforced).

88 *See id.*

89 *Id.* at 388–91 (§§ 670–75).

90 *Id.* at 368–69 (§§ 638–40).

91 Pomeroy did not mention Austin, and dated the Preface to his first edition December 22, 1863; Austin's Lectures on Jurisprudence were published earlier that year. The spirit of analytical jurisprudence, with its central distinction between the law that is (expository jurisprudence) and the law that ought to be (censorial jurisprudence) can be seen in Pomeroy's criticism of Blackstone's definition of law in terms of "right[] and . . . wrong" as "either tautological or incorrect," POMEROY, *supra* note 77, at 10–11 (§§ 16–18), and his account of the common law as having been "enacted" by the judges, *id.* at 20. In the preface to the 1883 edition of *Municipal Law*, Pomeroy praised Austin as a "profoundly able

Pomeroy's classification of substantive law was based upon primary rights, and unlike Blackstone he grouped remedies (Austin's "sanctioning rights") under primary substantive categories.[92] As a result, torts (a purely remedial category) formed no part of his conceptual structure. The common-law actions under the writs of trespass, trespass on the case, and trover were not treated together, but broken up and distributed as civil remedies enforcing the distinct primary rights to personal security, property, reputation, and the like.

As noted, Pomeroy showed his modernity, and further distinguished himself from the older Blackstone-Kent tradition, by treating contracts as a primary category of substantive law, equal in status to property. But the civilian division of "obligations" into contract and delict did not lead him to conclude that if contracts was a basic category, torts must be one as well. His book thus provided Holmes with a practical demonstration that torts was not a necessary component in a systematic and up-to-date account of the substantive law. An alternative categorical scheme, organized in good Austinian fashion around "primary rights," was entirely feasible.

III The Structure and Domain of Tort Law

Two years after declaring tort law not a proper subject, Holmes published "The Theory of Torts." It was the first serious attempt in the common law world to give torts both a coherent structure and a distinctive substantive domain. Though he would both amplify and modify his account in later and better-known writings,[93] the essential elements of "Holmes on Torts" can be found in this

and scholarly jurist," while claiming to have himself given a better account of common law adjudication. *Id.* at vii. *See also id.* at 19–20 (§§ 38–39), 23–26 (§§ 51–54), for his account of the quasi-legislative powers of common law judges. At the same time, Pomeroy expressed allegiance to traditional natural law thinking as the best guide to what the law ought to be. *Id.* at 7–8 (§ 11).

92 Pomeroy integrated the remedies enforcing individual rights with the rights themselves, whereas Blackstone had separated rights (Book 1) from remedies (Book 3). Both property and contracts, Pomeroy's other two basic divisions of law apart from "persons and personal rights," are proper legal subjects on Austinian principles, with each organized around a distinctive domain of "primary rights."

93 Holmes' other primary writings on torts are his article *Trespass and Negligence*, 14 AM. L. REV. 1 (1880), *reprinted in* 3 WORKS, *supra* note 7, at 76; his treatment of the subject in THE COMMON LAW, *supra* note 78, primarily Chapters 3 and 4; and his article *Privilege, Malice, and Intent*, 8 HARV. L. REV. 1 (1894), *reprinted in* 3 WORKS, *supra* note 7, at 371. Important supplementary aspects of his theory are found in the brief but significant passages on

remarkable 1873 article. Let me first summarize the main features of the account, and then show how the theory arose from his struggle to overcome the difficulties that had earlier led him to reject torts as a substantive category.

The central features of Holmes' account of torts, all of which remain influential to this day, were these:

- his account of negligence as conduct falling below the community's standard of reasonable care, with the determination of that standard treated as a question of law, but one usually involving the identification of social norms, and so a matter on which the judge could properly take the advice of the jury;
- the related idea that judges and other lawmakers have discretion to treat the requirement of due care either as a standard to be used in deciding individual cases, or as a principle to be specified into more particularized and determinate rules—with the consequence that many rules which make no reference to negligence or due care are nonetheless properly interpreted as falling under the negligence principle;
- the placement of liability for negligence at the doctrinal and practical center of the law of torts, covering "the great mass of cases;"[94]
- the division of tort law into three parts: intentional, negligence-based, and strict liability—with intentional and strict-liability torts treated as categories peripheral and subordinate to the central principle of liability for negligence;
- the idea that a plaintiff creates *prima facie* liability in tort by showing that the defendant has harmed him, and so does not have to show violation of an independently existing legal right or duty;
- the related idea of torts as a body of substantive law formed by the active accommodation of conflicting considerations of policy, in particular the prevention of harm, and the freedom to engage in valued activity—by contrast to the remedial conception of torts as the provision of compensatory damages for the breach of rights and duties found elsewhere in the law;

---

tort law in *The Path of the Law*, *supra* note 46, and *Law in Science*, *supra* note 7; and his concurring opinion in *Arizona Employers' Liability Cases*, 250 U.S. 400, 431 (1919). I am working on a full-scale study of Holmes' treatment of torts; here I summarize some of the conclusions of that study.

94 *The Theory of Torts*, *supra* note 32, at 327.

- the idea that the modern form of strict liability in tort redresses injuries caused by persons engaging in "extra-hazardous" activities,[95] who for reasons of policy are required to insure the safety of those they foreseeably harm.

Holmes' great breakthrough, the innovation that allowed him to treat torts as a "proper subject" after all, was his decision to organize tort law around the principle of liability for negligence. That principle gave torts a conceptual and doctrinal center, and implicitly designated its distinctive substantive domain as accidental injuries. With its own principle and subject matter, torts could overcome the difficulties that analytical jurisprudence placed in the way of making it a fundamental legal category. But before this could happen, Holmes had to do a good deal of work on the legal concept of negligence.

A *Negligence: The Background*

Negligence was becoming a subject of increasing practical importance around the time Holmes wrote "The Theory of Torts." The spread of factories, railroads, streetcars, and other technological innovations, and the associated rise in accidental injuries, meant that a good number of lawyers were making their living in whole or in part by bringing or defending negligence suits.[96] The growth in personal injury litigation had made negligence an appealing subject to commercial legal publishers, and the first treatise on the subject, by the Americans Thomas Shearman and Amasa Redfield, appeared in 1869, followed by two English monographs, by Robert Campbell and Thomas Saunders respectively, in 1871. The distinguished American legal writer Francis Wharton had also turned his attention to the subject, and his magisterial scholarly treatise appeared in 1874.

Unlike these more practical commentators, Holmes gave no indication that he was responding to the growth of negligence litigation in "The Theory of Torts." What motivated him to bring negligence to the center of tort law was neither a desire to sell books nor a practical concern about how the law should

95 *Id.* at 326–27.

96 Both the upsurge in accidental injuries and the corresponding growth of a personal injury bar around this time are documented, with a thorough discussion of the measurement difficulties and controversies, in John Fabian Witt, *Toward a New History of American Accident Law: Classical Tort Law and the Growth of the First-Party Insurance Movement*, 114 HARV. L. REV. 690, 713–22, 758–66 (2001). For a lucid statement of how new technology often produces more accidents (and more accidents that the law will properly judge to be caused by negligence, however socially advantageous the new technology may be), *see* Mark Grady, *Why Are People Negligent? Technology, Nondurable Precautions, and the Medical Malpractice Explosion*, 82 NW. U.L. REV. 293 (1988).

deal with accidental injuries. His ambition was rather to advance the project of developing a general conceptual map of the substantive law.

The conduct giving rise to negligence suits was a domain of "wrongs" that could be separated conceptually from breaches of contract, that did not involve invasions of property rights, and that were distinct from the more serious forms of wrongdoing that formed the primary focus of the criminal law.[97] Here was a piece of the legal map that needed a label, and the concept of tort, traditional in civil law and increasingly popular with common lawyers, seemed to fit it. What had to be worked out was the relationship between negligence and tort law.

Negligence was and remains a confusingly protean concept in the law, with at least three standard meanings, arising from two distinctions. First, it is a tort cause of action, whose conventional elements are (1) a duty of due care toward the plaintiff, (2) breach of that duty, (3) causing (4) injury to the plaintiff, with plaintiff's negligence either a defense or a factor reducing damages. This "cause-of-action" meaning, specific to tort law, is distinguishable from negligence as an element in a variety of civil actions and crimes, generally connoting the lowest legally cognizable level of fault. Negligence in this latter sense supplies the breach element of the negligence cause of action, and hence metonymically gives its name to the tort.

A second distinction then separates two competing versions of the "element" aspect of negligence—the "mental state" and the "conduct" versions. As an element, negligence might mean carelessness, a state of mind involving culpable inadvertence toward risk, or it might simply mean conduct that (irrespective of state of mind) was somewhat more risky than what a reasonable person would do. Thus under the "conduct" but not the "mental state" version, someone who proceeds after deliberately considering all risks can still be found negligent on the ground that the act was unreasonably risky when measured against the community standard.

With both distinctions in hand, we then have three senses of negligence: a "cause-of-action" sense, a "mental state (element)" sense, and a "conduct (element)" sense. Holmes argued for the "conduct" over the "mental state" version

97 Pomeroy had already identified property and contract as categories of substantive law properly justified by Austinian criteria. *See supra* text accompanying notes 78–82. Walker had offered a practical definition of crimes as the "more atrocious" of the class of legal wrongs, with their "atrocity" distinguishing them from the civil wrongs as a group. *See supra* text accompanying note 64.

of negligence as an element, a position which has since generally prevailed.[98] Though he was not original in treating negligence as conduct, he seems to have been the first to give a clear statement of the distinction between the two views. He then went on to make his formulation the basis of his primary innovation—yet another sense of negligence, an overarching principle, specific to tort law, covering both the ordinary negligence cause of action and also actions basing liability on specific conduct judged by lawmakers to be unreasonably unsafe. This formulation allowed him to give a coherent account of the relation between law and fact (and so between judge and jury) in ordinary negligence cases. It also supplied the basis for his claim that negligence, in the sense of his Negligence Principle, covered the central "great mass" of tort cases.[99]

1 The Negligence Cause of Action

At the time Holmes wrote, the relationship between negligence and torts was unclear and contested. After a long prehistory,[100] a "tort of negligence" had emerged from the action of trespass on the case to take fairly clear shape in a few prescient judicial decisions and bits of commentary during the 1860s. Thus the 1862 English opinion in the important *Swan* case stated its elements much as we understand them today: "The action for negligence proceeds upon the idea of an obligation on the part of the defendant towards the plaintiff to use care, and a breach of that obligation to the plaintiffs injury."[101] Of the four early treatise-writers on negligence, Saunders clearly recognized a dis-

98 Fowler V. Harper, Fleming James, Jr. & Oscar S. Gray, 3 The Law of Torts § 16.1 (2d ed. 1986). This standard treatise summarizes the debate over whether negligence is more properly defined as conduct falling below a certain standard, or as an indifferent or inadvertant state of mind. The notion of negligence as conduct promotes administrative simplicity because it is easier to judge conduct than mental state. Moreover, it avoids leaving the cost of unreasonable behavior on innocent victims. On the other side, the state of mind approach more closely links legal liability with the moral culpability of the defendant *Id.* In *The Theory of Torts,* Holmes distinguished between "negligence *latiori sensu*" (in the broader sense), the conduct version, and "negligence *stricto sensu*" (in the narrow sense), the state of mind version, and argued that the former defined the breach element in the negligence action. *The Theory of Torts, supra* note 32, at 334.

99 *See supra* note 94 and accompanying text.

100 The earliest intimations of an "action on the case for negligence" in English law dated back to the second half of the eighteenth century; for the history *see* M.J. Prichard, Scott v. Shepherd (1773) and the Emergence of the Tort of Negligence (1976), and David Ibbetson, *The Tort of Negligence in the Common Law in the Nineteenth and Twentieth Centuries, in* Negligence (E.J.H. Schrage ed., 2001).

101 Swan v. N. British Australasian Co., 31 Law J., Exch. 437 (1862).

tinctive negligence action, quoting the standard formulation-in his opening paragraph,[102] while Shearman and Redfield, as well as Wharton, more vaguely conveyed awareness of the tort action in their discussions of "general principles" of negligence.[103]

On the other hand, recognition of negligence as a separate tort was by no means universal. In his monograph, Campbell did not treat negligence as a distinct cause of action, and he explicitly declined to locate his subject within the law of torts, reiterating Austin's critique of the civilian tort-contract dichotomy.[104] As late as the beginning of the twentieth century, Sir John Salmond was still portraying negligence as a mental element in a number of separate torts on his view, but not a separate tort.[105]

The ambiguous conceptual status of negligence in the emerging law of tort was also reflected in its treatment in the two established torts treatises. As already noted, both Hilliard and Addison treated tort law in an unsystematic way, moving through the recognized tort causes of action in an order revealing no clear design. There was no chapter treating negligence as one of the recognized torts in either book. However each treatise began with a rudimentary

---

102 Thomas William Saunders, A Treatise Upon the Law Applicable to Negligence 1 (London: Butterworth's, ed., 1871) (quoting the description of the action from *Swan v. North British Austrelasian Co.*, 31 Law J., Exch. 437 (1862)).

103 Thomas G. Shearman & amasa A. Redfield, A Treatise on the Law of Negligence 1–14, esp. 3 (1869) ("Negligence, in respect to obligations imposed by law, is therefore called tortious negligence."). They discuss contributory negligence, an aspect confined to the tort action. *Id.* at 23–57. Wharton defines negligence as "such an inadvertent imperfection, by a responsible human agent, in the discharge of a legal duty, as immediately produces, in an ordinary and natural sequence, a damage to another." Francis Wharton, A Treatise on the Law of Negligence 3 (1874). We have here the elements of duty, breach, cause and injury; Wharton's discussion indicates that he sees negligence straddling contract and tort, but also has a full discussion of contributory negligence, a doctrine specific to the tort action. *Id.* at 264–366.

104 Robert Campbell, The Law of Negligence 12–13 (Stevens & Haynes ed., 1871). Campbell made the Austinian argument that a breach of contract is as much a civil wrong—a breach of primary duty—as are the actions conventionally recognized as delictual, and added the point that any subcategorization of civil wrongs had to take account not only of tort and contract but unjust enrichment—the Roman *obligatio quasi ex contractu*.

105 John W. Salmond, The Law of Torts: A Treatise on English Law of Liability for Civil Injuires § 2(3) (3d ed. 1912) ("Just as the criminal law consists of a body of rules establishing special offences, so the law of torts consists of a body of rules establishing specific injuries. Neither in the one case nor in the other is there any general principle of liability."). Salmond described negligence as a mental element, *see infra* note 121, but did not treat it as a distinct tort.

"general part" meant to address tort law as a whole, and each implicitly outlined the elements of the negligence action in this introductory part, though without any discussion of its relation to the other torts discussed in more detail in the later chapters.[106]

The first torts casebook produced at Harvard after the adoption of the case method, edited by James Barr Ames in 1875, contained no treatment of negligence at all, whether as a separate cause of action or an element; instead, it was limited to a treatment of torts involving intent or malice. Apparently this reflected the unfinished character of the teaching materials rather than a conscious decision to exclude negligence from the ambit of tort, but the omission of negligence from the most prestigious casebook for many years may well have influenced the profession's sense of the relative importance of the intentional and the accidental torts.[107]

Holmes himself apparently did not think of negligence as an individuated tort action before the conceptual breakthrough marked by his 1873 essay. He had occasion in one of his early articles on classification to formulate a list of recognized torts (under the heading of "duties of all the world to all the world"), and he came up with "assault and battery, libel, slander, false imprisonment, and the like, considered as causes of action *civiliter*." To the same purpose, as late as 1872, he gave a similar list.[108] Of course his main objection to torts as a legal category was that it was no more than the name of a list—an incoherent miscellany of civil causes of action apart from contract.[109] But in his mind that list of torts apparently did not include negligence.

2 The Negligence Element

The tentative treatment of the relation between tort law and negligence by early writers on those two topics was not surprising in light of a tradition that

106 *See* ADDISON, *supra* note 7, at 15–22; HILLIARD, *supra* note 7, at 131–39. Addison's first edition (1860) lacked any introductory general part on torts as a whole, or any account of the negligence action; its nearest approximation to the latter was a chapter, *supra* note 7, at 237–66, entitled "Of Trespasses and Injuries from the Negligent Use and Management of Chattels, and the Negligent Performance of Work."

107 When a second edition of the casebook was issued in 1893, it had an entire second volume devoted to negligence, the work of Jeremiah Smith, and a note by Ames indicated that the first edition had been left incomplete. JAMES BARR AMES & JEREMIAH SMITH, 2 A SELECTION OF CASES ON THE LAW OF TORTS, at v (2d ed. 1893).

108 *See Codes, and the Arrangement of Law*, *supra* note 36, at 216; *The Arrangement of the Law—Privity*, *supra* note 46, at 305.

109 Oliver Wendell Holmes, *Book Notice*, 5 AM. L. REV. 536 (1871), *reprinted in* 1 WORKS, *supra* note 7 at 241, 241–42 (reviewing CAMPBELL, THE LAW OF NEGLIGENCE (1871)).

had mainly considered negligence not as a distinct tort cause of action, but as an element of liability in a variety of civil actions ranging across a number of fields of law. In common-law commentary, negligence had mainly been treated under the law of bailments, which was considered either a fundamental legal category in itself[110] or a subdivision of property or contract law.[111] Negligence was the fault element in the bailor's claim against the bailee for lost or damaged property, and Lord Holt's judgment in *Coggs v. Bernard* in 1703 had brought into English law the civilian analysis of negligence into three degrees: gross, ordinary, and slight.[112] The early treatises on bailments by Sir William Jones in England and Joseph Story in America had solidified the tradition of considering negligence—and its three degrees—mainly as an element in bailment actions. Thus when Holmes wanted to insert a summary of his new negligence-centered theory of torts into his edition of Kent's *Commentaries*, he had to make it a footnote to the Chancellor's treatment of bailments.[113] And both Campbell's monograph and Wharton's treatise on negligence began with an exposition of the three degrees of negligence from bailment law, emphasizing the Roman-civilian roots of the doctrine.

A further traditional locus for the discussion of negligence involved yet another area that straddled the emerging categories of contract and tort—the responsibilities of common carriers and innkeepers for accidental personal injury, and for property loss or damage.[114] The largest group of suits of this kind

110 Bailment was actually the subject of both the first significant English-language treatise on any legal category, SIR WILLIAM JONES, AN ESSAY ON THE LAW OF BAILMENTS (1781), and also the first important American treatise, JOSEPH STORY, COMMENTARIES ON THE LAW OF BAILMENTS (1832). *See* Simpson, *supra* note 6, at 651–52.

111 Bailment was treated as part of the contract branch of the law of obligations in Roman Law, ZIMMERMANN, *supra* note 17, at 188 (chapter on *commodatum, depositum*, and *pignus*), 204 (comparison to English law of bailment), and was still treated as basically contractual in Campbell's 1871 book on the law of negligence, CAMPBELL, *supra* note 104, at 12. It was treated as part of the law of property by Blackstone and Kent. 2 BLACKSTONE, *supra* note 24, at 396, 451; KENT, *supra* note 53, at 558–611.

112 Coggs v. Bernard, 92 Eng. Rep. 107 (K.B. 1703). The *Coggs* trichotomy held that the bailee was liable only for gross negligence if the bailment was gratuitous to the bailor (looking after a friend's pet), liable for even the slightest negligence if gratuitous to the bailee (loaning a car to a friend), and liable for ordinary negligence where the bailment was for mutual benefit (a car rental).

113 KENT, *supra* note 53, at 561 n. 1.

114 *See* POLLOCK, *supra* note 29, at 339–40. Innkeepers and common carriers were required by law to serve all reasonable comers, refusal to serve was a tort (the origin of our law of antidiscrimination in public accommodations), and by extension injury to a customer in the course of the required service was also a tort.

were against common carriers, who were also bailees of shipped goods. As common carriage came to be a routine commercial service, the most contested issue with respect to these liabilities was whether they could be disclaimed by notice or agreement—a decision that we associate with the question whether the liability rule should be classified under contract or tort.[115]

Even the writers who recognized negligence as a separate tort action had to spend most of their time discussing it as an issue of bailment and carrier law. Shearman and Redfield wrote that if they treated negligence only as a tort this would leave the profession "without any information upon several important branches," and they went on to discuss bailment and carrier cases at length.[116] Wharton devoted a whole section of his treatise to cases in which the duty of due care arose out of contract, thus allowing the plaintiff to elect between suing for negligence in contract or tort.[117] And in the bulk of his book, after his clear statement of the elements of negligence as a tort action, Saunders also mainly discussed case law in the debatable middle ground.[118]

In short, negligence in 1870 was just emerging as a tort cause of action, and otherwise was a concept only loosely linked to the nascent law of torts. It was much more commonly considered an element or issue in bodies of law like bailment and common carrier liability; these in turn were understood

115 *See* Morton Horwitz, The Transformation of American Law, 1780–1860, 205–07 (1977); *see also* Kaczorowski, *supra* note 69, at 138–44 (describing nineteenth century trend toward making the strict liability disclaimable, once it was recognized that it was a form of compulsory insurance that commercial shippers should be free to decline). For us the main consequence of placing liabilities arising out of consensual relations in tort or contract involve disclaimability; thus the decisive shift of strict product liability from contract to tort came with decisions to the effect that disclaimers of liability for product defects would not generally be upheld where they involved threats to safety. This could occur in cases that were formally based on warranty (hence arguably contractual), *see e.g., Henningsen v. Bloomfield Motors*, 161 A.2d 69 (N.J. 1960), or in cases that explicitly based the liability on a new form of strict liability in tort, *see e.g., Greenman v. Yuba Power Products, Inc.*, 377 P.2d 897 (Cal. 1963).

116 Shearman & Redfield, *supra* note 103, at iv. The authors went on to make clear their allegiance to the tort-contract dichotomy, and to show their understanding of its civilian roots, when they wrote that "treatises expository of the common law... arranged in strict logical order" would have to await the coming of "some new Pothier" who would "do for America and England what the first Pothier did for France." *Id.* at iv–v.

117 Wharton, *supra* note 103, at 393–654.

118 Saunders, *supra* note 102, at 15–61 (evidence of negligence), 155–224 (negligence of attorneys, bailees, common carriers, innkeepers, physicians—the "non-stranger" situations of tort-contract ambiguity that provided most of the negligence cases).

either as freestanding legal categories, or as overlapping the line between contract and tort.

3 Mental Element or Conduct

The further question then arose whether negligence, regarded as an element, was to be understood as a mental state—culpable carelessness—or simply as conduct that departed from the standard of the reasonable man. Holmes' first scholarly engagement with negligence involved this question. He first endorsed the concept as sufficiently "philosophical" to be a proper topic for scholarly study in one 1871 book review,[119] but changed his mind later that year when reviewing Campbell's *Law of Negligence* forced him to focus on the Austinian analysis of negligence as a careless or inadvertent state of mind.[120] The mental-state view articulated by Campbell was widely held among nineteenth century commentators,[121] and Holmes apparently accepted it without question on this first encounter.

---

119 Oliver Wendell Holmes, *Book Notice*, 5 Am. L. Rev. 343 (1871) (reviewing Shearman & Redfield, A Treatise on the Law of Negligence (2d ed. 1870)).

120 *See* Oliver Wendell Holmes, *Book Notice*, 5 Am. L. Rev. 536 (1871) (reviewing Robert Campbell, The Law of Negligence (1871)); *see also* The Common Law, *supra* note 78, at 86 n. 48, where Holmes again cited Campbell "for Austin's point of view." In his detailed treatment of culpable mental states, Austin followed Bentham in distinguishing among "negligence," which in his terminology applied only to omissions, "heedlessness" or culpable inadvertance to risk, and "rashness," or culpable failure to give adequate consideration of a risk actually noted, the latter two of which applied to acts. *See Analysis of Pervading Notions*, *supra* note 49, at 425–34; Jeremy Bentham, *Introduction to the Principles of Morals and Legislation, reprinted in* 1 The Works of Jeremy Bentham, *supra* note 10, at 43–44. Later writers did not generally follow these elaborate distinctions, but treated acts and omissions, both advertent and inadvertent, under the single concept of negligence.

121 Thus Shearman and Redfield defined negligence as "carelessness ... want of care, caution, attention, diligence, or discretion, in one having no positive intention to injure the person complaining thereof." Shearman & Redfield, *supra* note 103, at 1–2. Wharton followed Austin in carefully analyzing negligence and intent as qualitatively distinct and mutually exclusive states of mind, to be inferred as a matter of fact from the evidence in each case. Wharton, *supra* note 103, at 11–17. The "state of mind" approach by no means passed away with the nineteenth century; it was still stated to be the law in Salmond's influential English treatise.

> "Negligence and wrongful intent are the two alternative forms of *mens rea*, one of the other of which is commonly required by law as a condition of liability. Each consists in a certain mental attitude of the defendant toward the consequences of his act ... He is

Holmes' point was that if negligence was a mental state to be alleged and proved as a fact to a jury, it could only serve as an element of liability in an incoherent collection of civil cases. In other cases involving similar issues, legislation or common law doctrine premised liability on proof of specific conduct, without any reference to state of mind. Negligence understood as a factual mental state would thus not be a promising concept around which tort law, or any distinctive portion of it, could usefully be organized.[122] Holmes' rejection of negligence as a fruitful concept for legal analysis thus fit well with his view, expressed later the same year, that tort was not a proper substantive legal category.

An alternative to the view of negligence as a mental fact, though, was available in standard definitions given by common law judges. These treated negligence simply as conduct falling below the standard set by the reasonable man, without any reference to an inadvertent state of mind. Thus, as Baron Alderson defined it in the *Blyth* case in 1856: "Negligence is the omission to do something that a reasonable man, guided upon those considerations which ordinarily regulate the conduct of human affairs, would do, or something which a prudent and reasonable man would not do."[123] If negligence was whatever the reasonable man would not do, it was irrelevant how carefully and thoroughly the party charged with negligence had contemplated the risks.[124] Specific authority to this effect was the 1837 English case of *Vaughan v. Menlove*, upholding the denial of an instruction that a defendant could not be found negligent if he had "acted bona fide to the best of his judgment." That the defendant had done his best did not mean that he had acted as a reasonably prudent man.[125]

B *Holmes' Innovations*

1 The Centrality of Negligence

Holmes made no reference to the "reasonable man" test as suggesting an alternative conduct-based conception of negligence in his 1871 review of Campbell's book. He was surely aware of the objective element in the standard negligence

guilty of negligence … when he … is … indifferent or careless whether they happen or not. …"

SALMOND, *supra* note 105, at § 5(1).

122 And quite consistently, Salmond, a leading proponent of the "state of mind" conception, denied that tort law as a whole had any defining structure. *See supra* note 105.

123 Blyth v. Birmingham Waterworks, 11 Ex. 781, 784 (1856).

124 Hover v. Barkoof, 44 N.Y. 113, 117 (1871) (testimony of defendant engineer that he believed all necessary steps for safety of bridge had been taken was properly excluded as irrelevant and potentially prejudicial).

125 Vaughan v. Menlove, 3 Bing. N.C. 468, 471, 132 Eng. Rep. 490 (C.P. 1837).

charge, but perhaps interpreted it as Tindal, C.J., had presented it in *Vaughan*, as an *ad hoc* practical concession to the difficulty of taking individual peculiarities into account in proving the actual mental state of the defendant.[126] As such, it was fully reconcilable in principle with the Austinian analysis, and this is how most of the early judges and commentators who dealt with negligence as a legal concept seem to have understood it.

But Holmes apparently continued to wrestle with the intuition that negligence was a promising concept around which to organize tort law, and at some point he broke through to the reformulation that he set out in "The Theory of Torts." Negligence was not, as ordinary usage suggested and as jurisprudential tradition maintained, a state of mind, and so a matter of fact, to be determined by the jury as present or not on the evidence in each case. Rather it was a complex legal conclusion, a determination that a public standard of conduct existed, that it applied to a party's conduct, and that the conduct fell below the standard. The "reasonable man" test was not a concession to the difficulties of proving individual capacities and states of mind, but rather a substantively distinct theory of liability.

Though Holmes was the first to formulate the point clearly, this much could have been pieced together from existing doctrine, taking account of the established elements of duty (due care as the standard of conduct) and breach (violation of that standard) in the usual formulation of the negligence cause of action. All that was needed was to join these to the objective ("reasonable man") aspect of the concept of negligence, which had been stated in *Vaughan* and *Blyth*.

Holmes' next step, though, was more inventive. He postulated an overarching principle of objective negligence, based on the general idea of a public standard of reasonable behavior, applicable to all conduct creating risks to others. He then argued that this principle was sometimes applied as an operative standard to the facts, as in a normal negligence case, but other times it was specified, legislatively or judicially, into more particular rules defining what would be considered reasonable or unreasonable in recurring situations. This expansion of the concept of negligence brought within its ambit a wide array of legislated and judge-made tort rules that did not in so many words require "due

---

126 *See id.* at 475.

> "Instead, therefore, of saying that the liability for negligence should be coextensive with the judgment of each individual, which would be as variable as the foot of each individual, we ought rather to adhere to the rule which requires in all cases a regard to caution such as a man of ordinary prudence would observe."

Id.

care" or make liability turn on "negligence." These rules could nonetheless be interpreted as defining what counted as reasonable conduct for the situations they covered. This was the innovation that allowed Holmes to say that negligence (thus expansively reconceived) covered "the great mass of [tort] cases."[127]

Holmes' formulation did more than widen the scope of negligence; it also supplied the first clear rationale for the respective roles of judge and jury in deciding the breach issue in ordinary negligence cases. When jurors decided whether someone had acted with due care, on Holmes' theory they were *not* simply finding facts, at least not adjudicative facts about an individual litigant's state of mind.[128] Rather, they were endeavoring to "suggest a rule of law to the court" by using their knowledge of a social fact: the existence of a social norm of conduct, "the practice of the average member of the community—what a prudent man would do under the circumstances." This practice or customary conduct then served as the standard in those cases where neither legislature nor court had further specified the elements of reasonable care.[129]

---

127 *See supra* note 94 and accompanying text.

128 This was the orthodox view, stated in an unsigned book review that, on the basis of its style and content, appears to have been written by Nicholas St. John Green. *See* Green, *Book Notice*, *supra* note 14, at 351.

> "As we understand the question it is as follows: 1) Does the law impose a duty or obligation? 2) What is that duty or obligation? These are questions of law. 3) Was the conduct under investigation a violation of that duty?... The legal duty which is generally imposed, is to take that forethought for the rights of others which under the particular circumstances of the case might be expected from a person of mature age who is not deficient in prudence. Whether that forethought has been exercised is a question of fact. Negligence is conduct arising from want of forethought which violates a legal duty. In our opinion negligence is a question of fact."

Id. at 351. Green's analysis is based on the Austinian theory, so Holmes seems not to have derived his importantly novel reconception of negligence from Green. The "mental fact" view of negligence was maintained in the face of Holmes' arguments by a great contemporary and sometime collaborator of his in James Bradley Thayer, *Preliminary Treatise on Evidence at the Common Law*, 226–29, 249–53 (1898) (negligence is a pure question of fact, but one on which, for reasons of policy, courts review the judgment of the jury more aggressively than usual).

129 *The Theory of Torts*, *supra* note 32, at 330. Holmes' account of the jury role in negligence determinations led him to propose his idea that judges would tend to reduce the standard of care to rule-like formulations in recurring situations, thereby cutting back the law-making role of the jury. His own judicial efforts in this direction were not successful in the United States. *See* Pokora v. Wabash Ry. Co., 292 U.S. 98 (1934). Some now regret this, *see* Kenneth Abraham, *The Trouble with Negligence*, 54 VAND. L. REV. 1187 (2001), but

Holmes thus brought to the center of tort law negligence reconceived in terms of conduct, which he here called "negligence *latiori sensu*" ("in the looser sense").[130] This focusing of tort law upon objective negligence was his most important innovation. He would again emphasize the centrality of negligence to torts in *The Common Law* by beginning his treatment of the subject with his Chapter 3, "Trespass and Negligence," which dealt with the choice of negligence over strict liability as the default principle for handling accidents. This left the intentional torts for subordinate treatment in Chapter 4, where Holmes applied the analysis in terms of conduct creating risk that he had already established in his discussion of negligence; intentional wrongdoing was causing harm by conduct more risky as a matter of degree than mere negligence. None of the other torts commentators or treatise writers of the nineteenth century followed Holmes in either this order of exposition or this conceptual priority.

2 The Tripartite Classification of Torts

Having placed objective negligence at the center of the spectrum of tort liability standards, Holmes portrayed it in "The Theory of Torts" as bracketed by "two extremes." At one end were rules of true strict liability, both ancient and modern; at the other were rules requiring true moral culpability—intent to harm, or malice, or "negligence *stricto sensu*," meaning Austinian negligence, a culpably careless "actual condition of the defendant's consciousness."[131] Here we find the familiar tripartite arrangement of torts into those involving serious fault, those involving only negligence, and those requiring no fault at all. This structure would be adopted by Melville Bigelow in his *Elements of Torts* in 1878, and by Sir Frederick Pollock in his treatise in 1887—the first modern treatise on tort law—from whence it went on to become the standard organizing scheme

---

Holmes' project was carried out to an extreme in England, where judicial formulations of separate type-situational standards of care proliferated to the point where more than 1000 pages of Beven's work on negligence were required to record them by 1928. Thomas Beven, Negligence in Law (4th ed. 1928). Shortly thereafter, jury trial in negligence cases was discontinued by statute. *See* Ibbetson, *supra* note 21, at 188–91. Holmes himself would not have wanted to go that far; he "believe[d] in our practice of leaving questions of negligence to" the jury, which helped to keep "the administration of the law in accord with the wishes and feelings of the community." *Law in Science*, *supra* note 7, at 418.

130 *The Theory of Torts*, *supra* note 32, at 334.

131 *Id.* at 327.

for the subject to this day.[132] Bigelow explicitly and Pollock more vaguely gave due credit to Holmes as the primary innovator.[133]

In *The Common Law*, Holmes would retain the basic idea of a tripartite structure dominated by objective negligence in the center, with strict liability at one end. At the other end, however, he placed, not torts involving malice or intent, but rather doctrines of privilege that protected conduct from liability, sometimes even conduct willfully or maliciously doing harm, on the basis of a judgment that the conduct in question required extra breathing room from the law.[134]

The categories of intentional (or malicious) torts on the one hand and privileged activity on the other are closely connected under Holmes' theory of torts. If, as Holmes argued, liability for negligence is the default rule in tort law, to require intent or malice for liability is to protect that class of risky conduct by a qualified privilege to inflict harm negligently. Holmes finally got his views clear on the relation between privilege and serious wrongdoing in "Privilege, Malice, and Intent" in 1894,[135] arguing that the law grants privileges protecting socially

---

132 Pollock, *supra* note 29, at 12–14. Pollock took the additional step of comparing the tripartite organization with the Roman law concepts of *dolus, culpa*, and *obligatio quasi ex delicto* respectively, and hence linking the common law scheme to civilian categories. In Roman Law, *dolus* meant "fraud," but could be expanded to encompass intentional wrongdoing more generally; *culpa* could mean fault generally, or the lesser variety of fault corresponding to negligence. Pollock's equation of the Roman liability *quasi ex delicto* with strict liability has not been uniformly followed; Austin thought the Roman category incoherent, and Pothier equated it with negligence, while treating the Roman *culpa* as intentional or malicious wrongdoing. *See Analysis of Pervading Notions, supra* note 49, at 343, 497–98; Pothier, *supra* note 52, at 73 (noting tort is an act causing damage through "fraud or malice," quasi-tort act causing damage "without malice, but through inexcusable imprudence"). A valuable analysis of Roman law influences on the nineteenth-century development of negligence doctrine is David Ibbetson, *supra* note 18.

133 Pollock, *supra* note 29, at vi; Melville Bigelow, Elements of the Law of Torts at v (1878). Eventually the tripartite scheme would become standard in the organization of American tort casebooks, at least with James Barr Ames & Jeremiah Smith, A Selection of Cases on the Law of Torts (Roscoe Pound ed., 1916).

134 The Common Law, *supra* note 78, at 128.

> "The theory of torts may be summed up very simply. At the two extremes of the law are rules determined by policy without reference of any kind to morality.
>
> Certain harms a man may inflict even wickedly; for certain others he must answer, although his conduct has been prudent and beneficial to the community. But in the main the law ... adopted the vocabulary, and in some degree the tests, of morals."

Id.

135 *Privilege, Malice, and Intent, supra* note 93.

valued conduct like the owner's free use of land, or the entrepreneur's freedom to start a business, but normally withdraws those privileges in cases of injury inflicted out of pure malice. In the 1894 essay, Holmes also returned to the tripartite structure as he had formulated it originally in 1873, and as we generally understand it today, dividing torts into those involving malice or intent, negligence (the general rule), and strict liability for mere "mischance."[136]

3 Objective Negligence as Compromise

Partaking of both moral fault and no-fault, objective negligence mediated between the two poles of the tort spectrum. "Actual fault" or blameworthiness was an important influence, invoking as it did socially defined standards of prudent conduct. But the objective element could also be seen as itself a kind of strict liability, motivated by each person's right to expect normal conduct of (even abnormal) others, and by a policy of putting deterrent pressure for safety on socially useful but more than usually risky activities. Thus the legal attribution of negligence was not ultimately constrained by moral (which in Holmes' usage meant purely internal) conceptions of personal virtue or wickedness.[137]

---

136 *Id.* at 371–72 ("If the manifest probability of harm is very great, and the harm follows, we say that it is done maliciously or intentionally; if not so great, but still considerable, we say that the harm is done negligently; if there is no apparent danger, we call it mischance."). *Privilege, Malice, and Intent, id.* at 372–77, also provided the structure of another of Holmes' innovations in tort theory, what became known as the doctrine of *prima facie* intentional tort. *See* Aikens v. Wisconsin, 195 U.S. 194, 204 (1904) (Holmes, J.); Kenneth Vandevelde, *A History of Prima Facie Tort: The Origins of a General Theory of Intentional Tort*, 19 HOFSTRA L. REV. 447 (1990). This doctrine provided the conceptual underpinnings for Holmes' celebrated dissents in labor injunction cases in the late 1890s, the opinions that probably convinced Theodore Roosevelt to appoint him to the United States Supreme Court. *See* Plant v. Woods, 57 N.E. 1011, 1015 (Mass. 1900) (Holmes, J., dissenting); Vegelahn v. Guntner, 44 N.E. 1077, 1079 (Mass. 1896) (Holmes, J., dissenting); *see also* WHITE *supra* note 78, at 300 (identifying labor dissents as "strong point in Holmes' favor" for Roosevelt).

137 *See* 2 HOWE, *supra* note 12, at 169–70, 176–78 (citing standard nineteenth century criminal law treatises for the individual moral approach to fault). Howe describes this approach as Kantian, referring to Kant's theory of personal ethics, which locates all virtue in the good will. This is a common misattribution. Kant, who insisted on a sharp separation of public justice from the ethics of private virtue, himself held an external theory of legal liability very much like Holmes' (as Holmes was quite aware—he had noted it in the French translation of the *Rechtslehre* that he read, *id.* at 178 n. 48). When Holmes speaks against confusing "morality" with law, it is almost always traditional Christian morality that he has in mind—the morality that "see[s] men as God sees them," THE COMMON LAW, *supra* note 78, at 86, and hence considers a sin in the heart to be of the same order as a sin in

In Chapter 3 of *The Common Law*, Holmes took care to emphasize that the principle of objectivity was not simply based on the evidentiary difficulties involved in taking account of "minute differences of character," the ground that had been given for the objective test in *Vaughn v. Menlove*.[138] A "more satisfactory" reason for the objective standard was substantive. A naturally hasty or awkward person's slips, he said, were "no less troublesome to his neighbors than if they sprang from guilty neglect." Tort liability in such cases, though not based on actual moral fault, was "necessary to the general welfare."

Holmes' point in this passage was that the victim's expectation of normal behavior from others in risky interactions deserves the law's protection as much as does the injurer's expectation that he will not be penalized if he does the best he can. Both expectations cannot be entirely fulfilled, and the law treats both equally when it strikes the compromise embodied in the objective standard. Moreover, Holmes made it explicit that the objective standard of negligence *was* a compromise between true fault and strict liability—a "middle point between the horns of this dilemma."[139] This middle way could be seen in two aspects: either as striking the equitable balance required by corrective justice,[140] or (more functionally) as a compromise between the two lines of deterrence-based argument favoring negligence and strict liability respectively.[141]

---

deed. Holmes' understanding of the Kantian distinction between external legal justice, and subjective and inner ethical virtue, is suggested by the conclusion of Chapter 1 of *The Common Law*, where he insists that on the one hand "the terminology of morals is still retained, and . . . the law does still and always, in a certain sense, measure legal liability by moral standards," while on the other hand "by the very necessity of its nature, [it] is continually transmuting those moral standards into external or objective ones, from which the actual guilt of the party concerned is wholly eliminated." THE COMMON LAW, *supra* note 78, at 33. Holmes' equivocation with the word "moral" here is consistent with a Kantian division of the realm of morality between a sphere of objective justice, and one of inner ethical virtue.

138 *See supra* note 126.

139 THE COMMON LAW, *supra* note 78, at 86.

140 As argued by WEINRIB, *supra* note 4, at 177–83.

141 For the deterrent case supporting strict liability, see *Arizona Employers' Liability Cases*, 250 U.S. 400, 431 (1919) (Holmes, J., concurring); negligence liability serves to deter unsafe conduct by designating individual unreasonably unsafe acts, rather than identifying risky activities that are the cheapest cost-avoider of injuries jointly caused by their interaction with other activities. Holmes was generally careful to preserve the neutrality of his account of tort law between a forward-looking account emphasizing deterrence, and a retrospective one based on corrective justice. *See* THE COMMON LAW, *supra* note 78, at 115 (aim of tort law to "prevent *or indemnify* from harm"); *id.* at 116 (purpose of tort law

4 Harm, and the Domain of Torts

In *The Common Law*, Holmes would explicitly formulate the evil against which tort law was directed as the doing of harm, rather than the infringement of rights or the violation of duties. The general question for the law to answer was when "a man is liable for *harm* which he has done."[142] The purpose of torts was "to secure a man against certain forms of *harm*," and to sanction the acts causing them "not because they are wrong, but because they are *harms*."[143] The general principle was that "[m]ost liabilities in tort... are founded on the infliction of harm which the defendant had a reasonable opportunity to avoid."[144]

Not every interest whose infringement counted as harm established a right; not every doing of harm violated a duty. The concrete rights and duties of the law had to be spelled out by striking a balance between the social interests in preventing the doing of harm on the one side, and protecting freedom of action on the other. To make every harm to an individual's interests a wrong "would interfere with other equally important enjoyments on the part of his neighbors." Hence the law privileged certain acts against liability even though the actor foresaw "that harm to another will follow from them."[145] Holmes' point in using this terminology was to emphasize that the rights and duties established in tort decisions were not premises taken from other bodies of law, but conclusions shaped by the judges' traditional common law power to strike the community's balance between freedom and security. Torts was thus an autonomous body of substantive law.

Holmes did not yet explicitly formulate the idea of harm as the trigger in "The Theory of Torts." But he avoided the conventional formulation of negligence as breach of a duty of care, which implied a standard of conduct based on pre-existing rights and duties found elsewhere in the law. Property

"to prevent *or secure indemnity from* harm at the hands of his neighbors"); *Privilege, Malice, and Intent, supra* note 93, at 371 (Tort law "recognizes temporal damage as an evil which its object is to prevent *or to redress*....") (emphasis added). In this he followed Austin, who distinguished civil relief from criminal punishment on the ground that whereas the latter was justified solely by its deterrent effect, the former served the dual purpose of prevention and redress. *See Analysis of Pervading Notions, supra* note 49, at 503–04; *see also supra* note 51.

142 The Common Law, *supra* note 78, at 64.

143 *Id.* at 115.

144 *Id.* at 116.

145 *Id.* at 115. In *Privilege, Malice, and Intent, supra* note 93, at 371–72, Holmes further refined his account: tort liability was triggered by "temporal damage" to plaintiff, by an act of the defendant whose "manifest tendency" was to inflict such damage, subject to privileges that exempted defendant from liability if his act was done with "just cause."

law spelled out such a body of independent rights, but there was no independent "law of bodily security" parallel to property law, and Holmes' innovations shifted emphasis toward the personal injury case. Instead of duty and breach, Holmes simply spoke of the "standard of conduct," and went on to offer his analysis of the respective roles of judge and jury in formulating that standard.[146]

Under the more familiar formulation in terms of duties (with their correlative rights), tort was essentially remedial, providing civil damage awards for violations of primary norms established in other departments of law. Thomas Cooley implied as much in his influential torts treatise of 1879, which thus failed to designate any distinctive primary conduct for tort law to govern.[147] By contrast, Holmes made torts a system of positive claims and liabilities aimed at preventing or redressing secular harms, thus rescuing the subject from his own Austinian critique of it as merely a remedial category.[148]

The connotations of the formulation in terms of harm gave torts a grander part indeed. A modern government's main job, specified by nineteenth century liberal theory as formulated by John Stuart Mill in *On Liberty*, was to deal

146 *The Theory of Torts*, *supra* note 32, at 327–31.

147 After a sophisticated discussion of the power of "judicial legislation" possessed by common law judges, THOMAS COOLEY, A TREATISE ON THE LAW OF TORTS OR THE WRONGS WHICH ARE INDEPENDENT OF CONTRACT 11–19 (1879), Cooley laid the basis for his presentation of tort doctrine with a chapter entitled "General Classification of Legal Rights," *id.* at 23, which dealt with "security in person," "security in the acquisition and enjoyment of property," and "security in the family relations[,]" *id.* at 29. The latter two classes of rights were defined elsewhere in the law, of course, and "personal rights" were defined by the protections offered them by criminal as well as tort law. The connections of tort law to other aspects of the law are emphasized by such an arrangement; but its unity and its coherence as a subject in its own right are not as clear. We still speak of many tort causes of action mainly in terms of the rights they protected—thus "the right of privacy," and the tort remedies for violations of constitutional rights by government officials. *See* David Leebron, *The Right to Privacy's Place in the Intellectual History of Tort Law*, 41 CASE W. RES. L. REV. 769, 769–92 (1990), for a good discussion of the distinction between right-based and harm-based accounts of tort law, using Cooley and Holmes as representatives of the two tendencies.

148 Holmes did not make a dogma out the formulation in terms of harm, but sometimes himself stated tort doctrines in terms of rights and duties, as with his justification of the last wrongdoer rule in *Privilege, Malice, and Intent*, *supra* note 93, at 377–79, and his denial of tort recovery for foreseeable pecuniary loss from a negligent breach of contract to someone who was neither a party to the contract nor an intended beneficiary. *See* Robins Dry Dock & Repair Co. v. Flint, 275 U.S. 303, 308–09 (1927).

with conduct doing "harm to others."[149] When contractual liability was treated in traditional liberal fashion as non-coercive because based on consent, the rules of tort liability could be seen as Holmes described them in *The Common Law*, as the law's authoritative baseline of "the conduct which every one may fairly expect and demand from every other, whether that other has agreed to it or not."[150]

Though in the 1873 article Holmes had yet to formulate tort law in terms of harm as such, he did anticipate the later move in his answer to his own earlier objection that torts had no proper substantive domain. He boldly affirmed that torts was indeed a proper subject because "an enumeration of the [tort] actions which have been successful, and of those which have failed, defines the extent of the primary duties *imposed* by the law."[151] Holmes' point was that it is mainly through tort law, its mildest vehicle of coercion, that the state draws the line between the acts it will regulate and those it will leave alone.[152] Tort thus deals with the space between contract and crime—imposing liabilities based on wrong rather than consent, but wrong that is not serious enough to merit punishment.[153] It is a space dominated by accidental injuries negligently caused. These wrongs constitute the special domain of torts, the subject-matter that makes it an important branch of the substantive law. The "law of bodily security" and its correlative "law of personal liberty" is made up of the rules of tort and criminal law, and because tort is the less drastic mode of the two modes of coercion, it draws the law's most basic line between freedom and protection.[154]

5 Strict Liability and Extrahazardous Activities

Holmes' centering of torts around its lowest cognizable level of wrongdoing, ordinary negligence, naturally raised the question whether his theory required

---

149 John Stuart Mill, On Liberty 1–2 (1859). Mill's formulation in terms of harm marks the modern shift of liberal theory away from the earlier Lockeian formulation in terms of natural rights.

150 The Common Law, *supra* note 78, at 63.

151 *The Theory of Torts*, *supra* note 32, at 331 (emphasis added).

152 *Cf.* New York Times Co. v. Sullivan, 376 U.S. 254 (1964) (treating a tort rule granting damages for defamation as a law abridging the freedom of the press).

153 And, we might add, wrongdoing that is not serious enough to justify either granting punitive damages to those injured by it, or prohibiting liability insurance as contrary to public policy.

154 Tort law of course overlaps with criminal law in the area of serious wrongdoing, where it provides redress for harms resulting from crimes. But its distinctive subject matter is the wrongs not serious enough to be made crimes.

that conduct must be wrongful (blameworthy) at all in order to be tortious. His answer was clear; both in "The Theory of Torts" and in *The Common Law* he accepted liability without fault as a legitimate if relatively peripheral part of tort law. Later he would come to recognize that the idea of enterprise liability might even make strict liability central, though he never actually endorsed recasting tort theory along those lines.[155] But from the first, Holmes recognized the English courts' modern recognition of strict liability in *Rylands v. Fletcher* as good law, and he never joined forces with the many prestigious judges and commentators of his period who believed that the conceptual purity of tort law, or liberal principles of formal equality and economic freedom, or a devotion to economic development, required rejection of tort liability without fault.[156]

---

155 "Our law of torts comes from the old days of isolated, ungeneralized wrongs ... But the torts with which our courts are kept busy today are mainly the incidents of certain well known businesses. They are injuries to person or property by railroads, factories, and the like. The liability for them is estimated, and sooner or later goes into the price paid by the public. The public really pays the damages, and the question of liability, if pressed far enough, is really the question how far it is desirable that the public should insure the safety of those whose work it uses."

The Path of the Law, *supra* note 46, at 397. Jury behavior in workplace injury cases shows that "the inclination of a very large part of the community is to make certain classes of persons insure the safety of those with whom they deal" *Id.*; *see also Arizona Employers' Liability Cases*, 250 U.S. 400, 432 (1919) (Holmes, J., concurring) (giving insurance rationale to justify constitutionality of statute imposing employer strict liability for workplace injuries). For my doubts that Holmes ever actually accepted enterprise liability, see *infra* note 170.

156 Most notable to this effect was *Brown v. Collins*, in which Judge Doe quoted Holmes' passage from *The Theory of Torts* interpreting *Rylands* as imposing liability for "extra-hazardous activities," and expressly repudiated it as carrying liability too far. Brown v. Collins, 53 N.H. 442, 445–46 (1873); *see also* Ives v. S. Buffalo Ry., 201 N.Y. 271 (1911) (striking down New York statute that held employers strictly liable for employee injuries on grounds that constitution prohibits liability without fault); Losee v. Buchanan, 51 N.Y. 476 (1873) (refusing to impose strict liability for exploding steam boiler, rejecting *Rylands*); COOLEY, *supra* note 147, at 81 ("That which is right and lawful for one man to do cannot furnish the foundation for an action in favor of another."); Smith, *supra* note 30 (proposing exclusion of strict civil liability from field of tort on ground that fault should be essential to tort liability); Ezra Thayer, *Liability Without Fault*, 29 HARV. L. REV. 801, 814–15 (1916) (stating that fundamental principle of the common law is that liability is linked to fault). For Pollock's more nuanced opposition to *Rylands, see* Frederick Pollock, *Duties of Insuring Safety: The Rule in Rylands v. Fletcher*, 2 L.Q. REV. 52 (1886), and POLLOCK, *supra* note 29, at 393 (explaining that "the ground on which a rule of strict obligation has been maintained and consolidated by modern authorities is the magnitude of the danger, coupled with the difficulty of proving negligence as the specific cause, in the particular event of

Nor did Holmes regard existing strict liability rules merely as survivals from a more primitive era.[157] In "The Theory of Torts," he explicitly distinguished between "ancient examples . . . traceable to conceptions of a much ruder sort," and modern rules based on "more or less definitely thought out views of public policy." He put the *Rylands* doctrine in the latter category, justified by "the principle that it is politic to make those who go into extra-hazardous employments take the risk on their own shoulders."[158] This is, so far as I know, the first use of the "extrahazardous" concept, though common-law courts had often justified pockets of strict liability by arguments of policy.[159]

Holmes supported strict liability for extrahazardous activities with an insight he had developed in the jurisprudence course he taught at Harvard in 1872.[160] He argued that civil liability did not always imply a legal duty, an "absolute wish" on the part of the sovereign to prohibit the conduct in question. Compensatory damages were sometimes imposed on permitted conduct to make the actor pay the price, as in the case of private eminent domain; and in other cases damages could be imposed to discourage an activity without prohibiting it, a kind of private analog to an excise tax on liquor or a protective

---

the danger having ripened into actual harm"). *See also* DAVID ROSENBERG, THE HIDDEN HOLMES 147–59 (1995) (showing that Holmes was not interpreted as a critic of *Rylands* in his own time).

157 *Cf.* James Barr Ames, *Law and Morals*, 22 HARV. L. REV. 97, 97–99 (1908). Holmes did believe that the generalized strict liability of employers for the torts of their employees, and of common carriers for loss or damage to goods, were survivals, and could not be justified at their full scope by the policies that were cited in their behalf. But he thought that enterprise liability might justify holding corporate or other business defendants responsible under these doctrines. *See* Oliver Wendell Holmes, *Agency I*, 4 HARV. L. REV. 345, 353–63 (1891), *reprinted in* 3 WORKS, *supra* note 7, at 347–54; Oliver Wendell Holmes, *Agency II*, 5 HARV. L. REV. 1, 14–23 (1891), *reprinted in* 3 WORKS, *supra* note 7, at 364–71; Oliver Wendell Holmes, *Common Carriers and Common Law*, 13 AM. L. REV. 609 (1879) [hereinafter *Common Carriers*], *reprinted in* 3 WORKS, *supra* note 7, at 60, 61, 74–75.

158 *The Theory of Torts*, *supra* note 32, at 326.

159 For example the strict liability of carriers for loss of goods was justified on the twin policy grounds of the shipper's lack of access to proof of a carrier's fault, and the need to deter carriers from colluding with robbers. *See* Kaczorowski, *supra* note 69, at 1135–37. Holmes thought these policy arguments were largely bogus rationalizations of a "survival" that derived from the ancient strict liability of all bailees, established at a time when the owner had no remedy over against a thief who stole from the bailee. *Common Carriers*, *supra* note 157, at 61.

160 *See* Oliver Wendell Holmes, *Law Magazine & Review*, 6 AM. L. REV. 723 (1872) [hereinafter *Law Magazine & Review*], *reprinted in* 1 WORKS, *supra* note 7, at 294, in which Holmes used the excuse of a book review to summarize what he had taught in the course.

tariff.[161] Where the sovereign had a genuinely mandatory intent, plenty of serious legal remedies were available—for example, criminal punishment, injunctions, and punitive damages. So the choice to impose compensatory damages as the sole remedial consequence of conduct left open the possibility that the lawmaker did not intend a prohibition.[162]

Austin had treated civil liability as equivalent to punishment, and so invariably expressing the sovereign's prohibition of the conduct in question. Holmes' point was that the relatively weak remedy of compensatory damages could be made available for harm caused by conduct that was thought justified as long as the price was paid. A primary example he had used in his jurisprudence course was the strict liability imposed for "injuries from extrahazardous sources." And to illustrate that the decision whether or not to impose tort liability could turn on policy considerations independent of the defendant's wrongdoing, he noted that the usual strict responsibility for straying animals

161 This insight, one of Holmes' most original, underlies much current literature—including the idea that civil liability characteristically charges a price, while criminal penalties inflict punishment, *see* Coffee, *supra* note 51; the distinction between property rules and liability rules, *see* Guido Calabresi & A. Douglas Melamed, *Property Rules, Liability Rules, and Inalienability: One View of the Cathedral*, 85 HARV. L. REV. 1089 (1972); the theory of efficient breach in contract, *see* RICHARD A. POSNER, ECONOMIC ANALYSIS OF LAW 107 (3d ed. 1986); and the idea that strict liability in tort might be used to encourage efficient activity levels for lawful forms of conduct, *see* S. SHAVELL, ECONOMIC ANALYSIS OF ACCIDENT LAW 5–46 (1987).

162 It is useful to keep Holmes' limited point about the compensatory damage remedy distinct from the more general skepticism he sometimes expressed about the grounding of law in a deontological morality of rights and duties. The two are often conflated (as they sometimes were by Holmes himself). *See, e.g.*, John C.P. Goldberg & Benjamin C. Zipursky, *The Moral of MacPherson*, 146 U. PA. L. REV. 1733, 1737–43 (1998). As the discussion in the text shows, the narrower doctrine depends on the existence of genuinely peremptory legal duties and rights, evidenced by remedies more stringent than compensatory damages. Under this analysis private law, where compensatory payment is the standard remedy, is then seen as an arena for the "civil" (in all senses) adjustment of human friction, and not involving rights that are to be "taken seriously" in the sense that they are meant to trump policy judgments.

Corrective-justice views of tort law are entirely consistent with this view, if, like Ernest Weinrib's version, they give no trumping effect to the rights they recognize, and so place no obstacle in the way of legislative decisions to limit or even abolish tort law public policy grounds. *See* WEINRIB, *supra* note 4, at 210–12. Taking private law as a domain of serious (trumping) rights comes most naturally to libertarians; it condemns workers' compensation as unjust, as in *Ives v. South Buffalo Railway*, 201 N.Y. 271 (1911), and carried out consistently would treat New Zealand as a human rights violator for its abolition of tort claims for negligent injury.

was relaxed in some western states, where the impracticability of fencing made it too much of a burden on essential economic activity.[163]

Holmes reiterated his support for the legitimacy of strict liability in his more complete treatment of torts in *The Common Law*. Again arraying tort rules along a spectrum, with objective negligence covering the great middle area, Holmes added for the first time a discussion of the imposition of strict liability on grounds of corrective justice as well as instrumental policy.[164] He also emphasized and amplified a point he had made in "The Theory of Torts"—that the rules resulting from specification of the negligence principle were often difficult to distinguish from strict liability rules laid down for reasons of public policy. Not only was strict liability legitimate in itself, but it also faded off by indistinct degrees into the category of rules specifying what should count as due care in recurring situations.[165]

On the basis of Chapter 3 of *The Common Law*, Holmes has often been misread as a champion of the principle of no liability without fault. His best-known torts passage is the one in which he argued that losses should presumptively lie where they fall, and that fault alone justifies shifting them. He counseled that if society wanted to cushion no-fault losses, such insurance decisions were better

---

163 *Law Magazine & Review*, *supra* note 160, at 297.

164 He did this in cases of private takings such as later theorists have discussed mostly in connection with *Vincent v. Lake Erie Transportation Co.*, 124 N.W. 221 (Minn. 1910). Holmes discussed the issue in connection with the old English case of *Gilbert v. Stone*, 82 Eng. Rep. 539 (K.B. 1648), in which the defendant stole plaintiff's horse under duress of a threat to his life, and was nevertheless held civilly liable to the owner. THE COMMON LAW, *supra* note 78, at 118. *Cf.* Spade v. Lynn, 172 Mass. 488, 489 (1899).

> "It is a question which deserves more discussion than it has received, whether a man is answerable for an injury inflicted upon an innocent stranger knowingly, or with sufficient notice of the danger, if the injury is an unavoidable incident of lawful self-protection. It might be said, and it has been held, when it is a question of paying damages, that a man cannot shift his misfortunes to his neighbor's shoulders."

Id. (citations omitted). For the classic discussions of the *Vincent* doctrine, *see* Francis Bohlen, *Incomplete Privilege to Inflict Intentional Invasions of Interests of Property and Personality*, 39 HARV. L. REV. 307 (1926); Robert E. Keeton, *Conditional Fault in the Law of Torts*, 72 HARV. L. REV. 401 (1959). Some corrective justice theorists analyze liability of the *Vincent* type as based on unjust enrichment rather than tort. *See, e.g.*, WEINRIB, *supra* note 4, at 196–98.

165 He discussed a number of older rules of strict liability to illustrate "the difficulty of distinguishing rules based on other grounds of policy [i.e. strict liability rules] from those which have been worked out in the field of negligence." THE COMMON LAW, *supra* note 78, at 121–26.

left to the market.[166] More decisively, shifting losses through tort would not insure the loss by spreading it, but would rather arbitrarily shift it to an individual defendant who was only the chance instrument of the plaintiffs loss. This would not only be unwise, but unjust.[167]

In that famous passage, Holmes was debating which principle should *generally* govern accidental injuries, fault or strict liability. He vigorously supported fault as the ruling general principle,[168] but we must remember that this is the

166 "The state might conceivably make itself a mutual insurance company against accidents, and distribe the burden of its citizens' mishaps among all its members ... Universal insurance, if desired, can be better and more cheaply accomplished by private enterprise." *Id.* at 78.

167

> "The undertaking to redistribute losses simply on the ground that they resulted from the defendant's act would ... be open to ... the still graver [objection] of offending the sense of justice. Unless my act is of a nature to threaten others ... it is no more justifiable to make me indemnify my neighbor against the consequences, than to ... compel me to insure him against lightning."

Id. at 77–78. The latter argument is the one he would qualify in the 1890s, recognizing that strict tort liability placed upon enterprises was indeed genuine (if compulsory) insurance, because its cost could be statistically predicted and spread to the customers. *See supra* note 155.

168 This is where David Rosenberg errs, in seeing Holmes as arguing, not for fault over strict liability, but for a restricted form of strict liability ("foresight-based") over a more extensive "cause-based") form. ROSENBERG, *supra* note 156, at 5–6. I believe that Rosenberg is led astray by the fact that Holmes' account of negligence treats the creation of a substantial risk of injury as culpable, without explicitly taking account of the cost of avoidance; this makes his version of negligence resemble some present-day descriptions of strict liability. But Holmes simply held to the "non-balancing" interpretation of negligence that was usual in his day, and that is still advocated by many, as a proper interpretation of what should count as culpable behavior. *See* Bolton v. Stone, 850 A.C. 867 (1951) (Lord Reid's speech provided the standard citation for the non-balancing conception of negligence in Commonwealth law); WEINRIB, *supra* note 4, at 147–52; Richard Wright, *The Standards of Care in Negligence, in* THE PHILOSOPHICAL FOUNDATIONS OF NEGLIGENCE 249, 251 (David G. Owen ed., 1995) (arguing that as a matter of positive law the Hand balancing test fails to explain how the courts treat negligence); Stephen Perry, *The Impossibility of General Strict Liability*, 1 CANADIAN J.L. & JURISPRUDENCE 147, 169–71 (1988). In American case law and commentary, the balancing conception of negligence did not become popular until at least a generation after Holmes wrote. *See* Michael D. Green, *Negligence = Economic Efficiency: Doubts*, 75 TEX. L. REV. 1605 (1997).

Holmes made very clear that the main standard of liability he argued for was fault-based (albeit objective) negligence, which was rooted in blameworthiness. Thus the reason there was no liability in the typical horse rundown case where nothing suggested special danger was that "the defendant is not to blame." THE COMMON LAW, *supra* note 78,

same Holmes who is famous for insisting that "general principles do not decide concrete cases."[169] Principles to him were not absolutes. This did not mean they were empty or useless; rather they served as guidelines and default rules, subject to exceptions and decreasingly applicable by degree as they diverged from their paradigm instances.[170]

The structure of Holmes' tort theory well illustrated these aspects of his treatment of legal principles. His general principle of liability was negligence, which provided the conceptual center for tort law, covered "the great mass" of cases, and supplied the default doctrine. But it allowed for exceptions at both ends of the continuum it dominated. At times something more than negligence was required for liability, as with the intentional torts. (Indeed, sometimes even intentional wrongdoing was not enough, and the law granted an absolute privilege.) Objective negligence shaded into deliberate wrongdoing at that end of the spectrum, as courts first found intent or malice from knowledge of facts suggesting a very high likelihood of injury, and then eventually came to equate intent or malice in the legal sense with this knowledge.

At the other end of the spectrum were another group of exceptions to the principle that based liability on objective negligence. Sometimes the law imposed strict liability for policy reasons of deterrence, as with extra-hazardous

---

at 75. And with respect to the early English cases "liability *in general*, then as later, was founded on the opinion of the tribunal that the defendant *ought to have acted otherwise, or, in other words, that he was to blame.*" *Id.* at 82 (emphasis added). He summarized "the *general notion* upon which liability to an action is founded" as "*fault* or *blameworthiness* in some sense." *Id.* at 85 (using "some sense" to refer to the objective test) (emphasis added). He referred in passing to "[t]he rule that the law does, in general, determine liability by *blameworthiness*," *id.* at 87 (emphasis added), and, again in a self-conscious summary, said that the law does not "*in general*" hold a man liable for unintended injury unless "he might and *ought* to have foreseen the danger, or, *in other words*, unless a man of ordinary intelligence and forethought would have been to *blame* for acting as he did," *id.* at 88 (emphasis added). In "*some cases*" (by contrast to the general case) lawmakers "put the mark higher… than the point established by common practice at which *blameworthiness* begins." *Id.* at 92 (emphasis added). And after the more extended discussion of the exceptional cases of strict liability in Lecture IV, Holmes finally summarized his doctrine as "*in the main*" deriving the test of tort liability from popular moral notions of blame, objectified, that is: "whether [defendant's] conduct would have been *wrong* in the fair average member of the community." *Id.* at 128 (emphasis added).

169 Lochner v. New York, 198 U.S. 45, 76 (1905) (Holmes, J., dissenting).

170 Indeed he gave the first formulation of this central idea of his jurisprudence in *The Theory of Torts*, *supra* note 32, at 330–31 (describing the "core-penumbra" structure of most general legal concepts). In the *Lochner* dissent, he noted that while general principles do not "decide" cases, they can "carry us far toward the end." *Lochner*, 198 U.S. at 75.

activities,[171] and other times it did so on the basis of a principle of corrective justice.[172] No sharp line divided the domains of fault and strict liability; they shaded into each other where rules could plausibly be characterized either as specifying negligence or as implementing the policies behind strict liability.[173]

IV Conclusion

Despite his famous jurisprudential slogans on behalf of a functional approach to legal theory, Holmes was not a jurist who habitually took careful account of social facts or even generally showed sound practical judgment on questions of public policy. As he admitted himself on occasion, he was really a philosophically-minded legal theoretician with deficiencies as a policymaker.[174]

---

171 "There is no more certain way of securing attention to the safety of the men... than by holding the employer liable for accidents... [T]hey probably will happen a good deal less often when the employer knows that he must answer for them if they do."
Arizona Employers' Liability Cases, 250 U.S. 400, 432–33 (1919) (Holmes, J., concurring). To make the deterrence argument convincing, the party to the interaction who is made strictly liable should have most of the opportunities for taking care. *See* William Jones, *Strict Liability for Hazardous Enterprise*, 92 COLLUM. L. REV. 1705, 1751 (1992); *see also* WILLIAM M. LANDES & RICHARD R. POSNER, THE ECONOMIC STRUCTURE OF TORT LAW, 310–11 (1987) (pointing out in regards to worker's compensation that making employers strictly liable reduces workers' safety incentives). Holmes may well have doubted that this asymmetry obtained in the hazardous employment situation, and it seems unlikely he would have voted for employer liability or worker's compensation laws as a legislator; thus he told a correspondent in 1908 that "little as I liked the Act" he had voted to uphold the constitutionality of the Federal Employers' Liability Act. THE HOLMES-EINSTEIN LETTERS: CORRESPONDENCE OF MR. JUSTICE HOLMES AND LEWIS EINSTEIN, 1903–1935, 33–34 (James Bishop Peabody ed., 1964).

172 This is the *Gilbert v. Stone* idea, which Holmes confined to intentional torts in *The Common Law. See supra* note 148. Later Holmes came to see that a version of the *Gilbert* argument supported forms of enterprise liability like workers' compensation. *See supra* note 155. Thus in the *Arizona* case he gave it as an alternative rationale for the statute:
"It is reasonable that the public should pay the whole cost of producing what it wants and a part of that cost is the pain and mutilation incident to production. By throwing that loss upon the employer in the first instance we throw it upon the public in the long run and that is just."
The Arizona Employers' Liability Cases, 250 U.S. at 433.

173 THE COMMON LAW, *supra* note 78, at 92–96, 121–26.

174 A point familiar to torts professors who every year teach *Baltimore & Ohio Railroad v. Goodman*, 275 U.S. 66, 70 (1927), *overruled by* Pokora v. Wabash Ry. Co., 292 U.S. 98. 105–06 (1934), the decision in which Holmes (who had never driven an automobile) under-

Had he been a more practical sort, we might imagine that he shrewdly observed the surge of litigation over accidental injuries stemming from technological and industrial developments, and then consciously shaped his theory of torts to center it around an idea (objective negligence) that was particularly well-suited to this newly dominant subject matter.

But given Holmes' intellectual proclivities, any such practical insight or motivation is unlikely, and there is no evidence for it in his writings on torts. Rather his published essays leading up to 1873 show him single-mindedly pursuing the jurisprudential project of systematic reclassification of the substantive law. Here as elsewhere, he wanted to connect his work in law to the great world of ideas, to science and philosophy. The reward he wanted was the approval of the few fellow legal scholars and thinkers whose opinion he respected. And his ultimate hope was that his ideas might enter into the fabric of the law and eventually exercise power over events.[175]

In the law, theories, however brilliant, do not thrive unless they also serve significant interests. John Norton Pomeroy had ideas about the organization of the law that, simply regarded as ideas, may have been as good as Holmes'—yet no one remembers them. Holmes' theory of torts turned out to have practical strengths that he never claimed for it, and that he may never have realized it possessed. Above all, his approach centered tort doctrine around its emerging primary source of litigation, accidental personal injuries. At the same time, it established a doctrinal framework flexible enough to allow a remedial structure originally grounded in intuitions of corrective justice to be adapted without too much strain to modern regulatory and compensatory uses.

It is natural to wonder how much Holmes' theory mattered. First, to what extent did his conceptual innovations influence the way we talk about torts today? And then, how much does the way torts teachers and academic

---

took to legislate for the whole nation a safety rule requiring motorists at railroad crossings to get out of their cars to look along the tracks when their view was obstructed. Holmes was aware of his deficiencies as a practical policy-maker; thus he contrasted Chief Justice White's attention to "the practical effect of the decision," properly its "ultimate justification," with his own tendency to "think of [the decision's] relation to the theory and philosophy of the law." HOLMES-SHEEHAN CORRESPONDENCE 58 (David H. Burton ed., 1976); *see also* Thomas C. Grey, *Molecular Motions: The Holmesian Judge in Theory and Practice*, 37 WM. & MARY L. REV. 19, 39–40 (1995) (providing similar Holmesian acknowledgements of falliability).

175 "To an imagination of any scope the most far-reaching form of power is not money, it is the command of ideas.... Read the work of the great German jurists, and see how much more the world is governed today by Kant than by Bonaparte." *The Path of the Law*, *supra* note 46, at 405.

commentators conceive and structure the subject affect the working tort law? On the first question, I would ascribe considerable influence to Holmes on the basis of the evidence I have set out here. On the second, though, little more than speculation seems justified. There is always room for skepticism, in an enterprise whose life is more experience than logic, about the influence of categorical arrangements and high-level doctrine on the law in action.[176]

The features of American tort law that seem best to fit Holmes' conceptual framework might have come out the same whatever the theories were, and indeed whether or not torts was accepted as a basic subject. Tort doctrines that combine regulatory with reparative purposes may have been inevitable in a federal system that generally left private law to the states, while authorizing the national government to regulate interstate commerce.[177] And attention to private damage suits as a substitute for social insurance seems to have been a likely development, independent of theory, in a country as individualistically resistant to safety-net legislation as the United States. Holmes' theory triumphed as theory, but in practice maybe it mattered and maybe not.

---

176 Thus writing about Holmes' influence on the law of torts, Brian Simpson pointedly distinguishes between "tort law" and "theorizing about tort law," and writes that "there is not the least evidence that Dean Langdell, the Continental Pandectists, or even the great Savigny over had any effect on the nineteenth-century common law of tort, either in England, the United States, or anywhere else." Holmes' "theory of tort law," he suggests, was "a purely philosophical enterprise," of the sort likely to be of interest only in "the world of high legal theory, so typical of the scholarship associated with American law schools." A.W.B. Simpson, *The Elusive Truth About Holmes*, 95 MICH. L. REV. 2027, 2032 (1997) (reviewing DAVID ROSENBERG, THE HIDDEN HOLMES: HIS THEORY OF TORTS IN HISTORY (1995)).

177 Congress and the courts have long had to confront the clash of federal regulatory purposes with the doctrinal structure of state tort law, in the contexts both of setting the limits to federal power where it enters the domain of private law, and determining the pre-emptive force of the valid exercise of that power. *See, e.g.*, Geier v. Am. Honda Motor Co., 529 U.S. 861 (2000) (the local tort law treating absence of airbag as design defect, pre-empted as interference with the purpose of a federal auto safety regulation, meant to encourage the introduction of airbags by gradual steps); Second Employers' Liability Cases, 223 U.S. 1 (1912) (holding that the federal statute eliminating employers' tort defenses in rail workers' negligence suits is a valid safety regulation of interstate commerce). Holmes himself helped develop this body of law, reading a federal safety statute broadly to override state tort defenses in his important opinion for a bare majority of the Court in *Schlemmer v. Buffalo, Rochester & Pittsburgh Railway*, 205 U.S. 1 (1907) (the Federal Safety Appliance Act's invalidation of assumption of risk as defense in suits involving conduct violative of Act's safety requirements implicitly prohibits using contributory negligence to defeat recovery in the area of overlap between the two doctrines).

One interesting possible consequence of Holmes' work remains to be considered. The accident-centered perspective that he promoted portrays American tort law in a way that makes it exceptionally salient in social and political terms, but at the same time leaves it curiously unstable. When the destiny of torts is tied to the problem of accidental injury, the subject as a whole becomes vulnerable to practical reassessments of the best public policy for dealing with that problem. If tort is essentially about accidents, it faces the risk of abolition as a significant body of law today.[178]

By contrast, corrective justice theorists, who think of tort as an abstract legal category organized around the distinctively bilateral character of certain paradigmatic wrongs, do not have to worry in the same way about losing their subject altogether. The intentional wrongs on which Aristotle founded his analysis of corrective justice[179] still remain torts in most legal systems today, even while these systems increasingly abandon tort as a way of dealing with accidental injury.

In our present American regime, we take torts for granted as a fundamental category, and we organize it (with some continuing dissent) around the problem of accidental injury and the concept of negligence. My argument has been that things need not have turned out this way. Working in the doctrinally fluid context created by the abolition of the forms of action, Holmes re-examined civil and common law traditions in the light of the latest nineteenth century jurisprudential notions, and out of the mix he formulated one plausible theory of torts. His account of the subject happened to fit with the flow of events and so took hold, and now it strikes us almost as common sense rather than theory. But we might not even have adopted torts as a basic legal category at all, much less taken that particular approach to it. So it is that the law sometimes arrives at a state that seems natural and even inevitable along a path shaped by—well, by accident.

---

178 Compare the titles of Stephen Sugarman's law review article and his subsequent book—*Doing Away With Tort Law*, 73 CAL. L. REV. 555 (1985), scaled back to DOING AWAY WITH PERSONAL INJURY LAW (1989). The original and more ambitious title in a sense stated the reality of the situation, given how widely held is the accident-centered conception of tort law that I trace back to Holmes.

179 ARISTOTLE, *supra* note 15.

Bibliography

Books

The Legal Enforcement of Morality (New York, Alfred Knopf, 1983) (editor, with introductory essay).

The Wallace Stevens Case: Law and the Practice of Poetry (Cambridge, Mass., Harvard University Press, 1991).

Articles (Short Cite Form: Bolded Date)

1973: The First Virtue (review-essay on John Rawls's A Theory of Justice), 25 Stanford Law Review 286–327 (1973).

1975: Do We Have an Unwritten Constitution? 27 Stanford Law Review 703–718 (1975).

1976: Property and Need: The Welfare State and Theories of Distributive Justice, 28 Stanford Law Review 877–902 (1976).

1977: Procedural Justice and Substantive Rights, Nomos XVIII: Due Process 182–205 (1977). Grey 1977

1978: Origins of the Unwritten Constitution: Fundamental Law in American Revolutionary Thought, 30 Stanford Law Review 843–893 (1978). Grey 1978

1979: Constitutionalism: An Analytic Framework, Nomos XX: Constitutionalism 189–209 (1979).

1980a: The Disintegration of Property, Nomos XXII: Property 69–86 (1980).

1980b: Eros, Civilization, and the Burger Court, 43 Law and Contemporary Problems 83–100 (1980).

1983: Langdell's Orthodoxy, 45 University of Pittsburgh Law Review 1–53 (1984).

1984: The Constitution as Scripture, 37 Stanford Law Review 1–25 (1984).

1985: The Hermeneutics File, 58 Southern California Law Review 211–236 (1985).

1986: The Malthusian Constitution (review-essay on Richard Epstein's Takings), 41 University of Miami Law Review 21–48 (1986).

1987: Serpents and Doves: A Note on Kantian Legal Theory, 87 Columbia Law Review 580–591 (1987).

1988a: The Original Understanding and the Unwritten Constitution, in Neil York (ed.), Toward a More Perfect Union: Six Essays on the Constitution 145–173, (Brigham Young Press: Provo, Utah, 1988).

1988b: The Uses of an Unwritten Constitution, 64 Chicago-Kent Law Review 211–238 (1988).

1989: Holmes and Legal Pragmatism, 41 Stanford Law Review 787–870 (1989).

1990a: Steel Against Intimation: The Motive for Metaphor of Wallace Stevens, Esq., 2 Yale Journal of Law & the Humanities 231–252 (1990).

1990b: Hear the Other Side: Wallace Stevens and Pragmatist Legal Theory, 63 Southern California Law Review 1569–1595 (1990).

1991a: Civil Rights vs. Civil Liberties: The Case of Discriminatory Verbal Harassment, 8 Social Philosophy and Policy 81–107 (1991).

1991b: Discriminatory Harassment and Free Speech, 14 Harvard Journal of Law & Public Policy 157–164 (1991).

1991c: What Good is Legal Pragmatism?, in M. Brint and W. Weaver (eds.), Pragmatism in Law and Society 9–27 (Boulder, Colo., Westview Press, 1991).

1992: Holmes, Pragmatism, and Democracy (The O'Fallon Memorial Lecture), 71 Oregon Law Review 521–542 (1992).

1993: Thayer's Doctrine: Notes on Its Origin, Scope, and Present Implications, 88 Northwestern Law Review 28–41 (1993).

1995: Molecular Motions: The Holmesian Judge in Theory and Practice, 37 William and Mary Law Review 19–45 (1995).

1996a: How to Write a Speech Code Without Really Trying: Reflections on the Stanford Experience, 29 U. C. Davis Law Review 891–956 (1996).

1996b: Freestanding Legal Pragmatism, 18 Cardozo Law Review 21–42 (1996), also in Morris Dickstein (ed.), The Revival of Pragmatism (Durham and London, Duke University Press, 1998).

1996c: *Hardwick v. Bowers* Diminished, 68 University of Colorado Law Review 373–386 (1996).

1996d: Modern American Legal Thought, 106 Yale Law Journal 493–517 (1996).

1997: Plotting *The Path of the Law*, 63 Brooklyn Law Review 19–58 (1997).

2000a: Cover-Blindness, 88 California Law Rev. 65–75 (2000).

2000b: Holmes on the Logic of the Law, in Steven Burton, editor, *The Path of the Law* and its Influence 133–157 (Cambridge University Press, 2000).

2001: Accidental Torts, 54 Vanderbilt Law Review 1225–1284 (2001).

2003: Judicial Review and Legal Pragmatism, 38 Wake Forest Law Review 473–511 (2003).

Index of Terms

www.ingramcontent.com/pod-product-compliance
Lightning Source LLC
LaVergne TN
LVHW010657300926
849161LV00005B/1146
* 9 7 8 9 0 0 4 2 7 2 8 8 0 *